THE
100
BEST
STOCKS
TO BUY IN
2019

PETER SANDER AND SCOTT BOBO

Adams Media

New York London Toronto Sydney New Delhi

Aadamsmedia

Adams Media
An Imprint of Simon & Schuster, Inc.
57 Littlefield Street
Avon, Massachusetts 02322

First Adams Media trade paperback edition December 2018

ADAMS MEDIA and colophon are trademarks of Simon & Schuster.

For information about special discounts for bulk purchases, please contact Simon &
Schuster Special Sales at 1-866-506-1949 or business@simonandschuster.com.

The Simon & Schuster Speakers Bureau can bring authors to your live event. For
more information or to book an event contact the Simon & Schuster Speakers
Bureau at 1-866-248-3049 or visit our website at www.simonspeakers.com.

Interior design by Colleen Cunningham

Manufactured in the United States of America

10 9 8 7 6 5 4 3 2 1

Library of Congress Cataloging-in-Publication Data has been applied for.

ISBN 978-1-5072-0894-6
ISBN 978-1-5072-0895-3 (ebook)

Contents

PART I

THE ART AND SCIENCE OF INVESTING IN STOCKS

By Peter Sander

The Art and Science of Investing in Stocks

Oh, no.

It happened *again*.

We lost. We lost to our old nemesis—the S&P 500 index—for a second year in a row.

For those of you new to the *100 Best Stocks to Buy* series, we measure ourselves against our closest no-brainer competitor—the S&P 500 index—which you could easily buy through one of many index funds and save yourself $16.99 or thereabouts plus tax on our book. Yes, you read that right—we *measure* our performance. That doesn't happen that often in the investing world, and it happens even less often in the investing *book* world! (Can you find another investing book that actually measures the results of its picks or its "proven system"?)

Our 2018 picks overall came up 1.2 percent short of the S&P, which means that if you had gone to the trouble to "buy the list" or a substantial portion thereof, you would have gained 12.6 percent including dividends—which would have fallen 1.2 percent short of the S&P's 13.8 percent gain. Now that sounds pretty bad, especially since we lost last year too. *Two years in a row.* Is it time for us to throw in the towel? Is it time for you to switch investing books? Is it time to simply throw your money over the wall to index funds? To a financial advisor who is likely to charge you 1 percent of your portfolio value *each year*?

Perish the thought!

Now you're probably anxiously awaiting a long list of excuses why this year was different, why we were on the right track until some unforeseen event like bad weather, bad debt, or bad politics knocked us unexpectedly off our saddles. Here it comes, right?

Nope, there are no excuses. But we do try to put our loss in perspective. It's a good habit to get into as an investor, and we think it's a rather good habit for investment writers like us to take on as well.

* * *

Now we offer some observations on our 2018 *100 Best Stocks* list performance:

First, we lost by less than last year. Our 2018 *100 Best* list lost by 1.2 percent. In 2017 we lost by 2.2 percent—so we can say we cut our loss in half!

Well, the claim is valid, but in the grand scheme a loss is still a loss—and the last two years of losses stand in contrast to our first seven years of wins! So, we're clearly not happy stock pickers, but we do realize it could have been worse.

Second, our long-term "style" has gone a bit out of favor. Those of you who have consistently bought our book over the years, followed our picks, and internalized our investing strategy know that we favor stocks that among other things pay dividends (until recently, 98 percent of our picks did) and have a regular and steadily growing dividend (typically 60–75 percent of our picks have raised their dividend steadily, that is, eight to ten years in a row). That philosophy has worked and has incidentally attracted us to a large number of steady-Eddie low-growth consumer staples stocks like Coke, Colgate-Palmolive, Procter & Gamble, General Mills, Campbell Soup, and the like: long-term picks bought especially for growing dividends. But rising interest rates, higher input costs, and other factors specific to these less-favored sectors caused a substantial portion of our list to underperform. Quite simply a high-yielding stock with growing dividends isn't as valuable when you can buy the same yield with a Treasury bond. Our consumer staples, REITs, and other strong payers faded this year, enough to affect the total list performance. So, for 2019, as we'll describe later in this narrative, we won't throw out the baby with the bathwater, but we made more changes than usual (14) and have injected some "growth" energy into our portfolio. This is not necessarily to say you should pick more high-flying growth stocks if you're not comfortable there—we're just adding a few more to our list for you to consider.

Third, we still think we beat the S&P on a risk-adjusted basis. Risk-adjusted? Now that sounds like Wall Street jargon, but the notion of risk as it applies to our list is really important here. Why? Because while our performance missed the mark, we always strive to make our list a little safer and less volatile than the S&P 500 and the market at large. We think we did, and to make our point and in keeping with our engineering-geek ways, we decided to measure *that* too. Read on…

* * *

When adjusted for risk, did we—*maybe*—really win this thing?

For years we've said that our list would do better than the market (and the S&P) in a *down* market. But for nine consecutive years now, we've never had the chance to test that claim. We haven't had a down market.

By making the claim, we maintain that most of our picks are less risky than the average stock market pick. That is, they have less *downside risk*, which equates roughly but not exactly to *volatility*. Like most others in the investment industry, we have relied on "beta" as a proxy for volatility. Beta measures the movement of a stock compared to the market as a whole. A beta of 1.00 means that a stock moves exactly with the market, which is a good thing when the market is going up, but a bad thing when it's going down. A beta of less than 1 is bad when the market is moving up and good when it is moving down. A beta greater than 1.00 means that stock moves more than the market (more up than the market when the market is up, more down than the market when the market is down). Beta doesn't really tell you how safe a stock is because (1) it compares to the market rather than measuring the intrinsic volatility of the stock, and (2) the indicator has been calculated against an "up" market for the past several years.

Okay, now we've really lost you in the weeds of Wall Street speak, have we not? We apologize; that is hardly our intent. Let's circle back to the original theme here: that our picks, while underperforming the market a bit, are more stable and more "sleep at night" than the market as a whole. For reasons just given, our industry standard "beta" measure falls short of being a true measure of volatility and especially *downside* volatility. What to do?

We sought to find a measure that would more closely measure true volatility, that is, the *up-and-down* fluctuations of a price of a stock, regardless of how closely it followed the market. Once we tallied this measure for all *100 Best Stocks*, we could make a definitive statement on the volatility of our portfolio as compared to the market at large.

We considered a measure or two of our own "chi-square" analysis but discarded them because we simply aren't statisticians and don't have enough number-crunching ability to feel comfortable creating our own measure. We wanted something off the shelf, and, as so often is the case, when we need a fact or figure on a company we turned to the Value Line Investment Survey, which in this case provides a neat singular measure known as "Price Stability." Bingo.

The Price Stability score, presented for every stock in the Value Line universe, ranks the stock's five-year standard deviation on a 1–100 scale—100 being the steadiest, or having the *lowest* standard deviation. Standard deviation is a singular measure of the up-and-down fluctuations over time of a series of data—the higher the fluctuation, the higher the standard deviation. So, the game became a matter of assigning a Price Stability score to each of the 2018 *100 Best Stocks*, averaging the scores, and comparing the result to the average Price Stability score for *all* S&P 500 stocks.

Despite the apparent complexity of this exercise, I think you can see where this is going.

- The average Price Stability score for the S&P 500 list was 68.03.
- The average Price Stability score for the *100 Best Stocks 2018* list was 76.87.
- Take the difference, and one can conclude that, on average, the *100 Best Stocks* list is about 9 percent more stable—less volatile—than the S&P 500.
- We were 1.2 percent less profitable but 9 percent more stable.

Think about it: if someone offered you a list of investments that would sacrifice a 1.2 percent gain (out of 13.8 percent total gain) for 9 percent greater stability, would you take it? Would you as an investor give up 1.2 percent of returns to enjoy almost 9 percent less risk? It's not a huge advantage, but it does support our claim that *while we fell short of the S&P 500 gain for 2018, we were measurably safer.* That's a good thing.

* * *

We pride ourselves on our long-term performance. In fact, if you had invested $100,000 across the board with us when we took over the *100 Best Stocks* series in 2010, you would now have $460,774. If you had invested $100,000 in the S&P 500 index, you would have $371,957, a difference of $88,817 (see Table 0.2). We've done well. Our investors have done well. We've done almost 24 percent better over time.

However, in the past two years we've lost a little ground to the S&P. While it's pretty difficult to keep any win streak alive, we're not happy about these losses; our prevailing thesis is that we can beat the S&P modestly *and consistently* while being just a little bit safer. We've got the "little bit safer" right as explained earlier, but we're starting to fall behind in the "beat the S&P modestly" part.

While we believe that all successful investors should stick with what made them successful, we also feel it is okay to tweak or adjust an investing style for the times. As mentioned, dividend-paying stocks have fallen out of favor due to high interest rates and the tendency for companies that pay them not to grow as much as others in a growing economy. For this year, as explained in detail later in this narrative, we have added some more "growth"-oriented stocks—stocks whose value is based on steady, predictable business growth, not just cash investor returns. While we still stay away from highfliers such as Facebook, Alphabet (Google), and Netflix, we have sprinkled in what we think are some dependable growth stories like Square, Analog Devices, and Zebra Technologies and have removed some of the redundant dividend-paying household products names like Kimberly-Clark, General Mills, and Colgate-Palmolive, as mentioned before. This isn't to say you shouldn't invest in these stocks—it's okay to keep your Coke and Procter—we just wanted to offer a few more growth choices if growth is what you seek.

* * *

Those of you who have followed us in recent years know that we've made an effort to keep our investment choices current with the millennial generation, those born with a digital silver spoon after 1982. They now outnumber the rest of us, and their tastes and needs harken much more to things digital and to experiences rather than things, among many other cultural differences. They eat healthy, balance life and work, and tend to do almost everything online or by digital messaging. They also prefer to do as much as they can from home, as it is digitally enabled; less hassle (especially in urban environments); and eco-friendly.

This has given birth to a whole new economy tagged by investing guru Jim Cramer and others as the "stay-at-home" economy. "Stay at home" means that you do as much as you can digitally from the home: ordering goods, services, and meals and groceries online; transacting banking and other business; healthcare; and so forth. This year we made a conscious effort to add "stay-at-home" and new age economy stocks; again, Zebra Technologies was added for its package-tracking devices, but we also added Sealed Air, which makes e-commerce packaging (including Bubble Wrap) to our list, which already includes Amazon, FedEx, UPS, Prologis, and others. We've covered the supply chain side pretty well with these picks and are on the lookout for other new concepts as they emerge. Table 9 now shows "Stay-at-Home Stars": companies destined to thrive in the emerging stay-at-home economy.

* * *

We've said it for years: good investors *admit their mistakes*. The worst thing you can do as an investor is "marry" a stock for life or blindly hold onto something—or avoid something—hoping for a different outcome despite overwhelming contrary evidence. Emotionally mature investors park their egos to the side and make the changes when necessary.

Such is what we did this year with GE, albeit (we're still learning!) a year too late. The GE story is well known—suffice it to say we fell for their marketing and their strategy to return to industrial roots—we just failed to comprehend how scattered and unhealthy those roots were. We liked their pitch about "smart" and connected industrial machinery, but it seems they've backed away from that promise, as well as a lot of that machinery. Gone for 2019.

And back on the 2019 list is Target. We cut Target last year because at the height of raging concern about the Amazon phenomenon eating up "bricks and mortar" retail, they announced a strategy to cut prices. Wrong path, and off the 2018 list they went. Since then they've reevaluated their strategy and are making it about shopping experience, something they've always done well and can't be so easily matched by Amazon. After a one-year hiatus, they're back on the list as the first stock we've cut, then added back the very next year. Target wasn't really a mistake but rather was an example of adapting our list more rapidly to change—something we investors all should do.

* * *

As usual, we continue to produce this book not only to give you our annual selections (fish) but also to provide a model for *how* we make our selections (teach you how to fish). This Part I narrative has elements of both—and we apologize once again for parts of it that might seem repetitive, year after year, for those of you faithful enough to buy each year's edition. (For those of you who would like still more insight on how to fish, I'll point to two of my other works: *The 25 Habits of Highly Successful Investors*, from this publisher, and *All About Low Volatility Investing*, from McGraw-Hill.) Anyway, for us, investing is a thought process that we hope you acquire over time—not just through our investment tenets and philosophies shared in the narrative but also by watching us *do* it (the *100 Best* list) and ultimately through your own experience.

Again, we continue to enjoy your feedback. We've fielded many fine questions that, frankly, we enjoyed answering. Not only do we appreciate the dialogues; we learn from them too. Keep them coming to Peter's email: ginsander@hotmail.com.

An Also-Ran *Again* for 2018…but Not Out to Pasture Yet

It's hard to believe it's been five years now since we created the "temporary" analysis and table comparing the performance of the *100 Best Stocks* list against major sector benchmarks as measured by Lipper, a division of

Thomson Reuters and a major supplier of quality financial information and analytics especially for the mutual fund sector. This year's analysis shows that while we lost to our "nemesis" the S&P 500 by a narrower margin (1.2 percent) than last year, it really shows how far we were off the leaders, the growth-oriented and international stocks that did so well this year. We turned in a decent and steady performance, but many of these leaders finished well ahead of us. But as you know, they finish near the back of the pack from time to time too. Table 0.1 shows the "race" and its finishing order.

Table 0.1 shows quite clearly how the improving global economy, much of which rides beyond US fences but is still impacted by Trump administration pro-business policies, kicked into high gear in 2018. China, of course, led the pack, while the still-strong "Science and Technology" group, which happens to include Internet highfliers like Amazon, Netflix, Facebook, and other high-energy picks, was number two. Most of the rest that beat us were in the various categories of growth (again helped along by these "FAANG" stocks and others) and in the international sector across the board. Again, these aren't the types of stocks we bet on for the most part, so, congratulations if you own them, and, as described in this opener, we put a little more growth impetus into the 2019 portfolio, but we stop short of thinking that we're riding the wrong horses. Again, remember that our *100 Best* list is intended for the most part to be a pretty "steady-Eddie" bunch, and if you prefer tortoises to hares, we may just have the right collection of stocks for you. You'll get to cash those bets in the long run.

▼ **Table 0.1: Performance Compared to Major Benchmarks**

100 BEST STOCKS 2018 **COMPARED TO LIPPER MUTUAL FUND INDEX BENCHMARKS**

Fund Benchmark	1-Year Return
China Region	36.2%
Science and Technology	27.5%
Pacific Ex-Japan	25.8%
International Small/Mid Cap Growth	24.9%
Pacific Region	24.2%
Emerging Markets	23.4%
Japan Region	23.4%
Latin American	22.7%

Fund Benchmark	1-Year Return
International Small/Mid Cap Core	20.1%
Global Multicap Growth	19.7%
International Multicap Growth	19.5%
Global Large Cap Growth	19.2%
International Large Cap Growth	17.1%
International Multicap Core	15.5%
International Large Cap Core	15.3%
International Small/Mid Cap Value	15.1%
Global Multicap Core	14.4%
International Large Cap Value	14.1%
European Region	14.0%
Global Large Cap Core	14.0%
S&P 500 with Dividends Reinvested	**13.8%**
Health/Biotech	13.8%
Financial Services	13.5%
International Multicap Value	13.0%
100 BEST STOCKS TO BUY 2018	12.6%
Global Multicap Value	10.4%
Global Large Cap Value	7.4%
Telecommunications	3.5%
Multisector Income	3.3%
High-Yield Bond	3.2%
General Bond	2.4%
Utility	2.4%
Intermediate Municipal Debt	1.9%
General US Treasury	1.5%
Inflation Protected Bond	0.7%
General US Government	0.1%
Short US Government	0.0%
Short/Intermediate US Government	-0.2%
Real Estate	-2.1%
Natural Resources	-5.5%
Precious Metals Equity	-8.2%

Source: Lipper/Thomson Reuters, *Barron's Weekly*

A Nine-Year Stretch Run

Back in 2010 we took over the publication of *The 100 Best Stocks to Buy* series from previous author John Slatter. Motivated by our own curiosity and a couple of poignant reader queries, we ask ourselves every year: So how well did we do? How are we doing over the *long term*? How well did we achieve the goals of applying solid, value-based, marketplace-influenced investing techniques and philosophies to picking great companies, the *100 Best* of them for you to invest in? More simply stated, would you have been better off to not buy our book, to not take the time to pursue individual stock investing and to throw it over the wall to a low-cost S&P 500 index fund, as so many are doing today—and as experts, even Warren Buffett himself, are now suggesting you do?

Being more sensitive now to this question than ever, for one, having endured our *second straight* losing year, and two, for now observing the groundswell, first toward "passive" and "index" investing and now toward growth, we continue to carefully monitor our long-term performance, now over a nine-year stretch. Even though we "lost" last year, upon checking the figures, we still find the long-term results pretty encouraging.

Table 0.2, another of those "temporary" tables not destined to disappear any time soon, shows our nine-year performance—and despite coming up short again in 2018, we're still pretty nicely ahead of the pack. If you had invested $100,000 in our 2010 *100 Best* list and adjusted your portfolio according to our annual adjustments, you would have $460,774 today, compared to $371,957 if you had invested in the S&P 500 through an index fund. You'd be $88,817, or just shy of 24 percent, ahead (less, of course, the cost of buying our book each year!). Upshot: we still think we're doing pretty well despite the 2017 hiccup and the less severe 2018 shortfall—again though losing by 1.2 percent to the S&P we still gained 12.6 percent for the year! Well worth the price of a book, in our not-so-unbiased view.

Individual Investor: This Book Is (Still) for You

If you bought this book, you're probably an astute and experienced individual investor who invests in individual stocks in individual companies—or at least *would like* to. Are you alone? Heck no. You have plenty of company.

Those of you who have followed our story (and our stock picks) over the years know that we are unrelenting advocates for the individual investor. We live by the old adage: "Nobody cares about your money more than you do." While we hold this still to be an essential truth, and while a 2013 study we cited for four years bears out the fact that in the wake of the Great Recession and in light of substantial investment advisory fees, more investors were

▼ Table 0.2: Performance Compared to Major Benchmarks

NINE-YEAR PERFORMANCE COMPARISON: *100 BEST STOCKS* VERSUS S&P 500

ANNUAL PERFORMANCE OF EACH *100 BEST* LIST AND COMPOUNDED CUMULATIVE PERFORMANCE

		2010	2011	2012	2013	2014	2015	2016	2017	2018
100 Best Stocks	Gain, percent	**62.5%**	**20.0%**	**5.5%**	**19.2%**	**23.8%**	**15.0%**	**2.65%**	**14.2%**	**12.6%**
	Compounded	62.5%	94.9%	105.6%	145.1%	203.5%	249.0%	258.2%	309.1%	360.8%
	$100,000 invested in 2010	$162,500	$194,919	$205,639	$245,122	$303,461	$348,980	$358,228	$409,097	$460,774
S&P 500	Gain, percent	**44.6%**	**13.1%**	**5.4%**	**15.6%**	**22.4%**	**12.5%**	**2.35%**	**16.4%**	**13.8%**
	Compounded	44.6%	63.5%	72.4%	99.3%	143.9%	174.4%	180.8%	226.9%	272.0%
	$100,000 invested in 2010	$144,600	$163,543	$172,374	$199,264	$243,899	$274,387	$280,835	$326,892	$371,957
Net advantage, $100K invested, *100 Best Stocks*		$17,900	$31,376	$33,265	$45,858	$59,562	$74,593	$77,393	$82,205	$88,817

For twelve-month periods beginning April 1 of previous year, dividends included after 2011 going alone than ever before. That said, we must now take more interest in *where* they were going alone. Recently, on the heels of recent recommendations of investment experts—even the Oracle of Omaha himself—and on the heels of recent investment performance, more and more investors are turning to so-called *passively* managed investments, notably index funds, as a favored alternative to stock picking or so-called *actively* managed funds, which pick stocks *for* you. In this year when even our supposedly "best" stock picks were once again beaten out by the S&P 500 index, we'd be foolish not to take note.

The Growing Popularity of Passive Investing

Pick up any financial journal from the last couple of years or listen to any financial commentator today, and you'll soon realize there has been a shift in sentiment today toward "passive," sometimes known as "index" investing. While passive investing to a large degree retains the notion that you can manage your investments better than a paid advisor can, this new "trendy" investment philosophy suggests that most if not all of you should invest in "passive" investments, that is, "baskets" of stocks defined by an index, rather than trying to pick individual stocks. In fact, this year's resurgence in international and growth stocks could well have been a product of passive investing—passive "index" products make such investing easier, especially for international stocks.

We, of course, as exponents of individual stock picking, take issue with passive investing as a panacea. We do believe it has its place as an anchor or foundation of your portfolio and is a way to play less familiar sectors, like international, especially if you do not have the time or inclination to manage your own stock picks. But beyond that, we still feel pretty strongly that stock picking has its place (else, would we write this book?). Let us share, in this section, the premises—and weaknesses—of passive investing.

It starts with an assessment of what it costs to "get help" with your investments. The first stop on this tour is to examine the cost of hiring a professional advisor to help you with *any* investments—passive or active. For most accounts, a professional advisor will cost 1 percent of your asset value at minimum. Trading commissions may be—and mutual fund fees *will* be—additional to that figure. Mutual fund fees, some of which are hidden, can be surprisingly high; we'll get to that in a minute.

Then there are hedge funds. Those glamorous parking places for rich folks' dough in years past, which charge 2 percent in fees and 20 percent of gains—only, as widely reported in the media, there hasn't been much in the way of gains recently! The decline in hedge fund hegemony was brought to the forefront last year by none other than Mr. Buffett himself.

The Bet: Warren Weighs In

Most of us think of Warren Buffett as the consummate stock picker—and, looking at his 50-plus-year record of picking individual stocks, who could argue? But that doesn't necessarily mean he advocates stock picking for the rest of us.

What gives?

Ten years ago, Mr. Buffett sneered at the performance of professionally managed funds—hedge funds specifically—where concentrations of investable wealth were managed by supposedly the best and the brightest professional stock pickers around: hedge fund managers. If they couldn't beat the S&P 500 index, who could? Were they worth the "2 and 20"—2 percent of assets plus 20 percent of gains—fee structure they routinely charge their clients, whether markets perform well or not?

Mr. Buffett, always eager to prove his postulations and to put his money where his mouth is, made a big bet on the notion that these high-powered funds *do* actually underperform. He bet $500,000 that five so-called "funds of funds" (funds containing other hedge funds) couldn't beat the S&P 500 index, as measured by the low-cost Vanguard S&P Index Fund over a ten-year period. Only one hedge fund manager would even step up to take this bet!

You know where this is going; Mr. Buffett won the bet handily! Over the first nine years (ending December 31, 2016) the funds of funds, hampered by a further 1 percent "funds of funds" fee on top of the "2 and 20," brought in an average of 2.2 percent return compounded annually versus 7.1 percent for the index fund! The actively managed hedge funds failed miserably, mostly due to their costs and fees. (Ha! Now we don't feel so bad with our "mere" 1.2 percent shortfall!)

He laments:

"A lot of very smart people set out to do better than average in securities markets. Call them active investors. Their opposites, passive investors, will by definition do about average. In aggregate, their positions will more or less approximate those of an index fund. Therefore, the balance of the universe—the active investors—must do about average as well. However, those investors will incur far greater costs… A number of smart people are involved in running hedge funds. But to a great extent their efforts are self-neutralizing, and their IQ will not overcome the costs they impose on investors."

He goes on to conclude:

- "Investors, on average and over time, will do better with a low-cost index fund than with a group of funds of [actively managed] funds" (and by association, the actively managed funds themselves);
- "The bottom line: When trillions of dollars are managed by Wall Street-ers charging high fees, it will usually be the managers who reap outsized profits, not the clients";
- "More than $100 billion has been wasted on bad investment advice in the past decade";
- (And thus) "Both large and small investors should stick with low-cost index funds."

The letter can be found on the Berkshire Hathaway website at www .berkshirehathaway.com/letters/2016ltr.pdf (see pages 21–24, "The Bet," for Mr. Buffett's prescient thoughts and conclusions).

And now, for a few conclusions of our own.

Why We Think Stock Picking Still Makes Sense

Where does this leave us as exponents of individual stock picking? Did Warren Buffett, our hero, our mentor, our guiding light to picking good businesses and stocks, suddenly abandon the entire principle by which we operate (and write)?

Not so fast. Of course, Mr. Buffett clearly believes that there is room at the top…room, that is, for stock pickers who really know what they're doing and have the time. (Otherwise would he not have jettisoned his entire $189 billion stock portfolio in favor of index funds?) We see no evidence that he is following this advice—instead, he still feels he can pick stocks, and who can argue? It may not surprise you that we think we can pick stocks too, and that you and we together can ride among the elite horses in this stock-picking race.

Why do we think this? Two reasons, primarily, each of which can be summed up into two three-word statements: (1) averages are averages and (2) cost is cost.

AVERAGES ARE AVERAGES…

What do we mean by "averages are averages"? Simply this: in order for a population (say, a group of stocks) to have an average, *some part* of that population must be above average. When you buy a "basket" of stocks defined by a broad or a sector index, it must by definition carry both the "good" and the "bad" stocks in a group. If you buy an S&P 500 fund, you will get, by definition, the "good" and the "bad" stocks in the S&P 500. If you buy a "sector" fund, say for Financials, or more broadly, "Small Cap Value" or some such, you will get both the good and the bad (and too, the ugly!) stocks in that group.

So why not try to pick out just the "good"? Although we held on to some clunkers like GE and Campbell Soup too long this year, we do think it's possible to pick more of the "good" than the bad as individual stock pickers. And the seven-year win streak that precedes the 2017 and 2018 "downers" bears that notion out.

...And Cost Is Cost.

What do we mean by "cost is cost"? Simply put, you can invest "cheaply" by buying an index fund or "expensively" by hiring an advisor to help you pick stocks (or a hedge fund manager if you're a higher roller) and/or by buying an actively managed mutual fund.

Just how expensive *are* actively managed funds, you might ask? More expensive than most people think.

Although "active" mutual fund and asset management fees have been coming down of late and are advertised at 1 percent or less in many cases, the true cost of mutual funds goes far beyond the well-publicized "expense ratio," which covers basic management, marketing, and distribution costs for the fund. At least three other cost factors add drag to mutual fund performance:

- *Transaction costs for trading securities*—including commissions but also the "spread" between bid and offer prices, which according to one study adds another 1–1.5 percent to costs
- *"Cash drag"*—in a fund, a certain amount of cash must be held for expenses and redemptions, another 0.8–1 percent
- *"Soft dollar" costs*—paid to professional advisory firms offering research and advice to the fund, another 0.5 percent or so

These cost factors may add another 2–3 percent to the cost of owning an actively managed mutual fund, in addition to the 1–1.5 percent "expense ratio" and another 1 percent if you're paying a professional advisor yourself to hold your account and recommend the fund in the first place.

You may be paying 5–6 percent of your asset value to achieve—what? Seven to 8 percent returns in a good year and 14–16 percent gains in an outstanding one? And what about a "down" year? Yes, you can really lose if the markets lay an egg.

Here's the bottom line:

We don't think, by any means, two bad years for our *100 Best Stocks* list should beget a change in your investing strategy.

The logic of trying to pick only the good stuff still prevails, so long as you have the time, energy, inclination, thought process, and tools to pick individual stocks. We think *The 100 Best Stocks to Buy* continues to provide you with a healthy head start in this direction, and we see no reason to abandon the individual stock picking approach as of now—for most of you anyhow. It's cheap, too: not 1 percent or 2 percent for an advisor or "2 and 20" for a hedge fund or 5–6 percent for an actively managed mutual fund— at $16.99 or less per year (and today's $4.95 discount broker commissions) you *can* actively manage your investments and win!

Now that we've made (remade) the case for the individual investor and for individual stock picking, where does *The 100 Best Stocks to Buy* really fit in? Every edition of *100 Best Stocks* is intended as a core tool for the individual investor, especially those investors inclined to buy individual stocks. Most of you probably aren't inclined to buy individual stocks for your entire portfolio—nor should you be unless you have the time and it's your thing to do. Sure, it makes sense to round out your portfolio with index-based funds and ETFs. You might like Japanese companies and products, but who can pick Japanese stocks? Buy the fund instead. Stumped on where to find the best China or international growth opportunities? Buy the fund instead.

It may even make sense, depending on your time and proclivity for this sort of thing, to build a base of index-based ETFs or passively managed funds, and then to "spark" it with a few individual stocks of your choosing. Start with the funds, add the stocks. Or, start with the stocks, add the funds. Either way, *The 100 Best Stocks to Buy* is designed to help.

If you accept the idea of picking individual stocks for some part of your investment portfolio, then it becomes a question of what tools and process to use. You need to start somewhere; if you're reading this, we think you've started in the right place! If nothing else, our book is far less expensive than 1 percent of your stock portfolio (we hope!).

In this vein, we'd like to share a review of *The 100 Best Stocks to Buy in 2018* recently posted by "buffettfan" on Amazon:

"I purchase this book each year and use it as one of the many resources to follow stocks I already own or that I may be interested in. This is an excellent book to use for research of larger well-known companies. It describes the business, its growth rate, dividend growth rate, reasons to buy, reasons for caution, etc. This is not a book for trading stocks. Most of the 100 stocks remain the same from year to year with only a handful of changes into and out of the recommended stocks. That is one of the reasons I continue to purchase the book each year. Buying an S & P Index Fund or ETF has become more in vogue recently but, for anyone preferring to own individual large company stocks, this is a useful addition to your library."

* * *

We know that *100 Best Stocks* is hardly the only tool available. The Internet has made this book one of hundreds of choices for acquiring investing information. With the speed of cyberspace, our book will hardly be the most current source. In fact, we know, despite recent changes to the publishing schedule, that we're still at least six months out-of-date. If you check our research, you'll be able to come up with two to three calendar quarters of more current financial information, news releases, and so forth.

Does the delay built into the publishing cycle make our book a poor source? Not at all. It works because the companies we choose don't change much and because they avoid the temptation to manage short-term, quarter-to-quarter performance. We chose these companies *because* they have sustainable performance, so who cares if the latest details or news releases are included? In *The 100 Best Stocks to Buy in 2019*, as with all previous editions, we focus on the *story*—the story of each company, the *intangibles*—not just the latest facts and figures.

To that same point, *100 Best Stocks* goes well beyond just being a stock screen or a study of stocks to invest in. Analysis forms the base of *100 Best Stocks*, but it isn't the rigid, strictly numbers-based selection and analysis so often found in published "best stocks" lists. Sure, we look at earnings, cash flow, balance sheet strength, and so forth, but we'll also look far beyond those things. We'll look at the intangible and often subtle factors that make truly great businesses—that is, companies—great. That is, once again, the company's *story*.

Great companies have good business fundamentals, but what makes them really great is the presence of intangibles and subtleties—the brands, the marketplace successes, the management style, the competitive advantages, the loyal customers—that will *keep* them great or make them greater in the future. In our view, *good intangibles today lead to better business fundamentals down the road.*

100 Best Stocks is not a simple numbers-based stock screen like many found on the Internet and elsewhere today. It is a selection and analysis of really good businesses you would want to buy and own, not just for past results but for future outcomes. Does "future" mean "forever"? No, not anymore. While the *100 Best Stocks* list correlates well with the notion of "blue-chip" stocks, the harsh reality is that "blue chip" no longer means "forever."

We feel that the 100 companies listed and analyzed in the pages that follow are the best companies to own for 2019 and, generally, beyond. That said, the word "own" has become a more active concept these days. Gone are the days of "own forever," like the halcyon days when Peter's parents, Jerry and Betty Sander, bought their 35 shares of General Motors, lovingly placed the stock certificate in their safe-deposit box, and henceforth bought nothing but GM cars. Today, there is no forever; the economy, technology, and consumer tastes simply change too fast, and the businesses that participate in the economy by necessity change with it. Ownership is a more active concept than it was even ten years ago.

So going forward, we offer the *100 Best* companies to own now and for 2019, those that have the best chances of not only surviving but evolving with—or even ahead of—the economy based on their current market position and approach to doing business. We think these are the best companies to (1) stay with or perhaps stay slightly ahead of business change, (2) provide short- and long-term returns in the form of cash and modest appreciation, and (3) do so with a measure of safety or at least reduced volatility so that you can burn your energy doing other things besides staring at stock quotes day and night. And—importantly—these are the picks we feel can beat the indexes, especially in the long run.

Bottom line: our intent is simple and straightforward. We provide a list and a written vignette composed from the facts and the story. You take the information as it's presented, do your own assessment, reach your own conclusions, and take your own actions. Anything more, anything less, won't work. You're in charge, and we suspect that you like it that way.

What's New for 2019

For those of you who've stayed with us over the years, you'll find that this edition takes the same approach as before. For those of you reading for the first time, here are some guidelines and ideas we follow.

First and once again: no changes to the author team of Scott and Peter (we'll introduce ourselves in a minute). Once again, no significant changes to the structure or format of our presentation. Continuing is our emphasis on sustainable value, strong market position and other intangibles, and sustainable and growing cash returns to investors, in the form of dividends and share buybacks as well as share appreciation. We continue to take interest in the persistency of dividend increases above and beyond the yield itself, and we continue to stay focused on total shareholder returns. For the most part, we are playing the hand that got us here.

However, although we say every year that our investing style and presentation has remained essentially the same, the style of the best artists, writers, or even software programmers evolve over time. As with any blend of science and art, investing most certainly included, the approach evolves; the style acquires a little of this and a little of that and loses a little of something else as time goes on. Experience matters and is taken into account. Changes in the world investing context and environment factor in—and, heck, we're getting older and perhaps a bit wiser. Maybe we see things a little differently than we did eight years ago…and certainly 35 years ago. All of these factors influence the mix; here are a few directions we've taken recently (or have continued with emphasis) with this edition:

- *A little more growth.* While we may wish we hadn't someday, we did turn our heads a bit toward the recent gains in growth stocks and the growing (not just recovering) economy we find ourselves in. As we say later in this section, growth is part of value, and in this edition, we have pulled some of the slow movers and replaced them with a bit more energy—growth stocks! We removed some redundant and perhaps overly "staid" issues like Colgate-Palmolive and Campbell Soup and made a few high-energy replacements like Intuitive Surgical and Trex. We replaced 14 stocks in all, 11 of them with "Aggressive Growth" companies. We went from four companies that didn't pay dividends last year to 11 such non-payers this year. While our total portfolio still largely consists of steady, defensive, dividend-paying issues, we think we have jazzed it up just a bit and sensibly.

- *Low-volatility bias.* We continue to think it's important to get good returns but also to sleep at night. *Steady* growth, *steady* returns, *steady* dividend increases—that's what we continue to prefer for the majority of our picks. While we present "beta" as a measure of market correlation, we look deeper into the actual patterns and history of earnings, dividends, cash flow, and yes, share price—and now the relative statistical stability as reported by Value Line. If it's a wild ride (or if there *are* no earnings, cash flows, etc.), we don't get on; we prefer to watch from the sidelines instead. You'll never find the likes of Twitter or Snap on our list. We know—as the markets continue to rise through the years, the chances for corrective "volatility" increase—there isn't a whole lot we can do about that except to stick to our knitting. That said, we're reaching a bit more outside our normal "core" type of holding for the third year in a row to pick up a few more aggressive companies that seem at the forefront of change. We continue to add a few smaller companies for the list, to add some energy and reap the benefits of these new companies still coming into their own (more on that in a minute).

- *Still playing defense.* While we look more for up-and-comers, we still stick to the more defensive stance taken starting in 2014 in light of market "exuberance" and in recognition of the fact that in our multiyear tenure at the reins of this book, we have yet to see a down year! Our lists continue to be constructed to provide enough growth opportunity to beat the market but also to beat the market in a *down* market, that is, to be down only 5 percent if the market dropped 10 percent. This position probably played a large part in our failure to win in 2017 and 2018. Quite honestly, many of our *100 Best Stocks* seem fully valued at this juncture. We were—and still are—nervous about riding them any further. Our strategy for dealing with this continues to be to evaluate all of our picks carefully using our "sell if there's something better to buy" philosophy and try to visualize how they would do "on a sloppy track." And while we are embracing growth-oriented issues, we continue to avoid "momentum" plays, as they have a tendency to beat a "mo" path downward at the slightest sign of change. Thus, to our peril, we have avoided Facebook, Netflix, Google, and others (although we do have two of the "FAANGs"—Amazon and Apple).

- *Focus on millennials.* The shift continues. A January 2015 *New York Times* headline summed up the inflection point perfectly: "Millennials Set to Outnumber Baby Boomers." There are now about 81 million millennials and 75 million boomers, with millennials counted as being born between 1982 and 1997 and, more importantly, with a digital silver spoon in their mouths. Hmm, we thought. Have we embraced this adequately in our stock picks, given that we like companies with at least steady, and preferably improving, brand strength and loyal customer bases? Millennials are typically portrayed as digitally fluent, preferring unstructured environments, having a taste for customizable products, healthy foods, immediate gratification—all with short attention spans and relatively less loyalty to companies and brands than their non-digital ancestors. We've had to ask ourselves—Do they drink Coke? Buy IBM? Shop at Target? Wash their clothes with Tide? Buy clothes emblazoned with polo ponies? Go to movie theaters?—and a thousand other questions. Are we seeing—or about to see—a major shift in consumer preferences as millennials gradually take charge of the commercial world? Do long-standing brands like Coke and Cheerios have cachet with these groups like they once did with us older folks?

We've seen considerable recent evidence in the retail world that the "millennial" megatrend is large and here to stay. Online shopping is no longer just a novelty—it has captured 9.5 percent of the US retail market as of Q1 2018 and is growing 16.5 percent per year. Shopping malls and mall stores in particular have seen sales and traffic declines. We took Walmart and Tiffany off the 2017 list and Macy's and Target off the 2018 list.

The "stay-at-home" economy is growing gangbusters, and we're still not sure we've fully embraced this shift. We have, however, incorporated a review of how a company will fare with this shift, keeping retailers like Costco and Ross or Kroger on the list as they appear relatively immune to e-commerce incursion (we hope we're right!). We have also put Target back on the list for 2019 out of respect for its physical store strengths, relative online success, and strong management. For every retailer, we ask ourselves: Can you get it (efficiently) on Amazon Prime? If yes—and if there's nothing otherwise compelling about the shopping experience—we're inclined to hit the delete button.

We think this stay-at-home trend is important enough that we've now dedicated Table 9 in our "stars" tables to capturing the Top 10 Stay-at-Home Stars: companies that will prosper most from the stay-at-home economy boom.

- *New focus on "smaller" companies.* For the most part, the "typical" *100 Best* company has been large, well known, steady, profitable—a "blue-chip" stock in old investing parlance. That is still true, but good investors try to find companies for which the best years are in front of them… or more precisely, they blend some of today's successful companies with some of tomorrow's. "Invest where the puck is going, not just where it has been" hockey great Wayne Gretzky might have said about this. To that end, we've started to identify smaller companies on the *100 Best* list. We now have a size indicator in the heading for each stock. "Large Cap" companies have a total market-share value (or "cap," number of shares outstanding times share price) greater than $5 billion. "Mid Cap" companies fall between $1 billion and $5 billion, and "Small Cap" companies have a total market worth of less than $1 billion. We added three Mid Caps and two Small Caps for 2019, so now of our 100 companies, 11 are Mid Caps and four of them, Daktronics, Schnitzer Steel, and this year's CalAmp and Craft Brew Alliance, are Small Caps. In future years we would like to have 15–20 Small Cap and Mid Cap companies to add a little energy and interest to our list; we're almost there.

Other than that, for 2019 and beyond we continue on a value-driven track, looking for the very best businesses to invest in with an emphasis on "sell if there's something better to buy." We look not just for stocks that will prosper in a short-term business-friendly tax-friendly environment as created by the Trump administration via the 2017 Tax Cuts and Jobs Act (*anybody* can do that!); we are looking for *long-term* value. Big jumps in net earnings from tax savings don't impress us! But it is nice not to have to write much about earnings and revenue shortfalls created by the stronger dollar— that short-term phenomenon seems to be over for now. That said, what will happen going forward with trade and currency is devilishly hard to predict at this juncture. Finally, even as international stocks get their day in the sun, we still prefer strong exporters as a way to play the global economy, and we expect a leveling dollar to make this approach look wiser going forward than it has in the past two years.

Finally, we're glad to see commodity prices recover after the "crash" cycle; we continue to stick with a few favorites like Chevron and Mosaic. They should prosper as (1) the commodity cycle reverses, and (2) they capitalize on the efficiencies that became necessary during the funk.

About Your Authors

If you're a regular reader of the *100 Best Stocks* series you've probably seen the following before. It's about us, and not much has changed about us, so feel free to skip this section if it's altogether too familiar—or if it doesn't matter much to begin with.

Peter Sander

Peter is an independent professional researcher, writer, and journalist specializing in personal finance, investing, and location reference, as well as other general business topics. He has written 51 books on these topics, as well as numerous financial columns, and has performed independent, privately contracted research and studies. He came from a background in the corporate world, having experienced a 21-year career with a major West Coast technology firm.

He is, most emphatically, an individual investor and has been since the age of 12 (okay, so Warren Buffett started when he was 11), when his curiosity at the family breakfast table got the better of him. He started reading the stock pages with his parents. He had an opportunity during a "project week" in the seventh grade to read and learn about the stock market. He read Louis Engel's *How to Buy Stocks*, then the preeminent—and one of the only—consumer-friendly books about investing available at the time. He picked stocks and made graphs of their performance by hand with colored pens on graph paper. He put his hard-earned savings into buying five shares of each of three different companies. He watched those stocks like a hawk and salted away the meager dividends to reinvest. He's been investing ever since. (Incidentally, Warren Buffett bought Cities Service preferred shares, Peter bought Burlington Northern preferred shares following much the same principles, and how ironic that Mr. Buffett came to own all of Burlington Northern. Perhaps Peter will come to own a big oil company someday.)

Yes, Peter has an MBA from Indiana University in Bloomington, but it isn't an MBA in finance. He also took the coursework and certification exam to become a certified financial planner (CFP). By design and choice, he has never held a job in the financial profession. His goal has always been to share his knowledge and experience in an educational way that is helpful for the individual (as an investor and a personal financier) to make his or her own decisions.

He has never earned a living giving direct investment advice or managing money for others, nor does he intend to.

A few years ago, it dawned on Peter that he has really made his living finding value and helping or teaching others to find value. Not just in stocks but other things in business and in life. What does he mean by value? Simply, the current and potential *worth* of something as compared to its price or cost. As it turns out, he's made a career out of assessing the value of people (for marketers), places (as places to live), and companies (for investors).

Scott Bobo

Peter and Scott have been friends and colleagues since, roughly, tenth grade (a long time!). Scott has been part of the team for nine years now and has been huge not only in identifying the *100 Best Stocks* but also analyzing them and explaining their pros and cons crisply and in plain English so that you can make the best use of the list. Having Scott on the team allows you to get the combined wisdom and observations of two people, not just one, in an arena where one plus one almost always equals something greater than two.

Scott has been an investor since age 14, when he made the switch from analyzing baseball box scores to looking at the numbers and charts in the business section. In his 20-plus years in engineering and technology management, he's learned that a unique product value proposition is important to the success of any company. He has also learned (the hard way) that proper financial fundamentals are critical. From a development manager's perspective, comprehending a new product's risk/reward proposition is one of the keys to a company's success. From an investor's perspective, it's also one of the keys to successful value investing in a dynamic, innovation-driven market.

Scott adds a strong analytical touch. But he is most at home as an applications engineer, explaining how a company's products work and how they apply to a customer's needs. Consequently, and in addition to analytical legwork, Scott adds an extraordinary and very real-world sense of how a company's products "fit" in the marketplace. Determining whether a company's products are relevant, best-in-class, and have a competitive advantage over others is an oft-overlooked core skill for a value investor. Scott brings this skill to the table in a big way.

How do these diverse experiences of Peter and Scott translate into picking stocks? Just like customers or places to live, we want companies that produce the greatest return, the highest value, *per dollar invested*—and *for the amount of risk taken*. The companies we will identify as among the *100 Best* have, in our assessment, the greatest and most persistent long-term *value*, and if you can buy these companies at a *reasonable price* (a factor that we largely leave out of this analysis because this is a book, and prices can change considerably), then these investments deliver the best prospects while keeping the downsides manageable.

Later we'll come back to describe some of the attributes of value that we look for.

Changes in the 100 Best Stocks List

When we first took over this series from John Slatter for the 2010 edition, we made 26 changes, not a revolution but perhaps a strong evolution of the philosophy toward core value principles, strong competitive advantages and intangibles, and healthy cash returns. After that first year we went back to more of a fine-tuning mode, changing 14 stocks for the 2011 list, 12 for 2012, and back to 14 for 2013. In 2014, we held the line in a measure of defense and the simple inability to find "better horses," and changed only eight stocks. For 2015 and with the heady gains in the markets (almost 24 percent) we felt that a few more of our horses might be ready to fade and brought in 13 fresh ones for that year's ride. The pattern continued mostly unchanged in 2016 when we changed ten stocks, and in 2017, we changed nine.

That number ticked up to ten in 2018 as we lost no fewer than four companies to takeovers and fine-tuned the list with six others. This year—for 2019—we're getting a bit more aggressive again: *14* changes in all. We had only two "taken out": Aetna and Qualcomm (the latter looks not to be taken out, but its business prospects seem sufficiently confused by legal challenges and their acquisition attempts that we're taking them off anyway). For the other 12, here's where we decided to slice off some of the humdrum household products names like Kimberly-Clark, Colgate-Palmolive, and Campbell Soup, and cut several winners like Aqua America, WD-40, and Otter Tail, which, while remaining excellent companies, had just grown a bit beyond our expectations and would seem to have little left for the next race.

We thought, in today's market, some of our new, more growth-oriented picks would fit our "sell when there's something better to buy" mantra. The overall methodology used for analysis and selection of the *100 Best Stocks* remains largely unchanged. We continue to focus on fundamentals that really count, like cash flow; profit margins and balance sheet strength; and those intangibles such as brand, market share, channel and supply-chain excellence, and management quality, which really determine success *going forward*. While we're adding a bit more growth focus, we continue to emphasize dividends and, more generally, investor returns. We still feel that investors should get paid something to commit their precious capital to a company; it's a sign of good faith to investors and provides at least some return while waiting for a larger return in the future—or if things go south later on. That said, we wanted to give you some choices that delay this gratification if that's okay with you as an investor. This year 89 of this year's *100 Best* pay at least some dividends—down from 96 in 2017. Our "legacy" non-payers are CarMax, Itron, Amazon, and First Solar. To that list we add Aptiv, CalAmp, Intuitive Surgical, Craft Brew Alliance, Myriad Genetics, Trex, and Square. These stocks are included because of other prospects; we can turn our heads the other way on the dividend for now but would expect some dividends or an outright sale eventually as the business models mature.

Despite the increased dabbling in growth, a "hallmark" factor differentiating our approach is our continued preference for companies with a track record for regular dividend *increases*. A few years ago, we started tracking, for each company, the number of dividend increases or *raises* (yes, you can think of them as comparable to a raise in your own wage or salary) in the past ten years. We are proud to report that of the 89 *100 Best Stocks* paying dividends in 2018, fully 65 of them (73 percent) raised their dividend from 2017 to 2018. This percentage was greater two years ago (88 percent). While we've seen some companies temporarily hold back dividends due to the commodity cycle and a greater emphasis on growth and investment in their businesses, others (like Apple, for instance) have enriched their raises as a consequence of the 2017 Tax and Jobs Act and resultant tax savings and repatriation of mounds of free cash. Of the 89 companies that pay dividends, 36 of them have raised their dividends in each of the past ten years, and 26 more have raised them each of the past eight or nine years (most of these took a year or two off during the Great Recession), adding up to 62 stocks that can be depended on for annual raises. Pretty good stuff, in our view.

As in all editions, we review the performance of our 2018 picks in some detail and continue with our "stars" lists identifying the best stocks in six different categories:

1. Yield Stars (stocks with solid dividend yields—Table 6)
2. Dividend Aggressors (companies with strong and persistent records and policies toward dividend *growth*—Table 6.1)
3. Safety Stars (solid performers in any market—Table 7)
4. Growth Stars (companies positioned for above-average growth—Table 8)
5. Stay-at-Home Stars (formerly Prosperity Stars—companies poised to do particularly well in today's modernized e-commerce—Table 9)
6. Moat Stars (companies with significant sustainable competitive advantage—Table 10)

So, if you're an investor partial to any of these factors, such as safety, these lists are for you.

2017–2018: An Improved Business Climate—with Uncertainty

Now we diagnose what happened in the year gone by and try to turn that into a prognosis for the coming year. Always a challenge in any year—and especially in one where we missed our overarching goal of beating the S&P 500 index—again.

Of course, the year followed an unusual one featuring the surprise election of Donald Trump. The advent of the Trump administration brought with it the prospect of sweeping, mostly pro-business change—less regulation, lower tax rates, more stimulus—and some antibusiness change in certain corners of the commercial landscape, including healthcare, environmental, and alternative energy businesses. The previous year ended with a "Trump trade" that benefited financial and tech firms in particular with the promise of less regulation, higher interest rates, and stronger growth.

Starting in 2017, some but not all of the Trump agenda came into existence. Some regulation was pulled back. Most anticipated cutbacks in the Affordable Care Act did not happen. The landmark piece of legislation that *did* happen was the Tax Cuts and Jobs Act of (late) 2017, which dramatically cut corporate (and personal) tax rates, gave corporations a path to repatriate piles of cash previously kept overseas, and limited corporate interest expense deductions in certain cases. As 2018 plays out into 2019, we will see more of what the net effect turns out to be, but higher reported corporate profits, spending on business investment, payouts to shareholders and, in certain cases, employees, and a general $1.5 trillion (over ten years) boost to the economy will result. Business will *look* better if in fact not *be* better. (Note to readers: higher profits based on tax cuts do *not* indicate improved business *performance*, at least in our view.)

Another Trump administration activity that gives us a "wait-and-see" at least at this point is the policy on trade. At the time of this writing, the Trump administration is dabbling in protective tariffs for certain basic industries such as aluminum and steel and is considering extension into other more high-value-add products like automobiles and machinery. Not surprisingly the rest of the world is responding in retaliatory fashion with tariffs of their own on US goods. We don't know where this is going, but for now it concerns us that, first, it introduces inflation, as the cost of everything could be eventually driven up by these tariffs, and, second, it introduces a level of unpredictability into all business everywhere, as many key business decisions like factory location are best made with years of policy stability on this front, not weekly gyrations. Finally, we are concerned about inflation in general as (1) the tax cut will increase the deficit and borrowing, (2) tariffs and other policies will increase the cost of landed goods, and (3) we emerge naturally from the recent commodity down cycle—all in a context of higher economic growth with people having more money to spend. So these "business-friendly policies" have a lot of possible offsets in this real world of uncertainty. We enter 2019 with questions: How much more money will new tax and spending policies put into individual and corporate pockets? How much will interest rates rise? And how fast will marketplace trends, such as the rise of millennials and the decline of bricks-and-mortar retail, change the business landscape? Here are six specific factors and trends that drove, and continue to drive, the markets:

- *Higher interest rates but predictable Fed policy.* In past years, we've written of an "accommodative" Fed, doing what it could to keep interest rates low, money supply high, and business and personal finances stimulated. Now the economy has recovered, and employment in particular has strengthened, so the Fed, rather than providing a tailwind, is trying to raise rates gradually to control inflation and temper money supply *without* capitating growth. Given this tough balancing act, in late 2016 they embarked on a plan to raise rates *gradually* and *predictably*, keeping everyone informed of what they plan to do as they go. The Fed as gentle tailwind is over for now; the Fed will probably keep a closer eye on inflation than employment, as unemployment recently hit a multiyear low of 3.8 percent. Interest rates are likely to be neutral to a slight negative in the markets over the coming year and a stronger risk to income-generating investments in our portfolio such as REITs—though we're hoping much of the risk has already been priced into these stocks for now (high-dividend payers are "worth" relatively less when one can get 3 percent or more from a completely safe government bond, which recently became the case). So long as the Fed retains its current course of moderation and transparency, we feel the markets shouldn't feel too much impact.

- *Trade friction.* The economy functions best when allowed to function without distortions, in our view. The trade wars and tariffs mentioned earlier don't usually accomplish much at the end of the day; one industry gets protected at the expense of the other, and the resulting tariff structures are inflationary and cause uncertainty, both of which hurt the economies they were designed to protect. In our opinion President Trump is experimenting with such protections because it is one of the few things he can do unilaterally without anyone's approval (this is as close as we'll come to becoming "political" in our book), and we hope he soon sees the consequences and moves on to more proven ways to manage the trade deficit. In the meantime, these actions could be very disruptive to certain industries such as autos, manufactured goods, logistics companies, and agriculture.

- *Exit from commodity down cycle.* As 2018 progresses we see that a combination of higher demand and rationalized supply has brought most commodity prices out of the deep doldrums if not to mid-2010s decade highs. Oil has recovered to about $70 a barrel from the low $30s (still short of the previous $100s), and most other commodities have, to a degree, followed suit. This is good for the many industries involved in producing these commodities (which have also become more efficient to survive the lean years), which will in turn spend more on equipment and services to produce. All good, unless demand once again outstrips supply and other distortions such as speculative futures trading come in to drive the prices of commodities unrealistically high—such inflation in this environment could be hazardous to many parts of the economy. For now, companies involved in producing commodities or supplying those companies with products and services should do well.

- *Emergence of the stay-at-home economy.* An offshoot of the millennial emergence, there has been a marked shift in the propensity to carry on daily activities, whether necessary or recreational, at home "while sitting on the couch." The emergence and success of Amazon Prime is, of course, glaring evidence of this trend. More and more households elect to order food and other staples, entertain themselves, and even interact with others at home through social media. CNBC's Jim Cramer and others suggest good times ahead for TV and video content providers such as Netflix, home food and pizza delivery (Domino's), video game and video game hardware makers (Activision, NVIDIA), social media, consumer electronics, home improvement, cloud computing, payment services providers, small-package logistics providers—you get the idea. Of course, the trend will hurt traditional retail, mall operators, and possibly even energy and automotive interests. We've embraced the trend to a greater degree but not wholly in our stock picks, adding Amazon, a couple of logistics providers, and now Square, Sealed Air, and Zebra Technologies, and de-emphasizing retailers.

- *US manufacturing growth—a resurgence?* For years, we've envisioned a steady, if not ground-shaking, reshoring of manufacturing to American soil. Companies finally got the memo that it isn't just about labor costs—long, inflexible supply chains and the inability to control quality negate the savings, sometimes in a big way. Chinese labor costs are going up, and improved availability and declining costs of US energy resources, especially natural gas, are helping even more. The Trump administration, through its "bully pulpit" so far, has aimed at slowing the offshoring of jobs if not an obvious repatriation of manufacturing from overseas. Now some industries like aluminum and steel are scoring more direct "protection." But thus far we haven't seen a wholesale repatriation—again the trade uncertainty will eat into this. True, some supply chains, especially for electronics products, simply aren't deep enough to support US manufacturing, although Apple supplier Foxconn's selection of a Wisconsin site for a major new plant suggests that it's not impossible to reshore such plants. Whether this "buzz" really results in a major upsurge in US manufacturing, which accounted for only 11.6 percent of GDP (down from 11.7 percent in 2016) and 7.9 percent of employment in 2016, remains to be seen. Many of our companies, like Illinois Tool Works, Prologis, FedEx, Eastman Chemical, and others will benefit from reshoring.

- *Persistence of share buybacks.* Companies have accumulated huge hoards of cash, as they have learned how to manage expenses and leverage their infrastructure to produce more for less. Although a big chunk of that cash is still parked overseas, companies continue to actively buy back shares, producing rather silent but persistent returns to existing shareholders.

S&P's Howard Silverblatt estimates that S&P 500 companies bought back an estimated $510 billion in 2017 compared to $536 billion in 2016, $573 billion in 2015, and $553 billion in 2014 (the record is $589 billion repurchased in 2007). The rise in share prices is at least partly responsible for the slight 2016 and 2017 dip. That said, cash provided by the tax cuts and repatriation may result in buybacks as high as *$800 billion in 2018* according to some estimates (we're concerned this could dry up a bit in 2019 as the windfall cash is exhausted). Many companies on our *100 Best Stocks* list could be classified as "buyback aggressors," retiring 10–20 percent and as much as 50 percent of outstanding float since 2004. This, of course, serves to increase returns, both to the shareholders who sell and to those who remain to enjoy a higher rate of return on the remaining shares. Notably, Apple spent $23.7 billion on buybacks just in the *first quarter* of 2018—a figure larger than the total market capitalization of many of the stocks on our list!

Whether companies continue buybacks at these rates depends on continued strong cash flows from general business results and from tax changes and whether they have alternative investments in capital goods, other equipment—or paying for inflation. Again, if inflation spikes unexpectedly we would anticipate an adverse effect on several fronts, buybacks included.

Report Card: Recapping Our 2018 Picks

Once again, we lost. Not quite as badly as with the 2017 list, but we lost to our major benchmark, the S&P 500. We could make excuses, but really the loss is mostly attributable to our investing style, which is biased toward companies with long-term stability and track records in paying and raising dividends. Simply put, the market—the aggregate investing community—did not value such stocks so highly in a year when interest rates were rising and so many strong growth opportunities were out there. We had too many big dividend payers and one major blowup—General Electric—that lost more than 50 percent of its value. These two items go a long way toward explaining our "failure" (though we don't really like to refer to a 12.6 percent gain as a "failure").

At this juncture, we'll once again do a short refresher on how we evaluate our gains. There are many ways to evaluate the performance of a group of stocks over time. Some are simplistic, such as averaging the percent gain in each share price. But such a method may not weight a portfolio very realistically, for it assumes you buy the same number of shares of Amazon at $1,600 as you would Daktronics at $8.50. We feel it's better to take the approach of an investor with $100,000 to invest—who invested $1,000 in each of the *100 Best Stocks* across the board, regardless of share price. Sure, you end up with some weird quantities of shares in your portfolio, but the portfolio, and thus the performance metrics, isn't weighted in favor of more expensive stocks.

The Bottom Line

If you had invested $100,000 in our *100 Best Stocks 2018* list on April 1, 2017—$1,000 in each of the 100 stocks—you would have ended up with $110,279 on April 1, 2018, not including dividends paid during that period for a decent 10.3 percent gain. Including dividends of some $2,353, you would have ended up with $112,632. The S&P, as measured by the buyable SPDR S&P 500 ETF Trust ("SPY"), was ahead 13.8 percent, including dividends ($113,786) during that period. We lost by $1,154 on a $100,000 investment—but still think we were winners particularly in the long term and taking risk into account as described at the beginning of this narrative.

Winners and Losers

The full list of the *100 Best Stocks 2018* and how they did through the comparison period can be found in Appendix A. At this point, we'll give an overview of what really worked and what didn't within the list. First, the winners:

▼ **Table 1: Performance Analysis:** *100 Best Stocks 2018*

TOP 20 WINNERS, 1-YEAR GAIN/LOSS, APRIL 1, 2017–APRIL 1, 2018

Company	Symbol	Price 4/1/2017	Price 4/1/2018	% change	Dollar gain, $1,000 invested (including dividends)
First Solar (*)	FSLR	$29.55	$70.98	140.2%	$1,402.03
Boeing (*)	BA	$180.47	$327.88	81.7%	$847.68
Amazon	AMZN	$886.75	$1,447.34	63.2%	$632.18
Schnitzer Steel	SCHN	$20.65	$32.35	56.7%	$602.91
AbbVie	ABBV	$65.16	$94.65	45.3%	$491.41
Novo Nordisk	NVO	$34.28	$49.25	43.7%	$474.04
Deere	DE	$108.86	$155.32	42.7%	$448.83
Valero	VLO	$66.29	$92.77	39.9%	$443.20
Abbott Labs (*)	ABT	$42.72	$59.92	40.3%	$427.90
Applied Materials (*)	AMAT	$40.28	$55.61	38.1%	$390.52
ResMed	RMD	$71.97	$98.47	36.8%	$387.38
Chemed (*)	CHE	$200.37	$272.86	36.2%	$367.27
UnitedHealth Corp.	UNH	$164.01	$219.87	34.1%	$358.88
Visa	V	$88.87	$119.62	34.6%	$354.34
Eastman Chemical	EMN	$80.80	$105.58	30.7%	$333.17
Columbia Sportswear	COLM	$58.75	$76.43	30.1%	$314.04
Fair Isaac	FICO	$128.95	$169.37	31.3%	$313.45
NextEra Energy	NEE	$128.37	$163.33	27.2%	$303.89
Union Pacific	UNP	$105.92	$134.43	26.9%	$294.00
Aetna	AET	$133.32	$169.00	26.8%	$282.63

* = New for 2018

The year 2018 gave us only 65 winners (stocks that were up) out of 100 compared to 77 in 2017, 57 winners in 2016, 79 for the 2015 list, and 89 for 2014. Simply put, we had too many losers in an otherwise strong year.

The winners hailed from many divergent parts of our list. To note first on our Top 20 Winners list (Table 1) are the stellar performances of some of our stronger "growth" names, including Amazon, First Solar, and Boeing, the latter two added for the year. Also notable are strong recoveries in Schnitzer Steel, Deere, Novo Nordisk, and ResMed. Our new picks did quite well, with six out of ten total new picks ending up on this top gainers list (notably, two of our top losers were also new picks!).

Now, for the losers:

▼ Table 2: Performance Analysis: *100 Best Stocks 2018*

TOP LOSERS, 1-YEAR GAIN/LOSS, APRIL 1, 2017–APRIL 1, 2018

Company	Symbol	Price 4/1/2017	Price 4/1/2018	% change	Dollar loss, $1,000 invested (including dividends)
Comcast	CMSCA	$37.60	$34.17	-9.1%	$(74.47)
Whirlpool	WHR	$171.33	$153.11	-10.6%	$(78.33)
Bemis	BMS	$48.86	$43.52	-10.9%	$(84.53)
Procter & Gamble	PG	$90.03	$79.28	-11.9%	$(88.75)
AT&T	T	$41.55	$35.65	-14.2%	$(94.58)
RPM International	RPM	$55.03	$47.67	-13.4%	$(111.21)
Kimberly-Clark	KMB	$131.63	$110.13	-16.3%	$(133.63)
Schlumberger	SLB	$78.10	$64.78	-17.1%	$(144.94)
Mosaic	MOS	$29.18	$24.28	-16.8%	$(155.93)
Steelcase	SCS	$16.75	$13.60	-18.8%	$(158.21)
Empire State Realty Trust	ESRT	$20.64	$16.79	-18.7%	$(166.18)
Kroger	KR	$29.42	$23.94	-18.6%	$(169.27)
Welltower	WELL	$70.82	$54.43	-23.1%	$(181.02)
CVS Health	CVS	$78.50	$62.21	-20.8%	$(182.04)
Dentsply Sirona (*)	XRAY	$62.87	$50.31	-20.0%	$(194.21)
General Mills	GIS	$59.01	$45.06	-23.6%	$(204.20)
Campbell Soup	CPB	$57.34	$43.31	-24.5%	$(215.03)
Fresh Del Monte	FDP	$59.23	$45.24	-23.6%	$(226.07)
Tupperware (*)	TUP	$68.91	$48.38	-29.8%	$(258.45)
General Electric	GE	$29.80	$13.48	-54.8%	$(523.49)

* = New for 2018

Our biggest losers list, as mentioned before, was anchored by über-failure General Electric, which surprised the entire investment world with its post-financial era malaise. We saw a lot of weakness in consumer staples (Campbells, General Mills, Procter & Gamble, Bemis) retail again (Kroger, CVS), resources (Mosaic, Schlumberger), and real estate investment trusts (Welltower, Empire State) where the prospects for higher interest rates hit hard. We thought all of these issues (except GE) would recover sooner than they did. Many—but not all—of these stocks came off the list for 2019, sticking to our "sell when there's something better to buy" mantra. Which brings us to...

Really, It's All about Value

Those of you who take in our book every year have seen this before, but we remain steadfast in the principles of value investing.

For intelligent investors, chasing the latest fad doesn't work; buying something and locking it away forever doesn't work anymore, either. Investors must make intelligent choices based on true value and follow those choices through time and change. It all points to taking a value-oriented approach to investing and to staying modestly active with your investments.

The next obvious task is to define what we mean by a "value" approach. Essentially, it is to think of buying shares in a company as buying the company itself; it is about putting yourself in an entrepreneurial frame of mind, not just an investment frame of mind. Would you want to own that business? Why or why not?

Fundamentally, whether or not you want to own the business depends on two factors: first, the *returns* you expect to receive on your investment in the near- and long-term future, and second, the *risk* you'll take in generating those returns. Fortunately, the third factor the prospective entrepreneur must consider—"Do I have the time to run this business?"—is less of an issue for the investor.

You are looking for tangible value—tangible worth—for your precious, scarce, and hard-earned investment capital. That return can come in the form of immediate cash returns (dividends), longer-term cash returns (dividends and especially growing dividends), or as growth in the value of assets longer term. If you realize your return in the form of owning a share of a larger company eventually, that's still a legitimate return. Cash flow received later in the form of a higher share price or a takeover is still cash return; it is just less certain because of the forces of change that may take place in the interim.

It is also theoretically worth less because of the nature of discounting—a dollar received tomorrow is worth more than a dollar received 20 years in the future.

The point: many investment experts distinguish between "value" and "growth" investing; in fact, mutual funds are often classified as being one or the other. We continue to dismiss this separation; growth can be an essential component of a firm's value. That growth can come either in the form of asset values or cash returns—i.e., growing dividends. This year, more than ever, we embrace growth as part of the value equation.

Value also implies safety. The safety comes in three forms. First is the quality and soundness of the firm's financial fundamentals—that is, income, cash flow, and the balance sheet. Value companies have plenty of reserves, a large enough *margin of safety*, to weather downturns and unforeseen events in the marketplace. Second, they have strong enough intangibles (brands, market position, supply-chain strength, etc.) to *maintain* their position in that marketplace and generate future returns. When we say this year, as we do *every* year, that our list should fare better in a *down* market than the S&P 500 as a whole; it's these safety factors and, particularly, the intangibles, that support our premise. Even though we are feathering in a few more "growth" stocks in the 2019 portfolio, we still think that overall the portfolio should fare better in a down market.

Third, if you're really practicing value-investing principles, you buy these companies at reduced prices, when the markets are down, when the company is out of favor. You're looking for situations where the price is less than what you perceive to be the value, although calculating the value that precisely is elusive. When you "buy cheap" you provide another margin of safety; that margin makes it less likely that the stock will drop further. It gives you room for error if you turn out to be wrong about a choice. Again, it's much like buying a business of your own—you want to pay as little as possible in case things don't turn out as you'd expect. In today's markets, admittedly it's hard to buy cheap, but many of the 14 new adds for 2019, for the moment at least, appear to have value relative to the market and the other choices we could have made. There are also many "bargains" in earlier entries to the list among the 35 of our stocks that actually went down last year. Sell when there's something better to buy.

Stay Active
What do we mean by "stay active"? Staying active means that you should remain abreast of your investment and, like any business you own, keep an

eye on its performance. Periodically review the business and the stock as you would your own finances to see if it is making money and generally doing what you think it should be doing. You should keep an eye on company-related news, financials, earnings reports, and so forth—it's all part of being an individual investor and owner of companies.

Beyond that, time permitting, you should listen in on investor conference calls (usually at earnings announcements) to see what management has to say about the business. In addition, you should watch your business in the marketplace. See how many people are going to your local Starbucks and whether they are enjoying the experience, and look for other signs of excellence. See how crowded the parking lots are at Costco and Target these days—maybe not so much so as in the past, as people are truly shopping from their couches (and from work using mobile devices and so forth). We're not talking about constantly monitoring the stock price. Instead, we're suggesting an oversight of the business as though it were one you happen to own that, while professionally managed, requires an occasional glance to make sure everything is still acting according to your best interests. We also recommend a periodic review—at least annually—of whether your investments are still your best investments. Evaluate each investment against its alternatives. If you still perceive it to be the best value out there, keep it. If not, consider a swap for something new. Sell if there's something better to buy.

The *100 Best Stocks* for 2019: A Few Comments

As we head into 2019 we expect the economy to still be growing in a generally favorable tax environment and a neutral to slightly negative interest rate environment. The Trump administration may provide a few more tailwinds in the form of US manufacturing support and infrastructure spending and may provide some headwinds in healthcare and other non-defense consumption industries. With trade, we just don't know; we expect a moderate recovery in energy and commodity prices as supply and demand gradually balance, stronger business investment, better news in the farm sector, and perhaps a little more certainty on trade and other economic topics as the 2018 elections wind down and the administration gains experience. We do think infrastructure spending will increase (as we did prior to the Trump administration).

Despite the enduring uncertainties, these external environmental factors should help our list achieve—and achieve better than the S&P 500 at large because we continue to tilt toward manufacturers, exporters, agriculture, and now growth and e-commerce plays with a couple of new energy plays to boot. We missed the boat on Financials and may continue to, as we simply aren't comfortable investing in companies we don't understand and that don't seem to add much real value to the economy.

But another important factor gives legs to corporate success and the stock market, despite the naysayers' notion that the markets are becoming grossly overvalued. Simply put, the dire times of the Great Recession motivated most quality US companies to clean up their act and operate more efficiently. They've not only "cut the fat"; they have also taken a more realistic view of how and where to deploy capital—the energy industry is a good example—to produce the best returns, rather than trying to do everything. Companies learned to "right-size," to spin off noncongruent businesses, and to invest and invest wisely. While this "efficiency cycle" endures, we think many firms will start spending more on business investment, especially with new cash in hand, which will help the likes of traditional *100 Best* entries like Oracle, Siemens, Itron, 3M, and Valmont.

Another factor that has become a bit more uncertain—a variable—to consider as we move forward to commit capital to businesses (that is, buy stocks) is interest rates. Now that the Fed is in motion after eight years of unprecedented accommodation, what's next? We feel this factor will remain a nonfactor, or at least in the background, so long as the Fed stays on course and continues to be "transparent." We are confident they will raise rates slowly enough so as to not knock the pins out from under our income-oriented stocks: REITs, utilities, etc. We did drop a couple of utilities—Aqua America and Otter Tail—due to valuation but are not advocating a mass exodus from income-oriented stocks.

We are very curious about exactly how far and how fast the "stay-at-home" economy will grow. We are committed to this concept especially after getting bludgeoned by Target and Macy's last year. But how big will the shift really be? Perhaps 5 percent of the population will start ordering all meals to be delivered at home (using a drone, maybe? Uber?), all at the expense of grocers and restaurants. As usual, there are early adopters, then all the rest come along at a measured pace. We don't know where this is going or how fast it will get there, but the best companies (like the ones on our list) will adapt. That all said, we've been surprised at how fast Amazon Prime is making headway at the expense of retailers (and have climbed on board ourselves), so once again we may be underplaying this trend. With e-commerce growing almost 15 percent a year, you can't ignore it. Maybe it does make sense to put Domino's Pizza on the list, though the price has risen tenfold in the past ten years and doubled in the past three. We'll buy in for extra cheese and pepperoni, but we're not sure we want to buy the stock.

All of this takes us to the usual place: we stick to companies with great business models, which have brand, marketplace, and financial strength sufficient to master the crosscurrents of change and the emergence of megatrends. We do factor in such megatrends as the couch, the cloud, the Internet of Things, the millennial preference for experiences *over* things, the demise of paper in the workplace, the "always-on" nature of personal connectivity (and the prospect of marketers taking advantage of it), autonomous vehicles, and the (for now) availability of healthcare for everyone. We've wanted to see a megatrend toward more energy wisdom; that one's been put on hold by cheap energy and new domestic energy supplies, although we're still betting on it for the longer term. We continue to see a "national" economy, where large national brands gradually usurp local favorites, providing extra lift for big brands and big names like Coke, Smucker, and Starbucks. (We do, however, especially with millennials in mind, watch for localization trends in key industries like food processing; the beer industry, where local microbrews have gained significant share, provides an example—and where now we have added Craft Brew Alliance to the list.) For 2019, as ever, we look for companies with good business models, which produce high-value-add things that people (or companies) need, do it efficiently, and generate a lot of cash. Good businesses. Not just companies that make a lot of money, but good businesses with a sustainable future. We think our "core" list is still pretty good regardless of what the market does; this year the fourteen changes we've made take in some of the themes we've already mentioned; occasionally we switched horses where we felt it made sense. Sell when there's something better to buy.

As is our custom, we'll start with the companies removed from the 2018 list:

▼ **Table 3: Companies Removed from 2018 List**

Company	Symbol	Category	Sector
Aetna	AET	Conservative Growth	Healthcare
Aqua America	WTR	Growth and Income	Utilities
AT&T	T	Growth and Income	Telecom Services
Campbell Soup	CPB	Conservative Growth	Consumer Staples
Cincinnati Financial	CINF	Growth and Income	Financials
Colgate-Palmolive	CL	Conservative Growth	Consumer Staples
General Electric	GE	Growth and Income	Industrials
General Mills	GIS	Growth and Income	Consumer Staples
Grainger, W.W.	GWW	Conservative Growth	Industrials
Kimberly-Clark	KMB	Growth and Income	Consumer Staples
Otter Tail	OTTR	Growth and Income	Energy
Qualcomm	QCOM	Aggressive Growth	Information Technology
Steelcase	SCS	Aggressive Growth	Industrials
WD-40	WDFC	Aggressive Growth	Industrials

This year's "cut" list includes a broad swath of household goods providers, acquisitions (there were two), companies that had become overvalued, and a few that had lost their way or underperformed for just too long. Aetna and Qualcomm were the acquisitions, though it appears that Qualcomm will stay independent at least for now. Household goods providers Kimberly-Clark, Colgate-Palmolive, Campbell Soup, and General Mills departed after dreary performances; we just had too many of these in our cupboard. AT&T was a late scratch, we just feel they've lost their way with the Time Warner merger, intense competition, cord cutting, and excessive debt; if we had $200 billion we're not sure *we* would want to buy that company (always a good test). Cincinnati Financial, Aqua America, Otter Tail, and WD-40 are all good companies but appear to have run as far as they can go. We got worried—perhaps prematurely—that Amazon was going to cut into W.W. Grainger's turf, and Steelcase just can't seem to get businesses to buy into its new office concepts. Then, of course, there's GE, which requires little further explanation other than a warning for investors not to get too caught up in sexy marketing pitches (as we did).

Sell when there's something better to buy. We did that in fourteen cases, and here they are:

▼ Table 4: New Companies for 2019

Company	Symbol	Category	Sector
Analog Devices	ADI	Aggressive Growth	Information Technology
Aptiv	APTV	Aggressive Growth	Industrials
CalAmp Corp.	CAMP	Aggressive Growth	Information Technology
Craft Brew Alliance	BREW	Aggressive Growth	Consumer Staples
Devon Energy	DVN	Aggressive Growth	Energy
Enterprise Products Partners	EPD	Growth and Income	Energy
Home Depot	HD	Aggressive Growth	Retail
Intuitive Surgical	ISRG	Aggressive Growth	Healthcare
Myriad Genetics	MYGN	Aggressive Growth	Healthcare
Sealed Air	SEE	Conservative Growth	Industrials
Square, Inc.	SQ	Aggressive Growth	Information Technology
Target	TGT	Growth and Income	Retail
Trex Company	TREX	Aggressive Growth	Materials
Zebra Technologies	ZBRA	Aggressive Growth	Information Technology

Once again, we've arrived at the part of the book many of you have been waiting for. Blow the "First Call" on the bugle, please: it is time to introduce our 14 new horses for the 2019 race! As pointed out already several times in this narrative, we "sell when there's something better to buy." Typically, we also try to keep the mix of sectors relatively constant for diversification's sake and so as not to overload in any sector or industry. While we try to give you some fresh investing ideas, we also try to stay true to the value-investing principles that got us here and that we believe in in the first place.

That all said, this year is a bigger year for change than most. Because the somewhat-changed investing climate more heavily discounts the value of current cash payouts, and because of returned strength of growth stocks, and because some of our stocks had grown to levels we felt to be difficult to grow further from, we made more changes than usual for 2019. We also jiggered the sector balance more than usual, dropping four Consumer Staples stocks (11 still remain) and four Industrials (12 still remain)—more on these changes in a minute. We introduced more "Aggressive Growth" stocks than usual; 11 of the 14 added, in fact, are classified as "Aggressive Growth." Now, mind you, this doesn't necessarily mean you need to become a growth investor. We are simply giving growth choices; you're still free to—and expected to—pick the stocks you want to own from this list according to your needs, interest, and risk tolerance. Now, let's examine the specific picks.

First, while we remain unsure about the retail sector as a whole, we decided that two retailers have good enough prospects even in the stay-at-home economy to add to the list. In a bit of an about-face (and to save face!) we brought back Target, which had earlier laid out a strategy of price cutting, which we thought made no sense, so we cut it last year. The management team, which we respect, revised the strategy to focus on store and online experience and merchandising, which we felt to be their strength from the beginning, so welcome back—and yes, we *can* admit that we were wrong (a very useful investing trait!). We've been wanting to add Home Depot for years; the company is largely Amazon-proof, has fixed operational issues, and is in the middle of a growing do-it-yourself movement. It has become the de facto supplier for many contractors as well.

While on the building products theme, we added Trex, an excellent small company dominating its niche in the supply of plastic/wood composite decking and related materials. People are constructing and rebuilding outdoor spaces in large numbers, and their materials are gaining share rapidly over natural lumber products. We only wish we had put this one on the list years ago! From there, we're starting to like what we see in the energy business and feel that *domestic* energy, particularly that which uses the latest "fracking" technologies, which have become much more efficient, will do well. To that end we picked Devon Energy, also a former *100 Best* member until the energy crash in 2015. And the stuff has to get to market, so Enterprise Products Partners becomes a *100 Best Stock* with its strong cash distribution track record as an added plus.

Where technology meets the stay-at-home economy, we added three more plays. Okay, Sealed Air (Bubble Wrap, etc.) isn't the latest technology, but somebody's got to apply new and existing technologies to make that large box-at-a-time supply chain more efficient, and "SEE" is our pick. We also like their fresh food packaging line in an era where fresh food has gained favor. Along those same lines, modern supply chains are heavily technology driven, and Zebra Technologies makes many of the barcode, RFID, and other technologies to help get stuff where it has to go. Finally, Square has invaded the payments-processing space in a big way for today's growing small and freelance businesses (and some large ones too) and is venturing into all-inclusive apps that not only process payments but also run the business—including pick-up and delivery—a big hit especially among millennial business owners.

Then come our more "pure" technology investments in companies dominating key niches in technologies. Analog Devices dominates its niche in analog (as opposed to digital) semiconductors, which make a lot of things work in ways most of us aren't familiar with. CalAmp is a Small Cap leader in telematics, the real-time remote distribution of digital information, which among other things helps thousands of UPS drivers optimize their delivery routes in real time. While we're on the subject of automating parts of the driving experience, Aptiv PLC is an enticing chunk of electronics technologies distilled out of the old Delphi Automotive Corporation heavily engaged in making your cars smarter than you are and stopping on a dime when you don't but should. In case your car *doesn't* stop on time and you end up in surgery, Intuitive Surgical puts their semiautomated da Vinci robotic surgical tools into your doctor's hands to get you up and running as soon as possible with minimal body damage. Of course, bad things can happen to you without ever touching the wheel of a car, and Myriad Genetics offers an ever-more-adopted set of tests to find out if you're predisposed to certain kinds of cancers or other diseases, and other tests to predict if certain treatments will work effectively for a variety of diseases *before* you start them. Finally, if all of this is too much to take in, and you simply want to relax with a tall cold one, Craft Brew Alliance, our fourth Small Cap pick, makes a nationally distributed line of refreshing brews flagshipped by their Kona brands. Mahalo.

As usual, we like to sum up the changes by sector after we do our picks. The sector balance is indicative at a high level of the nature of the changes we make each year. We don't like to change the sector balance too much unless there's a strong and compelling reason.

Table 5 sums up this year's 14 changes by sector. As mentioned earlier, we cut four Consumer Staples and four Industrials. We added four Information Technology firms (Analog Devices, CalAmp, Square, and Zebra), two Retail (Target, Home Depot), two Energy (Devon, Enterprise Products Partners), two Healthcare (Myriad and Intuitive Surgical) and replaced two of the Industrials (with Sealed Air and Aptiv PLC, not exactly "heavy" industrials). We added back one Consumer Staples (Craft Brew Alliance) and one Materials stock (Trex) to round out the list.

▼ Table 5: Sector Analysis and 2019 Change by Sector

NUMBER OF COMPANIES

Sector	On 2018 list	Added for 2019	Cut from 2018	On 2019 list
Business Services	2			2
Consumer Discretionary	4			4
Consumer Staples	14	1	-4	11
Consumer Durables	1			1
Energy	8	2	-1	9
Entertainment	0			0
Financials	5		-1	4
Healthcare	16	2	-1	17
Heavy Construction	0			0
Industrials	14	2	-4	12
Information Technology	8	4	-1	11
Materials	6	1		7
Real Estate	3			3
Restaurant	1			1
Retail	6	2		8
Telecommunications Services	3		-1	2
Transportation	6			6
Utilities	3		1	2

Yield Signs

While we did add a few more nonpaying "growth" stocks this year, we continue to like dividend-paying stocks. We like stocks that pay meaningful dividends and especially stocks that are likely to have their dividends raised over time.

With dividend-paying stocks, especially those inclined toward dividend increases, you get an attractive yield from the day you buy the stock, but you'll also get handsome raises over time. As we reported earlier, 65 of the 89 dividend-paying stocks on the 2017 *100 Best* list raised their dividends in 2016, and 36 of those have raised their dividends in each of the past ten years. We like this. We like it a lot. A company that raises its dividend

10 percent will roughly double the payout in just seven years. (Calculation? Rule of 72—divide the percent increase into 72 and you'll get the number of years it takes to double: 72/10 equals 7.2 years.) You could end up with twice the income in addition to any gains or growth in the price of the stock.

DIVIDEND-PAYING, DIVIDEND-RAISING STOCKS—NOW AND FOREVER

The Rule of 72 and dividend-paying stocks lessons should be taken to heart by prudent investors, particularly those who fret about the effects of rising interest rates on their income-oriented investments (and who follow such fret in the financial media). When interest rates rise, bond prices fall, as the implied yield must adjust somehow; that is, a bond that generates a fixed income stream is worth relatively less in a higher interest rate environment. Often, as we've seen this past year, dividend-paying stocks take a tumble along with their bond brethren anytime even the rumor of rising interest rates is unsheathed. But the rising dividend provides the difference, and we feel that most of the investing world, particularly those attempting to build a comfortable long-term retirement income stream, should take note.

If you invest in a bond over ten years, that bond will pay back its original principal at the end of the ten years, plus the interest as prescribed initially when the bond is sold. Nothing more, nothing less—so long as you wait ten years assuming no default. On the other hand, you might not get your original principal if you decide to sell the bond sooner in a rising interest–rate environment (note that the interest payments don't go up—only that the bond value goes down).

If you invest in a dividend-paying stock with a persistent dividend raise policy and track records, as some two-thirds of the *100 Best* list represents, you enjoy the benefits of—and the protection of—the rising dividend. If your company raises its dividend 10 percent each year, the dividend will double in 7.2 years, and if it's paying 3 percent today, that implies 6 percent in 7.2 years—or a *doubling in the stock price* if the same yield is maintained (which is affected by a lot of factors aside from the yield). If your company raises its dividend only 5 percent each year, it doubles in 14.4 years but is still up roughly 70 percent in the ten-year period just described. That's still a handsome payout as well as giving solid potential for stock appreciation.

This favorable scenario simply does not exist for bonds. Bonds may be a bit safer, as the interest payments are less likely to be cut (a cut is a default) and will be paid before dividends. But when we put a stock on the *100 Best* list, we feel that not only is the dividend itself fairly secure but so is the potential for *increase*. We should also add that most dividends receive favorable tax treatment for those of you holding investments outside of retirement accounts.

We continue to feel that investing in dividend-paying, dividend-growing stocks is the best way to save for a financially secure future.

A few years ago, we came to the realization that we use two simple and key indicators to suggest a good stock for further analysis: (1) strong and growing yield, and (2) the persistence of share buybacks. Like that pretty face at a party, those two features suggest that we should make the effort to learn the rest of the story. We continue to focus on those healthy companies willing to not only share a portion of their profits but also to give you, the investor, a periodic raise to recognize the value of your commitment of precious investment capital. In that spirit, in our presentation format we show the number of dividend increases in the past ten years in the header right after Current Yield. We know of no other financial publication that does this.

We also present the Dividend Aggressors list in our Stars lists, which you'll see shortly. Dividend aggressors are companies with substantial payouts that are also growing those payouts at a persistent and substantial rate. They have indicated through both words and performance that they continue to do so and have the resources to do it. It isn't enough to raise the dividend each year by just a penny; it must be substantial. It also isn't enough to raise the dividend each year but still only be yielding 0.5 percent. There are lists of "dividend achievers" floating around on the Internet, and there are even a few funds constructed around a dividend achievers index. Our Aggressors are—well—a bit more aggressive.

The climate for dividend growth continues to be favorable. After a few "slower" years the recent tax package is giving the companies the cash resources to more aggressively raise their payouts. Increases, which averaged 6–7 percent for S&P 500 stocks in 2016 and 2017, rose sharply to nearly 14 percent through midyear 2018 for companies that raised the dividend in the first five months of the year.

Dancing with the Stars

We continue developing and sharing our "star" categories—groups of stocks essentially the "best of the best" in categories we chose to highlight—yield stars, dividend aggressors, safety and stability stars, growth stars, prosperity stars (which we've now amended temporarily to be "Stay-at-Home Stars"), and moat stars. We provide these stars lists because we know that all investors have their own preferences, and thus there are no "best" stocks within our "best" list, that is, there is no number one, two, and so on within the list.

Table 6 shows the top 20 stocks on our *100 Best* list by percentage yield as of mid-2018.

▼ **Table 6: Top 20 Dividend-Paying Stocks**

Company	Symbol	Projected 2018 dividend	Yield %	Dividend raises, past 10 years
Enterprise Products Partners (*)	EPD	$1.72	6.6%	10
Welltower	WELL	$3.57	6.6%	10
Vodafone	VOD	$1.71	6.1%	5
Tupperware	TUP	$2.72	5.6%	6
Total S.A.	TOT	$2.93	5.1%	6
Public Storage	PSA	$8.00	4.0%	8
CenterPoint Energy	CNP	$1.08	3.9%	10
Chevron	CVX	$4.36	3.8%	10
Scotts Miracle-Gro	SMG	$2.30	3.6%	10
Procter & Gamble	PG	$2.76	3.5%	10
Coca-Cola	KO	$1.50	3.5%	10
Target (*)	TGT	$2.58	3.4%	10
United Parcel Service	UPS	$3.40	3.2%	10
CVS Health	CVS	$2.00	3.2%	10
Paychex	PAYX	$1.96	3.2%	8
Daktronics	DAKT	$0.28	3.2%	7
Whirlpool	WHR	$4.80	3.1%	6
Valero	VLO	$2.90	3.1%	9
Schlumberger	SLB	$2.00	3.1%	7
Archer Daniels Midland	ADM	$1.30	3.1%	9

(*) New for 2019

Table 6.1 shows our list of Dividend Aggressors for 2019:

▼ Table 6.1: Companies with Strong Dividend Track Records

Company	Symbol	Estimated 2018 dividend	Yield %	Dividend raises, past 10 years
3M Company	MMM	$4.88	2.2%	10
Boeing	BA	$5.57	1.7%	8
CenterPoint Energy	CNP	$1.08	3.9%	10
Chevron	CVX	$4.36	3.8%	10
Coca-Cola	KO	$1.50	3.5%	10
CVS Health	CVS	$2.00	3.2%	10
Enterprise Products Partners (*)	EPD	$1.72	6.6%	10
Johnson & Johnson	JNJ	$3.32	2.6%	10
NextEra Energy	NEE	$4.05	2.5%	10
Paychex	PAYX	$1.96	3.2%	8
Procter & Gamble	PG	$2.76	3.5%	10
Prudential	PRU	$3.15	3.0%	9
Public Storage	PSA	$8.00	4.0%	8
Siemens	SIEGY	$2.09	2.4%	8
Target (*)	TGT	$2.58	3.4%	10
Tupperware	TUP	$2.72	5.6%	6
United Parcel Service	UPS	$3.40	3.2%	10
Valero	VLO	$2.90	3.1%	9
Vodafone	VOD	$1.71	6.1%	5
Welltower	WELL	$3.57	6.6%	10

(*) New for 2019

REMEMBER, THERE ARE NO GUARANTEES

While dividends and especially high yields are attractive, investors must remember that corporations are under no contractual or legal obligation to pay them! Interest payments on time deposits and bonds are much more clearly defined, and failure to pay can represent default. With dividends, there is no such safety net. Companies can—and do—reduce or eliminate dividends in bad times, as most strikingly observed with BP in the wake of the Deepwater Horizon Gulf spill disaster in 2010 and most bank stocks after the 2008 dive. A few years ago, energy price declines have hurt many US oil producers, particularly more indebted ones engaged in the more expensive "fracking" process—and many of these players cut or omitted dividends. ConocoPhillips on our *100 Best* list is one example. Phosphate/potash miner Mosaic cut theirs too. And we all know what happened to GE—sliced in half, a big move for this one-time perennial blue chip. GE is a good example of why dividend investors should keep an eye out for changes in a company's business prospects and shouldn't put too many eggs in a single high-yielding basket. On the flip side, as investors become more conscious of returns, and as corporate management teams become more aware of such investor consciousness, we've seen a lot of companies loudly trumpet their recent dividend increases to their investors and the investing public. It's a nice sound that we hope to continue to hear.

Safety Stars

Safety stars are companies we think will hold up well in volatile and negative stock markets as well as recessionary economies. They have stable products and customer bases and long traditions of being able to manage well in downturns. We cut several from this list as we reduced utilities (Aqua America) and household products names (Kimberly-Clark, General Mills, Campbell Soup), but our list is still safe with adds of Abbott Laboratories, Archer Daniels Midland, Coca-Cola, and CenterPoint Energy.

▼ **Table 7: Safety Stars: Top 10 Stocks for Safety and Stability**

Company	Symbol
Abbott Labs	ABT
Archer Daniels Midland	ADM
Becton, Dickinson	BDX
Bemis	BMS
CenterPoint Energy	CNP
Coca-Cola	KO
Johnson & Johnson	JNJ
McCormick & Co.	MKC
Sysco	SYY
Waste Management	WM

Growth Stars

Looking at the other side of the coin and in light of our new growth stock picks, we made several revisions to our "Growth Stars" list, replacing Apple, Corning, and Starbucks (good growth companies, still) with Myriad Genetics, Trex, and Square.

▼ **Table 8: Growth Stars: Top 10 Stocks for Growth**

Company	Symbol
Amazon	AMZN
Myriad Genetics	MYGN
Boeing	BA
CarMax	KMX
Trex	TREX
First Solar	FSLR
ResMed	RMD
Scotts Miracle-Gro	SMG
Square	SQ
Visa	V

The next "Star" category has become our "utility" category, deployed to highlight ten "star" companies in an area of current interest. We've had "recovery stars," "prosperity stars," and "stars for a Trump economy." This year we shift it again, this time to "Stay-at-Home Stars." Table 9 shows ten companies that will do well in the growing e-commerce-based stay-at-home economy.

▼ **Table 9: Stay-at-Home Stars: Top 10 Stocks for an E-Commerce Economy**

Company	Symbol
Amazon	AMZN
Apple	AAPL
FedEx	FDX
Prologis	PLD
C.H. Robinson	CHRW
Sealed Air	SEE
Square	SQ
United Parcel Service	UPS
Visa	V
Zebra Technologies	ZBRA

Moat Stars

Finally, we get back to one of the basic tenets of value investing—the ability of a company to build a sustainable and unassailable competitive advantage. Value-investing aficionados call such an advantage a "moat," for it represents a barrier to entry for competitors that will likely preserve that advantage for some time. The moat can come in the form of technology, the use of technology, a brand, enduring customer relationships, channel relationships, size or scale, or simply a really big head start into a business that makes it hard or even impossible for competitors to catch up. The appraisal of a moat is hardly an exact science; here we give our top ten picks based on the size and strength (width?) of the moat. For 2019 we cut WD-40 from the *100 Best* list due to valuation, though it still has an excellent moat, and we added leading bearing supplier Timken to the Table 10 list.

▼ **Table 10: Moat Stars: Top 10 Stocks for Sustainable Competitive Advantage**

Company	Symbol
Amazon	AMZN
Apple	AAPL
Boeing	BA
Coca-Cola	KO
McCormick	MKC
Public Storage	PSA
Starbucks	SBUX
Timken	TKR
Visa	V
Vodafone	VOD

What Makes a Best Stock Best?

We have proclaimed that we could identify a good *100 Best* candidate based on two simple features: increasing dividend and declining share counts. But these, of course, aren't the whole story, especially in today's more growth-oriented investing climate. Where do we go from there? What comes next? What is it that defines excellence—*sustainable* excellence—among companies? That's been a topic of considerable debate for years, and with all the study that's gone into it, nobody has hit upon a single formula for deciphering undeniable excellence in a company. That may seem amazing at first, but when you think about it, it isn't.

That's largely because "excellence" isn't as scientific as most of us would like or expect it to be. Much like finding your "match" and life partner, it defies data and mathematical formulation. Take the square of net profits, multiply by the cosine of the debt-to-equity ratio, add the square root of the revenue-per-employee count, and what do you get? Some nice numbers, but not a clear picture of how things work together or how a company will sell its products to customers and prosper going forward. You certainly wouldn't want to select your ideal "match" this way.

Fundamentals such as profitability, productivity, and asset efficiency tell us how well a company has done and, by proxy, how well it is managed and how successful it has been in the marketplace. Fundamentals are about what the company has already achieved and where it stands right now. If a company's current fundamentals are a mess (or your potential partner is in bankruptcy court)—stop right now; there isn't much point in going any further.

In most cases, what really separates the great from the good are the intangibles: the "soft" factors of market position, market acceptance, customer "love" of a company's products, its management, its *aura*. These features create competitive advantage, or "distinctive competence," as an economist would put it, which cannot be valued. Warren Buffett and his sidekick Charlie Munger termed these distinctive advantages as the "lollapalooza effect"— the magic or secret sauce that makes truly good businesses work as a complex *system* transcending the basic facts, figures, and resources. Most importantly, these lollapalooza factors are less about the past and more about what a company is set up to achieve in the future. When you think about it, it's the intangibles that provide the spark for most of our personal matches too.

To paraphrase Buffett at his best: give me $100 billion, and I could start a company; but I could never create another Coca-Cola.

What does that mean? It means that Coca-Cola has already established a worldwide brand cachet; the distribution channels, customer knowledge, and product development expertise cannot be duplicated at any cost. When companies have competitive advantages that cannot be duplicated at any cost, they have an enduring grip on their markets. They can charge more for their products. They have a moat that insulates them from competition or makes it much more expensive for competitors to participate. They're perceived by loyal customers as having top-line products worth paying more for. They have plenty of lollapalooza.

A company with lollapalooza can control price and, in many cases, can control its costs.

Strategic Fundamentals

Let's examine a list of strategic fundamentals that define, or keep score of, a company's success. This list can be used as a checklist, although it's hard to find a company that shows excellence in all of these areas.

Are Gross and Operating Profit Margins Growing?

We like profitable companies; who doesn't? But what really counts is the size of the margin and especially the growth. If a company has a gross margin (sales minus cost of goods sold) exceeding that of its competitors, that shows that it's doing something right, probably with its customers and/ or with its costs. But competitive analysis is elusive; there is no dependable source of "industry" gross margins, and comparing competitors can be difficult because no two companies are exactly alike; it's easy to mix apples and oranges.

We like to see what direction gross margin is moving in—up or down. A growing gross margin also signals that the company is doing something right and is gaining strength in its markets and/or its supply chain. That isn't perfect, either; as the economy moved from boom to bust, many excellent companies reported declines in gross and especially operating margins (sales minus cost of goods sold minus operating expenses) as they laid off workers and used less capacity. Still, in a steady-state environment, it makes sense to favor companies with growing margins—and more and more, we tend to do so. In a declining market, companies that can *protect* their margins will come out ahead.

While net margins are also a good indicator of sustained or improving performance in many cases, for the next few years they will be distorted by tax savings from the 2017 Tax Cuts and Jobs Act; gross margins, which represent sales less direct cost of goods sold not including taxes, are unaffected and are thus a purer measure.

Does a Company Produce More Capital Than It Consumes?

Make no mistake about it—we like cash. Pure and simple, we also like it when a company produces more cash than it consumes.

At the end of the day, cash generation is the simplest measure of whether a company is being successful, especially over the long term. Sure, if a company buys an airplane or opens a factory or a bunch of stores in a given quarter, it will be cash-flow negative. But that should be a temporary thing; over the long haul, it should produce, not consume, cash. Companies that continually have to borrow or sell shares to raise enough cash to stay in business are on the wrong track.

How do you determine this? You'll have to become familiar with the Statement of Cash Flows or equivalent in a company's financial reports. "Cash flow from operations" is usually positive and represents cash booked from sales less cost of goods sold, with adjustments for noncash items like depreciation and for increases or decreases in working capital. In simple terms, is the cash going into the cash register from the daily operations of the business? Or from other sources?

"Cash used for investing purposes" or similar is a bit of a misnomer and represents net cash used to "invest" in the business—usually for capital expenditures but also for short-term noncash investments like securities and a few other smaller items usually beyond scope. This figure is typically negative unless the company sells some part of its infrastructure. Over the long haul, cash generated from operations should well exceed cash used to invest in the business.

Companies in expansion mode may not show this surplus, and that's where "cash from financing activities" comes in. That's the cash generated from issuing debt or selling securities—or paying off debt or repurchasing shares, if things are going well—and dividends are included here as well. Again, a successful company will produce more cash—capital—from the business than it consumes, just as a successful household does the same, or else it goes into debt. Smart investors track this surplus over time.

Are Expenses under Control?

Just like your household, company expenses should be under control, and anything else, especially without explanation, is a yellow flag.

The best way to test this is to check whether the "Selling, General, and Administrative" expenses (SG&A) are rising and, more to the point, if they are rising faster than sales. If so, that's a yellow, not necessarily a red, flag, but if it continues, it suggests that something is out of control, and it will catch up with the company sooner or later. In a downturn, companies that are able to reduce their expenses to match revenue declines scored more points too. Normally you won't have to dig through the financial statements for this; management usually points out its expense trends in conference calls and the "letter to shareholders" section of the annual report. It can be a little like watching children—if they're quiet on the topic, look out.

Is Working Capital under Control?

Working capital is a hard concept to grasp—even for small entrepreneurs who live with its ups and downs on a daily basis. Insufficient working capital is one of the biggest causes of death for small businesses, and working capital and especially changes in working capital can signal success or trouble.

Using a simple analogy, working capital is the circulatory lifeblood of the business. Money comes in and money goes out, and working capital is what circulates in the veins in between. In its purest sense, it is cash, receivables, and inventory, less short-term debts. It's what you own less what you owe aside from fixed assets like plant, stores, equipment, and long-term debt.

If receivables are increasing, that sounds like a good thing—more people owe you more money. But if receivables are rising and sales aren't, that suggests that people aren't paying their bills or, worse, the business has to finance more to achieve the same level of sales. Similarly, a rise in inventory without a rise in sales means that it costs the business more money—more working capital—to do the same amount of business. That costs twice, because unless the firm is lucky, more inventory means more obsolescence and potentially more deep-discount sales or write-offs down the road.

A sharp investor will check to see that major working capital items—receivables and inventory—aren't growing faster than sales; indeed, a company that generates more sales with a decrease in working capital is becoming more productive.

Is Debt in Line with Business Growth?

Like many other "fundamentals" items, you can tear your hair out looking at debt figures and trying to decide whether they're in line with asset levels, equity levels, and industry norms. A simpler test is to check to see whether long-term debt is increasing or decreasing, and in particular, whether it is increasing faster than business growth. Gold stars go to companies with little to no debt, and to companies able to grow without issuing mountains of long-term debt. It's also worth checking to make sure the company isn't simply issuing debt to buy back shares—a little of this is okay, but some companies take on expensive debt just to increase per-share earnings (and management bonuses). This isn't a good strategy; in fact, it isn't a strategy at all.

Is Return on Equity Steady or Growing?

Return on equity (ROE) is another of those hard-to-grasp concepts and another subjective measure when valuing assets and earnings. But at the end of the day, it's what all investors really seek: a return on their capital investments.

Like many other figures pulled from income statements and balance sheets, an ROE number, without any context, is hard to interpret. Does a 26.7 percent ROE mean, in itself, that a company is excellent? The figure sounds healthy, to be sure—it's a heck of a lot better than investing your money in a CD or T-bill. But because earnings and asset values are subjective, it may not represent true success. In fact, a company can increase ROE simply by borrowing money (yes!) and investing it into the business, even if it isn't invested as productively as other previous funds were invested. The math is complicated; we won't go into it here.

The true test of ROE success is to check whether it is steady or increasing. Increasing—that makes sense. Why *steady*? Because if a company makes profits in a previous period and reinvests them in the business, that amount of money becomes part of equity (retained earnings). If the company reinvests productively, it will produce more returns, and ROE will at least keep up. If the company can't reinvest those earnings productively, ROE will drop—and perhaps it should be paying the earnings to you as dividends instead of investing them unproductively in the business. So if ROE is steady, the company still has good investments to make, and management is probably doing the right thing.

We should note that many investment analysts today prefer "Return on Invested Capital" (ROIC) as a metric over ROE. ROIC is return, or profit, divided by total equity *plus* debt. This gets you past the distortions that adding debt to the balance sheet might cause. Since the traditional balance sheet equation holds that "Assets = Liabilities + Capital," you can simply use total assets as the denominator—essentially the measure is "return on assets." Some analysts prefer to go further by removing the cash balance from the asset denominator, to reflect the assets deployed and in use to generate returns and to get around the distortions of large reserve capital infusions often found at startup companies.

Does the Company Pay a Dividend?

Different people feel differently about dividends, and, as described previously, we place great emphasis on dividend-paying stocks and especially those that *grow* their dividends. After all, save for the eventual sale of the company to someone else, a dividend is the only true cash that an investor will realize from buying a stock in a corporation, other than by selling the stock. At least in theory, investors should receive some compensation for their investments once in a while.

Yet, many companies don't pay dividends or don't pay dividends that compete very effectively with fixed-income yields. Why do investors put up with this? Because, in theory anyway, a company in a good business should be able to reinvest profits more effectively than the investor can (or else why would the investor have bought the company in the first place?). Investors trust that reinvested profits will eventually bring the growth in company value that will be reflected in the share price, or eventual takeover, or an eventual payment of a dividend or, better yet, growth in that dividend.

That's the theory, anyway, but there are still lots of companies that get away with paying no dividend at all. Can we tolerate this? Yes, if a company is really doing a great job with their retained profits, like Apple before they started paying dividends seven years ago, or CarMax and Itron, or, now, Amazon and First Solar and the seven other non-dividend payers added this year. But while we embrace growth, we still have a soft spot for companies that offer at least something to their investors in the short term, some return on their hard-earned and faithfully committed capital. If nothing else, it keeps management teams honest and shows that management understands that shareholder interests are up there somewhere on the list of priorities. And getting an ever-*increasing* dividend—and owning a stock that has most likely appreciated because the dividend has increased—is like having your cake and eating it, too: a true favorite among investors, as noted in our previous sidebar (Dividend-Paying, Dividend-Raising Stocks—Now and Forever).

Strategic Intangibles

When you look at any company, perhaps the bottom-line question follows the Buffett wisdom: If you had $100 billion in cool cash to spend (and we'll assume the genius intellect to spend it *well*), could you re-create that company?

If the answer is yes, it may still be a great company, but it may not be great enough to fend off competition and keep its customers forever. If the answer is no, the company truly has something unique to offer in the marketplace, difficult to duplicate at any cost. That distinctive competence, that sustainable competitive edge—whatever it is, a brand, a patent, a trade secret, a unique customer experience, a lock on distribution or supply channels—may be worth more than all the factories and high-rise office buildings and cash in the bank a company could ever have.

What we're talking about are the intangibles, the "soft" factors that make companies unique and that add up to more than the sum of their parts, the factors that ultimately drive future revenues. Intangibles not only define excellence; they define the future, while fundamentals mainly define the past. Seven key intangibles follow, although you'll think of more, and some industries may have some unique ones of their own, like intellectual property in the technology sector.

DOES THE COMPANY HAVE A MOAT?

A business moat performs much the same role as its medieval castle equivalent—it protects the business from competition. Whatever factors create the moat, ultimately those are the factors that prevent you, with your $100 billion, from taking their business. Moats are usually a combination of brand, product technology, design, marketing and distribution channels, and customer loyalty all working together to protect a company. A moat doesn't just protect the existence of a company, it helps it command higher prices and earn higher profits.

Whether a company has a narrow moat, a wide moat, or none at all is a subjective assessment for you to make. However, you can get some help at

Morningstar (www.morningstar.com), whose stock ratings include an assessment of the moat.

Coca-Cola has a moat because of the sheer impossibility of surpassing its brand and brand recognition worldwide. CarMax has a moat because it is further along in putting retail-style dealerships on the ground and applying management information technologies to its business than anyone else; it would take years for a competitor to catch up. Amazon has a moat because of its immediately recognized brand, its size, and its technology leadership in delivering an industry-leading e-commerce experience. McCormick has a moat because it has kicked nearly all other spice makers off the store shelf; others are left with small niches only. The Moat Stars list presented earlier identifies the top ten stocks with a solid and sustainable competitive advantage.

DOES THE COMPANY HAVE AN EXCELLENT BRAND?

It's hard to say enough about brand, especially in today's fast-moving, highly packaged, highly national and international marketplace. A strong brand means consistency and a promise to consumers, and consumers sold on a brand will prefer it over any other, almost regardless of price. People still buy Tide; Starbucks is still synonymous with high quality and ambience. Good brands command higher prices and foster loyalty, identity, and even customer "love."

Ask yourself if a company has a sought-after brand, a brand that customers would pay extra to buy or align with, a brand that would be difficult to duplicate at any cost. Would customers rather fight than switch? Think about Apple, Starbucks, Coca-Cola, Allstate, Smucker's, Scotts, Southwest, or Nike, or the brands within a house, like Minute Maid (Coke), Tide (P&G), KitchenAid (Whirlpool), iPhone (Apple), or Varathane, DAP, or Rust-Oleum (RPM International).

IS THE COMPANY A MARKET LEADER?

Market leadership usually—but not always—goes hand in hand with brand. The trick is to decide whether a company really leads in its industry. Often—but not always—that's a factor of size. The market leader usually has the highest market share, and the important point is that it calls the shots with regard to price, technology, marketing message, etc.—other companies must play catch-up and often discount their prices to keep up. Apple is a market leader in digital music, Public Storage in self-storage units, McCormick in spices, Nike in sports apparel, Square in app-based transaction processing, and Starbucks in beverages—and so forth.

Excellent companies tend to be market leaders, and market leaders tend to be excellent companies. However, this relationship doesn't always hold true—sometimes the nimble but smaller competitor is the excellent company and *headed for* market leadership. Examples like Craft Brew Alliance, Valero, Columbia Sportswear, and Southwest Airlines can be found on our list.

Does the Company Have Channel Excellence?

"Channels" in business parlance means a chain of players to sell and distribute a company's products. It might be stores, it might be other industrial companies, it might be direct to the consumer. If a company is considered a top supplier in a particular channel, or a company has especially good relations with its channel, that's a plus.

Excellent companies develop solid channel relationships and become the preferred supplier in those channels. Companies such as Deere, Fair Isaac, McCormick, Nike, Novo Nordisk, Procter & Gamble, Scotts Miracle-Gro, Sysco, Visa, and Whirlpool all have excellent relationships with the channels through which they sell their product.

Does the Company Have Supply-Chain Excellence?

Like distribution channels, excellent companies develop excellent and low-cost supply channels. They are seldom caught off guard by supply shortages and tend to get favorable and stable prices for whatever they buy. This is not an easy assessment unless you know something about a particular industry. Fresh Del Monte, Nike, Starbucks, Costco, Home Depot, Craft Brew Alliance, and Procter & Gamble are examples of companies that have done a good job managing and innovating their supply chains.

Does the Company Have Excellent Management?

It's not hard to grasp what happens if a company *doesn't* have good management: performance fails, and few inside or outside the company respect the company. It's not easy for an investor to determine if a management team does a good job or acts in shareholder interests. Clues can include candor and honesty and the ability of company management to speak in accessible, easily understood terms about the company and company performance (it's worth listening to conference calls as a resource). A management team that admits errors and eschews other forms of arrogance and entitlement (i.e., luxury perks, office suites, fancy aircraft) is probably tilting its interests toward shareholders, as is the management team that can cough up some decent returns to shareholders once in a while in the form of a dividend.

This may be the most subjective and elusive assessment of all, as few investors work with these folks on a daily basis. Still, over time, you can garner a strong hunch about whether a management team is effective and on your side. Clearly presented investor materials like those found at RPM International, Timken, or Whirlpool are signs that management knows what it's doing, knows what's important, and has nothing to hide. Of course, be careful: it can be difficult to separate the "business B.S." from the true indicators of excellence. It becomes largely a matter of gut feel and personal assessment of what they say—again, we're back to what it takes to make that relationship "match."

Are There Signs of Innovation Excellence?

This question seems pretty obvious, but it's not just about the products that a company sells. True, if the company is leading the industry in innovation, that's usually a good thing, for "first to market" definitely offers business advantages.

The less obvious part of this question is whether the company makes the best *use* of technology to make operations and customer interfaces as efficient and effective as possible. Southwest Airlines may have missed our list in years gone by because of the difficulty of achieving excellence in an industry where players can't control prices or costs. While airlines have enjoyed better times, we still don't like them in general—but Southwest continues to make our list today, not only because of brand and management excellence but also innovation excellence. Why? Simply because, after all of these years, amazingly, it still has the best, simplest, easiest-to-use flight booking and check-in in the industry. Sometimes such innovations mean a lot more than bringing new, fancy products and bells and whistles to the market. You can also look to Amazon, Apple, CarMax, CenterPoint Energy, FedEx, Itron, Novo Nordisk, ResMed, C.H. Robinson, Square, Starbucks, UPS, and Visa on our list for more obvious examples of companies that have deployed technology and innovative customer interfaces to achieve sustainable competitive advantage.

Choosing the *100 Best*

With all of this in mind, just how was this year's *100 Best Stocks* list actually chosen?

The answer is subtler than you might think. If we could give you a precise formula, you wouldn't need this book. You'd be able to do it yourself. In fact, every investor would be able to do it on his or her own. Our book would simply be the result of yet another stock screener, and every investor would invest in the same stocks. Is that a feasible or practical solution? Hardly. Everyone would scramble to buy the same 100 best stocks. The prices would be sky high, and the price of other stocks would melt to nothing.

SIGNS OF VALUE

Following are a few signs of value to look for in any company. This is not an exhaustive list by any means, but it's a good place to start:

- » Rising dividends
- » Declining share count
- » Gaining market share
- » Can control price
- » Loyal customers
- » Growing margins
- » Producing, not consuming, capital (free cash flow)
- » Steady or increasing ROE
- » Management forthcoming, honest, understandable

SIGNS OF UNVALUE

...and signs of trouble, or "unvalue":

- » Declining margins
- » No brand or who-cares brand
- » Commodity producer, must compete on price
- » Losing market dominance or market share
- » Can't control costs
- » Must acquire other companies to grow
- » Management in hiding, off message, making excuses, difficult to understand, or in the news for all the wrong reasons

Fortunately or unfortunately, however you want to look at it, it isn't that simple. There are so many fundamentals, so many intangibles, and so many unknown and unknowable weighting factors to combine the fundamentals and intangibles that—well—it just wouldn't work. No screener could re-create the subtle judgment that gets applied to the cold, hard facts. It's that judgment, the interpretation of the facts and intangibles, that makes it worth spending money on a book like this.

While we didn't apply a specific formula or screener to the universe of stocks, we did take a few measurable factors into account to narrow the list from thousands to a few hundred issues. Those factors came from several sources, but at this point we must perennially tip our cap to Value Line and the research and database work they do as part of the Value Line Investment Survey. If you aren't familiar with Value Line, it's worth a look for any savvy individual investor, either online at www.valueline.com or, in many cases, at your local library. It is an excellent resource.

When to Buy? Consider When to Sell

We've said it over and over: *Sell when there's something better to buy.*

Selling is hard. So is removing something from our *100 Best* list (unless it became part of a takeover transaction). If it's hard to figure out when to buy a stock, it's even harder to figure out when to sell. People tend to get married to their investment decisions, feeling somehow that if it isn't right, maybe time will help and things will get better. It's human nature.

Or they're just too arrogant to admit that they made a mistake. That's also human nature.

There are lots of reasons why people hold on to investments for too long a time.

Here's the fundamental truth: buying and selling should be much the same process. Let's look at it from the point of view of selling. When should you sell? Simply, as we've said repeatedly, when there's *something else better to buy*. Something else better for future returns, something else better for safety, something else better for timeliness or fit with today's go-forward worldview; a *megatrend* as we've referred to it. That something else can be another stock, a futures contract, or a house, or any kind of investment. It can also be cash—sell that stock when...when what? When cash is a better investment. Or when you need the money, which is another way of saying that cash is a better investment—at least it's safer for the time being.

Similarly, if you think of a buy decision as a best possible deployment of capital because there's no better way to invest your money, you'll also come out ahead. It really isn't that hard, especially if you've done your homework. It's also made easier if you avoid rash overcommitments; that is, you avoid buying all at once in case you've made a mistake or in case better prices come later down the road.

Our Annual ETF Report: Good News for Individual Stock Investors

Finally, we reach our annual treatise on Exchange Traded Funds (ETFs) as an alternative to investing in individual stocks. While our chosen ETFs continue to offer an alternative to individual stock picking for all or part of your portfolio, this year as it turns out our individual stocks beat our chosen ETFs handily. In a year where victories were hard to come by against our old nemesis S&P 500 and many other stock indices—we'll take it!

The 100 Best Stocks to Buy series continues to be about the 100 best *individual companies* in which you can buy shares to build into your investment portfolio. The objective is to use these selections as a starting point to build a customized portfolio of your very own, a portfolio that earns decent, better-than-market, long-term returns from excellent companies while—because they're excellent companies—taking less risk than you would with most investments. Because you're doing it yourself, you save money on fees and expenses and come away with the pride of ownership of doing it yourself.

That said, not everyone has the time or inclination to do this. Not everyone wants to sail through the treacherous channels of company financial information and the foggy mysteries of intangibles and marketplace performance to figure out which companies are really best to own and to keep a finger on the pulse to make sure they stay that way. You may want to own individual stocks. But just as buying a kit makes many aspects of building a new outdoor deck easier, so does buying a stock "kit": a product or package of stocks to do what you might otherwise have to struggle through on your own. If you could get such a kit product cheap enough and aligned to your needs, why wouldn't you? It will save time, and you'll be firing up the barbecue and enjoying those outdoor parties with your friends a lot sooner. Or, perhaps at the risk of more tiring analogies, buying individual stocks is like ordering à la carte from a menu. You're not sure if what you're getting works together, so why not do a *prix fixe* to let the chef do some of the driving? Okay, enough…

Such is the impulse to find investment products—packages, *prix fixe* menus—that mimic the performance of the *100 Best Stocks*. Honestly, we would *still* love it if some fund company would come to us and "buy" our index to build a fund you could buy, but that hasn't happened yet (but we as optimists never give up hope!). In that spirit—and because we've written a lot about the merits of individual stock versus fund investing—and because of current trends noted earlier where people are buying more passive investments and index funds—we continue to offer this special section about using exchange-traded funds (ETFs) as a path to own portfolios crafted with many of the *100 Best Stocks* principles in mind.

The ETF Universe

We're talking about ETFs here, not traditional mutual funds—and we're talking about ETFs built around a fairly specific index, not the S&P 500 or Russell 2000 as a broad basket. Although total traditional mutual fund assets still outweigh ETF-held assets by a factor of six to one, traditional mutual funds are more expensive and haven't performed as well as ETFs—or the market benchmarks—over time. Therefore, we will limit this discussion to ETFs, but if you're working with a professional advisor or are limited to traditional funds through your 401(k) or some other investment platform, the discussion can apply to traditional funds too.

ETFs are packaged single securities trading on stock exchanges (rather than directly through a mutual fund company), which create a basket of securities that track the composition of specially designed indexes. With most ETFs (excluding "actively managed" ETFs) there are no fund managers making individual stock purchase or sale decisions—they are *passively managed*. The fund follows the index. It follows the good, the bad, and the ugly.

These indexes started out as broad, bland, and obvious—the first ETF, the SPDR S&P 500 ETF Trust, has tracked the S&P 500 index since 1993. Since that inception, hundreds of new indexes have been created to track everything from broad baskets of stocks to the price of certain commodities in Australian dollars. Five years ago, we made an attempt to identify the indexes, and the funds built around them, that mimic *100 Best Stocks* principles.

As of mid-2018, there are about 2,000 exchange-traded products traded in North America, of which about 1,800 are ETFs and 200 are so-called "exchange-traded notes," or ETNs, which are actually fixed-income securities adjusted in value to track an index without actually owning the components of the index. Growth in the ETF space has slowed as recently some funds have closed due to the lack of interest; the total number has stayed relatively constant over the past three years. Total assets were about $3 trillion, or 14 percent of the total "fund" market at the end of 2014. There are generalized and specialized ETFs covering stocks, bonds, fixed-income investments, commodities, real estate, currencies, and the so-called "leveraged and inverse" funds designed to achieve specialized investing objectives. Within each of those groups, the segments available could fill a chapter in and of themselves with divisions by market cap, style (growth versus value), industry, sector, strategy, country, and region—just to name a few.

ETF Advantages

There are numerous advantages of ETFs over traditional funds—reasons why they are "where the puck is going" in packaged investments:

- *Easy to research.* ETFs are relatively easy to understand and easy to screen using commonly found screening tools at online brokers. Among the tools we've used, Fidelity offers some of the best.
- *Transparency.* It's easy to learn what individual stocks an ETF owns and what comprises the underlying index, both through the online portals and through the index providers' websites. (Want to know what's in the Focus Morningstar Health Care Index? Just put the index name into a search engine, and you'll find out.)
- *Low fees, low cost.* Fees typically range from 0.1 percent for the most generic index funds to 0.2–0.8 percent for more specialized funds—about half of the typical figures found in traditional mutual funds. One fund provider—Vanguard—has traditionally been the lowest-cost provider in this regard; however, Charles Schwab recently introduced a series of broad index ETFs with annual fees in the 0.03–0.06 percent range. We expect others will follow.
- *Easy to buy and sell.* It's like buying and selling an ordinary stock.
- *Easy to match your objectives and style.* New funds are showing up every day, and many match a quality, low-volatility, value-oriented style we're aligned with.

Dining with the 100 Best: A Special ETF Menu

Our *100 Best Stocks* list doesn't really follow any investment style. It isn't just growth or value. It isn't just Large Cap, it isn't just high yield, nor is it just tied to certain industries or sectors of the economy. It is a blend of excellent companies in the right businesses, doing well in those businesses, with a potential for strong, steady, and growing investor returns. There is no index or any other screenable classification to select those companies. If there were, there'd be little reason to publish this book.

As we search for ETFs that run with the same tailwinds as our *100 Best* list, we start with the name of the fund and the index that the fund follows. "Dividend Achievers" or "Buyback Achievers" tells us we're looking on the right part of the menu. Then we dig in and look at the actual portfolio composition (again, most investing portals and brokerage sites let you do this—we use Fidelity [www.fidelity.com]). If we see lots of *100 Best Stocks* on the list, it confirms that we're on the right track.

Five years ago, we selected eight ETFs that we thought most closely followed our *100 Best* style and principles and could be used to build or supplement parts of your portfolio. We share the list in Table 11, and in the typical spirit of our presentations, we show the performance of these eight funds during our measurement period.

How Did We Do in 2018?

As we've lamented repeatedly, our 2018 *100 Best Stocks* list did "okay"— up 12.6 percent for our measurement year—but nothing to get excited about, especially in that it lost to the "simple" S&P 500 index by 1.2 percent. But in comparison to the ETFs that match our style, as Table 11 indicates, we did quite well, handily beating the field of competing ETFs. Why? We think it's because of two factors. First is the general bugaboo about fund and index investing: that with an index and a fund created from the index you get not just the "good" but also the "bad" and the "ugly" of any companies that comprise a group. You get the GEs with the Honeywells and the United Technologies (okay, we had all three in our portfolio too, but you get the idea—and at least we have the option to chuck GE for 2019, which we did).

Second, the market turned pretty sour on steady dividend payers during the year in anticipation of higher interest rates. It's likely that our ETFs, each being more focused on a singular investing style than our broader *100 Best* list, got caught with more losers than we did. In a market heavily favored to the *100 Best* "style," ETFs can do better than we do because they're "all in," whereas we dabble in growth kickers like Amazon and Schnitzer Steel. In a bad year for the *100 Best* style, our list might actually do better because our "outside the box" stocks give us some kick. Such is our explanation for 2018, and it serves as a reminder not to go "all in" on anything including *100 Best*–style ETFs. A good portfolio might have some ETFs but isn't fully committed to ETFs in our "style."

▶ Table 11: *100 Best Stocks*—ETF "Imitators"

ETFS WITH STRONG "100 BEST" COMPOSITION AND STRATEGIES

ETF	Symbol	Sponsor	Total assets	Expense ratio (%)	Price 4.1.2017	Price 4.1.2019	% gain share value	2017–8 dividend	Yield %	Total return	What attracted us
100 Best Stocks 2018 Portfolio										12.6%	
Market Vectors Wide Moat Etf	MOAT	Van Eck	$1.4B	0.46%	$38.30	$42.03	9.7%	$0.46	1.2%	10.9%	Compelling strategy
Powershares Buyback Achievers Portfolio	PKW	Invesco	$1.31B	0.63%	$52.17	$56.93	9.1%	$0.46	0.9%	10.0%	Compelling strategy
Ishares Msci Usa Minimum Volatility Index Fund	USMV	Blackrock	$14.50B	0.15%	$48.39	$52.04	7.5%	$0.95	2.0%	9.5%	Low volatility focus, lots of *100 Best Stocks*, low cost
Powershares S&P High Quality Portoflio	SPHQ	Invesco	$1.37B	0.29%	$27.61	$29.58	7.1%	$0.55	2.0%	9.1%	Growth and stability of dividends, lots of *100 best stocks*
Ishares Dow Jones Select Dividend Index Fund	DVY	Blackrock	$16.9B	0.39%	$91.50	$96.32	5.3%	$3.03	3.3%	8.6%	Growth plus income, lots of *100 Best Stocks*
Powershares S&P 500 Low Volatility Portfolio	SPLV	Invesco	$7.0B	0.25%	$43.84	$46.60	6.3%	$0.96	2.2%	8.5%	Low volatility focus, lots of *1100 Best Stocks*, low cost
S&P Spdr Dividend Etf	SDY	State Street	$15.4B	0.35%	$88.66	$90.88	2.5%	$4.53	5.1%	7.6%	Diverse portfolio, "dividend aristocrats" index
First Trust Morningstar Dividend Leaders	FDL	First Trust	$1.5B	0.45%	$28.50	$28.20	-1.1%	$0.97	3.4%	2.4%	Lots of *100 Best Stocks*

Selecting ETFs is an art in itself and was covered in a now-dated but still relevant earlier book we did in this series called *The 100 Best Exchange-Traded Funds You Can Buy 2012*. Unfortunately, that book didn't find a large enough market to be updated each year, but it is still useful in its original form and is still available. There are many other ETF resources, again at your online broker or through a specialized ETF portal called ETFdb (www.etfdb.com). This portal and its classification page (www.etfdb.com/types) can be helpful in finding individual ETFs that suit your taste.

We'll leave the ETF discussion here for this year; the good news continues to be that you can invest in ETFs and still follow the *100 Best* style.

Part II

THE 100 BEST STOCKS TO BUY

Finally, it's post time. Let the "First Call" trumpet fanfare announce *The 100 Best Stocks to Buy in 2019* as they approach the starting gate...

Index of Stocks by Company Name (*New for 2019)

Company	Symbol	Category	Sector
3M	MMM	Conservative Growth	Industrials
—A—			
Abbott Labs	ABT	Growth and Income	Healthcare
AbbVie	ABBV	Aggressive Growth	Healthcare
Allstate	ALL	Conservative Growth	Financials
Amazon	AMZN	Aggressive Growth	Retail
*Analog Devices	ADI	Aggressive Growth	Information Technology
Apple	AAPL	Aggressive Growth	Consumer Discretionary
Applied Materials	AMAT	Aggressive Growth	Information Technology
*Aptiv	APTV	Aggressive Growth	Industrials
Archer Daniels Midland	ADM	Conservative Growth	Consumer Staples
—B—			
Becton, Dickinson	BDX	Conservative Growth	Healthcare
Bemis	BMS	Conservative Growth	Consumer Staples
Boeing	BA	Aggressive Growth	Industrials
—C—			
*CalAmp Corp.	CAMP	Aggressive Growth	Information Technology
CarMax	KMX	Aggressive Growth	Retail
Carnival Corporation	CCL	Aggressive Growth	Consumer Discretionary
CenterPoint Energy	CNP	Growth and Income	Utilities
Chemed	CHE	Aggressive Growth	Healthcare
Chevron	CVX	Growth and Income	Energy
Coca-Cola	KO	Conservative Growth	Consumer Discretionary
Columbia Sportswear	COLM	Aggressive Growth	Consumer Staples
Comcast	CMCSA	Aggressive Growth	Telecommunications Services
ConocoPhillips	COP	Growth and Income	Energy
Corning	GLW	Aggressive Growth	Information Technology
Costco Wholesale	COST	Aggressive Growth	Retail
*Craft Brew Alliance	BREW	Aggressive Growth	Consumer Staples
CVS Health	CVS	Conservative Growth	Retail
—D—			
Daktronics	DAKT	Aggressive Growth	Information Technology
Deere	DE	Aggressive Growth	Industrials
Dentsply Sirona	XRAY	Aggressive Growth	Healthcare
*Devon Energy	DVN	Aggressive Growth	Energy
DowDuPont	DWDP	Growth and Income	Materials

Index of Stocks by Company Name (continued)

Index of Stocks by Company Name (continued)

Index of Stocks by Company Name (continued)

3M Company

Ticker symbol: MMM (NYSE) ❑ Large Cap ❑ Value Line financial strength rating: A++
❑ Current yield: 2.6% ❑ Dividend raises, past 10 years: 10

Company Profile

"Science. Applied to Life" is the slogan of the 3M Company, originally known as the Minnesota Mining and Manufacturing Co. It is a $32 billion diversified manufacturing technology company with leading positions in industrial, consumer and office, healthcare, safety, electronics, telecommunications, and other markets. The company has 81 manufacturing operations in 29 US states and in total 132 manufacturing operations in more than 36 countries. It serves customers in nearly 200 countries; 61 percent of the company's sales are international. 3M also operates 37 laboratories worldwide and spends about 5.8 percent of revenues on R&D. Due to the breadth of their product line and the global reach of their distribution, the company has long been viewed as a bellwether for the overall health of the world economy.

3M's operations are divided into five business segments (approximate revenue percentages in parentheses):

- The Industrial business (34 percent of 2017 sales) serves a variety of vertical markets, including automotive, automotive aftermarket, electronics, paper and packaging, appliance, food and beverage, and construction. Products include industrial tapes, a wide variety of abrasives, adhesives, specialty materials, filtration products, closure systems for personal hygiene products, advanced ceramics, automotive insulation, filler and paint system components, and products for the separation of fluids and gases.
- The Safety and Graphics business (19 percent) serves a broad range of markets that increase the safety, security, and productivity of workers, facilities, and systems. Major product offerings include personal protection, like respirators and filtering systems, safety and security products such as reflectorized fabrics and tapes, energy control products, traffic control products including reflective sheeting for highway signs, building cleaning and protection products, track and trace solutions, and roofing granules for asphalt shingles.
- The Healthcare business (18 percent) serves markets that include medical clinics and hospitals, pharmaceuticals, dental and orthodontic

practitioners, and health information systems. Products and services include medical and surgical supplies, skin health and infection prevention products, drug-delivery systems, dental and orthodontic products, health information systems, and antimicrobial solutions. The Healthcare business is the most profitable, with operating margins of 31.7 percent versus margins in the low 20s for the other four businesses.

- The Electronics and Energy segment (16 percent) serves the electrical, electronics, communications, and renewable energy industries, including electric utilities. Products include electronic and interconnect solutions, microinterconnect systems, high-performance fluids and abrasives for semiconductor and disk drive manufacture, high-temperature and display tapes, telecommunications products, electrical products, and optical film materials that support LCD displays and touch screens for monitors, tablets, mobile phones, and other products.

- The Consumer segment (15 percent) serves markets that include retail, home improvement, building maintenance, office, and other markets. Products in this segment include office supply products such as the familiar Scotch tapes, Post-it notes, Scotch-Brite cleaning abrasives, stationery products, construction and home improvement products, home-care products, protective material products, and consumer healthcare products. This segment grew considerably with the 2012 acquisition of the Avery Dennison office products line.

Near-term strategies include streamlining the organization structure, combining 40 businesses into 26, a more general cost-containment effort, and a greater emphasis on leveraging and promoting the brand across all businesses. The company has adjusted its portfolio once again with several small acquisitions and divestitures. The cost containment ("transformation" in company lingo) is intended to save $600–$700 million in costs and $500 million in working capital by 2020. A new $150 million laboratory opened in 2016 in St. Paul will help "strengthen the scientific edge." It appears that continued small acquisitions and an emphasis on fast-track R&D will continue to be themes going forward.

Financial Highlights, Fiscal Year 2017

Strong overseas sales, a stabilizing dollar, and some recovery in the energy industry led to a 5.7 percent FY2017 revenue gain. Cost efficiencies, operating leverage, and some raw material cost decreases led margins higher, in turn producing an 11 percent earnings gain; share buybacks upped the per-share gain to 12 percent. By segment revenue, Electronics and Energy and Safety and Graphics led the way while Consumer and Health Care lagged a bit. By region, Asia Pacific grew 10.9 percent while the US grew only 1.5 percent. The outlook for 2018 calls for a substantial 15–16 percent per-share earnings gain on a 6–7 percent revenue gain; growth slows a bit to an 8–9 percent EPS gain on a 4–6 percent revenue gain in 2019—still healthy for a company this size. 3M continues to reward shareholders, with a 6 percent dividend raise and a 2 percent share buyback; the company has retired 15 percent of its float since 2011.

Reasons to Buy

For years, 3M has served as a classic example of a "conservative growth" stock and is a classic exercise in brand excellence, marketplace and niche strength, and steady performance. The company makes and distributes many repeat-sale products essential to manufacturing and day-to-day operations of other companies and organizations and seemingly essential to most of us, e.g., Post-it notes and Scotch tape. The company appears to do better than the markets during strong periods and also holds value better than most during downturns. There is a persistent focus on innovation here, both in its products and in its internal operations and marketing—and it's more the slow, steady variety than a flash in the pan. Pro-US manufacturing policies from the Trump administration could boost domestic businesses. Cash flows are strong and growing and continue to be shared liberally with shareholders.

Reasons for Caution

3M is, and always will be, vulnerable to economic cycles, but in general the business holds up pretty well in down cycles. There's plenty of pressure from the investment community to get the top line moving forward, and we worry that 3M could go on a larger acquisition rampage to boost growth, but we continue to be comfortable with the types of acquisitions the company has made. Further, profit growth has been good for such a large company, so why the angst about revenue growth? Shares have gained a lot in the past two years, but we still think there's value here—once again we suggest placing a Post-it on this page to pick up a few shares when the price is right.

SECTOR: Industrials ◻ **BETA COEFFICIENT: 1.14** ◻ **10-YEAR COMPOUND EARNINGS PER-SHARE GROWTH: 6.0%** ◻ **10-YEAR COMPOUND DIVIDENDS PER-SHARE GROWTH: 9.0%**

	2010	2011	2012	2013	2014	2015	2016	2017
Revenues (mil)	26,662	29,611	29,904	30,871	31,821	30,274	30,109	31,657
Net income (mil)	4,169	4,283	4,445	4,659	4,956	4,833	5,050	5,620
Earnings per share	5.75	5.96	6.32	6.72	7.49	7.58	8.16	9.17
Dividends per share	2.10	2.20	2.36	2.54	3.42	4.10	4.44	4.70
Cash flow per share	7.43	7.85	8.35	9.09	10.02	10.29	10.93	12.04
Price: high	91.5	98.2	95.5	140.4	168.2	170.5	182.3	244.2
low	40.9	68.6	82.0	94.0	123.6	124.0	134.6	173.5

Website: www.3m.com

GROWTH AND INCOME

Abbott Laboratories

Ticker symbol: ABT (NYSE) ◻ **Large Cap** ◻ **Value Line financial strength rating: A++** ◻ **Current yield: 2.0%** ◻ **Dividend raises, past 10 years: 10**

Company Profile

In 2013 longtime *100 Best* stalwart Abbott Laboratories split itself in two, spinning off their research pharmaceutical firm known as AbbVie, which found its way back onto our list two years ago. The remaining healthcare products maker and distributor Abbott Labs, which kept the original company name, made it back last year, as the split appeared to be headed in the right direction for both companies. Last year's successful acquisition of cardiovascular, neuromodulation and diabetes device maker St. Jude Medical, Inc.—another *100 Best* stock—sealed the deal for us. After all the changes, we continue to like this story and present the evolved Abbott Labs again for 2019.

Today's Abbott engages in the discovery, development, manufacture and distribution of medicines, diagnostics, nutrition, and vascular products. The business continues to operate in four segments:

- Established Pharmaceuticals (15 percent of 2017 revenue) contains a portfolio of over 1,500 established and mostly generic prescription products including flu vaccines, hormone replacements, enzyme replacements, antibiotics, and other routine remedies for common ailments (in contrast to expensive, "sexy" treatments for rare diseases). This group is particularly strong in emerging markets.

- Nutritional Products (25 percent of revenue) makes and markets a portfolio of baby formulas under the "Similac" brand and an assortment of nutritional supplements targeted to adults (Ensure and Glucerna are major brands), electrolyte replenishment ("Pedialyte"), and other nutritional products and supplements. The company claims a number one market position in adult and pediatric nutritionals.
- Diagnostic Products (21 percent of revenue) makes and markets a broad line of diagnostic systems and tests for blood banks, hospitals, commercial labs, and alternate-care testing sites—this group holds a number one position in standard and advanced blood chemistry testing and monitoring. One exciting new product is the "FreeStyle Libre," a continuous electronic glucose monitoring system that eliminates finger pricks. This new product made the *Popular Science* "Best of What's New" list for 2016 and launched in Q4 2017.
- Medical Devices (formerly Vascular Products, 38 percent of revenue, was 14 percent of revenue in 2016 before St. Jude) markets a broad line of coronary, endovascular, structural heart, and other physical and electronic products. Recent product breakthroughs include Confirm Rx, the world's first smartphone-compatible Insertable Cardiac Monitor. Abbott products are sold in about 150 countries, with about 65 percent of total sales occurring overseas and 42 percent from emerging markets.

The acquisition of St. Jude brought a well-established product line of structural heart repair devices, including heart valve repair and replacement technologies, heart failure remedies, cardiac rhythm management devices, cardiovascular care devices including imaging devices and stents, and neuromodulation devices to manage chronic pain and movement disorders. The St. Jude acquisition makes Abbott a number one or number two supplier into these important high-growth markets.

Financial Highlights, Fiscal Year 2017

Global FY2017 sales rose 32 percent; while the vast majority of that rise was due to St. Jude, double-digit gains were also brought in by the Diagnostics and Pharmaceuticals groups, which had no St. Jude influence. Net income also spiked ahead 34 percent. The numbers are hard to compare looking backward or forward, with the AbbVie split, a 2015 sale of some generic pharmaceuticals businesses to Mylan (N.V., Netherlands), the St. Jude acquisition, and the more recent acquisition of diagnostic products maker Alere. Going forward the company projects a 13–14 percent revenue gain for 2018, about half of which comes from the Alere acquisition, and a 12–13 percent net income gain. For 2019, projections settle into a 6–8 percent annual revenue gain but still an 11–12 percent net income gain as margins improve. Modest buybacks will boost per-share earnings at a somewhat greater rate.

The company raised its dividend modestly in 2017 for a forty-sixth consecutive year of dividend increases (not counting the drop when AbbVie split off). The share count increased about 15 percent with the St. Jude acquisition but will drop 1–2 percent annually thereafter.

Reasons to Buy

Abbott is an established leader in important, stable, and mostly recurring healthcare markets and needs. Most of the product portfolio to date consists of products and diagnostics used over and over, including blood tests, diabetes remedies, cardiovascular devices, and nutritional products. We like that position.

The St. Jude acquisition brings Abbott to a leadership position in key cardiovascular markets, a good position with today's demographics and a relatively higher-margined business. Abbott's net margins had been tracking in the 15–16 percent range; with the St. Jude acquisition, net margins in the 17–18 percent range are more likely.

Reasons for Caution

Abbott operates with a solid business base but has been heavily involved in acquisitions since its 2012 split with AbbVie. While much of it makes sense from a strategic standpoint, it is disruptive and carries some risks. The $23.6 billion acquisition price for St. Jude may have been too high (for a company with $6 billion in annual revenue) and will create some goodwill write-offs down the road. We don't see too many risks with the core businesses, and we do expect the company to slow down or stop the acquisitions. While the business model makes sense, it is relatively difficult to evaluate Abbott's numbers with the large changes taking place in the past five years.

SECTOR: **Healthcare** ❑ BETA COEFFICIENT: **1.5** ❑ 10-YEAR COMPOUND EARNINGS PER-SHARE GROWTH: **NM** ❑ 10-YEAR COMPOUND DIVIDENDS PER-SHARE GROWTH: **NM**

	2010	2011	2012	2013	2014	2015	2016	2017
Revenues (bil)	35.2	38.9	39.9	21.9	22.3	20.4	20.9	27.4
Net income (bil)	6.5	7.3	8.2	3.2	3.5	3.3	3.3	4.4
Earnings per share	4.17	4.66	4.99	2.01	2.28	2.15	2.20	2.50
Dividends per share	1.75	1.88	2.01	0.56	0.88	0.96	1.04	1.06
Cash flow per share	5.90	6.61	6.91	3.17	3.35	3.21	3.20	3.70
Price: high	56.8	56.4	72.5	38.6	46.5	51.7	45.8	57.8
low	44.6	45.1	54.0	31.6	35.7	39.0	36.0	38.3

Note: Figures before 2013 are for combined company. See AbbVie, another *100 Best Stock*.

Website: www.abbott.com

AGGRESSIVE GROWTH

AbbVie, Inc.

Ticker symbol: ABBV (NYSE) ❑ Large Cap ❑ Value Line financial strength rating: A ❑ Current yield: 3.0% ❑ Dividend raises, past 10 years: 4

Company Profile

Spun off from the former combined Abbott Laboratories in 2013, AbbVie is a leading research-based biopharmaceutical company specializing in developing and marketing treatments and therapies for a range of complex diseases. The former Abbott was a perennial *100 Best Stock*. The other half of the split, still called Abbott Laboratories, specializes mainly in making and distributing a line of medical supplies. AbbVie's products help treat conditions such as chronic autoimmune diseases in rheumatology, gastroenterology, and dermatology; oncology, including blood cancers; virology, including hepatitis C virus (HCV) and human immunodeficiency virus (HIV); neurological disorders, such as Parkinson's disease and multiple sclerosis; metabolic diseases, including thyroid disease and complications associated with cystic fibrosis, as well as other serious health conditions. AbbVie also has a pipeline of new medicines, including more than 50 compounds or indications (20 in late-stage development), such as immunology, virology/liver disease, oncology, neurological diseases, and women's health. Its product portfolio includes Humira, Imbruvica, HCV products, additional virology products, metabolics/hormones products, and endocrinology products, among others.

Accounting for 65 percent of FY2017 sales and holding the title as highest-grossing drug in the world at $18.3 billion in annual sales, Humira is by far AbbVie's largest product—really, it's a franchise. An immunological agent initially developed to treat rheumatoid arthritis, the company (and the FDA) have found it quite useful for treating other immunological diseases such as psoriasis, psoriatic arthritis, and a number of other diseases in the rheumatology, gastroenterology, and dermatology space. The patent for the "composition of matter" expired at the end of 2016—and normally with 65 percent of the business this would be a huge red flag—but the company has an extensive "patent estate" of several dozen patents for the product covering other uses, formulations, manufacturing processes, and other patents extending well into the next decade. Amgen has recently delayed a generic launch in 2023, and the company plans several major launches in other drug categories as noted here. By 2020 the company expects Humira to account for about 50 percent of sales and a large share of profits—and steadily less as the post-Humira era unfolds.

Other major emerging drug platforms include Imbruvica, a hematology (blood oncology) and HCV drug acquired through the 2015 acquisition of Pharmacyclics, which is projected to reach 13 percent of sales by 2020, Viekira for Hepatitis C (8 percent by 2020), and Duopa for Parkinson's disease (3 percent by 2020). As exemplified by the Humira platform, the company continually looks for ways to extend existing and modified formulations into additional disease categories with new delivery and dosage models added in where feasible (Duopa uses an implant to provide steadier levels of dopamine for advanced Parkinson's patients, for example).

The company markets its products in 170 countries; about 38 percent of sales are overseas.

Financial Highlights, Fiscal Year 2017

Making the most of its existing and new platforms, AbbVie has emerged in four short years to produce some of the best results among its research pharma peers. In part driven by acquisitions, FY2017 revenues advanced 10 percent on a constant currency basis, down a bit from last year. Margins grew slightly aside from tax effects; net earnings grew 14 percent over 2016. The overall net profit margin stands at a very healthy 31.9 percent. Per-share cash flows advanced 13 percent supporting a 12 percent dividend increase; the dividend is up 60 percent in the four years since the company split from Abbott in 2013.

A healthy combination of organic growth, new drug launches, broader Humira penetration, and acquisitions will keep revenues rising at about a 15–16 percent clip through 2018, with per-share earnings well exceeding that pace into a 35–40 percent growth range as volume efficiencies and manufacturing process improvements take effect. The pace moderates a little in 2019 to a 10–12 percent EPS gain on a 5–7 percent forecasted revenue gain.

Reasons to Buy

Research pharma companies are quite often too complex for our simple minds and tastes, so we take on this sector with great care, as we also did with diabetes drug specialist Novo Nordisk a few years back. Here, we find a bit more complexity since yes, as stated, AbbVie specializes in the treatment of complex and advanced diseases. We won't pretend to understand how its products actually work.

What we do like and think we understand is the underlying business strategy. AbbVie focuses on a few key drug platforms like Humira and Imbruvica, making the most of them while offering extendable solutions for other complex oncological, immunological, and neurological indications as well. While it's unfortunate that there are so many of these complex diseases around to treat, we like AbbVie's focus on this relatively more profitable, defensible end of the market.

The financial track record speaks for itself—any company with a 30 percent–plus net profit margin that shares its success with its shareholders comes as pretty good medicine for us.

Reasons for Caution

Complexity is probably our number one issue—this company could fail miserably in one or more of its markets, and we laypeople would probably be none the wiser. The dependence on Humira naturally raises the specter of patent expirations, from which the company appears to position itself quite well to minimize the potential damage. Healthcare industry consolidation and power shifts may lead to reduced drug prices and margins, which would hurt AbbVie and others in the group. Finally, we do worry a bit about the growth-by-acquisition tendencies, though we do think acquisitions so far make sense and are done *on top of* a pretty sound and successful business.

SECTOR: **Healthcare** ❑ BETA COEFFICIENT: **1.61** ❑ 10-YEAR COMPOUND EARNINGS PER-SHARE GROWTH: **NM** ❑ 10-YEAR COMPOUND DIVIDENDS PER-SHARE GROWTH: **NM**

	2010	2011	2012	2013	2014	2015	2016	2017
Revenues (mil)	—	—	—	18,790	19,960	22,839	25,638	28,216
Net income (mil)	—	—	—	5,066	5,375	7,060	7,904	9,011
Earnings per share	—	—	—	3.14	3.32	4.29	4.82	5.60
Dividends per share	—	—	—	1.60	1.66	2.02	2.28	2.56
Cash flow per share	—	—	—	3.44	3.62	4.64	5.23	5.73
Price: high	—	—	—	54.8	70.8	71.2	68.1	99.1
low	—	—	—	33.3	45.5	45.4	50.7	59.3

Website: www.abbvie.com

CONSERVATIVE GROWTH

Allstate Corporation

Ticker symbol: ALL (NASDAQ) ❑ Large Cap ❑ Value Line financial strength rating: A+ ❑ Current yield: 2.0% ❑ Dividend raises, past 10 years: 7

Company Profile

Allstate is the nation's second-largest publicly held, full-line "P/C" (property/casualty) insurance provider, offering the gamut of auto, home, renters, and business insurance, and has become a larger player in life insurance, retirement, and annuity segments as well (although it still is ranked only nineteenth among US life insurers. The company serves 16 million households through a network of 36,000 total agents with almost a billion and a half policies in force in all 50 states plus DC and Canada. It prides itself on its four-tiered brand and channel strategy for delivering choice and advice to customers where, when, and how they want it.

The company sells its own Allstate product through 10,430 exclusive Allstate agencies and its "Encompass" subbrand through independent agencies. It estimates that the Allstate brand alone owns 9 percent of the traditional P/C market, with a 10 percent share of the auto market and an 8 percent share for homeowners. The company owns and operates the e-commerce insurance portal Esurance and also sells its product directly, along with other insurance brands, through its "Answer Financial" phone portal for self-directed consumers looking for choices. That said, the lion's share of premiums ($28.9 billion, or 91 percent of policies in force) is earned through the Allstate brand, while Encompass and Esurance contribute about $1.7

billion, or about 6 percent for Esurance and 3 percent for Encompass. By product line, auto leads the way with about 69 percent of premium dollars, homeowners with 24 percent, with the rest coming from life, commercial, and other business lines. Increasingly, the company is using analytics to "microsegment" and tune the premium/cost mix.

Recent acquisitions have brought in Arity, a user of data and analytics to better manage risk, enhancing a broader strategy to deploy analytics across the business, and SquareTrade, an innovative provider of protection plans and support services for the consumer electronics buyer.

Financial Highlights, Fiscal Year 2017

Higher premiums, improved investment income, and the SquareTrade acquisition drove FY2017 revenues 5.4 percent higher, while net income jumped some 25 percent, recovering from a poor showing in 2016 and reflecting tax savings and lower claims expense (surprising, given the hurricanes in late 2017; the company managed to avoid the worst of this). The "combined ratio," which includes underwriting expenses (claims) and operating expenses, improved to 93.6 percent, that is, $6.40 in pretax profit is generated for every $100 in premiums received—this figure is down from around 9 percent in 2016. Going forward, the company expects premium growth in the 3–7 percent range annually through 2019 supported by price increases, which in turn are supported by news headlines (2017 catastrophes) and a stronger economy. Net income could jump another 20–25 percent in 2018 due to tax changes, price increases, and investment income gains but are expected to stay relatively flat in 2019. Dividend increases and share buybacks will be moderate after an expected 25 percent dividend increase in 2018, again related to tax changes. Allstate has reduced its share count 48 percent since 2004.

Reasons to Buy

We like the market position, brand strength, channel strategy, increased stability, and upside potential both in underwriting and in investment performance. The company has gained a solid strategic hold on its reputation, brand, and channel strategy. Esurance and other "direct" models are gaining traction, while the company is also offering a better product mix and better cross-selling opportunities through its traditional agencies. Increased investment income will also help. Allstate has all the earmarks of a well-managed company.

The Allstate brand is ever stronger, turning from a slight negative years ago to a solid positive through stronger advertising, product offering, and general branding initiatives. The company now proudly places its name on "adjacent" businesses such as Allstate Roadside Services. Another branding example is the new "Package" policy, combining auto and homeowners into a single policy sold under the Encompass brand. All of this combined with solid shareholder returns makes Allstate in our view a solid blue-chip performer in a difficult industry with a pretty decent upside going forward.

Reasons for Caution

Competition is stiff and another hurricane-infested year like 2005 could also hurt, although Allstate is more geographically diverse than some of its competitors—and we saw how this helps: 2017 did *not* turn out to be a disaster. Higher auto claims rates, driven by smartphone use, greater mileages driven because of cheap gas, and a generally faster pace of life are also a concern but should be covered by price increases eventually. Interest rates on the industry's traditional investment instruments, while improving, are still historically weak, and another major stock or bond market correction could hurt too. For years, the brand suffered from a reputation for poor claims performance and an overly sales-y approach. Although the company is more aware of its relatively erratic past and seems to be doing something about it, the prior volatility of its results in revenues, earnings, and especially dividends paid is hard to ignore. Finally, we'll admit that we find insurers (as most Financials) difficult to understand because of terminology and somewhat different ways of measuring and reporting financial performance; you may also find this company difficult to understand well enough to commit your capital comfortably. Proceed carefully.

SECTOR: **Financials** ❑ BETA COEFFICIENT: **0.85** ❑ 10-YEAR COMPOUND EARNINGS PER-SHARE GROWTH: **1.0%** ❑ 10-YEAR COMPOUND DIVIDENDS PER-SHARE GROWTH: **-0.5%**

	2010	2011	2012	2013	2014	2015	2016	2017
Property/casualty premiums (mil)	25,957	25,942	26,737	27,618	28,929	30,309	31,407	32,300
Net income (mil)	1,535	699	2,143	2,756	2,379	2,119	1,785	2,382
Earnings per share	2.83	1.34	4.34	5.70	5.42	5.21	4.69	6.71
Dividends per share	0.80	0.83	1.09	0.75	1.12	1.29	1.29	1.45
Underwriting inc. per share	(0.58)	(4.19)	2.49	4.95	4.22	4.06	3.34	5.82
Price: high	35.5	34.4	42.8	54.8	71.5	72.9	74.8	105.4
low	26.9	22.3	27.0	40.7	49.2	54.1	56.0	73.0

Website: www.allstate.com

AGGRESSIVE GROWTH

Amazon.com, Inc.

Ticker symbol: AMZN (NASDAQ) ❑ Large Cap ❑ Value Line financial strength rating: A+
❑ Current yield: Nil ❑ Dividend raises, past 10 years: NA

Company Profile

"Alexa, buy ten shares of Amazon."

Such a fantasy hasn't arrived quite yet—that we know of—but who knows, it may soon be part of this juggernaut's amazing streak of innovations and conveniences destined to transform our shopping world.

Simply put, Amazon.com makes us feel old. We can remember a mere 23 years ago when Amazon was just a retailer—a *book* retailer. A huge one, granted, but the first thought that came to mind at the mention of its name was a great place to buy a book *cheap* without having to drive somewhere to find it.

Then they started selling other stuff.

Amazon.com has become the world's largest e-commerce retailer, but the company's scope has grown beyond even that in the past several years. Amazon Web Services (AWS) is now the world's largest provider of cloud computing services, with a market share larger than that of the next five largest players combined. Amazon Video is a provider of video on-demand services, competing with both traditional cable providers as well as IP (Internet)-based rivals such as Hulu. They are also producing award-winning original movies and series. Amazon Go is testing the waters in the grocery business with an eventual goal of 2,000 stores in the US, an effort that may well be accelerated with their recent purchase of Whole Foods. Amazon Prime has now dented the rest of the retail and consumer universe with millions of customers willing to pay $10—no, now $12—a month for "Prime" priority shipping services, creating a steady flow of little brown boxes wrapped in black tape to our doorsteps—5 *billion* such packages in 2018 (and oh, by the way, you get access to Amazon Prime video and other stuff too). Add to that our new friend "Alexa"—the family of Echo voice-recognition products transforming our kitchens and living rooms to on-demand music centers and convenience stations—and oh, by the way, enabling us to order that stuff on Prime with a simple voice command. Then, to top it off in one of the more irony-laden business moves of recent memory, Amazon is now rolling out a test of retail bookstores.

Among such a laundry list of superlatives, who can fail to note a stock that has gone up from the mid-600s when we first added it to the 2017 *100*

Best Stocks list to over $1,400 as we compose this narrative today? When else have we had anything to do with a stock that sells for $1,400? Only for an extraordinary company on a relentless, and successful, journey to transform the universe, that's Amazon today.

Financial Highlights, Fiscal Year 2017

Overall, FY2017 produced a 31 percent increase in revenues, with "product" sales up 24 percent to $119 billion, and "service" sales up 43 percent to $59 billion. North American sales increased 33 percent while International increased 24 percent, and AWS gained 43 percent. AWS continues to produce the lion's share of operating income, while International continues to operate at a loss, mostly due to increased outlays for increased fulfillment capacity and technology. FY2018 projections call for a 24 percent revenue gain and a doubling of net income as infrastructure investments moderate, scale improves, and new revenue streams from Whole Foods and Echo technology become more fully realized.

Reasons to Buy

There are many good reasons to own a piece of AMZN right now, as the company is at the heart of the "stay-at-home" trend; in fact, it is driving it with services like Amazon Prime and the Amazon Marketplace. The Marketplace, really an online shopping mall, makes it possible for vendors and customers around the world to connect and transact business without a physical storefront. And who doesn't know about Amazon Prime's bundle of one-click ordering, free two-day shipping to most places, music, movies, free books, and other goodies? Amazon has been at the very forefront of making Internet shopping safe, secure, convenient, cost-competitive for the seller and price-competitive for the buyer—and it is disrupting most of the retail industry. It's a safe bet that you, or at least your neighbors, are ordering mundane household items like laundry detergent and Hershey's Kisses using Prime. We do—and no, we're not millennials (although we still struggle with having Alexa do it for us).

Okay, so it's a successful business model and a good place to shop. Does that mean it's a good stock to own? Even at today's prices? Obviously, we think so.

The single best reason to own a piece Amazon is that it continues to deliver on nearly every promise made since its founding. Jeff Bezos predicted the company might take a decade to become profitable. This scared away many investors, but in retrospect, it was a brilliant piece of expectations management, having the additional benefit of being the truth. Fifteen years after making *that* statement, Bezos continued to tell investors that new Amazon projects had a five-to-seven-year horizon, on the theory that very few companies had the patience to take on projects that took that long to develop. In Bezos's view, this meant there was effectively zero competition for these longer-term opportunities. Right again.

At that time, e-commerce was growing five times faster than the overall retail market, and Amazon was growing twice as fast as e-commerce as a whole. Fast-forward five years to today, and Amazon has carved out an enormous chunk of the US (and worldwide) retailing market by being willing to take on projects of enormous scale and complexity and executing on them with a vengeance. Alexa gives us a great example, and more is likely in store as they consolidate Whole Foods into an online grocery service and local delivery point. Next may be a headlong foray to transform prescription drug delivery and healthcare in general. "We're very stubborn," Bezos once said.

As another example, Amazon Web Services, the company's on-demand cloud computing platform, launched in 2003 as an Amazon-internal IT project for managing certain aspects of transaction data. A year later, it was launched as a service for public use. Today, AWS accounts for over $17 billion in revenue and $4.3 billion in operating profit, exceeding the rest of the company's profit combined.

The list of accomplishments, new products, and platforms is unparalleled in Corporate America—it's two full pages of bullet points just in the most recent quarterly report, and far too much to cover here. Quite simply, Amazon is transforming retail, web services, and the living room at a pace heretofore unknown—and expanding its influence steadily into international markets too. The company is truly living up to its name "Amazon."

Reasons for Caution

As much as we like the company, its customer value proposition and execution excellence, there's no getting around the cost of these shares. With a share price approaching $1,500, up *another* 50 percent in a year, the valuation (price to earnings) is astronomical while even the forward ratio (based on 2018 projections) is around 145 (compared to 21 for the S&P 500). Although profitability is growing, and sales are growing dramatically, simply maintaining this kind of stock price may require an almost unimaginable sustained financial performance. Amazon has rewarded the bold and faithful handsomely in the past, but the timid and doubtful among us cannot be faulted for treading gingerly through the stacks of this very special bookstore.

SECTOR: **Retail** ❏ BETA COEFFICIENT: **1.63** ❏ 10-YEAR COMPOUND EARNINGS PER-SHARE
GROWTH: **10.5%** ❏ 10-YEAR COMPOUND DIVIDENDS PER-SHARE GROWTH: **NA**

	2010	2011	2012	2013	2014	2015	2016	2017
Revenues (bil)	48.1	61.9	74.5	89.0	107.0	130.0	136.0	177.9
Net income (mil)	631.0	130.0	274.0	(241.0)	596.0	2,485	2,371	2,244
Earnings per share	1.37	0.29	0.59	(0.52)	1.25	5.20	4.90	4.55
Dividends per share	—	—	—	—	—	—	—	—
Cash flow per share	3.77	5.04	7.68	9.70	14.60	18.60	21.99	21.60
Price: high	246.7	264.1	405.6	408.1	696.4	685.5	847.2	1213
low	160.6	172.0	245.8	284.0	285.3	474.0	474.0	747.7

Website: www.amazon.com

AGGRESSIVE GROWTH

NEW FOR 2019

Analog Devices, Inc.

Ticker symbol: ADI (NASDAQ) ❏ Large Cap ❏ Value Line financial strength rating: A+ ❏ Current yield: 2.1% ❏ Dividend raises, past 10 years: 10

Company Profile

Analog Devices designs, manufactures, and markets high-performance analog, mixed-signal, and digital signal–processing chips used in a multitude of electronic devices. Founded in 1965, they have grown to be one of the largest semiconductor houses in the world by focusing almost exclusively on a segment of electronic design known as signal processing. They do not make large-scale microprocessors, discrete digital logic, or memory, but concentrate instead on real-time applications such as front-end signal acquisition, analog/digital conversion, signal conditioning, and amplification.

Analog's high-value-add components find their way into products such as medical imaging equipment, cellular base stations, digital cameras and televisions, industrial process controls, defense electronics, factory automation systems, satellites, and automobiles. In all, the company derives nearly half its revenue from the Industrial market, with Communications, Automotive, and Consumer markets accounting for the other half in nearly equal shares. They make thousands of products, with the ten highest revenue products in total accounting for just under 8 percent of revenues.

The company fabricates many of its own analog parts at any of its four manufacturing facilities ("fabs"), located in Massachusetts, Santa Clara, CA, and Limerick, Ireland. ADI also employs third-party suppliers (primarily

TSMC in Taiwan) for fabrication of its sub-micron CMOS die. The company closed its wafer fabrication facility in Massachusetts at the end of fiscal 2009 and now sources its blank wafers from third parties.

In March 2017 the company completed its acquisition of Linear Technology, another analog semiconductor design house but with a highly complementary product line focused primarily on power devices and associated controllers.

Financial Highlights, Fiscal Year 2017

Fiscal 2017 data includes approximately two-quarters of combined results for ADI and Linear Technology (LT). In 2017, revenue rose 49 percent to $5.1 billion with gross margins of 60 percent and net margins of 33 percent (up 5 percent from 2016). Results for the first quarter of 2018 are similarly strong, with revenues of $1.52 billion and gross margins of 68.2 percent. The structure of the LT acquisition added 60 million shares to the ADI share base (an increase of 20 percent), and EPS on this new basis came in at $1.42, meeting expectations.

Projections through 2019 call for significant growth in revenue to $6.24 billion, with further gains in net profit margin, driving 2019 earnings to near $2.13 billion as redundancies created by the LT acquisition are reduced.

Reasons to Buy

The technology sector in general and the semiconductor industry in particular are central to the current sea change in the way computing intelligence affects our lives. Intelligence once confined to datacenters or home PCs has been moved further and further out into the very edges of our experience. Why is this happening now? Because intelligence follows the availability of data for it to manipulate. We have computers in our cars only because our cars can now generate data for the computers to act upon. Where does this data come from? It comes from sensors and other devices that translate the impulses and streams of analog information from our human existence into the realm of digital data. These analog components have become faster, smaller, smarter, and cheaper, and this has led to their ubiquity in the devices we employ in our daily lives. This is the market that ADI targets, and as a consequence of this distributed intelligence, times have never been better for analog suppliers.

We've looked at ADI almost every year as a possible *100 Best* stock, and while we liked what we saw, there were always one or two stronger prospects in the technology sector. ADI was always steady but not necessarily stellar.

This year, however, ADI prospects look much brighter due in large part to the Linear Technology acquisition. Founded in 1981, LT quickly established a reputation for design excellence and unparalleled support. Their customers were more than willing to pay higher premiums for LT's parts that were either on the leading edge of new designs or were simply better than what the competition offered. This led to net margins that were the envy of the industry (35.2 percent in 2015) and helped to support an engineering-driven company culture that boasted remarkable talent retention. LT billed itself as "the company that no one leaves." In short, ADI received (for the fairly high price of ten times LT's 2015 revenues and a quarter of an ADI share for each LT share) not just a catalog of parts and customers, but one of the industry's leading pools of talent and a potent product development environment. The addition of LT's customer base (whose design cycles tend to be longer) will also raise the quality and longevity of ADI's revenue streams.

To that end, analog chip suppliers tend to hold design wins and customers for the life of a customer's product. In critical circuits, products are designed with the characteristics of key components in mind, and a change of suppliers often necessitates a redesign or a re-spec of the final product. For this reason, ADI's earnings have been more reliable than those of the suppliers of commodity ICs; the LT acquisition should only improve things.

With the acquisition, ADI will also gain LT's fabrication facilities. Fab ownership is a double-edged sword. If the fab is not fully utilized during a down cycle in the economy, the higher fixed costs lead to lower operating margins. As someone once said, "It's like owning a bunch of elephants—you can get a lot of work done, but they have to eat." During an up cycle, however, you're paying yourself rather than someone else to build your dies, effectively capturing what would have gone out the door to a vendor. In the end, fabs are nearly always a net positive if kept fully utilized. Owning the fab also allows control and the ability to modify its operation very specifically to get the most out of product designs. This is a real benefit to a maker of analog parts, as fab tuning for analog processes tends to be as much art as it is science.

Fun fact: ADI's logo is a schematic symbol for a gain stage, which takes in a small signal and amplifies it into a larger version of that signal. If there's a better parallel for "buy low, sell high" we can't think of it.

Reasons for Caution

When your recent annual revenues are around $3 billion, and you buy another company for around $15 billion, it puts a bit of strain on your budget and adds risk and complexity. Although ADI still has a reasonable cash position, future acquisitions of significant size are probably not in the cards. Smaller, tactical buys, however, are still on the menu.

SECTOR: Information Technology ❑ BETA COEFFICIENT: **1.10** ❑ 10-YEAR COMPOUND EARNINGS PER-SHARE GROWTH: **10.0%** ❑ 10-YEAR COMPOUND DIVIDENDS PER-SHARE GROWTH: **12.5%**

		2010	2011	2012	2013	2014	2015	2016	2017
Revenues (mil)		2,762	2,993	2,701	2,634	2,865	3,435	3,421	5,108
Net income (mil)		712	839	651	674	763	1,001	959	1,688
Earnings per share		2.33	2.72	2.13	2.14	2.40	3.16	3.07	4.68
Dividends per share		0.86	0.97	1.20	1.36	1.48	1.60	1.68	1.80
Cash flow per share		2.79	3.21	2.53	2.52	2.82	3.62	3.55	5.11
Price:	high	38.6	43.3	42.7	51.2	58.0	69.0	74.9	94.0
	low	26.3	29.2	34.3	41.7	42.6	50.6	47.2	71.0

Website: www.analog.com

AGGRESSIVE GROWTH

Apple, Inc.

Ticker symbol: AAPL (NASDAQ) ❑ **Large Cap** ❑ **Value Line financial strength rating: A++** ❑ **Current yield: 1.5%** ❑ **Dividend raises, past 10 years: 6**

Company Profile

Now easily the world's most valuable company with a market capitalization just short of $900 billion, Apple, Inc. remains an admired bellwether for consumer innovation and design for a wide swath of consumers from preteen to seniors (and a growing number of commercial customers). We hardly need to review what the company makes and sells, but we will once again anyhow; it's still kind of fun.

Apple designs, manufactures, and markets computers, smartphones, tablets, portable music players, digital watches and related software, peripherals, downloadable content, and services. It sells these products through its own retail stores, online stores, and third-party and value-added resellers. The company also sells digital content through its iTunes store. The company has become a big player in the "digital wallet" mobile payment space, with its Apple Pay apps and network. Finally, although we haven't heard much about it lately, the company is probably still investigating large-scale technologies such as the automobile business.

The company's products have become household names: the iPhone, iPod, iPad, and MacBook head up the list of hardware products. While the software may be less well-known, QuickTime, iOS, MacOS, tvOS, and WatchOS are important products. Even more important is Services, which have been growing at a double-digit pace into a profitable $30 billion–dollar business, bundling together the iCloud, iTunes, iBooks, Apple Pay, Apple Music, the Mac App Store and other content delivery, and AppleCare support services. Breaking down sales by product family: Smartphones account for $141 billion of the $229 billion in FY2017 sales—fully 62 percent. Mac (personal computers) accounts for 12 percent, iPad 8 percent, "Other Products" for 4.5 percent, and, not to be left out, Services now accounts for 13 percent of revenues: $30 billion a year. Annual growth: Smartphones 3 percent, iPad (–7 percent as competition eroded prices), Mac 13 percent, Services 23 percent, and "other" 11 percent.

It's hard to imagine the current consumer tech landscape without Apple's presence at the top of the heap. Its product line, while comparatively narrow, is focused on areas where the user interface is highly valued, and, increasingly, where some kind of content or service can be sold after the hardware sale. The company has leveraged this focus to become one of the most profitable companies in history, with net profit margins exceeding 20 percent.

Apple is the flagship case study in creating extraordinary value through innovation, innovative leadership, and marketing excellence. They are broadening product lines such as the iPhone to include more high-end and low-end offerings; the iPhone X is now $1,000+. It looks as if wearable technology is the next best opportunity, but who knows?

Financial Highlights, Fiscal Year 2017

Sales resumed their upward march in 2017 after a soft 2016, with the top line advancing 6 percent; profits marched upward hand in hand as margins stayed the same; at $48 billion the company still generates more profits than most companies do sales! Their bread-and-butter iPhone sales sagged a bit (down 1 percent to 77 million units, but the average selling price rose 15 percent—one must watch trends in both figures to own this stock). Expansion in services, China and the overall installed base is driving a 13–15 percent revenue gain forecast for 2018, with earnings up a massive 16 percent with scale, services expansion, and tax effects. This is a huge percentage gain when taken on such a large base. Revenue growth moderates to 4–6 percent in 2019, but earnings plow ahead another 10–12 percent. Share buybacks in the 100 million range annually (roughly 2 percent) drive per-share earnings some 35 percent higher in all in 2019 as compared to 2017.

Reasons to Buy

Innovation. Market leadership. Brand strength. Growth. Profitability. Cash flow. Cash returns. And now, the steady and growing "Services" revenue and profit stream. Best in class across the board. How could Apple *not* be a *100 Best Stock*? We certainly like the results, but mostly we continue to admire (and believe in) the business and innovation excellence that got Apple there in the first place.

Apple's best-known product, the iPhone, seems ubiquitous. They're everywhere, and you can be forgiven for thinking that the market for this product is saturated. Everyone thought it was getting too expensive as lower-priced Android products started to flood the market, and everyone wondered what would happen in China. But the truth is, by improving quality, and gradually improving feature sets, Apple is once again gaining share in the smartphone market. Moreover, we seem to have come to a sweet spot on the replacement cycle as many previous iPhone customers are upgrading to the latest generation. New services, particularly Apple Pay, cloud storage, and the music service, are growing rapidly—and that's just sales. The profitability and cash-flow story is even better. Net profit margins of 21–23 percent for a company of this size alone are remarkable—and they're *growing*—suggesting that the company's products are far from becoming commoditized. On the shareholder-return front, the recent emphasis on returning cash to shareholders has plenty of distance to go.

While many are concerned about Apple's ability to innovate, and while there has been something of a slowdown in the creation of whole new businesses, like iPods and tablets, we continue to feel that Apple still has room to create blockbusters in the "wearable" technology space—smartphone technology integrated into clothing, for example, and in flexible display technologies (see Corning, another *100 Best* pick) and even into flexible *phones*. We foresee other major "vertical" applications of iPhone/iPad form and technology in cars (check out "CarPlay") and in the healthcare space for remote patient monitoring and such. The company has also broken ground in content development, perhaps someday to rival Netflix or Amazon Prime.

We still favor Apple as a long-term investment, though the price has once again started to track the progress. Buy when the price looks right.

Reasons for Caution

Our biggest concern is simple: smartphones make up 62 percent of the business. That brings a risk of saturation and competition that has made us uncomfortable in the past, but the current success of the iPhone 8 and X series mitigates the concern. That said, similar concerns prevail in the tablet space, where competition from Microsoft Surface and others is getting stronger. But this segment is only 8 percent of the business—a good thing in this case. In the main, we continue to admire Apple's ability to generate income, and now, to distribute it to shareholders. The franchise is the world's most valuable, but nobody can sit on their laurels, especially when their laurels are this high off the ground and in plain sight of every competitor. Apple must continue to feed the innovation machine.

SECTOR: **Consumer Discretionary** ❑ BETA COEFFICIENT: **1.19** ❑ 10-YEAR COMPOUND EARNINGS PER-SHARE GROWTH: **37.5%** ❑ 10-YEAR COMPOUND DIVIDENDS PER-SHARE GROWTH: **NM**

	2010	2011	2012	2013	2014	2015	2016	2017
Revenues (bil)	65.2	108.2	156.5	170.9	182.8	233.7	216.8	229.2
Net income (bil)	14.0	25.9	41.7	37.0	39.5	53.4	45.7	48.4
Earnings per share	2.16	3.95	6.31	5.66	6.45	9.22	8.31	9.21
Dividends per share	—	—	0.38	1.63	1.82	1.98	2.18	2.40
Cash flow per share	2.35	4.26	6.85	6.96	8.09	11.59	10.53	11.41
Price: high	46.7	61.0	100.7	82.2	119.8	134.5	118.7	177.2
low	27.2	44.4	58.4	55.0	70.5	92.0	89.5	114.8

Website: www.apple.com

AGGRESSIVE GROWTH

Applied Materials

Ticker symbol: AMAT (NASDAQ) ❑ Large Cap ❑ Value Line financial strength rating: A+ ❑ Current yield: 1.4% ❑ Dividend raises, past 10 years: 6

Company Profile

Founded in 1967 in the heart of the Silicon Valley, Applied Materials is the world's leading supplier of semiconductor fabrication equipment. The company also has allied product lines that are used in the production of LCD and OLED displays, solar panels, as well as a film deposition product line used in the production of high-tech packaging and other applications requiring precision films. Services and support for these advanced products constitutes an additional (and significant) business line.

The largest part of the business is the wafer-processing line. "Wafers" are thin discs made of a crystalline silicon base, upon which are constructed the electrical circuits that constitute the core of the customer's final target product, whether it be a memory chip, a processor, an operational amplifier, or any of thousands of other semiconductor types. AMAT's equipment processes raw silicon wafers (produced by outside foundries) through many dozens of processing steps into finished integrated circuit chips. A single 12-inch diameter processed wafer may have as many as a thousand identical finished products ("chips") etched onto its surface. Different types of semiconductors (including the familiar integrated circuits used in computing equipment) require different types of processing, and AMAT produces equipment and support for dozens of complete end-to-end production processes.

AMAT's customers are among the largest integrated circuit fabricators in the world: Intel, GlobalFoundries, Taiwan Semiconductor, Micron Technology, and others. These companies use AMAT's equipment to produce not only their own products for sale but also finished integrated circuits ("ICs") on contract for the hundreds of "fabless" (factory-less) semiconductor design houses around the world.

In 2006, AMAT entered both the display and solar panel manufacturing equipment markets, only to exit photovoltaics in 2010. The display segment is still active and is participating in the development of the organic light-emitting diode (OLED) display market. Today the company also derives significant revenue from its software and services operation, which provides management tools and technical support for its products.

Financial Highlights, Fiscal Year 2017

AMAT had a great FY2017—without reservation, one of its best years on record. Revenues up 34 percent, earnings up nearly 100 percent, per-share earnings up 110 percent...all while actually improving operational efficiency and strengthening their already solid balance sheet. Their 50-year anniversary also brought healthy increases in backlog (a key indicator for long-sales-cycle products), with orders for semiconductor equipment up nearly 50 percent to $3 billion and display equipment up 31 percent. Overall, backlog increased 33 percent to $1.5 billion.

The company's three reportable segments are Semiconductor Systems, Applied Global Services, and Display and Adjacent Markets. All returned excellent performance in FY2017, with Semiconductor Systems netting a 38 percent increase in sales and a 7 percentage-point increase in operating margin. Applied Global Services showed a 17 percent increase in sales, while Display grew sales 58 percent with a 6 percentage-point increase in operating margin. Good news all around for the company in a very good year.

As has been the case for several years, nearly 90 percent of AMAT's sales were in Asia Pacific (Korea, Taiwan, China, Japan) with the rest going to the US and Europe, reflective of the geographies in the chip-manufacturing business.

The overall improvement in net profit is not entirely due to increased operational efficiencies, however. The company completed an inversion in FY2015, incorporating in the Netherlands, and the already-lowered tax rate fell from 14 percent in FY2016 to 8 percent in FY2017. This rate should hold steady for the foreseeable future.

Reasons to Buy

As we mentioned in last year's edition, the semiconductor equipment industry has been notoriously cyclical, with business levels rising and falling with both demand in the underlying semiconductor market as well as advancements in the state of the art of manufacturing. Demand for semiconductors tends to follow the consumer market (with a base of steadier industrial and commercial demand), while cycles in the semiconductor equipment business have been much longer, typically three to four years. Recent advances in transistor structures, 3D fabrication, and embedded and "stacked" memory have served to accelerate demand for new equipment, and AMAT has been investing heavily in technology and personnel to get out in front of the curve they were largely responsible for creating.

We mention this history only as a lead-in for the bigger picture going forward as the economics of the integrated circuit economy are about to shift in a couple of important ways. First, mainstream CMOS transistors now use about 40 percent less power to operate at the same speed as earlier devices. This has a lot of implications, but primarily it will enable the possibility of many new classes of portable devices. Second, the availability of cheap computing power will further drive the ubiquity of these devices. As an example, you can buy a new "project" computer for $20 that has 300 times the computing power of our first $1,000 laptop, with far more memory, faster I/O, and better graphics. Third, momentum down the flash memory technology curve is accelerating to the point where it's no longer crazy to talk about the eventual elimination of the hard disc drive altogether. Finally, the automotive market will be going through a revolution over the coming decade, with electric cars, self-driving cars, and in-car telematics and entertainment systems driving an enormous incremental demand for sensor, power, logic, and memory devices. This is all supplemental, steadier, and higher value-add volume in the semiconductor market compared to what AMAT supports today.

Put this all together, and we think the cyclical nature of this equipment market is fundamentally changed, at least for the next four to five years. Collectively, part of this fundamental shift shows up in the market as IoT, or the Internet of Things. These new devices will demand the latest in fabrication technologies, and as a result we think the demand for fab capacity will be increasing steadily for several more years.

AMAT has few competitors and is well positioned with fab partners in low-cost geographies, particularly in the rapidly growing Chinese market. Sales of AMAT equipment in China are growing rapidly and may soon surpass sales in the Taiwan region, long a mainstay for AMAT.

Another emerging business worth mentioning is the roll-to-roll thin film process used to make familiar packaging materials for foods like coffee beans, candies, and packaged potato chips. The process deposits flexible films that provide a gas/moisture barrier to extend the shelf life of foods. Derived from the company's vacuum deposition process, the product extends the company's applications from computer "chips" to the kind of "chips" we like to eat!

Finally, as part of the tax windfall and following the pattern set by other corporations in similar circumstances, AMAT is stepping up its dividend and stock buyback plans. In the most recent quarter AMAT returned over 40 percent of cash from operations as dividends and share repurchases. We believe the company will buy back an additional 2–3 percent of its shares and double the current dividend through 2018.

Reasons for Caution

AMAT is the world leader in semiconductor equipment sales, but one major competitor, Lam Research, is of similar size with a solid record of growth. We feel AMAT has certain advantages in their technology and operations, but it is worth keeping a weather eye on competitors for technology announcements. That same "weather eye" should also watch to make sure the health of the current high-demand cycle will indeed extend well into the early 2020s, as appears currently to be the case.

SECTOR: **Information Technology** ❑ BETA COEFFICIENT: **1.15** ❑ 10-YEAR COMPOUND EARNINGS PER-SHARE GROWTH: **7.0%** ❑ 10-YEAR COMPOUND DIVIDENDS PER-SHARE GROWTH: **9.5%**

	2010	2011	2012	2013	2014	2015	2016	2017
Revenues (mil)	9,549	10,517	8,719	7,509	9,072	9,659	10,825	14,537
Net income (mil)	1,333	1,926	529	256	1,072	1,377	1,720	3,434
Earnings per share	1.00	1.45	0.42	0.21	0.87	1.12	1.54	3.17
Dividends per share	0.26	0.30	0.34	0.38	0.40	0.40	0.40	.40
Cash flow per share	1.23	1.66	0.79	0.55	1.19	1.51	1.96	3.62
Price: high	14.9	16.9	13.9	18.2	25.7	25.6	33.7	60.9
low	10.3	9.7	10.0	11.4	16.4	13.2	15.4	31.7

Website: www.appliedmaterials.com

AGGRESSIVE GROWTH

NEW FOR 2019

Aptiv PLC

Ticker symbol: APTV (NYSE) ❑ Large Cap ❑ Value Line financial strength rating: B++ ❑ Current yield: 1.4% ❑ Dividend raises, past 10 years: 2

Company Profile

We sometimes begin our company profiles with a bit of company history, often including the origin story of the business: where it began, how it evolved, etc. While we feel it's important to understand a *little* of how Aptiv got here, telling the story from just 1994 forward would take more space than we have. Suffice it to say that after no fewer than three IPOs, two bankruptcies, several spin-offs, and at least one lawsuit against its own investors, the company once known as Automotive Components Group, Delphi Automotive Systems, Delphi Corporation, Delphi Incorporated, and now (as of December 2017) Aptiv, is in a good place. Or perhaps even a better one, for as we go to press we see they've relocated their headquarters from the UK to Ireland.

Aptiv is probably best recognized as the partial remnants of a once-captive and later spun off major parts supplier to General Motors. Over the years many parts of the business have been either discontinued of disposed of, most significantly the December 2017 spin-off of the entire Powertrain Systems segment into a new, independent company named (of course) Delphi Technologies PLC. The grimy details of all of the paring down of the original business are well documented—what's important to know at this point is Aptiv is a much leaner, more tightly focused business than in its past. They no longer make brake hoses, door handles, air-conditioning parts, batteries, fuel injectors, wheel bearings, dashboards, suspension components, drivetrain components, or any of dozens of other associated automotive parts. These operations have all been sold off over the past decade; the company is now focused mainly on electric vehicles and autonomous (driver-assist and driverless) technology.

The company organizes its businesses into two segments: Signal and Power Solutions, and Advanced Safety and User Experience. Signal and Power Solutions provides hardware and systems for the complete design, manufacture, and assembly of a vehicle's electrical architecture. The goal here is to create the vehicle's signal distribution and computing backbone with particular emphasis on reduced emissions, higher fuel economy, and an open framework for increased content and future electrical upgrades. The Advanced Safety and User Experience unit provides components, controls, configured systems, and software development platforms for safety features, security, comfort, and vehicle operation. These products are the basis for features such as autonomous driving, active safety systems (airbags and active braking, etc.), heads-up displays, and integrated infotainment systems. Overall their charter is to reduce driver distraction and improve vehicle safety in an enhanced occupant environment. Throw in a map to all the Stuckey's on I-75 south of the Ohio River, and you've got the makings of a pretty good road trip!

Financial Highlights, Fiscal Year 2017

Reviewing the numbers for a year in which the company divested of nearly 25 percent of its business makes for some tricky analysis, but on paper, the business had a good year overall. Revenues (obviously) were off, as were earnings, but net margins were up nearly a percentage point, and cash flow was down (predictably) but steady. Looking forward to 2018/2019 the company should benefit from significant improvements to margins on a growing top line—earnings should grow 20 percent per year to record levels (though it looks like the dividend may suffer somewhat).

Note: Certain historical financial measures are not directly attributable to Aptiv PLC, and this is reflected in the tables at the end of this entry.

Reasons to Buy

There's little doubt that the high-value-add segment of the volume automotive market is in the future of autonomous vehicles. Automobile manufacturers are highly motivated to move quickly on a burgeoning trend: people are simply fed up with driving or want to improve the ease and safety of the driver experience.

In order to enable the autonomous vehicle vision, you first have to create and integrate a lot of the technologies that replace the automobile's current control CPU: the human driver. You have to give the automobile vision, the ability to analyze and comprehend those visual inputs, and the ability to react appropriately and, when necessary, quickly enough to avoid trouble. In other words, you have to have 100 percent reliable safety systems. This is one of the baseline attributes of autonomous transport, and it's one of the most difficult to engineer.

Aptiv is one of the leading competitors in this field and has customized and sold systems to a number of the major automotive Original Equipment Manufacturers (OEMs). OEMs have a strong preference for this sort of outsourcing as it's simply more cost-competitive to buy versus starting from scratch with an in-house development project. It also provides for the ability to gain from their competitor's experience, assuming they're buying the same systems.

Aptiv's current driver-assist products are doing very well in the market with sales to all of the top 25 automotive OEMs and a product presence in 86 percent of the top-selling vehicles in the US, the EU, and China. The company maintains a local presence of both manufacturing and technical support in its largest regions. Comprehensive localized presence is often a requirement to entry in many economies, but Aptiv feels this strengthens its business as well.

In addition to their mainline business with automotive OEMs, Aptiv has also been contracted by Singapore to develop a fleet of autonomous vehicles targeted for full deployment in 2022. Municipalities in the US and Europe are already engaged in similar projects to mobilize their own transportation systems, hopefully avoiding the costs, disruption, and roll-the-dice results of light-rail and projects of similar scale. Using the roads that are already in place, but using them more efficiently, holds a great deal of appeal in large urban areas. Boston has also entered into an agreement for a similar program.

With the disposal of much of its traditional nuts and bolts operations, Aptiv is embracing this concept of "mobility" (sorry, but they use this word a lot in their marketing materials); the idea is that going forward, people don't necessarily value the ownership of a vehicle—they just want to get where they want to go. This is a trait often written off as a "millennial" thing, but once you've used any of the current for-hire services, you begin to understand the appeal. Aptiv understands that being a competitor in an industry that makes products that are on what appears to be an inexorable path to commoditization is a race you don't really want to win. So, you exit all the parts of the automobile business that require huge capital investments in tooling and materials, and you remain in the parts of the business that will grow faster than the auto industry as a whole. This makes for a "mobile" business. Good move.

Reasons for Caution

A more intelligent and efficient vehicle transportation usage model could make for downward pressure on the unit sales of vehicles themselves. Any decline due to this effect is probably several years out, though, and would be preceded by a significant up-tick in unit volumes as part of the rollover. There's always the possibility that autonomous vehicle adoption will be delayed or nixed altogether by accidents and technical problems.

SECTOR: **Industrials** ◻ BETA COEFFICIENT: **1.25** ◻ 10-YEAR COMPOUND EARNINGS PER-SHARE GROWTH: **NA** ◻ 10-YEAR COMPOUND DIVIDENDS PER-SHARE GROWTH: **NA**

	2010	2011	2012	2013	2014	2015	2016	2017
Revenues (mil)	13,817	16,041	15,519	16,463	17,023	15,165	16,661	12,884
Net income (mil)	631	1,145	1,077	1,212	1,351	1,176	1,149	990
Earnings per share	NA	2.72	3.33	3.89	4.48	4.14	4.21	3.81
Dividends per share	—	—	—	0.68	1.00	1.00	1.16	1.38
Cash flow per share	NA	2.72	3.33	3.89	4.48	4.14	4.21	3.81
Price: high	NA	22.9	38.3	60.4	74.9	90.6	84.8	105
low	NA	19.2	21.8	37.2	58.2	66.1	55.6	66.6

Website: www.aptiv.com

CONSERVATIVE GROWTH

Archer Daniels Midland Company

Ticker symbol: ADM (NYSE) ◻ Large Cap ◻ Value Line financial strength rating: A+ ◻ Current yield: 3.0% ◻ Dividend raises, past 10 years: 9

Company Profile

ADM is one of the largest food processors in the world. It buys corn, wheat, oilseeds, and other agricultural products and processes them into food, food ingredients, animal feed and ingredients, and biofuels. It also resells grains on the open market. ADM produces and distributes intermediate components for food product manufacture and is by far the largest publicly traded company in this business. "*ADM Feeds Your Food Business*" is their motto.

Among the more important products are vegetable oils, protein meal and components, corn sweeteners, flour, biodiesel, ethanol, other food and animal feed, and now, specialty ingredients. Foreign sales make up about 47 percent of total revenue.

The company is highly vertically integrated and owns and maintains facilities used throughout the production process. It sources, transports, stores, and processes agricultural materials in 76 subsidiary countries on six continents, with 270 processing and ingredient plants, 500 procurement facilities, 230 bulk storage terminals, and its own extensive sea/rail/road network. The company owns or leases 28,600 rail cars, 2,300 barges, 31 ocean vessels, and a fleet of trucks. There are 44 innovation centers worldwide.

The company currently operates in four business segments: Oilseeds Processing (37 percent of FY2017 sales, 31 percent of operating profit), Corn Processing (15 percent, 34 percent), Agricultural Services (43 percent, 22 percent), and the recently acquired WILD Flavors and Specialty Ingredients and other (6 percent, 11 percent). The Oilseeds Processing unit processes soybeans, cottonseed, sunflower, canola, peanuts, and flaxseed into vegetable oils and protein meals for the food and feed industries. Crude vegetable oils are sold as is or are further refined into consumer products, while partially refined oils are sold for use in paints, chemicals, and other industrial products. The solids remaining from this processing are sold for a number of applications, including edible soy protein, animal feed, pharmaceuticals, chemicals, and paper.

The Corn Processing segment milling operations (primarily in the US) produce food products too numerous to list but include syrup, starch, glucose, dextrose, and other sweeteners. Markets served include animal feeds and the vegetable oil market. Fermentation of the dextrose yields ethanol, amino acids, and other specialty food and feed products. The ethanol is processed for beverage stock or industrial use as the base for ethanol-blended gasoline and other fuels. Within this group, ADM owns a 40 percent interest in the Red Star Yeast Company.

The Agricultural Services segment is the company's storage and transportation network. This business is primarily engaged in buying, storing, cleaning, and transporting grains to/from ADM facilities and for export. It also resells raw materials into the animal feed and agricultural processing industries.

Acquired in 2015, the expanding WILD Flavors and Specialty Ingredients segment produces many existing nutrients product lines, including high-fiber and nutritional supplements like natural-source vitamin E and Omega-3 DHA. This group, and the recent acquisition of Harvest Innovations, a producer of gluten-free and minimally processed soy proteins and oils, has expanded ADM's presence in the specialty corners of the food business. In mid-2016 the company divested some of its Brazil ethanol business in a strategic shift from commodity to higher-value-add businesses. In 2017 the company made several small acquisitions, including contract and private label pet food maker Crosswind Industries. More significantly, in early 2018 ADM made an offer to acquire rival grain merchant Bunge Ltd. (a former *100 Best Stock*) in a deal that would have created the largest food commodity trading giant and given ADM's international business a boost. At the time of this writing the merger talks have stalled.

In March 2018 the company announced a realignment of its business segments to "enhance agility, drive innovation and drive operations to further improve the customer experience." A new Carbohydrate Solutions business unit will include the current Corn and Milling operations including ethanol. Nutrition will include the WILD Flavors and Specialty Ingredients business as well as animal nutrition products. The Oilseeds business will remain unchanged while Origination will be the current Agricultural Services business less the corn milling operations.

Financial Highlights, Fiscal Year 2017

Acquisitions, spin-offs, currency effects, fluctuating prices, and fluctuating costs of agricultural commodity inputs make any yearly comparison of ADM results challenging. FY2017 was no exception. Mostly due to softness in the oilseed business, total revenues dropped about 2.4 percent, while earnings dropped accordingly by 5 percent. Tax rate changes and a $200 million cost savings initiative, combined with stronger market conditions, should bring more than a return to normalcy; for 2018 profits are expected to recover and rise 22–25 percent on a 2–3 percent revenue gain. For 2019 ADM looks for a 7–9 percent earnings gain on similar revenue growth. "Right-sizing," mix improvement, and cost containment will be priorities and will expand the naturally thin margins measurably. Steady dividend increases and modest share buybacks should continue.

Reasons to Buy

Although near-term results have been weak, we still like ADM for the longer term. Agriculture is still a key strategic business on a global basis, and increased demand for food and especially middle-class Western diets from emerging market customers bodes well. The company is and has been a strong player in the biofuels industry. While uncertainties continue in the ethanol and biofuels segment, the company's experience and scale in ethanol and biodiesel are strong positives, and the company should win as other smaller players exit the market.

There are four major suppliers that dominate the world market for commodity foodstuffs: Archer, Bunge, Cargill, and Dreyfus—the "ABCD" of world foods—and ADM has made an overture to acquire the "B," which would improve its position in the market and probably drive costs down. ADM continues to grow its presence in the emerging markets of Asia, South America, and Eastern Europe. ADM's presence and extensive transportation capability give it a decided advantage over its smaller competitors, many of which are focused only in certain markets or certain industries. The company is fine-tuning its business mix, disposing of smaller low-margin product lines in favor of a higher-value-add in the food chain with the addition of WILD and other product lines; we like the increasing emphasis on this business. We like the solid track record for growth in dividends and overall shareholder value.

Reasons for Caution

We've seen how agricultural cycles and production can negatively impact this company, and it will try the patience of the most patient investors. The WILD acquisition may signal a move to the "wild" side in more specialized, less commoditized business, which seems like a good strategy but does add some risk. Also, the company may be late to this party, though it is well positioned as a "bulk" supplier of these key ingredients. ADM is heavily invested in the corn-ethanol-fuel processing chain, which has had its own ups and downs as well as detractors. Federal government policy toward ethanol subsidies bears watching. Finally, the company does produce that nasty-sounding but in fact relatively benign high fructose corn syrup; a pickup in nutritional health sentiment in the food and especially the beverage industry won't help. There are more than the usual concerns short term for ADM, but we still consider ADM a long-term play in a healthy and vital industry.

SECTOR: **Consumer Staples** ▫ BETA COEFFICIENT: **1.01** ▫ 10-YEAR COMPOUND EARNINGS PER-SHARE GROWTH: **2.5%** ▫ 10-YEAR COMPOUND DIVIDENDS PER-SHARE GROWTH: **12.5%**

	2010	2011	2012	2013	2014	2015	2016	2017
Revenues (mil)	61,692	80,676	89,038	89,804	81,201	67,762	62,346	60.828
Net income (mil)	1,959	2,036	1,496	1,342	2,248	1,849	1,280	1,216
Earnings per share	3.06	3.13	2.26	2.02	3.43	2.98	2.16	2.13
Dividends per share	0.58	0.62	0.69	0.76	0.96	1.12	1.20	1.28
Cash flow per share	4.49	4.54	3.56	3.42	4.80	4.59	3.80	3.84
Price: high	34.0	38.0	34.0	44.0	53.9	53.3	47.9	47.4
low	24.2	23.7	24.2	27.8	37.9	33.8	29.9	38.6

Website: www.adm.com

Becton, Dickinson and Company

Ticker symbol: BDX (NYSE) ◻ Large Cap ◻ Value Line financial strength rating: A++ ◻ Current
yield: 1.4% ◻ Dividend raises, past 10 years: 10

Company Profile

Gotten a flu shot or any other "delivery" of medicine lately? Chances are
the "device" used to make the delivery had a prominent "B-D" logo on the
package. "B-D" stands for "Becton, Dickinson," one of the premier medical
supply and technology companies on the planet.

Becton, Dickinson is a global healthcare technology player focused on
improving drug delivery, enhancing the diagnosis of infectious diseases and
cancers, and advancing medical lab work and drug discovery. The company develops, manufactures, and sells medical supplies, devices, laboratory instruments, antibodies, reagents, and diagnostic products through its
two segments: BD Medical and BD Life Sciences. These products are sold
to healthcare institutions, life science researchers, clinical laboratories, the
pharmaceutical industry, and the general public. With the 2015 acquisition
of CareFusion, B-D became a big player in the automated medicine delivery
market, a growing segment that reduces medicine delivery errors while also
reducing costs for medical providers. This acquisition added roughly 45 percent to the company's top and bottom lines starting in 2016.

We had thought the company would stop there, but in fact it made another
big acquisition in 2017, a $25 billion acquisition of C.R. Bard, a former *100
Best Stock* and a major developer and supplier in the vascular, urology, oncology,
and surgical spaces. Bard will add about 20 percent to the revenue base and,
with higher margins, 30–40 percent to profits, and will be initially managed as
a separate reporting segment called "BD Interventional." With the acquisition,
B-D will become one of the world's five largest healthcare suppliers.

International sales account for about 46 percent of the total. The B-D
brand is found throughout the range of clinics, medical offices, and hospitals
and is well recognized in the medical community.

The company now operates in two worldwide business segments: BD
Medical (67 percent of FY2017 sales) and BD Life Sciences (formerly
Biosciences—33 percent). The former Diagnostics segment was folded into
Medical, and the CareFusion business resides there as well. As mentioned
earlier, a new BD Interventional segment will report starting in 2018, which
will account for about 15–20 percent of the total business.

The BD Medical segment produces a variety of drug-delivery devices and supplies, including "sharps" (hypodermic needles and syringes) and related disposal products, infusion therapy devices, intravenous catheters, insulin injection systems, regional anesthesia needles, diabetes care systems, and automated delivery and prefillable drug-delivery systems for pharmaceutical companies. What was once the Diagnostics unit offers system solutions for collecting, identifying, and transporting blood and other specimens, as well as instrumentation for analyzing these specimens. Testing systems include those for sexually transmitted diseases, microorganism identification and drug susceptibility, and certain types of cancer screening.

BD Life Sciences provides research tools and reagents to accelerate the pace of biomedical discovery. Clinicians and researchers use BD Life Sciences' tools to study genes, proteins, and cells to understand disease, improve technologies for diagnosis and disease management, and facilitate the discovery and development of new therapeutics. Products include reagents, fluoroscience cell-activated sorters and analyzers, monoclonal antibodies and kits, and cell imaging and reagent solutions, among others.

The BD Interventional unit, formerly Bard, offers some 15,000 products targeted to clinical, surgical, and maintenance applications in biosciences, cancer screening, diabetes care, drug delivery, genomics, and infection prevention.

Financial Highlights, Fiscal Year 2017

FY2017 reported revenues showed a moderate 3 percent drop after a large 2016 gain due to CareFusion; the main reasons were a divestiture of a respiratory products business that came with CareFusion and accounting changes for some contract services. Most BD Medical and BD Life Sciences segments grew in the 3–5 percent range during the year. Net income advanced almost 11 percent as acquisition synergies took hold and margins increased significantly. FY2018 results will include Bard and are projected to advance about 30 percent in total, followed by a 10–12 percent advance in 2019; earnings will jump some 40 percent in 2018 and another 10–12 percent in 2019 commensurate with revenue growth. Modest dividend increases should continue, but share counts will rise about 17 percent with the Bard acquisition—to be bought back gradually with more emphasis placed on paying off the $10 billion of debt used to buy Bard before the end of the decade.

Reasons to Buy

Becton, Dickinson continues to be a classic "blue-chip" company, still as recession-proof as any stock on our list. The steady upward share price march since 2013 is classic, and the stock has risen faster in the past year as these acquisitions have been added—all in an environment where some healthcare stocks have sold off due to uncertainties about drug costs and business models. Earnings, cash flow, and dividend growth over the years have been steady, and net profit margins are both healthy (15 percent) and growing to record levels (17–18 percent) recently. The company will benefit from becoming a full-line supplier of a wide variety of mostly consumable medical products and will also continue to benefit through the broadening of healthcare offerings into developing nations, from the automation of medicine delivery, and from a greater emphasis on preventative care, e.g., flu shots.

Reasons for Caution

CareFusion was a big bet and one that lay a bit outside of the core supplies and diagnostics business presenting some additional risks, but everything has gone well. The Bard acquisition is similar but bigger. It appears that B-D manages acquisitions well and makes the most of market and operational synergies, but we won't know how well the Bard takeover is working until the end of 2018. Possible changes in the Affordable Care Act and more recently the ad-hoc healthcare delivery consortium started by Amazon, Berkshire Hathaway, and JPMorgan Chase also add some downside and uncertainty. Recent healthcare cost scrutiny may hurt some supplies and testing product lines but should help lines devoted to preventative care and efficient care delivery, like CareFusion. All said, Becton continues to be one of the best, safest, steadiest, and most well-managed players in the industry—and now it's becoming one of the biggest.

SECTOR: Healthcare ❑ BETA COEFFICIENT: 1.12 ❑ 10-YEAR COMPOUND EARNINGS PER-SHARE GROWTH: 9.5% ❑ 10-YEAR COMPOUND DIVIDENDS PER-SHARE GROWTH: 12.0%

	2010	2011	2012	2013	2014	2015	2016	2017
Revenues (mil)	7,372	7,828	7,708	8,054	8,446	10,282	12,453	12,093
Net income (mil)	1,185	1,272	1,123	1,159	1,236	1,480	1,869	2,072
Earnings per share	4.94	5.61	5.36	5.81	6.25	7.16	8.59	9.48
Dividends per share	1.48	1.64	1.80	1.98	2.18	2.40	2.64	2.92
Cash flow per share	7.25	8.27	8.30	8.79	9.37	11.25	13.99	13.56
Price: high	80.6	89.4	80.6	110.9	142.6	157.5	181.9	229.7
low	66.5	72.5	71.6	78.7	105.2	128.9	129.5	161.5

Website: www.bd.com

Bemis Company, Inc.

Ticker symbol: BMS (NYSE) ❑ Mid Cap ❑ Value Line financial strength rating: A ❑ Current yield: 2.7% ❑ Dividend raises, past 10 years: 10

Company Profile

A long-term investor should be prepared to stick with a company through thick and thin. There will always be lean years, some of which will leave you scratching your head. But if the business is right, the niche is strong, the intangibles like brand and management are right, you may well choose to stick with a company through a bad stretch, particularly if they have plans in place to address the problems. If nothing else, the dip presents a good buying opportunity. There can be no better example of this choice than Bemis, which, despite a terrible 2017, we are keeping on the list in advance of what we feel are much better prospects going forward, prospects that will reward investor patience in the long run. Let this one be a lesson, good or bad—we'll see what happens in 2019. But wait a minute. As we exit our edit cycle in late 2018, there seems to be a cash offer on the table…

You open a stick of string cheese. You pull the little tab at the end and out pops the stick of cheese, which has been happily stored in its little plastic sack through thousands of miles of trucks, warehouses, more trucks, a stock-room or two, the store, your refrigerator, and now maybe your lunch bucket or bag. You enjoy the string cheese with a sandwich made from lunchmeat packaged in a little zippered plastic bag. Afterward, you take your regular dose of allergy medication, packed up in one of those 12-tablet plastic trays with a metal foil backing to tear through.

Who makes this stuff? Did you ever stop to think about it? How it makes our lives easier, as well as those of manufacturers and distributors of these products? Neither had we, until our search for strategic and vital niche holders led us to this quiet, understated Wisconsin firm.

"Where inspired packaging solutions take shape" is the slogan, and it goes a long way to explain their value add in the food chain. Bemis makes all kinds of semirigid and flexible packaging solutions mostly out of plastic and mainly for the food, beverage, health and hygiene, building materials, and chemicals markets. Flexible packaging products include bags, wraps, and containers, many with a pressure-sensitive or zipper closure, all set up to be filled with standard packaging line equipment and all labeled for the client's products. "Raw" packaging materials roll out of 60 facilities to the end of packing lines in 11 countries. About 35 percent of sales are international; most of that is in Latin America, China, and Australia.

A key strategy is to help customers (mostly consumer products and industrial manufacturers) find economical solutions that improve product quality, safety, shelf life, and shelf presence—they attempt to differentiate a customer's product through the package. The company believes that its leadership position "rests on its strong technical foundation in polymer chemistry, film extrusion, coating and laminating, printing and converting" and that "material science continues to be the primary instrument for creating sustainable competitive advantage."

An unfavorable product mix, a poor operational software implementation, Latin America weakness, and an oversized, outdated infrastructure delivered a strong wakeup call in 2017, with a significant slump in earnings as related later on. The company has embarked on a new operational restructuring program called "Agility," which will examine everything from plant infrastructure and location to office space. Additionally, the company has had a stake taken by activist investor Starboard Value, which added four new directors (now 12 total) to the board to help guide change. These aggressive actions, while not without risk and cost, give an opportunity to take this strong niche player to a more efficient level.

Additionally, while we see some challenges in the packaged foods area as many younger consumers seek "fresh" items, we think the crosscurrent of greater e-commerce food (and pharmaceutical) sales and in special packaging solutions even for "healthy, fresh and convenient" foods such as bagged salads bode well for specialty packaging in this dynamic category.

Financial Highlights, Fiscal Year 2017

FY2017 revenues were roughly flat; the aforementioned difficulties during the year led to a 28 percent slide in net earnings. Despite the plunge, the company raised its dividend, albeit modestly, for a thirty-fifth consecutive year, bought back about 2 percent of its stock, and issued a relatively optimistic forecast—factors that led us to the "keep this stock" side of the fence. Revenues are likely to remain roughly flat through 2019 with a stronger advance predicted after that; profits are expected to recover beyond previous levels as restructuring measures take hold, with a 45–50 percent recovery in 2018 and a 10–12 percent further advance in 2019. We're betting a lot on these figures and in continued dividend increases and share repurchases.

Reasons to Buy

This is not an exciting company, but it is a strong niche player providing critical packaging technologies to the industries it serves. New and innovative food-packaging designs are becoming more desired as convenience, quality, and health and safety outweigh cost as a priority in most consumer markets these days. The new packaged salads are a good example of packaging for a product not packaged before; new ziplock containers for lunchmeats, cheeses, etc., show how the package is moving up the value-add scale. The company is investing in new technologies and applications such as package design enhancements for microwaving, easy-open packages for elderly customers (we continue to applaud this one!), new technologies to replace common plastic bottles and tin cans, and new technologies and delivery systems for the healthcare and pharmaceutical industries. Cash flow and cash returns to shareholders have become a priority and are steady and increasing; the issue continues to have appealingly low volatility and is a good defensive play. In all, we think they're in the right business if they can solve their operational challenges; we're willing to wait at least one more year.

Reasons for Caution

All restructurings carry risk and usually extra costs; the outcomes can be uncertain and painful, especially when an outsider activist is involved. We're taking a chance here. Growth has been hard to come by lately, but we think new innovations in the pipeline should address that. The basic need for this sort of product—while changing—is intact.

SECTOR: **Consumer Staples** ▫ BETA COEFFICIENT: **0.86** ▫ 10-YEAR COMPOUND EARNINGS PER-SHARE GROWTH: **3.0%** ▫ 10-YEAR COMPOUND DIVIDENDS PER-SHARE GROWTH: **4.0%**

	2010	2011	2012	2013	2014	2015	2016	2017
Revenues (mil)	4,835	5,323	5,139	5,030	4,344	4,071	4,004	4,046
Net income (mil)	203.3	212.4	225.3	237.0	233.1	242.0	236.0	172.6
Earnings per share	1.83	1.99	2.15	2.28	2.30	2.47	2.48	1.87
Dividends per share	0.92	0.96	1.00	1.04	1.08	1.12	1.16	1.20
Cash flow per share	3.84	3.87	3.66	4.19	4.21	4.21	4.30	3.76
Price: high	34.3	34.4	33.9	42.3	47.2	49.4	54.2	52.0
low	25.5	27.2	29.5	33.7	34.3	38.9	42.4	40.6

Website: www.bemis.com

Boeing Company

Ticker symbol: BA (NYSE) ❑ Large Cap ❑ Value Line financial strength rating: A++ ❑ Current yield: 2.0% ❑ Dividend raises, past 10 years: 8

Company Profile

Way back in 2011, we "grounded" Boeing.

At the time, the airline industry was suffering from weak demand and high costs—high fuel prices in particular. They were financially strapped and weren't buying many aircraft. As well, back then the company was having trouble getting its 787 Dreamliner to market, with one production delay after another. Europe's Airbus consortium was making share gains in key aircraft markets, winning deals even with US airlines. The military and defense market wasn't doing so well either under the Obama administration.

That was then; this is now. Boeing has navigated these air pockets, some internal, some external, with flying colors. Now it has blended several tailwinds—lower fuel prices, healthier airline customers, higher defense spending, tax policy changes, and a strong and more fuel-efficient product catalog—into a smooth, steep takeoff that doesn't look to descend any time soon.

Boeing has delivered on its new aircraft, including new, larger, and more efficient versions of its ever-popular 737 series (the new 737-MAX can carry up to 200 passengers over 4,000 miles on 8 percent less fuel than an older 737; 4,300 are on order since launch). The company is well positioned in good areas in the defense and space sectors including satellites and unmanned guided weapons that appear to have strategic advantage going forward. The backlog is over $500 *billion* on unfilled orders for some 5,800 aircraft. The company values its potential ten-year market opportunity at $10 *trillion*. Boeing clearly exceeded our expectations since we put it on the list last year; the only question is when things will level off—2019 looks like another excellent year.

Boeing is the world's largest aerospace company. Its leading commercial aircraft lines include the familiar 737, 767, 777, and 787 platforms, but it also produces business jets and a variety of defense aircraft including F-15 and F/A-18 fighters, CH-47 (Chinook) and AH-64 (Apache) helicopters, Osprey vertical landing and takeoff aircraft, and Harpoon guided weapons. The company has delivered 3,644 new commercial airplanes and 1,041 military aircraft and satellites in the past five years. It also is involved in space and security systems, managing the International Space Station and selling various kinds of satellites.

The company is organized into two principal segments: Commercial Airplanes and Defense, Space & Security. Commercial Airplanes accounts for about 61 percent of 2017 revenues, while the Defense, Space & Security group, which includes Boeing Military Aircraft and Network & Space Systems, brings in about 26 percent; Global Services & Support and Other brings in about 13 percent. The company is the US's largest exporter and has operations in 65 countries, with foreign sales accounting for 55 percent of 2017 revenues.

Financial Highlights, Fiscal Year 2017

Timing of deliveries and product mix (more single-aisle, fewer twin-aisle commercial aircraft) caused FY2017 revenues to level off a little more, while operational efficiencies and lower R&D costs among other factors elevated net income about 3 percent. For 2018 the company expects the tailwinds of continued strong orders and backlog as airlines worldwide update their fleets, high-volume deliveries, tax effects and operating leverage to raise earnings some 30–35 percent on a 4–5 percent revenue increase, with another 8–10 percent earnings increase in 2019 on a similar revenue updraft. Net profit margins, helped considerably by the new tax law, will approach 10 percent after navigating through the 5–7 percent range for many years. Dividend increases have been substantial—24 percent in FY2017; increases in the 20–30 percent rate going forward appear likely at least for the next two years. The company has repurchased over 21 percent of its shares in the past five years and has returned $40 billion to shareholders overall during that period.

Reasons to Buy

When we originally "grounded" Boeing eight years ago, they were suffering from weak external markets, competition, and internal execution issues. What a difference eight years makes! New products, strong execution, and a much healthier "customer" industry have created a *good* perfect storm for Boeing—and revenues in general and profitability in particular have responded well. Airline fleets are eager to replace aging, less fuel-efficient aircraft. Increased defense spending will also help. The company is reaping the success of massive R&D investments in recent years and is achieving scale, which also improves profitability. It also helps to have such large backlogs, as the company doesn't have to guess on production requirements, product mix, etc.

Reasons for Caution

Throughout its history, Boeing has been subject to cyclical turbulence as the airline industry and defense spending go through cycles of their own. Some of these cycles have been severe. That said, the current positive cycle seems to have longer legs, and the company's products in our view have a stronger and more sustainable competitive advantage in technology and scale that should help avoid the kinds of sharp downturns seen previously—if the airline business softens they will still buy new aircraft in an effort to become more efficient. Additionally, new competition has arrived at the gate in the form of new Chinese-built airliners, which have not yet been certified for US carriage but still bear watching. Finally, one cannot ignore the steep share price ascent starting in early 2017—and any pilot knows that such sharp ascents bring with them a greater chance for a stall and fall. We took a hard look at this one and feel the company's current excellence and prospects outweigh share price risk, but do book your flights carefully in this stock.

SECTOR: **Industrials** ◻ BETA COEFFICIENT: **1.37** ◻ 10-YEAR COMPOUND EARNINGS PER-SHARE
GROWTH: **10.5%** ◻ 10-YEAR COMPOUND DIVIDENDS PER-SHARE GROWTH: **14.0%**

		2010	2011	2012	2013	2014	2015	2016	2017
Revenues (bil)		64.3	68.7	81.7	86.6	90.8	96.1	94.6	93.9
Net income (bil)		3.3	3.6	3.9	4.6	5.5	5.2	6.9	7.1
Earnings per share		4.46	4.82	5.11	5.96	7.38	7.44	10.84	11.71
Dividends per share		1.68	1.68	1.76	1.94	2.92	3.64	4.36	5.68
Cash flow per share		6.85	7.08	7.56	8.60	10.40	10.51	14.36	15.59
Price:	high	76.0	80.6	77.8	142.0	144.6	158.8	160.1	299.3
	low	54.1	56.0	66.8	72.7	116.3	115.1	102.1	155.2

Website: www.boeing.com

AGGRESSIVE GROWTH

NEW FOR 2019

CalAmp Corp.

Ticker symbol: CAMP (NASDAQ) ◻ Small Cap ◻ Value Line financial strength rating: B ◻ Current
yield: Nil ◻ Dividend raises, past 10 years: NA

Company Profile

CalAmp, founded as California Amplifier, Inc., in 1981, is a provider of telematics hardware and services to the automotive, freight, construction, and emergency services industries, among others. "Tele-what?" you may ask (we sure did). "Telematics," broadly defined, is the acquisition and communication of data from remote, and often mobile, sources (the "tele" part).

Usually, no operator intervention is required or involved (the "matic" part). Telematics is a rapidly developing field, paralleling and in some cases part of the current developments in autonomous vehicles. CalAmp's products are typically embedded in new vehicles in the form of hardware, software, and services to provide fleet operators data on location, speed, and other information critical to their business. An automotive dealership, for example, would be able to locate all of its vehicles across an arbitrarily large geography and find out (for example) which cars are ready for sale or which cars need to have their batteries charged. A freight operator can track vehicles, trailers, and containers in real time and can predict service delays based on vehicle-supplied data. All of this data is communicated, maintained, and analyzed using cloud services provided by CalAmp and tailored to each customer's specific needs. The company's products and services are marketed and sold worldwide.

This focus is relatively new for the company. CalAmp's first business was as a supplier of hardware components and finished products to the commercial/consumer satellite communications industry, but their primary customer was the Department of Defense. The end of the Cold War forced the company to refocus its efforts on commercial and consumer applications, and it carved out a healthy niche in the wireless cable and satellite television markets. CalAmp became the primary supplier for the microwave electronics used in the now-ubiquitous DirecTV and Dish Network satellite receivers.

Following a series of acquisitions in the early 2000s, the company expanded its product base with a focus on software and terrestrial communications, from which the company's current products evolved. Recognizing the declining margins in the market, in 2016 the company exited the satellite television market entirely via a sale of its satellite operations to EchoStar, the owner of Dish Network.

Financial Highlights, Fiscal Year 2017

CalAmp exited the fiscal year as a company without a satellite communications operation for the first time in its history. Nonetheless, the company amassed record revenues of $365 million, up 4 percent, and record earnings of $31 million, rebounding from the prior year's losses. Operating margins were up 31 percent, and cash flow more than tripled. Overall, it was a solid full-year report.

A few months after the conclusion of the sale of the company's satellite operations, CalAmp announced the acquisition of LoJack Corporation for

$134 million in cash. LoJack, a provider of vehicle theft recovery systems and fleet management solutions, is a complementary acquisition from both a product and marketing perspective, with its own network of worldwide sales channels.

Market expectations for fiscal years 2018 and 2019 are for continued growth in revenue in the 8 percent/year range with more conservative estimates for total earnings of around 4 percent/year.

Reasons to Buy

The last few years have seen the growth and acceptance of "smart" vehicle capabilities at a pace that surprises many, even industry insiders. Providers of various forms of vehicle intelligence have brought forth a wealth of potential products, and the auto industry, eager to differentiate their vehicles in what has rapidly become of a market full of nearly identical offerings, has begun to design new features at a dizzying pace.

Paralleling the explosion of customer-facing technology in the consumer space is the growth of dealer and owner/operator-facing technology in the commercial space. The cost of intelligence in an automobile, a commercial truck, an ambulance, or a piece of construction equipment is getting cheaper every year as a percentage of total asset value, and an investment in the security and utility maximization of that asset is money well spent. CalAmp's solution for consumer vehicle status and security benefits automotive dealers, leasing operators, financing operations, and other security scenarios. CalAmp's acquisition of LoJack gives them the only recovery system directly integrated with law enforcement services, which could well lead to sales to other municipal fleet and public safety operations.

The trucking industry has a number of established players in the tracking market. CalAmp's telematics cloud offers a set of application programming interfaces (APIs) and web services that integrate data from their own devices as well as their competitors, offering fleet operators an opportunity to integrate their data operations across a disparate asset base and/or retrofit outdated technology. This is a unique offering in the industry.

The company's heavy-equipment market is highlighted by its relationship with Caterpillar, which should generate revenues of $11 million per quarter in FY2018 and beyond. Shipments to a second large heavy equipment OEM began in March 2018.

In effect, nearly any ground-based mobile asset is a potential target for CalAmp's hardware, but we have to point out the company's service revenue chain that accompanies these products. Software and Subscription Services revenues have grown nearly 60 percent over the past two years and now constitute close to 17 percent of the company's total revenues with very strong gross margins.

CalAmp is one of the smallest companies we've covered in our series, one of two "Small Cap" stocks riding along with LED digital sign maker Daktronics on our *100 Best* list. Normally we would advise a level of caution here, but we like what we see here in terms of the company's management and agility. This is a company that has seen the complete evaporation of its primary markets more than once in its history, and each time it's been prepared and ready to move in a new direction and consistently grow in the process.

Having bid farewell to the satellite market, CalAmp was prepared for a full pivot to telematics with a clear view of the opportunities made available by trends in the cost of computing, industry modernization, and asset management. We expect these trends to be persistent and accelerate over the next several years, and so we're very excited to find an established player with a broad vision in this nascent, largely fragmented market. Keep on truckin'.

Reasons for Caution

The company has been hit with a couple of lawsuits over potential patent violations over the past few years, with one $10 million suit pending. On the other hand, they're also the beneficiary of an action that should provide a significant offset to this potential liability. Patent trolls pop out from under their bridges nearly any time the words "communication" and "computer" are combined in a product description, but we expect that a recent shift in acceptance standards in patent lawsuits toward a more rigorous proof of standing will ameliorate this risk significantly.

SECTOR: **Information Technology** ◻ BETA COEFFICIENT: **1.20** ◻ 10-YEAR COMPOUND EARNINGS PER-SHARE GROWTH: **3.5%** ◻ 10-YEAR COMPOUND DIVIDENDS PER-SHARE GROWTH: **NA**

	2010	2011	2012	2013	2014	2015	2016	2017
Revenues (mil)	114	139	181	236	251	281	351	365
Net income (mil)	(3.3)	5.2	15.4	11.8	16.5	16.9	(7.9)	31
Earnings per share	(.12)	.18	.51	.33	.45	.46	(.22)	.85
Dividends per share	—	—	—	—	—	—	—	—
Cash flow per share	(.03)	.27	.52	.56	.71	.74	.44	1.50
Price: high	3.8	5.1	9.7	29.7	34.8	21.8	20.5	24.7
low	2.0	2.6	4.0	8.0	14.7	14.0	12.1	14.5

Website: www.calamp.com

AGGRESSIVE GROWTH

CarMax, Inc.

Ticker symbol: KMX (NYSE) ❑ Large Cap ❑ Value Line financial strength rating: B+ ❑ Current yield: Nil ❑ Dividend raises, past 10 years: NA

Company Profile

"The Way Car Buying Should Be" is the appropriate slogan used by this clean-cut chain of used vehicle stores and superstores and its new big-box, retail-like model for selling cars. CarMax buys, reconditions, and sells cars and light trucks at 181 retail centers in 89 metropolitan TV markets in 39 states, mainly in the Southeast, Midwest, and California, but is gradually moving to a more nationwide footprint. The company specializes in selling cars that are under six years old with less than 60,000 miles in excellent condition; the cars are sold at a competitive price, typically in the $10,000 to $34,000 price range, for their condition in a no-haggle environment. The price is the price; the emphasis is on the condition of the vehicles and on a helpful and friendly sales and transaction process. Sales representatives are compensated for cars they sell but not in such a way that drives them to push the wrong car on a customer. The company sold some 721,512 used vehicles in 2017, up 7.5 percent from 2016 and up 77 percent from the 408,080 sold in 2011. The average selling price for 2017 was $19,757, up 0.9 percent from the previous year as used car prices have softened a bit—but the average gross margin was $2,173 per vehicle, up slightly from the previous $2,163.

CarMax is gaining footholds in new markets such as Denver, Minneapolis-St. Paul, the Pacific Northwest, Philadelphia, Boston, and smaller markets such as Boise, Grand Rapids, Mobile, and El Paso. Most reports suggest they are gaining market share in the markets they serve with a high degree of customer satisfaction. CarMax plans to open 15 more new stores in 2018. Ten of these will be in metro areas of fewer than 600,000 residents, including Greenville, NC, Santa Fe, NM, Macon, GA, and Corpus Christi, TX. Other larger markets include Buffalo, NY, Vancouver, WA (Portland, OR), Jensen Beach, FL (Fort Lauderdale), and McKinney, TX (Dallas/Ft. Worth). They will open 13–16 new stores in 2019. From 181 stores total today, they anticipate 225 stores in place by the end of the decade, including new presence in the Seattle, New York City, and San Francisco areas and more small-format stores in smaller markets like Harrisonburg, VA, and Jackson, TN. The overall strategy is to build a national footprint and brand, achieve economies of scale, and make the most of online marketing initiatives.

The health of the economy and consumer spending has swung car buying into a higher gear, but with newfound consumer prudence. Many of these purchases are heading to the one- to six-year-old used car sector of the business, where prices are 40–60 percent lower than comparable new cars. The new car boom of recent years has led to a large number of lease returns, which, while depressing used car prices somewhat, also provides a major source of low-cost supply for CarMax's inventory. In addition to "retail" used car sales, CarMax is a big player in auto wholesaling, having moved about 409,000 units mostly taken in trade; the company is the world's largest used car buyer. The company also earns income through its financing unit, known as CarMax Auto Finance, or CAF. The unit finances about 43 percent of the company's sales.

CarMax also has service operations and sells extended warranties and other products related to car ownership. The company has state-of-the-art web-based and mobile tools as well as other aids designed to make the car selection, buying, and ownership experience more personalized, more "self-service," and generally easier. As CarMax puts it, customers expect four things when they buy a car:

1. Don't play games
2. Don't waste my time
3. Provide security
4. Make car buying fun

The company's offering is aimed at reducing these concerns and providing the right experience. The offering continues to be largely unique in the industry, and competitors would have a long way to go to catch up.

Financial Highlights, Fiscal Year 2017

The 2017 year was a good one overall but started to hit the brakes toward the end. Total sales rose a bit over 9 percent, although sales took a 3 percent dip in the final quarter. For the year, comparable store sales rose 2 percent while dipping 8 percent in the final quarter—a drop felt to be in line with a "macro" slowdown in the auto industry. Earnings rose 8 percent, while per-share earnings rose a bit over 12 percent on the back of a 3 percent share repurchase. Management expects sales and earnings to return with slightly higher margins and is forecasting an 18–20 percent earnings-per-share increase on a 4–5 percent top-line increase for 2018 and another 10–12 percent per-share earnings increase in 2019 on a sales gain of 6–8 percent. Success factors included a significant growth in online and mobile vehicle shopping activity, and higher conversion rates in the store with an assortment of physical and process tweaks.

The company announced its first share buyback program in 2012 and has pursued it aggressively every year since then, clearly set up as a shareholder return vehicle in lieu of dividends. Since then they have retired 20 percent of the float and are on track to retire a third of that 2012 225-million-share count by the end of the decade.

Reasons to Buy

CarMax states its purpose clearly: "To drive integrity in the automotive industry by being honest and transparent in every interaction." Quite simply, CarMax continues to be a buy if you believe the traditional dealer model is broken and if you believe people will continue to see value in late-model used vehicles. CarMax as a brand is gaining national recognition as a "go-to" in the car buying (and selling) process.

Additionally, CarMax brings the latest in business intelligence and analytic models to the car-marketing process, in procurement, merchandising, pricing, and selling the vehicles. Do green Jeep Cherokees sell well in Southern California? Then let's find some, put them on the lot there, and set at a market-based price. KMX is well ahead of the industry in making analysis-based supply and selling decisions and has quite successfully deployed analytic tools to adjust prices and inventories quickly to market conditions. They point out the large amounts of data accumulated through selling 10.5 million vehicles, hosting 65 million customers in their history, and handling 200 million digital interactions per year—a distinct competitive advantage that bodes well for the future.

CarMax is increasingly a big player in the 40-million vehicle used car market (versus 17 million for new cars), taking market share from traditional used car dealers, but there's fertile ground to capture more. The company estimates that it has only 5 percent of the current market for zero-to-ten-year-old used vehicles in markets in which it operates, and only 3 percent of the total nationwide—all while being the largest player and twice the size of the nearest competitor.

The company is positioned well both for organic growth through market share and for geographic growth; there is still plenty of fertile ground for new growth, especially in the Northeast and Northwest and smaller metro areas. The footprint is slowly but surely becoming a nationwide one, which will not only help volumes but also brand recognition, pricing power, buying power, and cost absorption.

Earnings momentum has been strong lately, in part due to the aggressive share repurchase program.

Reasons for Caution

As the softening auto market in early 2018 once again reminds us, CarMax will always be somewhat vulnerable to economic cycles, the availability of credit, and the availability of quality used vehicles to resell. Recent concerns about vehicle availability have morphed into concerns about oversupply as lease returns flood the market. Lease returns are an important source of supply for the company, so there is good news in this as well.

A new trend toward longer six- and seven-year new car financing periods may keep people in their cars longer, but it may also incentivize people to buy used to avoid the long financing period in the first place. As this company is still in the growth phase, and new dealerships involve putting lots of new cars on the ground, working capital needs are extensive, long-term debt has risen, and cash returns to shareholders have not met our norms; however, the share repurchase program takes a big step toward fixing that.

SECTOR: Retail ❑ BETA COEFFICIENT: 1.55 ❑ 10-YEAR COMPOUND EARNINGS PER-SHARE GROWTH: 15.5% ❑ 10-YEAR COMPOUND DIVIDENDS PER-SHARE GROWTH: NA

	2010	2011	2012	2013	2014	2015	2016	2017
Revenues (mil)	8,975	10,004	10,963	12,574	14,269	15,150	15,875	17,120
Net income (mil)	380.9	413.8	425.0	492.6	583.9	628.6	633.8	684.0
Earnings per share	1.67	1.79	1.87	2.16	2.68	3.05	3.30	3.70
Dividends per share	—	—	—	—	—	—	—	—
Cash flow per share	1.95	2.19	2.00	2.70	3.35	3.93	4.30	4.81
Price: high	30.0	37.0	38.2	53.1	68.7	75.4	66.6	77.6
low	18.6	22.8	24.8	38.0	42.5	50.6	41.3	54.3

Website: www.carmax.com

AGGRESSIVE GROWTH

Carnival Corporation

Ticker symbol: CCL (NYSE) ❑ Large Cap ❑ Value Line financial strength rating: B+ ❑ Current yield: 3.1% ❑ Dividend raises, past 10 years: 5

Company Profile

Carnival Corporation is the world's largest leisure travel company, providing cruises and cruise vacations to destinations throughout the world. The company operates under ten individual cruise brands or separate cruise lines in two segments—North America, and Europe, Australia, & Asia (EAA). The North America segment includes Carnival Cruise Line, Princess Cruises, Holland America Line, and The Yachts of Seabourn (a luxury line) cruise brands. The EAA segment includes Costa Cruises, Cunard Cruises, AIDA Cruises, P&O Cruises (UK), and P&O Cruises (Australia). Together, these cruise lines operate 103 modern ships (with 18 more on the way between now and 2022) with more than 232,000 berths, and the company claims about 48 percent of the worldwide cruise market. The company operates a few port facilities, Alaska tours, and some other adjacent travel operations. About 64 percent of revenues come from the North American brands. For those of you who feel from experience that cruise ships must make most of their money selling alcohol on board, indeed about 25 percent of their revenue is classified as "onboard and other."

The ships are modern, really, floating hotels, and the travel experience is all-inclusive and easy for guests. The typical cruise is set up for all age groups, with plenty of varied activities and foods for all, including new specialty restaurants and celebrity chefs on board and big names such as Crosby, Stills & Nash in the entertainment lineup. The *Carnival Vista*, launched in 2016, has an onboard brewery, an IMAX theater, and an aerial "Skyride." Also launched in 2016, the Holland America Line's *Koningsdam* allows patrons to blend their own wine and enjoy Lincoln Center Stage, Billboard Onboard, and B.B. King. The *Majestic Princess*, launched in 2017, is tailor-made for the Chinese market and features the largest shopping space on any cruise ship as well as karaoke and mah-jongg rooms. The 2017 *AIDAperla* features a microbrewery, ice rink, climbing walls, and an expansive German spa for the German cruise market.

The company adds two to three new ships per year and sells one to two per year, with a targeted capacity growth of about 5 percent compounded annually. The company plans to introduce 7 LNG-fueled ships in the coming years and has already reduced fuel consumption 29 percent through various conservation measures.

Fares are "all-inclusive," but travelers will find plenty of add-ons such as Internet service and alcoholic beverages, which run up an additional tab while on board. Cruises range from short three- and four-day "Love Boat" cruises out of Los Angeles, to three- and four-week and longer passages through entire regions such as the Middle East or Southeast Asia.

Customer service is paramount and has become a recent emphasis of the Carnival lines. Live agents are available before, during, and after the cruise to answer any questions ("Can my 17-year-old bring his skateboard?"

"Yes, but he'll have to stow it while on board the ship; he can access it for ports of call."). The experience is turnkey and much simpler than the typical land-based vacation, especially if multiple destinations are involved. The company and its lines have gotten smart about attracting repeat customers through loyalty programs and "perks"—some wealthier retirees might spend half a year on the company's ships as a simpler, less-expensive alternative to owning a large motor home or vacation property. Retirees have always been prime targets, but the offering is becoming more attractive to families and younger customers as well—to a degree, because cruises have become more "hip."

Recent directions include "green cruising" where ships are powered by liquefied natural gas, new cruises to Cuba (the first embarked in early 2016), and more originations and availability from China to serve the growing traveling middle class there. To that point, there are an estimated 135 million outbound travelers in China today, a figure estimated to grow to 200 million by 2020—and currently only 5 percent of the company's capacity serves China.

Financial Highlights, Fiscal Year 2017

After many years of rocky seas, particularly during the Great Recession, Carnival has finally, through a combination of marketing and operational excellence, found calmer waters and steady tailwinds on the revenue front, and in most expense categories FY2017 revenues rose just under 7 percent, while cost efficiencies and better capacity utilization were offset by a 36 percent increase in fuel costs (which are about 8 percent of total expenses) to cap net income at a 1 percent gain over last year. Strong cash flows, however, supported two dividend increases (totaling 18 percent) through the year and a healthy buyback program (4 percent of shares in two years). Going forward, the company expects capacity increases, strong bookings, and more efficient ships to guide the course toward 8–9 percent revenue growth in 2018 followed by 5–7 percent in 2019; earnings should sail forward 25–30 percent after the soft 2017, followed by another 10–13 percent gain in 2019, with a robust combination of debt reduction, dividend increases, and buybacks occurring through the early part of the decade.

Reasons to Buy

We continue to think cruising has come into its own as a mainstream regular travel alternative, not just a niche business providing a once-in-a-lifetime honeymoon or retirement cruise to Alaska. Cruises are more complete and easier than in past years, and there is something for everyone. The new ships are spectacular.

The marketing story is solid—strong brands, customer service, and customer loyalty leading the way. Millennials, who once probably would never have thought of a cruise, now are attracted to the activities, special meals, and entertainment, and the experience as a whole. It is no longer just for Grandma and Grandpa. As this group is more and more likely to shun material goods for experiences, cruise operators, especially those offering "interesting" itineraries, are in the right dock at the right time. We also think their strategy to capitalize on growing China tourism is on course, as are their efforts to attract other significant national markets such as Germany and the UK.

Financially, we consider shareholder returns to be on the right heading.

Reasons for Caution

It's hard not to think about how economic cycles can affect this industry; fancy vacations are usually the first thing to go when times turn tough. We'd counter that cruises don't have to be "exotic," and many are affordable even on a modest family budget—there's something for everyone here. High fixed costs (ships, especially today's ships, are expensive!) present some financial challenges especially in bad times. Fuel prices bear watching, and competition in this industry is fairly intense, but we feel that Carnival has the strongest position, the best brands, and the best overall offering. You should no longer need a life jacket to buy this company, but watching the horizon is important as it is for any stock.

SECTOR: **Consumer Discretionary** ❑ BETA COEFFICIENT: **0.84** ❑ 10-YEAR COMPOUND EARNINGS PER-SHARE GROWTH: **1.5%** ❑ 10-YEAR COMPOUND DIVIDENDS PER-SHARE GROWTH: **2.5%**

		2010	2011	2012	2013	2014	2015	2016	2017
Revenues (mil)		14,469	15,793	15,382	15,456	15,884	15,774	16,389	17,510
Net income (mil)		1,978	1,912	1,464	1,078	1,516	2,103	2,580	2,606
Earnings per share		2.47	2.42	1.88	1.39	1.99	2.70	3.45	3.59
Dividends per share		0.40	1.00	1.00	1.00	1.00	1.10	1.35	1.60
Cash flow per share		4.30	4.36	3.84	3.44	4.06	4.83	5.95	5.99
Price:	high	47.2	48.1	39.9	40.5	46.5	55.8	54.9	69.9
	low	29.7	28.5	29.2	31.4	33.1	42.5	40.5	51.7

Website: www.carnivalcorp.com

CenterPoint Energy, Inc.

Ticker symbol: CNP (NYSE) ❑ Large Cap ❑ Value Line financial strength rating: B+ ❑ Current yield: 4.1% ❑ Dividend raises, past 10 years: 10

Company Profile

Based in Houston, TX, CenterPoint Energy is in the electricity delivery (not production, but delivery) business, serving more than 2.4 million customers in a 5,000-square-mile service territory in the greater Houston area and is in the retail gas delivery business, serving more than 3.4 million metered customers in Louisiana, Arkansas, Minnesota, Mississippi, Oklahoma, and Texas (including Houston). It is the nineteenth-largest investor-owned electric utility and sixth-largest gas distribution company in the US by customer base. It is also—as of this writing—in the natural gas production and distribution business, with a 54 percent interest in a master limited partnership called Enable Midstream Partners, which produces and distributes wholesale gas and some oil mainly from Texas and Oklahoma. Finally, the company operates an unregulated CenterPoint Energy Services arm, which sells gas to commercial, industrial, and wholesale customers in 33 US states and provides an assortment of consulting services for other utilities.

CenterPoint intrigues us because, first, it does not own generating assets but instead distributes electricity to its customers produced by 18 providers, some green. It owns the wires, the meters, and the customer contact, while such messy problems as fuel costs and environmental risks are left to someone else. Second, in its distribution business, the company has learned to use technology to drive efficiency and improve the customer experience, with advanced implementations of smart grids, smart metering, and other technologies from companies such as Itron, Inc. (another *100 Best* pick). The company has installed smart meters for almost all of its customer base—more than 2.4 million "advanced" meters—automating meter reading and frequent readouts on electricity use. Customers are never left in the dark for long—these technologies manage the grid to reduce consumption, access the least expensive source, and keep the lights on more reliably.

Finally, as mentioned previously, we like the idea of a gas distributor acquiring some upstream assets to control costs and assure supplies—only it backfired as energy prices cratered in late 2014. The company took a $1.8 billion noncash write-down of the asset value of Midstream and is reconsidering its ownership. CNP appears likely to divest Enable to take some of the commodity price risk out of its business, but the timing is far from certain. We're good with either direction CenterPoint decides to go with this investment—sell, spin-off, or retain—the decision may be made in 2018 but would probably be carried out over a few years. The midstream gas business is in far better shape than it was two years ago.

Electricity transmission and distribution accounts for 31 percent of FY2017 revenues; regulated retail gas distribution accounts for 38 percent, unregulated wholesale gas sales 29 percent, and services 2 percent. The company recognizes no revenue from its Enable investment, but it earned about $265 million pretax in 2017 as "Equity in earnings (losses) of unconsolidated affiliates"—far better than the $1.6 billion paper loss it took in 2015.

Financial Highlights, Fiscal Year 2017

With the limited partnership interest and the large unregulated sales unit, revenues and earnings can vary more widely than with most large utilities. In 2017, we also had Hurricane Harvey, a $1.1 billion gain booked as a result of the Tax Cuts and Jobs Act, a recovery in Houston's all-important energy industry (most high-rises in downtown Houston are occupied once again), and favorable seasonal weather patterns. The net for FY2017 was a recovery beyond successful 2014 levels, with revenues up 27 percent and earnings up some 57 percent—all excluding the tax changes. Although it cost in excess of $120 million, Hurricane Harvey's net effect will be zero after insurance payments and future rate recovery.

Rate relief, a steady 1–2 percent rise in the customer base, expense control operating efficiency, and the predicted relative stability of Enable results are projected to bring revenue gains in the 2–3 percent range for 2018, followed by a 5–6 percent gain in 2019, with net income relatively flat for 2018 and rising 7–9 percent in 2019. Depletion and depreciation allowances typically keep cash flows well ahead of earnings for this type of company. As such, cash flows are well ahead of the pace of earnings and nearly four times the indicated dividend, making it secure though significantly higher than the national utility average.

Reasons to Buy

CenterPoint is a progressive-minded utility located in what has been a high-growth market that simply cannot do without electricity. We look at the electricity business as a key business anchor with decent growth prospects, and we like the deployment of leading-edge technologies in that business. We like their positioning as a low-cost producer and wholesaler in the gas business with a built-in outlet in the regulated business for their product. We think the Enable "pendulum" has swung back from "problem" to "opportunity," and that any good news in this sector, including a sale, will only help from this point forward. The dividend is still high compared to peers and appears secure and poised to grow about 4 percent a year; we think they could afford more. CenterPoint combines the safety and yield of a quality utility with a bit of appreciation potential in the energy production and distribution business.

Reasons for Caution

We worry that another slowdown in the energy economy could temper Houston's growth, creating a soft patch in its own right. CenterPoint shares have performed quite well and perhaps a little beyond anticipated growth; prudent investors should look for "value" entry points.

SECTOR: **Utilities** ◻ BETA COEFFICIENT: **0.57** ◻ 10-YEAR COMPOUND EARNINGS PER-SHARE GROWTH:**1.5%** ◻ 10-YEAR COMPOUND DIVIDENDS PER-SHARE GROWTH: **7.0%**

	2010	2011	2012	2013	2014	2015	2016	2017
Revenues (mil)	8,765	8,459	7,452	8,106	9,226	7,386	7,528	9,614
Net income (mil)	442	546	581	536	611	465	432	679
Earnings per share	1.07	1.27	1.35	1.24	1.42	1.08	1.00	1.57
Dividends per share	0.78	0.79	0.81	0.83	0.95	0.99	1.03	1.07
Cash flow per share	3.14	3.43	3.89	3.54	3.85	3.40	3.68	4.03
Price: high	17.0	21.5	21.8	25.7	25.8	23.7	225.0	30.5
low	5.5	15.1	18.1	19.3	21.1	16.0	16.4	24.5

Website: www.centerpointenergy.com

AGGRESSIVE GROWTH

Chemed Corporation

Ticker symbol: CHE (NYSE) ◻ Mid Cap ◻ Value Line financial strength rating: B++ ◻ Current yield: 0.4% ◻ Dividend raises, past 10 years: 9

Company Profile

"Call Roto-Rooter, that's the name, and away go troubles down the drain" is the affable slogan of this well-known "root" business of the two-company conglomerate Chemed. Yes, if Roto-Rooter is the root, then those roots have sprouted a "tree" in an entirely different business: end-of-life health—hospice—care. Today's Chemed is two businesses for the price of one: the VITAS Healthcare Corporation (69 percent of FY2017 revenues) and the original Roto-Rooter, now 31 percent of revenues (up from 29 percent in 2016). Consider this new-to-our-list Mid Cap company a healthcare business, one for your health at the end of life, and one for the health of your home plumbing.

As the name sounds like one of a chemical company, the name "Chemed" deserves some explanation. Its roots (sorry!) go back to a Cincinnati soap products maker (a familiar theme) known as DuBois Chemicals, which eventually made a name in the industrial cleaning products business. Chemed Corporation came on to the scene in 1971 when W.R. Grace, which had bought DuBois in 1964, spun it off as "Chemed." Chemed bought and ran Roto-Rooter franchises, and as the saying goes, liked the business so much it bought the entire company in 1980 (it had been founded in 1935). Chemed decided to quit the capital-intensive and environmentally sensitive commodity chemical business in 1991 and sold DuBois. The company bought VITAS in 2004. After a few other acquisitions and divestitures, we arrive at today's Chemed, a parent company of two distinct businesses. Both businesses are operated as wholly autonomous entities; the Chemed ownership or brand does not appear on either subsidiary's website except under a well-subordinated "parent company" tab at the bottom of the VITAS page (www.vitas.com) and a bare mention on Roto-Rooter's "About Us" page.

Founded in 1978 as a volunteer organization by a United Methodist minister and his oncology nurse wife, today's VITAS business provides noncurative hospice and palliative care services to its patients through a network of physicians, registered nurses, home health aides, social workers, clergy, and volunteers. Included are spiritual and emotional counseling to both patients and their families. In 2017, VITAS provided over 6 million days of care in 14 states for over 82,000 patients and their families; about 98 percent of that in their home (2 percent in dedicated inpatient units). VITAS operates in an industry dominated primarily by small, nonprofit, community-based hospices. About 97 percent of revenue is from Medicare or Medicaid sources.

The name "Roto-Rooter" is probably more familiar to most of us. Roto-Rooter originally was created to offer round-the-clock drain cleaning and maintenance services using the familiar "snake" equipment they pioneered and now manufacture and sell. Today's Roto-Rooter has expanded into providing a full line of on-site, often emergency-based plumbing and water restoration services both to residential and commercial customers; plumbing now accounts for about half of the subsidiary's revenue. The business operates through 110 company-owned branches and independent contractors and 400 franchisees. The company covers 90 percent of the US and 40 percent of Canada's population.

Financial Highlights, Fiscal Year 2017

FY2017 revenues rose almost 6 percent overall, although beneath the surface Roto-Rooter revenues increased 14.7 percent while VITAS, again hampered by a negative change in Medicare hospice reimbursement rates, advanced only 2.2 percent. Net earnings were up almost 30 percent on margin expansion at Roto-Rooter and a much lower tax rate. VITAS earnings continued to lag from the Medicare cutbacks. For 2018 the company expects moderate growth and utilization on the hospice front and continued growth and margin expansion with selective price increases for Roto-Rooter; the net is a 22–25 percent earnings gain on a 3–5 percent revenue increase. Revenue and earnings growth stabilize into the 4–6 percent range in 2019. Share buybacks in the 2 percent range will drive the already-low (16 million) share count lower, while dividend increases in the 10 percent range will sweeten the pot a little.

Reasons to Buy

Although this one performed better than expected in 2017 and early 2018, leaving less room for gains, we still like the potential here. Chemed offers the opportunity to buy into not one but *two* good businesses; both have a component of stability with ample growth opportunity. Both are leaders and recognized brands in highly fragmented industries; what other brand of plumbing services do you know aside from Roto-Rooter? Although the 14 states with current operations represent a populous cross section of the US, there is plenty of potential for geographic expansion in the VITAS business toward becoming a nationally, and possibly internationally, recognized name. Also, increased understanding and use of home hospice services over more pricey hospitalization in end-of-life stages will help. The combined business exhibits improving margins, operating leverage, low debt, and strong cash generation and a willingness to return it to shareholders, mainly in the form of share buybacks. The small share count (16 million shares) is attractive so long as things are going well; there are relatively few shares to go around for institutional investors as the word gets out about Chemed.

Reasons for Caution

One may always wonder about the merits of managing two such completely disparate, unrelated businesses; as well, there is always a good possibility another (perhaps unrelated) company may be brought into the mix. Two disparate businesses may be manageable but as many learned in the late 1960s and early 1970s conglomerate boom, *too many* is not.

Chemed has already gained some appeal with the investment community; that and the low share count has driven recent share prices to high levels. The low share count can bring upside but also downside volatility if business conditions deteriorate. Shop carefully; otherwise your investment results may be headed for life support—or worse, down the drain.

SECTOR: **Healthcare** ❑ BETA COEFFICIENT: **1.05** ❑ 10-YEAR COMPOUND EARNINGS PER-SHARE GROWTH: **14.0%** ❑ 10-YEAR COMPOUND DIVIDENDS PER-SHARE GROWTH: **14.5%**

	2010	2011	2012	2013	2014	2015	2016	2017
Revenues (mil)	1,281	1,356	1,430	1,413	1,456	1,543	1,580	1,667
Net income (mil)	81.8	86.0	89.3	77.2	99.3	110.3	108.7	141.1
Earnings per share	3.55	4.10	4.62	4.16	5.57	6.33	6.48	8.43
Dividends per share	0.52	0.60	0.68	0.76	0.84	0.92	1.00	1.08
Cash flow per share	5.21	6.06	6.47	6.23	7.84	8.56	8.86	11.00
Price: high	65.0	72.3	72.1	82.0	112.0	160.1	164.1	251.0
low	45.9	47.7	49.1	61.7	72.5	100.5	124.8	158.8

Website: www.chemed.com

GROWTH AND INCOME

Chevron Corporation

Ticker symbol: CVX (NYSE) ❑ Large Cap ❑ Value Line financial strength rating: A++ ❑ Current yield: 3.9% ❑ Dividend raises, past 10 years: 10

Company Profile

Over the past three years, Chevron has become a poster child for strong, stable, entrenched businesses in can't-lose industries suddenly rocked out of bed by changes beyond their control—namely the 70 percent drop in the price of its chief product, oil. The "poster child" reference includes the company's response and recovery—which as of early 2018 isn't complete but is certainly headed in the right direction.

As with everyone else in the energy and most other commodity industries, the downturn forced tough decisions on cost cutting and "right-sizing," all while maintaining the course for investors. For the most part Chevron stayed the course by selling some assets, issuing debt, and pulling back capital expenditures. They maintained the dividend, and even increased it, albeit by one cent in 2016 and three cents in 2017 to keep their 30-year string of raises intact. A moderate improvement in oil prices to $60/barrel and a leaner, meaner cost structure brought the company well into the black in 2017, though not back to the heady days of 2008–2014. Chevron has become a good example of how to steer a large ship through a major revenue slump.

Chevron is the world's fourth-largest publicly traded, integrated energy company based on oil-equivalent reserves and production. It is engaged in every aspect of the oil and gas industry, including exploration and production, refining, marketing and transportation, chemicals manufacturing and sales, and power generation.

Active in more than 180 countries, Chevron has reserves of about 11.1 billion barrels of oil equivalent (57 percent liquids, 43 percent gas), with a production rate of 1.7 million barrels of oil equivalent (flat from 2016) and 6.0 billion cubic feet of gas per day (up 15 percent). In addition, it has global refining output of more than 2.7 million barrels per day (bpd) and operates more than 10,000 retail outlets around the world. Oil-equivalent production is concentrated in the US (27 percent), Kazakhstan (16 percent), Thailand (9 percent), Nigeria (9 percent), Indonesia (8 percent), Angola (5 percent), Australia (5 percent), Bangladesh (4 percent), Canada (4 percent), and 13 percent other. For the most part, with minimal Middle East exposure, these locations are relatively low risk and high potential compared to many competitors' production holdings. Although it increased the overall exposure to the 2014–15 oil price swoon, Chevron is more concentrated in oil (less in gas) than some of its competitors. That said, it has stepped up its new shale developments, particularly in gas, while reducing development costs substantially. Chevron also has active global downstream businesses in manufactured products including lubricants, specialty chemicals and additives, specialty refining units for aviation and maritime markets, and various logistics activities, including pipelines, shipping, and a global trading unit.

The company's global refining network comprises ten wholly owned and joint-venture facilities. Gasoline and diesel fuel are sold under three well-known consumer brands: Chevron in North America; Texaco in Latin America, Europe, and West Africa; and Caltex in Asia, the Middle East, and southern Africa.

Chevron is the number one jet fuel marketer in the US and third worldwide, marketing 500,000 barrels per day in 80 countries. The company's fuel and marine marketing business is a leading global supplier and marketer of fuels, lubricants, and coolants to the marine and power markets, also with about 500,000 barrels of sales per day.

The company's traditional emphasis in oil hurt the company as prices fell almost 70 percent in 2014–15, severely affecting the bottom line and causing a rare annual net loss in 2016. In 2017 a combination of cost and capital containment, more flexible spend, asset sales, and a return to $50 to $60 per barrel oil brought the company back to a cash flow positive state, after increasing borrowings considerably to cover the dip. Chevron's strategy is to go "lean and mean" and capitalize on relative strength in oil (versus gas) and strength in downstream refining and marketing while maintaining shareholder returns, which will break even at $50 oil and bring solid positive cash flow at $60 and $70 oil.

Financial Highlights, Fiscal Year 2017

FY2017 revenues were up a substantial 24 percent as oil prices recovered and production volumes increased—and would have been stronger without the October Gulf Coast hurricanes, which disrupted refinery production. Net profit rose to $7.1 billion from a half a billion deficit in FY2016. Production increases, steady $60/barrel oil, and efficiency gains (nothing like a severe downturn to bring these on!) are forecast to bring a 10–12 percent 2018 revenue gain followed by a 2–5 percent gain in 2019, which could prove conservative if strong energy demand drives higher prices. Earnings should rise some 50–60 percent in 2018 as prices stay north of breakeven; then a more modest 4–6 percent in 2019. Dividend growth should resume a more normal 3–4 percent annual track, while share buybacks look to be on hold as the company expands production.

Reasons to Buy

We are obviously betting on the long term; taking a long-term view of Chevron's strengths and response to business adversity; Chevron appears to be doing quite well on both counts.

For exploration and production strength and geographic and technological diversity, few companies exceed Chevron's strengths. The 155 percent reserve replacement ratio (new finds versus depletion) is among the tops in the industry. The company is in some of the best sectors and geographies in the business and has established a good brand and track record for discovery, production, and downstream operations. We like the diversification into refining, which generally benefits from lower input prices. Long term, the company has a solid record and emphasis on cash generation and distribution. We think shareholders will be well rewarded with growing cash returns in the long run—especially as energy prices normalize even to the diminished $60 level. With a little patience, we continue to think CVX is among the best in a difficult industry.

Reasons for Caution

Of course, recent energy price shifts continue to put a dent in CVX's universe. The price shifts have been an opportunity for some of the wiser—and more cash rich—players such as Chevron to streamline operations and to acquire productive assets more cheaply. The biggest long-term negative is an almost doubling of long-term debt to $35 billion to keep the home fires burning. It remains to be seen how quickly, if at all, the company plans to lose that debt. This business may take some time to return to its previous glory, but it is still a safe play and likely winner in today's leaner circumstances.

SECTOR: **Energy** ❑ **BETA COEFFICIENT: 1.15** ❑ 10-YEAR COMPOUND EARNINGS PER-SHARE GROWTH: **-5.0%** ❑ 10-YEAR COMPOUND DIVIDENDS PER-SHARE GROWTH: **9.0%**

	2010	2011	2012	2013	2014	2015	2016	2017
Revenues (bil)	204.9	253.7	241.9	228.8	212.0	138.4	114.5	141.7
Net income (bil)	19.0	26.9	26.2	21.4	8.9	4.6	(0.5)	7.2
Earnings per share	8.48	13.44	13.32	11.09	10.14	2.45	(0.27)	3.79
Dividends per share	2.84	3.09	3.51	3.90	4.21	4.28	4.29	4.32
Cash flow per share	15.99	19.98	20.05	18.61	19.17	13.70	10.05	13.90
Price: high	92.4	111.0	118.5	127.8	135.1	113.0	119.0	126.2
low	66.8	102.1	95.7	108.7	100.1	69.6	75.3	102.6

Website: www.chevron.com

CONSERVATIVE GROWTH

The Coca-Cola Company

Ticker symbol: KO (NYSE) ❑ Large Cap ❑ Value Line financial strength rating: A++ ❑ Current yield: 3.5% ❑ Dividend raises, past 10 years: 10

Company Profile

The Coca-Cola Company is the world's largest beverage company. For more than 100 years, the company has mainly produced concentrates and syrups, which it then bottles or cans itself or sells to independent bottlers worldwide.

Then in 2010 it took a big step to "own" the supply chain with the acquisition of bottler Coca-Cola Enterprises' North American operations; CCE still handles distribution for Europe. Independent bottlers add water (still or carbonated, depending on the product), sugar, and other (often local) ingredients, then bottle and distribute the products to restaurants, retailers, and other distributors. Now it is taking another big step—"refranchising"— selling many of these bottlers off to generate cash, to focus on the core businesses, and to dramatically increase profitability. It is almost finished with that important step, and as a confirmation of the strategy, it reported a 1.4 percent drop in net profit in 2007 on a 15 percent drop in revenues as it shed the bottling operations. Finally, Coke is making many moves to diversify beyond its core carbonated beverage base. Yesterday's staid Coke is changing, and for the most part, we applaud the changes.

Coke operates in more than 200 countries and markets nearly 500 brands of concentrate and finished beverages, which are bottled into more than 3,900 different branded products, including Coca-Cola; 21 of those brands bring in over $1 billion annually—a figure that has doubled since 2007. The numbers are staggering: Coke ships over 29 billion cases annually, which works out to 637 billion servings sold per year, 1.9 billion beverages consumed per day—or 21,990 servings per second. Currently it is all processed through 250 bottling partners operating 900 plants moving product through 24 million retail outlets.

As a breakdown of revenue, 65 percent of all sales are overseas—16 percent in Latin America, 30 percent in Europe, the Middle East, and Africa, and 19 percent in the Pacific.

The product line continues to adjust to today's health-conscious, often millennial consumer. New acquisitions and product development have followed a multipoint strategy: (1) leveraging the power of winning brands (the popular smaller 7-ounce cans, multiple flavorings for Diet Coke); (2) creating premium experiences (Schweppes 1783 premium flavored tonic mixers) and (3) pursuing on-trend nutrition (AdeS soy-based beverages). The company has also invested in Monster Beverage and others. Some 19 of their 21 billion-dollar brands have low- or no-calorie alternatives. The new "Freestyle" machine found in a growing number of fast-food restaurants allows drinkers to customize their drinks. It's fun, and remember— customization is one of today's biggies. And did you know? It now collects data so that Coca-Cola can see what tastes are preferred; what a laboratory! (The dispenser team has its own website—check out www.coca-colafreestyle .com.) Other innovations include mass-customized cans and bottles with people's names on them, and something we've all awaited: a return to the original Coke bottle shape and format where possible.

Importantly, Coke now views their business as a total portfolio containing "category clusters," with marketing and branding strategies for each cluster. Their vision includes the following clusters and representative products:

- Traditional soft drinks—50 percent plus: Coke, Sprite, Fanta, etc.
- Energy drinks—through Monster stake—15 percent: Monster, Burn, NOS brands
- Water, enhanced water, sports—15 percent: DASANI, Smartwater, Vitaminwater, Powerade, Schweppes
- Ready-to-drink coffee, tea—15 percent: Gold Peak, FUZE Tea, Barista Bros., Dunkin' Donuts Iced Coffee
- Juice, dairy, plant-based—10 percent: Minute Maid, Simply Orange, Fairlife, Core Power, AdeS

The point is simple: Coke is diversifying into a comprehensive ready-to-drink beverage provider.

As mentioned earlier, the company is reversing its strategy to own its US distribution channel—specifically its bottling network. Coca-Cola is embarking on a "21st Century Beverage Partnership Model," essentially a franchising model, in which the company works closely with its bottling franchisees but does not carry the asset base, employee base, or the headaches of that relatively low-margin business. Commodity price risks also move over to the franchisees. The impact on margins is significant, raising net profit margins some 7–10 percent (to 27–30 percent) as currently implemented.

Financial Highlights, Fiscal Year 2017

As highlighted earlier, the FY2017 story is mainly one of de-franchising; revenues took a 15 percent "hit" without this business while net margins increased about 3 percent and net profits only declined 1.4 percent. With a moderate buyback, per-share earnings remained unchanged. Remaining de-franchising will take revenues down another notch, 12–13 percent. But a 3 percent rise in "organic" revenues combined with tax benefits and productivity measures are forecast to drive earnings some 45 percent higher in 2018 (as "currency and structural headwinds abate" in company parlance), an act to be followed in 2019 by a 6–9 percent earnings gain on a 3–4 percent rise in revenues. Cash returns to investors continue to be decent on both the buyback and dividend front, with dividends growing in the mid-single-digit range and share buybacks reducing share counts in the 1–2 percent range annually.

Reasons to Buy

The well-conceived de-franchising strategy is icing on the cake for this already hugely profitable corporation. Who, besides Apple, makes 30 percent *net* profit margins? Coke does with this move.

While the traditional fizzy drink business is becoming a bit passé in today's world, Coke is adapting to the change and in our view, continues to be solid. The company has category leadership, especially globally, in soft drinks, juices and juice drinks, and ready-to-drink coffees and teas. They're number two globally in sports and energy drinks, water, and ready-to-drink teas.

The Coca-Cola name is probably the most recognized brand in the world and is almost beyond valuation. Indeed, Mr. Buffett once uttered the classic line about its brand strength and intangibles: "If you gave me $100 billion and said take away the soft drink leadership in the world from Coke, I'd give it back to you and say it can't be done."

That's all pretty old news now; what's important is that Coca-Cola has also shown us, in today's world, that it isn't just going to sit around and go flat while we investors sit around and cry in our beer. We see signs that the company "gets it" and will not only adapt but will eventually have a chance to remain the number one brand even with a full new mix of beverages and packages for the modern world. Coca-Cola has traditionally been a steady defensive stock and offers a solid dividend with a constant track record of dividend growth. The company boasts—quite rightly—about having raised dividends in each of the past 55 years. It is also fairly pure play on international business.

Reasons for Caution

Coca-Cola is under our constant scrutiny for relevance in today's increasingly millennial-dominated market. Sales of traditional sparkling beverages in established markets—the US and Europe, and now Latin America—are in a slow decline due to interest in health and reducing obesity.

For the future, these market changes could provide some speed bumps. One wonders how the Coke culture will resonate with today's millennial beverage requirements—less sugar, fewer artificial ingredients, more customization and transparency—and one wonders further whether the new-age consumer will adapt well to healthy or fun drinks sold by Coca-Cola. Therein lies the 64-ounce question: Can they deliver change? Fast enough? Can they get the message out? In time to make a difference as traditional sugary beverages decline? Right now, our bet is "yes."

Overall, this is a slow, steady growth story, which may be too slow for many, with new risks the company didn't face when Mr. Buffett bought his 400 million shares years ago.

SECTOR: Consumer Discretionary □ BETA COEFFICIENT: **0.72** □ 10-YEAR COMPOUND EARNINGS PER-SHARE GROWTH: **5.0%** □ 10-YEAR COMPOUND DIVIDENDS PER-SHARE GROWTH: **8.5%**

		2010	2011	2012	2013	2014	2015	2016	2017
Revenues (mil)		35,123	46,554	48,017	46,854	45,998	44,294	41,863	35,410
Net income (mil)		8,144	8,932	9,019	9,374	9,091	8,797	8,354	8,340
Earnings per share		1.75	1.92	1.97	2.08	2.04	2.00	1.91	1.91
Dividends per share		0.88	0.94	1.02	1.12	1.22	1.32	1.40	1.43
Cash flow per share		2.09	2.41	2.46	2.58	2.53	2.49	2.37	2.23
Price:	high	32.9	35.9	40.7	43.4	45.0	43.9	47.1	47.5
	low	24.7	30.6	33.3	36.5	36.9	36.6	39.9	40.2

Website: www.coca-colacompany.com

AGGRESSIVE GROWTH

Columbia Sportswear Company

Ticker symbol: COLM (NASDAQ) □ **Mid Cap** □ **Value Line financial strength rating: B++** □ **Current yield: 1.1%** □ **Dividend raises, past 10 years: 10**

Company Profile

As we select our *100 Best Stocks* each year, among the many types of materials we use as sources we read a lot of corporate histories. The history of clothing maker Columbia Sportswear pretty much tops them all:

"Born and raised in Portland, Oregon, Columbia Sportswear Company has been making gear so that Pacific Northwesterners can enjoy the outdoors for more than 70 years. At the helm for over 40 years has been our Chairman, Gert Boyle. Her Tough Mother persona has grown Columbia into the global sportswear company that it is today—still based in Portland, still making no-nonsense apparel and footwear to keep you WARM, DRY, COOL and PROTECTED no matter what. Our unique Pacific Northwest heritage and Boyle family irreverence is what sets us apart from the competition."

Typically we don't lift content verbatim from such corporate writings. But this one not only describes Columbia's colorful past; it also quite aptly describes what the company has become today. As described—and still led by the 94-year-old Ms. Boyle (Chairperson of the Board) and her 68-year-old son Timothy (President and COO)—Columbia makes a line of practical, functional, and tastefully styled active wear that is increasingly used in non-active situations. Most of you have seen a Columbia vest or jacket or two on the streets or in the woods during your daily travels. Rainwear is a specialty—given its Portland roots—but the company makes and distributes high-quality, conservatively designed shirts, pants, hoodies and fleece wear, tops and bottoms for women, shoes, and accessories, among other products. The clothing and shoes are designed for outdoor wear and for skiing/snowboarding and other rugged activities, but they are casual enough and of high enough quality to fit in well for Casual Friday at work and casual anything outside of work; you won't get turned away at your favorite nice restaurant if you show up wearing Columbia. You probably won't notice Columbia—until you notice it. It's all about one of our favorite themes: "elegant simplicity."

Apparel, accessories, and equipment accounted for about 78 percent of 2017 sales, with footwear making up the rest. The company has expanded its own direct-to-consumer channel through Columbia-branded stores and through its website. US distribution is a mixed wholesale and direct model, with 3,300 wholesale customers on the wholesale side; the "DTC" (direct to consumer) side added 11 stores to reach 105 outlet retail stores, 24 branded retail stores, and 4 brand-specific e-commerce sites (see later in this section for some of the specialty brands). About 38 percent of sales are overseas, with Asia-Pacific and Latin America accounting for about half of that. Through a joint venture, the company has 86 retail locations and an online sales presence in China. All apparel and footwear are manufactured by contract manufacturers to spec; the company operates no manufacturing facilities.

Columbia has also expanded into more specialty lines, such as yoga clothing. Columbia also owns and distributes Mountain Hardwear, a respected climbing-inspired line of high-end performance outerwear, and other "lifestyle" brands including SOREL (women's wear), prAna ("stylish, sustainable active wear"), and Montrail (high-performance running footwear). SOREL is the largest subbrand, accounting for about 9 percent of 2017 revenues;

the others account for less than 5 percent each. The Columbia brand itself accounts for just over 80 percent of revenues.

On the innovation front, a new performance technology called "OutDry Extreme," including jackets made from 21 recycled plastic bottles, has received excellent reviews in the rainwear category, and the technology has been extended to gloves and footwear. A new line of performance fishing wear has also recently come to market. Comfort is a major theme; "Clothing that feels as good as it looks" is one of their mottos.

Financial Highlights, Fiscal Year 2017

After a bumpy 2016 highlighted by the exit of Sports Authority and others, strong international sales, strong brands, and better execution brought a 4 percent increase in 2017 sales, an 0.5 percent increase in operating margin (a significant increase in the thin-margined apparel industry), and a 10 percent increase in net income. Going forward, international strength, operational improvements, and greater emphasis on direct channels should produce earnings gains in the 8–10 percent range annually on sales gains in the 3–6 percent range. Dividends have been ascending to the summit slowly but surely, while share buybacks have stopped for the moment at the side of the trail.

Reasons to Buy

Three years ago we looked for a company to replace the stumbling Ralph Lauren on our *100 Best* list, and we still think we found it in Columbia Sportswear. The brand has slowly but surely expanded its international reputation for functionality, performance, good design, quality, and value. It has the conservative, enduring qualities of Ralph Lauren products without being showy or pretentious; its understated elegance has resonated with millennials much better than Ralph, and its appeal is much wider than just millennials. Go out on a rainy day (or any other) and see what people are wearing.

As the brand has solidified and gone global, the company has woken up from the financial doldrums too. Sales, margins, and profits are all on a decent uptrend in a tough retail market as the products become more standard and are distributed more widely in varying retail channels including direct (you must no longer trek to REI to buy Columbia).

Reasons for Caution

The clothing business is by nature notoriously cyclical and trendy, and we don't pretend to be able to follow these trends, let alone pick the companies that will ride ahead of them. That's why we like Columbia—it is trendy because it isn't trendy. That said, even this strength can fall on its ear as it has with Ralph Lauren, Eddie Bauer, and many of its brethren. (We think those two names experienced other problems, namely Ralph's hoity-toity snob reputation and Eddie's poor quality, which Columbia may not experience if it stays on track.) Competition from the likes of Patagonia and Marmot is also substantial, but neither produces as complete a line nor has achieved as wide a distribution as Columbia. Oh, and about distribution: channel partners can be fickle too—or even go bankrupt. We hope they don't reach too far down market (e.g., Walmart) to boost volumes; as any mountain climber knows, it's easy to make mistakes in this industry and hard to recover.

SECTOR: Consumer Staples ◻ **BETA COEFFICIENT: 0.89** ◻ 10-YEAR COMPOUND EARNINGS PER-SHARE GROWTH: **4.5%** ◻ 10-YEAR COMPOUND DIVIDENDS PER-SHARE GROWTH:1 **9.0%**

	2010	2011	2012	2013	2014	2015	2016	2017
Revenues (mil)	1,483	1,694	1,670	1,685	2,100	2,326	2,377	2,466
Net income (mil)	77	103	100	94	137	174	192	210
Earnings per share	1.13	1.52	1.47	1.37	1.94	2.45	2.72	2.98
Dividends per share	0.37	0.43	0.44	0.46	0.57	0.62	0.69	0.73
Cash flow per share	1.71	2.19	2.07	1.95	2.74	3.33	3.61	3.86
Price: high	31.1	35.3	29.2	39.7	45.9	74.7	63.6	72.5
low	19.1	20.6	21.6	23.9	34.3	41.1	43.6	51.6

Website: www.columbia.com

AGGRESSIVE GROWTH

Comcast Corporation

Ticker symbol: CMCSA (NASDAQ) ◻ **Large Cap** ◻ **Value Line financial strength rating: A** ◻ **Current yield: 2.1%** ◻ **Dividend raises, past 10 years: 10**

Company Profile

Comcast is one of the nation's leading providers of communications services and information and entertainment content passed through those services. The company is in five businesses: Cable Communications, Cable Networks, Broadcast Television, Filmed Entertainment, and Theme Parks.

The Cable Communications core business is Comcast Cable, the familiar cable TV delivery network that has evolved into a conduit for delivering bundled high-speed Internet services, phone services, scheduled TV, studio shows and movies, and on-demand content, and even theme parks. This business serves some 22 million video subscribers and 26 million Internet subscribers in 39 states.

Comcast Cable is an assortment of content properties delivered primarily through cable and includes regional sports networks such as Comcast Sports Network Bay Area and national channels such as MSNBC, CNBC, Syfy, Bravo, Oxygen, the Golf Channel, and E! (an entertainment channel) as well as Fandango (a moviegoer's website), and others. The Broadcast Television business is centered on NBCUniversal, which includes the familiar NBC broadcast network and studios but also Telemundo and NBC Universo, all acquired in 2013. Filmed Entertainment includes Universal Pictures, DreamWorks Animation (acquired in 2016), Focus Features and Illumination brands of feature-length films and other entertainment. The Theme Parks business includes Universal theme parks in Hollywood, Orlando, and Osaka, Japan. Finally, "other" business interests include ownership of the Philadelphia Flyers hockey team and the Wells Fargo Center arena in Philadelphia. With these businesses, Comcast has become one of the largest integrated content development and distribution businesses in the US.

Comcast places a lot of emphasis on connectivity and penetration in its customer base. In 2017, they estimated a total opportunity ("homes and businesses passed") of 57.2 million locations; that is, 57.2 million locations they could serve with currently installed cable lines. Out of that opportunity, they estimate 22.4 million video subscribers (39 percent penetration), 25.9 high-speed Internet subscribers (45 percent), and 11.6 million voice telephone subscribers (20 percent). There are about 2 million business subscribers for high-speed Internet, a recent focal area. The company also emphasizes selling multiple products (i.e., cable TV and Internet), much of it through its bundled "Xfinity X1" bundled brand, and estimates about 19 million multiple product customers.

For management purposes, Comcast breaks down its business into two major segments:

- Cable Communications (61 percent of total revenues and 70 percent of operating income) houses the "delivery" business, including video, high-speed Internet, and voice services (collectively, "cable services") and the Xfinity bundle.
- NBCUniversal (39 percent of revenues, 30 percent of income) houses the content creation and entertainment businesses, including Cable Networks—12 percent of total revenues, Broadcast Television (11 percent), Filmed Entertainment (9 percent), and Theme Parks (7 percent).

Not surprisingly, the Comcast network has long been built on acquisitions, starting with the cable network and continuing more dramatically with the acquisition of NBC, Universal, and DreamWorks properties. In an effort to make a dent in international markets, the company recently launched a $30.5 billion bid for Sky, a European pay-TV provider.

Financial Highlights, Fiscal Year 2017

Strength across all businesses turned Comcast into a 5 percent revenue increase for 2017, excluding an irregular upside bump for broadcasting the Rio Olympics in 2016. Gains in the Cable Communications and NBCUniversal businesses were roughly equal. The Filmed Entertainment segment did particularly well, up 20.4 percent primarily on the success of *Despicable Me 3*, *Fifty Shades Darker*, and *The Fate of the Furious*. Higher volumes and margins delivered a 16 percent increase in net earnings; a 100-plus million share buyback drove per-share earnings some 18 percent higher. Revenue gains should run around 5 percent in 2018 and somewhat smaller in 2019; with per-share earnings gains somewhere in the 20–25 percent range for 2018 slowing to 5–7 percent for 2019—all depending on what happens with the Sky and other possible acquisitions.

Reasons to Buy

The addition of Comcast to the 2013 *100 Best* list was one we debated out of concern about cable companies in general. However, it continues to pay off handsomely; the shares have tripled since our decision. We like the company's strategic and operational focus—the acquisitions make sense, and the metrics they present truly describe what's important in the business—not just size and volume but also making customer relationships better and more profitable. The different pieces of the company fit together well.

As regular watchers of CNBC, MSNBC, Comcast Sports, and others, and admirers of the DreamWorks and other film platforms, we like the content assortment—it may not be the biggest, but it is one of the best content franchises. We expect content to become a bigger part of the business than the 20 percent it brings today. Comcast (and its competitors) are becoming a larger version of what the big three television networks once were. They own not only the content development and marketing but also the content delivery infrastructure, giving them a step up on most other content providers. There are no franchises or distributors to deal with, and they are free to develop independent content and compete with their own live and streamed content as they see fit. This is an extremely dynamic market model, and Comcast holds a leadership position.

The growth in market dominance, improved branding, and new revenues from the increased adoption of Xfinity all bode well, as does what we think will become the eventual reality of on-demand content as a standard—and profitable—product from suppliers such as Comcast.

Reasons for Caution

Although Comcast is certainly big enough to survive on its own, the trend toward industry consolidation brings the usual risks associated with acquisitions. The company is big and complex to manage, and faces extreme competition in most of its markets, although it may have at least a temporary bandwidth advantage at present. It's a lucrative and growing market; there will always be competing technologies and services for what Comcast has to offer.

SECTOR: **Telecommunications Services** ❑ BETA COEFFICIENT: **1.26** ❑ 10-YEAR COMPOUND EARNINGS PER-SHARE GROWTH: **21.5%** ❑ 10-YEAR COMPOUND DIVIDENDS PER-SHARE GROWTH: **16.5%**

	2010	2011	2012	2013	2014	2015	2016	2017
Revenues (mil)	37,937	55,842	62,570	64,657	68,775	74,510	80,403	84,526
Net income (mil)	3,535	4,377	6,203	6,816	8,380	8,171	8,485	9,850
Earnings per share	0.65	0.79	1.14	1.28	1.47	1.63	1.74	2.06
Dividends per share	0.19	0.23	0.33	0.39	0.45	0.50	0.55	0.61
Cash flow per share	1.85	2.22	2.68	2.83	3.24	3.45	3.80	4.33
Price: high	11.2	13.6	19.2	26.0	29.7	32.5	35.7	42.2
low	7.6	9.6	12.1	18.6	23.9	25.0	26.2	34.1

Website: www.comcast.com

GROWTH AND INCOME

ConocoPhillips Company

Ticker symbol: COP (NYSE) ❑ Large Cap ❑ Value Line financial strength rating: B++ ❑ Current yield: 1.7% ❑ Dividend raises, past 10 years: 8

Company Profile

Like the rest of the industry, ConocoPhillips was hit hard by the 50–70 percent haircut in the price of their main products, namely, oil and gas three years ago. You won't typically find companies that lose money, especially two years in a row, on our *100 Best* list. But we hung on to this one, first of all, because we expected a cyclical recovery in the price of oil (which indeed has happened) to cover about two-thirds of the dip. Second, and most importantly, we liked the different approach COP took, truly downsizing (or right-sizing) its business and retaining capital instead of borrowing to pay shareholders.

Thanks to the 2012 spin-off of refiner Phillips 66, ConocoPhillips is now a pure play in the "E&P" (exploration and production) sector. Although lower oil and gas prices have turned ConocoPhillips from a $54 billion multinational "E&P" company into a $29 billion one of late (with the refining unit, it was once a $240 billion company), COP is still one of the world's largest E&P enterprises. Headquartered in Houston, TX, the company operates in 16 countries (down from 30) with about 11,400 employees (down from over 19,000).

The company's E&P operations are geographically diverse, producing most of its resources in the US, including a large presence in Alaska's Prudhoe Bay. The company also has a large presence in US shale "fracking" regions, including Eagle Ford and Permian regions in Texas and the Bakken region in North Dakota. (Fracking was once "good"; then considered "bad" because of its relatively high cost. It's becoming "good" again as great strides in efficiency are lowering the breakeven cost.) As well, the company produces in Norway, the United Kingdom, western Canada, Australia, offshore Timor-Leste in the Timor Sea, Indonesia, Malaysia, Brunei, China, and Libya (but no longer Vietnam, Senegal, Nigeria, Algeria, or Russia). The top five producing regions, accounting for 75 percent of oil-equivalent production, are US Lower 48 (29 percent), Alaska (13 percent), Canada (12 percent), Australia/Timor Sea (12 percent), and Norway (10 percent).

Over the years, ConocoPhillips had become a strong natural gas play and a strong domestic energy player, with some 42 percent of total oil equivalents coming from the US (including Alaska). Recently the company has been focusing on "shorter cycle," less capital-intensive projects, selling non-producing gas assets and has been slowing deepwater exploration and stepping up "unconventional" plays—shale—all to optimize the balance sheet and cash flow. About $16 billion in "non-core" asset sales occurred in 2017, which dragged down reported earnings but kept cash flows strong; asset sales will likely curtail before 2019.

Financial Highlights, Fiscal Year 2017

In 2017, the average realized price for a barrel of crude oil equivalent was $51.96, 27 percent above the $40.86 received in 2016 but still well off pre-2015 levels. This plus a 4 percent production increase led to a 23 percent rise in revenues. Asset sales, many at less than book value, took a hit to reported earnings, which managed a modest positive figure for the first time in three years. Cash flows were healthy and ten times reported earnings, giving evidence to the fact that asset impairments were a big factor in reported earnings; the actual cash intake was fine. Continued energy price recovery and some production gains and asset purchases are expected to drive revenues 18–20 percent higher in 2018 and 8–10 percent higher again in 2019. Per-share earnings should recover dramatically into the $4.00 to $5.00 range by 2019 and well beyond that into the early part of the decade. Dividend increases, slow at first, will begin to chip away at the large 2016 cut but won't achieve those levels any time soon, while the company appears to have used the 2015–16 slump adroitly to repurchase shares—some 5 percent of them—and will proceed with modest buybacks through 2019. The company also retired about $10 billion in debt, some incurred during the crisis, and now has 25 percent less debt than it had before the crisis started.

Reasons to Buy

As CEO Ryan Lance put it, "ConocoPhillips has taken a leadership stance with a new approach to the E&P business, one designed to deliver predictable performance and superior returns across a wide range of commodity prices." The strategy of disposing assets, generating capital through asset sales and dividend cuts while still paying a constant percentage of cash flows to shareholders, reducing long-term debt, and making itself profitable at sub-$50 oil all seems to have paid off and is laying groundwork for a pretty strong future, with per-share earnings estimated north of $7 in a few years. For a company of Conoco's size, we think they're making the right moves.

We like the domestic slant on the production mix; it is lower cost and more stable than most. We don't have to add a measure of geopolitics into the long list of risk factors. With these factors plus the likelihood of a "leaner meaner" company emerging from the downturn, plus a still-decent dividend likely to rise substantially upon any favorable oil price movement, we think the future looks bright.

Reasons for Caution

The story of ConocoPhillips has been a story of change over the past five years. The company successfully divested the refining operations to gain focus—only to gain focus on the most volatile part of the business (which became far more volatile in 2015–16). E&P is risky by nature even with a steady oil price (although COP's domestically oriented portfolio reduces this risk); when you add in price volatility it makes for…well, a volatile mix. COP has taken its pain in stride, but the possibility of a continuing glut as more producers come on line with lower cost production could keep the headwinds blowing.

SECTOR: Energy ❏ BETA COEFFICIENT: **1.21** ❏ 10-YEAR COMPOUND EARNINGS PER-SHARE GROWTH: **NM** ❏ 10-YEAR COMPOUND DIVIDENDS PER-SHARE GROWTH: **NM**

	2010	2011	2012	2013	2014	2015	2016	2017
Revenues (bil)	189.4	244.8	62.0	54.4	52.5	30.7	23.7	29.1
Net income (bil)	8.8	12.1	7.4	8.0	6.2	(1.7)	(3.2)	0.7
Earnings per share	5.92	8.76	5.91	6.43	4.96	(1.39)	(2.52)	0.61
Dividends per share	2.16	2.64	2.64	2.70	2.84	2.94	1.00	1.06
Cash flow per share	12.50	15.63	11.47	12.57	11.79	5.97	4.77	6.44
Price: high	68.6	77.4	78.3	74.6	87.1	70.1	53.2	56.4
low	48.5	68.0	50.6	56.4	60.8	41.1	31.0	42.3

Website: www.conocophillips.com

AGGRESSIVE GROWTH

Corning Incorporated

Ticker symbol: GLW (NYSE) ❏ Large Cap ❏ Value Line financial strength rating: A ❏ Current yield: 2.5% ❏ Dividend raises, past 10 years: 7

Company Profile

When you think of Corning, you think of glass. The ticker symbol, in fact, reflects the company's name when it joined the NYSE—Glass Works. Although the company may have been best known for some time as a producer of common housewares such as drinking glasses and dinnerware (anyone remember Corelle?), Corning has long been at the cutting edge (ouch) of glass and ceramics research. In 1932 the company produced the enormous mirror for the Palomar Observatory's main telescope, a 102-inch behemoth that required a full year to cool once cast. Corning also developed and produces viewing glass for spacecraft and high-pressure submersibles. And, of course, the company's invention of high-transmissibility fiber-optic cable (and the production techniques required for efficient manufacturing) revolutionized modern telecommunications by providing high-speed, low-power data connections that were immune to electrical interference.

Corning is well known today as the producer of Gorilla Glass, the optically clear, mechanically tough, and electrically conductive material that makes smartphones possible. First employed in the original iPhone, Gorilla Glass is now ubiquitous in the smartphone market. But this isn't their only display-related business, as they also provide glass for LCD and OLED products. Recently, the company is showing interest in wireless (fiberless?) markets with acquisitions of two network hardware providers in anticipation of the rollout of 5G wireless technology.

These targeted acquisitions, though, are a relatively minor part of Corning's overall business strategy. Corning has historically grown organically via internally developed technologies and product development programs. The company continues to spend on R&D (7 percent of their top-line revenue last year), and you wouldn't go too far wrong in thinking of Corning as a materials science and research company with several "killer app" businesses that pay the rent, and then some.

Corning operates in five segments, nearly all centered on the glass business. Display Technologies (30 percent of FY2017 sales) is the world's largest producer of glass substrates for liquid crystal displays (LCDs) in Japan, China, Taiwan, and South Korea for the television and computer markets. Optical Communications (35 percent) makes fiber-optic cable and an assortment of connectivity and other products related to fiber for telecommunications companies, LAN, and data center applications. Specialty Materials (14 percent) provides a wide assortment of high-tech, glass-based materials, including the well-known Corning Gorilla Glass, so named for its endurance characteristics. This product is even gaining traction in automotive and architectural markets. Also out of this division comes a new bendable display substrate known as Willow Glass and a host of glass and ceramic products and formulations used in the semiconductor industry, precision instruments, and even astronomy and ophthalmology. The Environmental Technologies segment (11 percent) makes ceramic substrates and filters for emission control systems, mostly for gasoline and diesel engines. The Life Sciences segment (9 percent) makes laboratory glass and plastic wares. An "All Other" segment accounts for less than 1 percent.

The company competes with a number of suppliers, mostly Japanese, on a variety of fronts, and in 2016 acquired a 40 percent equity interest in Hemlock Semiconductor Group, a producer of high-purity polycrystalline silicon used in the semiconductor and solar industries.

Promising innovations include the adaptation of its "Willow Glass," thinner than a dollar bill, for ultrathin, ultrasensitive touchscreens to improve size and weight characteristics of mobile devices. Eventually this will evolve into bendable, curved, and curving glass displays, allowing us to literally wear our devices—an exciting prospect that companies such as Apple, Samsung, and a host of others are investing in heavily.

Gorilla Glass continues to find new applications in architectural and automotive designs—such as the company's new "Dynamic Windows," architectural glass panels, which automatically darken, reducing energy consumption, and new lighter windshields, sunroofs, and other glass products for cars.

Financial Highlights, Fiscal Year 2017

Corning's FY2017 benefited from a strong fourth quarter, and overall the year brought gains in most segments. Companywide, sales were up 8 percent while earnings gained 30 percent, a strong showing in what was expected to be a tepid year. Displays saw some moderation in pricing pressures as the year wore on, and volumes were improved, but revenues were still off 7 percent. Corning expects similar volume increases in both 2018 and 2019, with their own volumes outpacing the market and costs improving as they bring a new generation fab on line. Optical was the star in 2017, with healthy gains in both sales and income (some due to acquisitions), and a promising outlook in 2018. Overall, estimates call for 6 percent gains in revenues and 12–14 percent gains in income for both FY2018 and FY2019, reflecting a more favorable product mix and improved pricing and cost bases for both Display and Environmental.

Reasons to Buy

It's always great when you develop a product that's accepted in the market as a standard. Even better is when your customers come to you directly and ask you to develop a product that meets their needs. It's so much easier to sell something to someone when they already want to buy it.

Corning seeks out these opportunities, and as a business model it works well. In fact, two of their mainstay products (Gorilla Glass and catalytic cores) were developed in close partnership with the end customer. In this vein, the company announced in July of 2017 the development of Valor Glass, a line of packaging solutions for the injectable medicines market. Compared to existing products, Valor Glass provides much higher levels of chemical stability and mechanical strength. It is the first purpose-built glass for the containment of medicines and vaccines and was designed in partnership with two of the biggest players in the pharma business, Merck and Pfizer. The finished product offers longer shelf lives, improved durability, higher yields, and higher processing speeds for the packaging of the contents. Corning expects to invest $4 billion in additional R&D and production facilities for the Valor line.

As Corning puts it, we are now in the "Glass Age"—many promising new technologies are built on a foundation of high-tech glass products, and Corning is the best pure play in this niche. We like companies that stand to benefit no matter how a market plays out. Our CarMax pick benefits whether Ford or Toyota or Hyundai wins; CarMax sells used cars no matter what. At least for glass displays, Corning is in the same position—whether Samsung or Apple or LG wins the smartphone contest, Corning wins. The explosion in smart devices and the new technologies Corning is likely to bring to that space create some excitement down the road. We think the inevitable advent of wearable mobile computing devices will be a big spark for this company.

Aside from the short-term speed bump in display technologies, the core businesses like fiber optics are doing well, and we expect some of the new technologies like Gorilla Glass and the self-darkening glass products to become core businesses. The advent of 5G wireless will create opportunities for new and clever implementations of fiber optics, and Corning will be at the center of it with their fiber and connector businesses. Wireless 5G (compared to traditional wireless cell technology) consists of a multitude of shorter-range RF transceivers interconnected with fiber to provide much higher bandwidth with much lower latencies.

Also worth noting is Corning's stated intent to return plenty of cash to shareholders both in the form of dividends and the share buybacks and appears positioned to do so going forward, especially on the buyback front. By the end of 2018, Corning will have reduced share count almost 50 percent from 2010, with an expected dividend increase of 30 percent by the end of 2019.

Reasons for Caution

While its product portfolio is broader than it was 15 years ago, supplying well beyond the telecom industry, the company is still subject to business and inventory cycles. Glass, without the right amount of innovation, is a commodity business with plenty of foreign competition.

SECTOR: Information Technology ❑ **BETA COEFFICIENT: 1.25** ❑ 10-YEAR COMPOUND EARNINGS PER-SHARE GROWTH: **4.5%** ❑ 10-YEAR COMPOUND DIVIDENDS PER-SHARE GROWTH: **20.0%**

		2010	2011	2012	2013	2014	2015	2016	2017
Revenues (mil)		6,632	7,890	8,012	7,819	9,715	9,111	9,390	10,116
Net income (mil)		3,275	2,620	1,728	1,961	2,472	1,339	1,013	1,325
Earnings per share		2.07	1.76	1.15	1.34	1.73	1.00	0.98	1.48
Dividends per share		0.20	0.23	0.32	0.39	0.52	0.36	0.54	0.62
Cash flow per share		2.64	2.49	1.85	2.12	2.79	2.15	2.21	2.81
Price:	high	21.1	23.4	14.6	18.1	23.5	25.2	25.3	32.8
	low	15.5	11.5	10.6	11.6	16.5	15.4	16.1	24.1

Website: www.corning.com

AGGRESSIVE GROWTH

Costco Wholesale Corporation

Ticker symbol: COST (NASDAQ) ❑ Large Cap ❑ Value Line financial strength rating: A+ ❑ Current yield: 1.0% ❑ Dividend raises, past 10 years: 10

Company Profile

Every year we take a hard look at Costco, for it has become so large that we wonder how it possibly could keep growing—and how could the stock possibly keep going up—and it does. That remains the case even after a sharp dip in late 2017 due to general indigestion in the retail sector over Amazon's presence.

Every year we wonder if Costco has any room to grow, whether it is long in the tooth as a retailing concept, too small in the margins, too expensive to buy as a stock, and too "mass" intensive to appeal to today's variety of custom-demanding millennials. Now we have to judge it regularly against the hard realities of e-commerce. We almost ditched our four-wheel flatbed two years ago and headed for the exits. But we didn't—and we're still impressed with Costco's appeal both to cost-conscious millennials and to a whole lot of cost-conscious "older folks" like us as well. And we don't really think e-commerce has yet become a major threat to the sort of shopping that requires four-wheel flatbeds. As such, this powerful retailer still keeps its spot on the 2019 *100 Best* list.

Costco Wholesale Corporation operates a multinational chain of membership warehouses, mainly under the Costco Wholesale name, that carry brand-name merchandise at substantially lower prices than are typically found at conventional wholesale or retail sources. The warehouse sales model was designed to help small- to medium-sized businesses reduce costs in purchasing for resale and for everyday business use, but as most know, the individual consumer has been their big growth driver. The company capitalizes on size and operational efficiencies, such as "cross-docking" shipments directly from manufacturers to stores, to deliver attractive pricing to its customers. Based on sales volume, Costco is the largest membership warehouse club chain and second-largest general retailer in the world.

Costco carries a broad line of product categories, including groceries, appliances, television and media, automotive supplies, toys, hardware, sporting goods, jewelry, cameras, books, housewares, apparel, health and beauty aids, tobacco, furniture, office supplies, and office equipment. Approximately 21 percent of sales come from packaged food and beverages, 14 percent from "fresh food" and 20 percent from "sundries"—snack foods, candy, alcohol, and cleaning supplies. Another 16 percent comes from hardlines—electronics, appliances, hardware, automotive, office supplies, and health and beauty aids—and 12 percent from softlines—primarily clothing, housewares, media, jewelry, and domestics. The rest, including gasoline, pharmacy, optical, and other services, form a catchall "other" category. The emergence of Costco as a grocer of choice cannot be missed, with its appeal to the more cost-conscious set of trend-conscious food consumers.

Additionally, Costco Wholesale Industries, a division of the company, operates manufacturing businesses, including special food packaging, optical laboratories, hearing aid centers, and jewelry distribution. The company operates 536 discount gas stations worldwide. "Ancillary" businesses such as jewelry, optometry, gasoline, and others, of course, are designed to bring people into the stores. A wide and growing variety of products are sold under its "Kirkland" private label; at $35 billion in sales the brand accounts for about 27 percent of the business.

Costco is open only to members of its tiered membership plan, the higher "Executive" tier at $120 annually (versus $60 for the standard membership) gaining access to reward points and other perks and discounts. Executive members account for about one-third of the base and two-thirds of the sales. In all, there are 90.3 million members (up 4 percent), with a 90 percent membership renewal rate in the US and Canada.

As of the end of 2017 Costco has 746 locations: 518 in the US and Puerto Rico (up from 506), 98 in Canada (versus 94), 37 in Mexico (versus 36), 28 in the UK (unchanged), 26 in Japan (versus 25), 13 in South Korea (12), 13 in Taiwan (12), 9 in Australia (8), and 2 in Spain (2). Costco added two new countries, one store each: France and Iceland. The company also has a significant and growing e-commerce presence at www.costco.com. It still accounts for only 4 percent of revenues, and the company is experimenting with same-day delivery through its Costco Grocery service, which hasn't gained much traction to date but may do so as customers seek to avoid crowds at the stores. The point is that—even though the "flatbed" shopper isn't easily lured by e-commerce—the company is investing on future customer experiences.

Financial Highlights, Fiscal Year 2017

After a flat 2016, same store sales rose 4 percent in FY2017, leading the way to a 9 percent sales gain overall (which also includes a slight bump due to the 53-week year). Revenue from membership fees, helped along by a midyear price increase, rose 8 percent to $2.85 billion, not coincidentally slightly exceeding the total net income for the year of $2.56 billion, itself up just over 9 percent for the year. The opening of 23 to 26 new stores, a gain in market share after some Sam's Club closings (about 10 percent of their base), international expansion, tax cuts, and general execution improvements are forecast to bring an 18–20 percent earnings gain on a 7 percent rise in revenue in 2018, followed by a 10–12 percent earnings gain on a 7 percent revenue rise in 2019. Modest dividend increases and share buybacks look to continue.

Reasons to Buy

Costco is in an attractive best-of-both-worlds niche: it is a price leader consistent with the attitudes of today's more frugal consumer, yet it enjoys a reputation for being more upscale than the competition. We've all heard the boast, "I got it at Costco" from even our most affluent and high-minded friends—and of course, there's everybody else.

We also continue to like the international expansion and think the formula will play well overseas—although their ambitious European and Asian plans may be tempered a bit by local preferences for small package sizes and the general lack of storage space. Any US resident who has hosted a visitor from abroad knows that Costco is a favored destination during the visit. We expect international expansion will be one of the company's primary growth drivers over the next ten years. We also applaud the recent move to switch exclusive credit card use from American Express to a co-branded Citigroup Visa credit card (in addition to accepting ordinary Visa and MasterCard debit cards). This card is less expensive and more accessible to most members and has broadened sales appeal. Costco also gets high marks for employee pay, satisfaction, and loyalty, and for corporate citizenship in general.

In all, the company has a strong brand in a highly competitive sector relatively immune from the Amazon threat and is well managed.

Reasons for Caution

The major concern today is the emergence of e-commerce. More frequent visits and lower tickets already suggest a convenience model is taking hold, and eventually these consumers could defect altogether. Or could they? True, you can buy much of what you get at Costco online. But is it really more convenient to receive huge packages on your front doorstep? Or just to go out once a week and get what you need? Or get it delivered locally? Time will tell, but Costco has the advantage of ease, we think, when it comes to shopping for large quantities of basic, and not so basic, needs. Another concern is the dependence on low-margin food and sundry lines. That said, food does get customers into the store and gets them there more than once a week. More store traffic means more and more regular store sales overall.

We do fret over the high share price, low margins, and dependence on membership fees for profitability. All three bring a measure of vulnerability to the stock—a misstep could be costly. On the flip side, management has shown its ability to navigate through difficult periods, the brand is strong, and the prospects for a global footprint, above all else, are encouraging for the future. There are a lot of headwinds in today's retail space, but we think Costco is unique enough and strong enough to prosper.

SECTOR: **Retail** ❑ BETA COEFFICIENT: **0.96** ❑ 10-YEAR COMPOUND EARNINGS PER-SHARE GROWTH: **10.0%** ❑ 10-YEAR COMPOUND DIVIDENDS PER-SHARE GROWTH: **13.5%**

	2010	2011	2012	2013	2014	2015	2016	2017
Revenues (bil)	77.9	88.9	99.1	105.1	112.6	116.1	118.7	129.0
Net income (mil)	1,307	1,462	1,741	1,977	2,058	2,334	2,350	2,564
Earnings per share	2.93	3.30	3.97	4.49	4.65	5.27	5.33	5.82
Dividends per share	0.77	0.89	1.03	1.17	1.33	1.51	1.70	1.90
Cash flow per share	4.85	5.34	6.13	6.69	7.05	7.90	8.24	9.00
Price: high	73.2	88.7	106.0	126.1	146.8	169.7	169.6	195.4
low	53.4	69.5	78.8	98.6	109.5	117.0	138.5	175.8

Website: www.costco.com

AGGRESSIVE GROWTH

Craft Brew Alliance, Inc.

Ticker symbol: BREW (NASDAQ) ❑ Small Cap ❑ Value Line financial strength rating: B
❑ Current yield: Nil ❑ Dividend raises, past 10 years: NA

Company Profile

Five years ago we added a "consumer hotline" in the form of coauthor Peter's personal email address to field questions, get feedback, and to overall make this book serve the readers' needs—*your* needs—better. We've received plenty of good feedback, fielded a lot of excellent questions, and have in some cases found out about new investment ideas or better ways to present the ones we have. One of the more common questions has been to the effect of "Why don't you include any of the major brewing or other alcoholic beverage makers?" Like most other questions, we pondered this carefully and pretty much stuck to our knitting by keeping them off the list. Why? Not because we are abstainers or teetotalers—not hardly! It was because of intense competition and our reluctance to declare that we understand fickle consumer tastes. But 2019 is a new year, and we're bringing you a brewer. A craft brewer. Really, a small conglomerate of craft brewers making the best of big and small—small brewing, big distribution—to bring differentiated, interesting brews efficiently to all parts of the country. That small brewing conglomerate is called Craft Brew Alliance.

Craft Brew Alliance, Inc., is the sixth-largest craft brewing company in the US and is a leader in brewing, branding, and bringing to market world-class craft beers. It was largely formed by the 2008 merger of Portland, Oregon's Widmer Brothers (Widmer Hefeweizen and others) and Seattle's Redhook (Redhook Ale and others) and bolstered considerably by adding Hawaii's Kona Brewing Co. (Longboard Island Lager and others) in 2010. Additionally, the company founded gluten-free brewer Omission Brewing Co. in 2012 and created brewing and distribution relationships with three local partner brands: Appalachian Mountain Brewery in western North Carolina, Cisco Brewers in New England, and Wynwood Brewing Company in the Miami, FL, area. Finally, the company launched a hard cider brand called Square Mile in 2013. Kona is now by far the largest brand, accounting for 58 percent of the volume and growing at 7 percent annually. Widmer accounts for 17 percent and declined 17 percent in 2017; Redhook accounts for 13 percent and declined 26 percent, Omission accounts for 6 percent and grew 3 percent, and "all others" (partnerships) accounted for 6 percent and grew 34 percent.

The strategy is to bring the best of craft brew to a broad US market (and to specific markets in the case of the three partner brands just mentioned) efficiently with a wide audience and strong brand recognition. Key to this strategy is a 2016 master distributor agreement with Anheuser Busch, which allows Craft Brew access to A-B's national distribution network: Craft Brew reps sell the product, then deliver it nationally to all 50 states through A-B's wholesalers so that Craft Brew does not have to warehouse, end-distribute, or collect from national and local accounts. Most craft brewers, if they attempt national distribution at all, can't scale enough to handle their own distribution; Craft Brew's A-B alliance gives it a significant leg up on many of its craft brew brethren.

Craft Brew operates three major breweries in Oregon, New Hampshire, and Hawaii, in addition to an "innovation brewery" in Seattle for small-batch blends; the other three major breweries also have small-batch capability. The company also utilizes the A-B brewery in Fort Collins, CO, to brew up to 300,000 barrels a year as part of the partnership agreement. Another agreement made in 2018 allows A-B to brew some of its craft beers in Craft Brew's Oregon and New Hampshire facilities.

In addition to the packaging, Craft Brew also owns and operates five brew-pub restaurants in towns as part of a consumer awareness and R&D effort. The brew pubs generate about 13 percent of revenues and about 3 percent of gross profit.

Financial Highlights, Fiscal Year 2017

FY2017 was the first full year that Craft Brew realized the benefits of the A-B agreement; while revenues rose modestly by 2.5 percent, net income moved out of negative territory to $2.6 million, one of the best levels since inception. The Kona brand continues to excel even in a flat (pardon the pun) to declining national beer market (total sales slightly negative, craft brews up only 1.4 percent in total for 2017). The company is looking for ways to bolster its two classic brands, Widmer and Redhook, through adding specialty seasonal offerings and varieties. The national cost structure will get continued focus—all leading to a projected 3–4 percent sales gain for 2018 and a near tripling in net income; the bubbles should continue to rise to a 7–8 percent sales gain for 2019 and a 50 percent increase in net income.

Reasons to Buy

Craft Brew operates in the best of both worlds in the beer industry: it captures the high-value-add, differentiated experience, and panache of the individualized craft brew, while enjoying the benefits of national distribution to expand the market and lower costs. Profits are expected to increase dramatically over the coming years. The business strategy is strong and enduring (the A-B agreement lasts until 2028), and may lead to more international distribution, more brands under the umbrella, and possibly even an A-B or some other acquisition as the model proves itself. The flagship Kona brand continues to be a solid winner in the market—mahalo!

Reasons for Caution

As a percentage of alcoholic beverage consumption, total beer consumption has been declining. No matter how you look at it, the beer industry is ultra-competitive, and the craft brew segment has been at the center of that competitive struggle. When Widmer and Redhook got together in 2008 there were 200 "craft" brands; now there are over 5,000. Craft is the key trend in the beer industry, but it's drawing a lot of competition and has always had to look over its shoulder at competitive international brands (Corona, Heineken, etc.) and at ersatz "craft" brands offered by major brewers like Blue Moon (Molson Coors). While we applaud their strategy—even a good strategy will yield thin margins and results under such a competitive load—we also find the recent decline in the Redhook and Widmer brands unsettling, though Kona is more than making up the difference, and Omission seems like a winning concept as well. Consumer tastes in this area are fickle, and who knows what people, especially millennials, will be drinking five years from now. Pop the top on this new Small Cap, and even if you don't make money you'll enjoy the experience.

SECTOR: Consumer Staples ❑ **BETA COEFFICIENT: 0.45** ❑ **10-YEAR COMPOUND EARNINGS PER-SHARE GROWTH: NA** ❑ **10-YEAR COMPOUND DIVIDENDS PER-SHARE GROWTH: NA**

	2010	2011	2012	2013	2014	2015	2016	2017
Revenues (mil)	131.7	149.2	169.3	179.2	200.0	204.2	202.5	207.5
Net income (mil)	1.7	2.9	2.5	2.0	3.1	2.2	(0.3)	2.6
Earnings per share	0.10	0.15	0.13	0.10	0.16	0.12	(0.02)	0.14
Dividends per share	—	—	—	—	—	—	—	—
Cash flow per share	0.46	0.53	0.52	0.53	0.61	0.62	0.56	0.68
Price: high	9.9	10.2	8.9	18.7	18.0	14.3	22.4	20.1
low	2.2	5.1	5.6	6.3	10.1	6.8	6.8	12.0

Website: www.craftbrew.com

CONSERVATIVE GROWTH

CVS Health Corporation

Ticker symbol: CVS (NYSE) ❑ Large Cap ❑ Value Line financial strength rating: A++ ❑ Current yield: 3.0% ❑ Dividend raises, past 10 years: 10

Company Profile

Stanley and Sid Goldstein were distributing health and beauty products in the early 1960s when they decided to branch out into retailing, opening their first Consumer Value Store in Lowell, MA, in 1963. The CVS chain had grown to 40 outlets by 1969, the year they sold the business to Melville Shoes. Melville underwent a restructuring in the mid-1990s, spinning off CVS and other retail units.

Stan and Sid should be proud. CVS is now the largest pharmacy healthcare provider in the US and ranks seventh on the *Fortune* 500 list—and could be headed higher. In keeping with its mission, three years ago it changed its name from "CVS Caremark" to "CVS Health." Its flagship Retail Pharmacy domestic drugstore chain operates 9,803 retail and specialty pharmacy stores and 1,134 walk-in healthcare clinics in 49 states, the District of Columbia, Puerto Rico, and Brazil. The company holds the leading market share in 88 of the 100 largest US drugstore markets, more than any other retail drugstore chain, and holds a 24 percent share of the US retail pharmacy market. Over time, it has expanded through acquiring other players in the category—Osco, Sav-On, Eckerd, and Longs Drugs. CVS's purchase of Longs Drugs in 2008 vaulted the company into the lead position in the US drug retail market, ahead of Walgreens.

With the 2007 acquisition of pharmacy benefits manager Caremark, the 2015 acquisition of 1,700 Target pharmacies and 80 health clinics, and the 2016 acquisition of nursing home pharmacy provider Omnicare, the company took its biggest step forward in late 2017 announcing the plan to acquire leading health insurer Aetna (up to now, another *100 Best Stock*) for $77 billion. This is a truly disruptive acquisition; the result would be a vertical combination of a payer (Aetna) and a provider (CVS core businesses) leading to a new level or at least a different kind of cooperation between these elements in the healthcare food chain. What remains to be seen is (1) regulatory approval, which we think will happen, and (2) how well the vertical combination will work in practice—will insurance competitor UnitedHealth push business away from CVS because the latter owns archrival Aetna?

Anyway, let's return to CVS in its current form. Its stores are situated primarily in strip shopping centers or free-standing locations, with a typical store ranging in size from 8,000–13,000 square feet. Most new units include a drive-thru pharmacy. Prescriptions generate over 75 percent of Retail Pharmacy sales, which in turn makes up about 46 percent of the company's total sales and is far more profitable, generating 80 percent of gross profits.

The Caremark acquisition transformed CVS from strictly a retailer into the nation's leading manager of pharmacy benefits, the middleman between pharmaceutical companies and individuals with drug benefit coverage. The Caremark acquisition forms the core of the company's Pharmacy Benefits Management (PBM) operations, and the Pharmacy Services segment now makes up about 62 percent of sales—but only 20 percent of gross profit. This is a low-margin business, with gross profit of about 5 percent of revenue versus more than 30 percent for the Retail Pharmacy segment. CVS estimates that they own 30 percent of the US PBM market.

Part of the Retail Pharmacy segment, the company's MinuteClinic concept is especially interesting in today's climate of managing healthcare costs. CVS now has 1,134 clinics (including 80 new clinics in Target stores) in 33 states and DC, offering basic health services like flu shots given by 2,200 nurse practitioners and physician's assistants in a convenient retail environment. Plans are to grow MinuteClinic into 1,500 locations in 35 states by 2019. The concept gradually is gaining mainstream acceptance with 28 million patient visits to date—and of course, those clinics located in CVS stores bring traffic to those stores. We see the MinuteClinic concept playing well with Aetna in a joint effort to reduce doctor visits and lower costs.

Financial Highlights, Fiscal Year 2017

FY2017, aside from the Aetna news, was kind of a mixed year. Revenues in total rose 5.7 percent, but Retail sales were off 2.6 percent due to withdrawal from participation in certain networks—and, who knows—a minor Amazon effect? (We do think the convenience factor makes much of CVS's retail business immune from Amazon, but now Amazon has announced its intention to enter the prescription market—stay tuned). Pharmacy sales were up 9 percent, but as shown earlier, this is a lower margin business. In total, net earnings decreased 4.6 percent as a result. Forecasts, not including Aetna, call for a 2–4 percent revenue rise yearly through 2019 with 3–6 percent net earnings increases. What happens after the merger remains to be seen, but we know it will increase debt levels and share counts. Dividend growth has accelerated recently, but again we don't know what will happen after Aetna.

Reasons to Buy

Clearly the Aetna combination will change the CVS landscape as well as the whole healthcare sector. We expect it to work in CVS's favor, perhaps strongly, but it may take time. The ability to vertically integrate major pieces of the healthcare system to reduce costs and cut friction will be tested in the merger. Cost efficiencies and competitive advantages are the hopeful result; time will tell. Typically, we take companies going through major strategic shifts like this off the *100 Best* list until the dust settles, but in this case, we like the combination enough to stick with it; additionally, the uncertainty has driven the stock price down through much of 2017 and 2018, giving a good buying opportunity.

CVS is already a smartly diversified market leader. Cross-selling of prescriptions, retail products, and health services all seems to be working well and is an important part of the strategy. Now Aetna is added to this powerful crucible.

Reasons for Caution

The acquisition is huge. There is execution risk, as well as marketplace risk if rival players (UnitedHealth, Walgreens, to name a few) align their stars to compete, and channel conflict, as described earlier, is also a risk. One also cannot ignore Amazon's stated intentions on this market. Beyond these, old risks still linger: some of the features of the Trump administration agenda create new uncertainties for CVS, including drug pricing and the Affordable Care Act. All together, the environment CVS is operating in has become less stable than years past, but we think the company has the footprint, the resources, and the management qualities to effectively manage through the change—and we feel the Aetna combination should be looked at as an opportunity.

SECTOR: **Retail** ❑ BETA COEFFICIENT: **1.03** ❑ 10-YEAR COMPOUND EARNINGS PER-SHARE GROWTH: **14.5%** ❑ 10-YEAR COMPOUND DIVIDENDS PER-SHARE GROWTH: **25.5%**

		2010	2011	2012	2013	2014	2015	2016	2017
Revenues (bil)		98.0	107.2	123.1	126.7	139.4	153.2	177.5	185.8
Net income (mil)		3,700	3,766	4,394	4,902	5,255	5,810	6,332	6,042
Earnings per share		2.67	2.80	3.43	4.00	4.51	5.18	5.84	5.90
Dividends per share		0.35	0.50	0.65	0.90	1.10	1.40	1.70	2.00
Cash flow per share		3.75	4.10	4.99	5.74	6.30	7.18	8.27	8.40
Price:	high	37.8	39.5	49.8	72.0	98.6	113.6	106.7	84.7
	low	26.8	31.3	41.0	49.9	64.9	81.4	69.3	66.8

Website: www.cvs.com

AGGRESSIVE GROWTH

Daktronics, Inc.

Ticker symbol: DAKT (NASDAQ) ❑ Small Cap ❑ Value Line financial strength rating: B+ ❑ Current yield: 3.1% ❑ Dividend raises, past 10 years: 7

Company Profile

You're driving down the highway. You're thinking about getting rid of a month's worth of grime and dirt and crud from your car. Suddenly, in vivid Technicolor, you see a billboard ahead on your right. Not just any old indifferent and ignorable billboard displaying the same old thing months on end. It's brightly lit. It flashes an offer. Five Star Car Wash, at this exit, has a "Today Only—25 Percent Off" special. Twenty minutes ago, you passed a high-resolution, multicolor electronic sign flashing "Road Work Ahead—Current Delay 30 Minutes" with a colorfully mapped detour and plenty of color emphasizing important street names and route numbers. So, you tap the brakes, hit the right lane, and off the interstate you go. A win-win—you have a clean car, and the car wash, having a lighter day than usual and temporarily pricing its services accordingly, gets another unit through their system.

How great Wayne Gretzky made famous the idea of "skating where the puck is going," and it's still one of our favorite investing maxims. Like it or not, we think such real-time, highly visual signage is where the puck is going in marketing: real-time visual displays to complement your real-time mobile devices. Give it time, and it will come. Give it time (and we've given it a lot; this particular puck has taken longer than we expected when we added Daktronics five years ago), and there will be real-time visual graphic displays on park benches and subway entrances. Give it time, and there will be "digital street furniture" and such just about everywhere. Give it time, and there will be large video displays in entertainment venues, gambling casinos, and the like. Give it time, and vividly colorful video displays will become standard architectural elements on modern office buildings.

How do you invest in this looming megatrend? There's a small company located almost literally in the middle of nowhere—Brookings, SD—that makes this stuff. Chances are this company made both of the signs mentioned previously. "Digital Street Furniture" is actually one of their product lines. Their core and founding business is really the large multimedia scoreboards in place in a growing number of sports arenas. The company, Daktronics, has a hand in an assortment of places where digital display technology can make a difference in outdoor environments, from $40 million scoreboards to the variable dollars-and-cents-per-gallon digital displays outside your local gas station.

Daktronics—a rare "Small Cap"' pick on the *100 Best* list—is the world's leading supplier of electronic scoreboards, large electronic display systems, digital messaging solutions, and related software and support services for sporting, commercial, and transportation applications. Business segments include Commercial, Live Events, High School Parks and Recreation, Transportation, and International: these groups are organized around customer segments and are all set up to create and sell unique applications of the core product lines of the company, which include video display systems, scoring and timing systems, digital billboards, digital street furniture, and simpler message displays like price, time, and temperature displays. Most of the company's products are based on LED technology with low to high resolution and embedded digital controllers. Here is a bit more "color" on the five segments:

- Commercial (25 percent of FY2017 revenue) sells a variety of digital signage to auto dealer, restaurant, gaming, retail petroleum (gas stations), and shopping center markets. Vivid video displays used for architectural or commercial purposes as part of the full building design is another emerging subsegment of this business.
- Live Events (36 percent of revenue) produces the traditional and some highly customized scoreboards, as well as signs for entertainment venues, including programmable displays, parking information signs, and even specialized signs for places of worship.
- High School Parks and Recreation (14 percent) includes not only digital-age marquee signs for theaters and other venues but also for the box office, merchandise sales areas, and others.
- Transportation (9 percent) covers the freeway signs; there is also plenty of digital signage in airports, train stations, public parking areas, and other public transit facilities.
- International (15 percent) sells all applications into international markets.

Overall, Daktronics has about a 30 percent share of the LED video display market, making it the number one player, and as much as 70 percent of the variable message highway sign market in the US. In early 2016 the company acquired Canadian digital media solutions provider ADFLOW

Networks, signaling a greater emphasis on providing complete solutions, not just LED hardware. In early 2017 the company rolled out new lines of ultra–high definition visual displays, and in early 2018 the company unveiled a next-generation full-color no-maintenance overhead variable message sign that is winning praise in the industry.

The company has 2,709 employees—including, somewhat unusually, about 400 interns and students on the payroll mostly from the local South Dakota State University. Retired cofounder and chairman Aelred J. Kurtenbach, a PhD electrical engineer and professor at SDSU, owns 5.1 percent of the shares. His son, Reece A. Kurtenbach, runs the company. The website, at www.daktronics.com, is a fun and instructive ride.

Financial Highlights, Fiscal Year 2017

Several crosscurrents affected the business once again in FY2017, as the different segments turned in mixed results. Declines in billboard shipments in the Commercial segment were offset by $9.9 million in revenue reported by the new ADFLOW group. Completion of some live-event projects helped revenues in that group, Transportation was flat; international was soft. The net was a 55 percent gain in net income from $10.3 million to $16 million on slightly higher margins and a 7 percent sales increase. Backlogs were up about 10 percent. Forecasts into 2018 and 2019 call for 3–4 percent revenue gains (which we feel is a bit conservative) with net income gains in the 20–25 percent range annually. The dividend, which was cut in 2016, may start a return to and go beyond previous levels in 2018.

Reasons to Buy

Since beaches and surf weren't part of the landscape when we were growing up in the Midwest, like any normal kids we were fascinated with signs of all kinds. Daktronics takes signs to a new level.

We continue to feel that such digital signage is a big part of the future of mass, real-time marketing communications—a "system" including your mobile device plus electronic signage—like it or not. Overall, we like situations where a core technology is applied successfully to an ever-larger number of end markets. We also think as such digital signage becomes more mainstream, the company will be able to produce in larger volumes, even mass-produce more of their applications, which should drive down unit costs and increase profitability. We see advantages in the South Dakota ("Dak-tronics?" We didn't get it for a long time) location, too—a dedicated workforce and low cost of doing business. As well, the company has virtually no debt.

All this said, Daktronics hasn't performed as well as hoped for when we added it to our *100 Best* list in 2015 in an attempt to get a bit of niche technology and Small Cap growth "energy" into the mix. The company just hasn't hit its stride (nor its own production capacity) with its business, though backlogs and order flows are getting stronger. Market acceptance of digital signage on a broad scale just hasn't happened yet. We hope to see a significant near-term advance in Transportation and Commercial applications—this is where we think the bulk of future expansion really lies. Our patience is paid for in part by the attractive dividend (though it was cut in mid-2016), and we hope for an eventual "breakout" in this enticing market. We're hoping we're not wrong, just early.

Reasons for Caution

While the company is the top player in most of its markets, there is plenty of product and price competition in the form of major Japanese firms like Mitsubishi (and if you've been to Tokyo, you know how mainstream digital signage can be). We do also wonder if environmental movements will rise up to quell what could easily become overstimulating visual "pollution," but so far to our knowledge this hasn't happened on a large scale.

More conventionally, Daktronics clearly has a riskier profile than most of our picks. Order flow and delivery timing can vary considerably especially in the Live Events segment, and performance overall has been more erratic than we would like. But we continue to think the business will smooth out and prosper once electronic commercial signage becomes more mainstream.

SECTOR: **Information Technology** ❏ BETA COEFFICIENT: **1.19** ❏ 10-YEAR COMPOUND EARNINGS PER-SHARE GROWTH: **-6.5%** ❏ 10-YEAR COMPOUND DIVIDENDS PER-SHARE GROWTH: **20.0%**

	2010	2011	2012	2013	2014	2015	2016	2017
Revenues (mil)	442	489	518	552	616	570	590	625
Net income (mil)	14.2	8.5	22.8	22.2	20.9	2.1	10.3	16.0
Earnings per share	0.34	0.20	0.53	0.51	0.47	0.05	0.23	0.35
Dividends per share	0.10	0.10	0.22	0.23	0.39	0.40	0.40	0.27
Cash flow per share	0.81	0.62	0.91	0.85	0.82	0.43	0.85	0.75
Price: high	17.3	16.7	11.9	16.1	15.6	13.2	10.9	11.1
low	7.1	8.0	6.3	9.4	10.8	7.2	5.9	7.6

Website: www.daktronics.com

Deere & Company

Ticker symbol: DE (NYSE) ❑ Large Cap ❑ Value Line financial strength rating: A++ ❑ Current yield: 1.5% ❑ Dividend raises, past 10 years: 8

Company Profile

We finally got our way with Deere.

As the slogan tells us, "Nothing Runs like a Deere." And for the past year and a half, you could also say, "Nothing Runs like Deere Stock." A pleasant surprise, for sure—we almost gave up on this one as the business, the stock, and farm economy languished through the middle part of the decade. Deere became a severe test of our mettle and our conviction to stay with good businesses for the long term. The brand and business are best in class, but mid-decade business conditions of agricultural surpluses, a strong dollar, declining exports, low farm prices, and low farm incomes had Deere and most other ag-related companies stuck in the knee-deep mud of cyclical lows. Inventories of both new and used product were piling up at dealerships. But due to brand strength, loyalty (ours and its customers'), the propensity of good companies to use downturns to become more efficient, and our long-term belief in agriculture, we hung on to Deere. We're glad we did, and it has become a classic example of why one should hang on to a business strong to its core, its shares having more than doubled since its 2016 lows.

Founded in 1837, Deere & Company grew from a one-man blacksmith shop into a worldwide corporation that today does business in more than 160 countries and employs more than 56,000 people around the globe. Deere has a diverse base of operations reporting into three segments: Agriculture and Turf, Construction and Forestry, and Financial Services.

Deere has been the world's premier producer of agricultural equipment for nearly 50 years. The Agriculture and Turf segment produces and distributes tractors, loaders, combines, harvesters, seeding, mowers, hay baling, tilling, crop care and application, and other equipment. If it's used on a farm and requires an engine, Deere likely offers it.

Additionally, over the years, the company has developed and expanded lines of turf and utility equipment, including riding lawn equipment and walk-behind mowers, golf course equipment, utility vehicles, and commercial mowing and snow-removal equipment. Deere also offers a broad line of associated implements: integrated agricultural management systems technology and solutions; precision agricultural irrigation equipment and supplies; landscape and nursery products; and other outdoor power products.

With the Construction and Forestry segment, Deere is also the world's leading manufacturer of forestry equipment and a major manufacturer of heavy construction machines (Caterpillar is still the market leader in this segment). Major lines include construction, earthmoving, material-handling, and timber-harvesting machines including but not limited to backhoe loaders; crawler dozers and loaders; four-wheel-drive loaders; excavators; motor graders; articulated dump trucks; landscape loaders; skid-steer loaders; and log skidders, feller bunchers, log loaders, log forwarders, log harvesters, and related attachments. This segment, currently about 22 percent of the business, is about to expand significantly with the acquisition of German road construction equipment maker Wirtgen Group Holding GMBH. Wirtgen makes paving, compaction, mixing and rehabilitation machines and sells them in 100 countries. Wirtgen will add about 70 percent or about $3 billion to the Construction and Forestry segment sales and about 12 percent to Deere's sales overall.

As the company reports it, FY2017 revenue for the Agriculture and Turf segment is about 78 percent of the $25.9 billion in FY2017 product revenue; the Construction and Forestry segment makes up the remainder. The Financial Services segment rolls its revenue into the other segments, and only segment profits are reported, but that segment produces about 20 percent of total net profit.

The Financial Services segment includes John Deere Credit, which is one of the largest equipment finance companies in the US, with more than 1.8 million accounts.

Overall, international sales account for 39 percent of the total.

Financial Highlights, Fiscal Year 2017

When fortunes reverse in a cyclical product sector, the results can be dramatic. Strong international markets, a declining dollar (finally!), strengthening agricultural economics, infrastructure spending and recent improvements in energy, mining, and forestry businesses drove a 12 percent increase in FY2017 revenues, with similar organic increases projected annually through 2019 and a $3 billion one-time bump thrown in for 2018 from Wirtgen. Much-improved scale and product mix drove earnings some 42 percent higher in 2017 (no wonder the stock price surge!) with another 25–28 percent increase projected for 2018 and 18–20 percent for 2019.

After a two-year hiatus, Deere will probably start raising its dividend again; similarly, share buybacks are on hold now pending the acquisition.

Reasons to Buy

Deere has become a classic case study in managing—and investing in—a cyclical company. We had placed our bets that the cycle would end and the heavy use of Deere machinery, coupled with the inevitable long-term growth in agriculture would put the company back on top of its game in just a few short years. Who could argue about the long-term growth in agriculture, as the global population is predicted to increase 30 percent by 2050 and as global standards of living increase on top of that? Indeed, the company reminded us that global grain demand had already increased 35 percent just from 2000 through 2015.

We're also big fans of the brand and historic excellence. As far as industrial companies go, Deere continues to be a poster child for US industrial ingenuity and excellence. It has an outstanding brand (and one of the most popular logos for hats, jackets, and so on, worn by people who have barely seen a farm field!) and reputation in the agriculture industry, and we see the ag industry as strong and strategic far into the future as global living standards improve and emerging markets develop.

Longer term, farm incomes should rise worldwide, and the company continues to invest in developing markets. We also think that innovation is a plus—Deere leads its competitors in R&D investment (5.9 percent of sales), bringing the Internet and GPS to farming and farming machines; new engines also promise greater fuel economy and reduced emissions.

Beyond its products, Deere has established an almost unassailable brand leadership with its services and customer-centered innovations. Deere, more than others, puts its people in the field (literally) to figure out what agriculture professionals really need, and they work with their customers closely to sell their products through a solid dealer network.

"Sell when there's something better to buy"—and we couldn't come up with anything better in this important manufactured goods segment two years ago. Good thing.

Reasons for Caution

The company plowed through an extraordinarily difficult period giving us a test of our long-term commitment. Now the stock price has doubled—too much, too soon given the slow, steady recovery?

Deere is, and always will be, vulnerable to cycles in the farm sector. The normal cycle, and in particular indelible memories of 1980s farm difficulties, can cause the farmers who buy this stuff to get cautious pretty quickly. All in all, farming will always be with us, both in the US and overseas, and there will always be a demand for machines and especially smarter, more efficient ones—Deere has an enormous brand and long-term track record.

SECTOR: **Industrials** ❑ BETA COEFFICIENT: **0.75** ❑ 10-YEAR COMPOUND EARNINGS PER-SHARE GROWTH: **5.5%** ❑ 10-YEAR COMPOUND DIVIDENDS PER-SHARE GROWTH: **12.0%**

	2010	2011	2012	2013	2014	2015	2016	2017
Revenues (mil)	23,573	29,466	33,501	34,998	32,961	25,775	23,387	25,885
Net income (mil)	1,865	2,799	3,065	3,533	3,162	1,937	1,524	2,159
Earnings per share	4.35	6.63	7.64	9.08	8.53	5.76	4.81	6.68
Dividends per share	1.16	1.52	1.79	1.99	2.22	2.40	2.40	2.40
Cash flow per share	5.72	8.34	9.56	11.45	11.45	8.62	7.39	9.32
Price: high	84.9	99.8	89.7	95.6	94.9	98.2	104.6	159.4
low	46.3	59.9	69.5	79.5	76.9	71.9	70.2	103.1

Website: www.deere.com

AGGRESSIVE GROWTH

Dentsply Sirona

Ticker symbol: **XRAY (NASDAQ)** ❑ **Large Cap** ❑ Value Line financial strength rating: **B++** ❑ Current yield: **0.6%** ❑ Dividend raises, past 10 years: **9**

Company Profile

Last year, in between checkups, we switched horses, replacing dental supply provider Patterson Dental with Dentsply Sirona. We've long been fans of the dental supply business, with its high margins and steady demand growth as people like us age and our teeth become decayed and fall out. We had become disillusioned with Patterson (PDCO), which had made a major acquisition into the relatively lower-margin veterinary supply space. We switched horses, midstream as it were, to Dentsply as a purer play in the dental space, which has become a leader in dental treatment technology as well with their 2016 acquisition of Sirona Dental Systems, formerly a unit of Siemens (another *100 Best Stock*). Although we haven't gotten wet yet, our "horse" still seems to be standing midstream, but we think this one will be a winner for patient investors (and investor patients!) over time. With the merger, Dentsply Sirona is now the world's largest maker of professional dental products and technologies and offers a complete solution ("The Dental Solutions Company" is their slogan) of equipment and consumables to cover the needs of any dental practice, clinic, lab, or distributor in the field.

The Sirona acquisition brought among other things a core competency in new dental technologies like digital and 3D imaging systems, CAD/CAM tools for custom manufacture of lab products, and the single-visit "CEREC" crown-making system. It added about 50 percent to Dentsply sales and a strong international footprint.

Prior to the Sirona acquisition, Dentsply's sales breakdown was about 50 percent dental specialty products, including root canal instruments and materials, digital scanning and x-ray products, and implant materials, 29 percent ordinary dental practice consumables, 10 percent dental lab materials such as crown and bridge materials, and 12 percent consumable medical device products such as drills and catheters. After the merger, the reporting segments are Dental and Healthcare Consumables (accounting for 53 percent of revenue) and Technologies (accounting for the remaining 47 percent). The combined company has 40 distributors and a sales presence in 120 countries accounting for 66 percent of sales overseas.

Financial Highlights, Fiscal Year 2017

FY2017 revenues jumped about 5.5 percent while earnings softened slightly due to acquisition costs. As merger synergies and other cost measures come into play, the company expects a 10 percent bump in 2018 earnings on a 5 percent revenue rise, with a similar earnings rise in 2019 on a heftier 8–9 percent sales gain. Share buybacks in the 4–5 percent range annually will push annual per-share earnings growth into the 15 percent range, while the dividend, though still small, is slated to grow more than 10 percent annually.

Reasons to Buy

Dentsply Sirona is well positioned to capitalize on several growth vectors in the dental industry. First, there's the international and emerging market opportunity, as modern dental health becomes a standard in overseas and especially developing markets. Second is the greater integration of digital technologies in the dental practice, from x-rays to 3D and CAD/CAM automation of lab work such as crowns to the management of patient records; the company is well positioned to cross-sell all parts of this operational food chain. Third is the increased presence of single-visit outcomes, where a crown can be mapped, created, and installed in one day using the CEREC technologies. Fourth is the stream of licensee revenue other distributors bring in for deploying Dentsply technologies like CEREC. (As an example, Patterson also offered CEREC as a licensee.)

Of course, these geography- and technology-related growth vectors are additional to the growth already slated for the industry coming in the form of an aging population, greater and longer retention of natural teeth, greater acceptance and practice of dental implants, and the gradual automation and digitization of dental practices.

We like the stronger positioning of the combined company as a one-stop shop for all technology and consumables needed to run any kind of dentistry-related practice, as well as the greater extension into higher-margined technology products and the greater presence overseas. Of course, we like the higher gross and net margins this all is bringing to the bottom line.

Finally, in today's expensive stock market, Dentsply Sirona seems relatively reasonably priced given future prospects.

Reasons for Caution

Dental markets can be cyclical, as we found out during the Great Recession as patients put off more elective procedures and dental practices stopped spending on equipment and supplies. The company increased its float 50 percent albeit to bring in a 50 percent sales increase with the acquisition but seems intent to buy back the new float as quickly as possible.

SECTOR: **Healthcare** ▫ BETA COEFFICIENT: **1.17** ▫ 10-YEAR COMPOUND EARNINGS PER-SHARE GROWTH: **7.0%** ▫ 10-YEAR COMPOUND DIVIDENDS PER-SHARE GROWTH: **9.0%**

	2010	2011	2012	2013	2014	2015	2016	2017
Revenues (mil)	2,221	2,537	2,928	2,951	2,922	2,674	3,765	3,950
Net income (mil)	277.2	290.9	319.2	340.7	360.4	373.0	616.0	600.0
Earnings per share	1.90	2.02	2.22	2.35	2.50	2.62	2.75	2.65
Dividends per share	0.20	0.21	0.22	0.25	0.27	0.29	0.30	0.33
Cash flow per share	2.42	2.56	3.20	3.33	3.51	3.62	3.40	4.05
Price: high	38.2	40.4	41.4	51.0	56.3	63.4	65.8	69.0
low	27.8	28.3	34.8	39.4	43.0	49.4	53.4	52.5

Website: www.dentsply.com

AGGRESSIVE GROWTH

Devon Energy

Ticker symbol: DVN (NYSE) ❑ Large Cap ❑ Value Line financial strength rating: B++ ❑ Current yield: 0.6% ❑ Dividend raises, past 10 years: 5

Company Profile

As recently as 2014 we had five major energy stocks on the *100 Best* list. We pruned out Marathon Oil due to a company split and ExxonMobil due to sheer size and difficulty replacing reserves. We held onto Chevron, ConocoPhillips, and Total S.A., which continue on the list today. But for the 2015 list we were left wondering if we were now underexposed to this key cash-producing economically important sector. So, we added a diversified energy company to replace Marathon and ExxonMobil—Devon Energy—to the 2015 *100 Best Stocks* list.

We all know what happened. That "add" was just in time for the rout in oil prices that started in 2015, continued full force in 2016 to a nadir almost 70 percent lower than the peak, and started to recover in 2017. When the price of your chief product drops 70 percent, you're in trouble—especially if you're relatively small and don't have the resources to easily bridge the gap.

We hastily dropped Devon from the 2016 list.

That was then, this is now. Oil prices have rebounded and, at around $70/barrel, are within 30 percent of the $100-barrel norm seen in mid-decade. Inventories are dropping (finally) as the strong economy drives worldwide demand, and natural gas has taken over as the fuel of choice for utilities and many industrial processes.

As such we wanted to once again expand our exposure to the sector, and to find a company that would give the right kind of exposure to the recovering energy industry. We had a few criteria in mind. First, we wanted a company well positioned to take advantage of the "fracking" (hydraulic fracturing) boom producing a bounty of energy right here in North America. In line with that, we wanted a company with less international exposure, one comfortable with new technologies, one expanding its reserves faster than production, one qualifying as a good corporate citizen, and one with a sizeable presence in the natural gas business. The 2017 production mix was 45 percent oil, 37 percent natural gas, and 18 percent natural gas liquids.

Devon Energy produces almost exclusively in six locations all within North America. In order of size its six major operations are:

- Barnett Shale in north Texas—28 percent of company total and a particularly strong concentration of gas
- Canada Heavy Oil—from the Athabasca Oil Sands—24 percent
- STACK in western Oklahoma—20 percent
- Eagle Ford in west Texas—11 percent
- Delaware Basin in southeast New Mexico and west Texas—10 percent
- Rockies Oil—mostly in Wyoming—3 percent

Devon is involved in "upstream" exploration and production and in "midstream" processing, mainly the separation of natural gas liquids (propane, butane, etc.) from the gaseous methane for sale and shipment. Devon owns a 64 percent stake in ENLAKE, a midstream producer and transporter of energy products. The company's strategies include investing in more innovative oil and natural gas liquids (NGL) production techniques, and in keeping critical mass in relatively few areas to reduce operating costs and concentrate on knowledge of those areas.

The company has doubled production since 2011 and is most excited about innovative "multizone" approaches to development especially in the Delaware and STACK areas. This approach, where several taps are placed strategically in a shale formation, can increase output as much as 20 percent while reducing costs 10–30 percent.

Led by these new state-of-the-art projects, the company expects to increase overall production 18 percent a year and reduce expenses 5–10 percent. The company currently breaks even at $50 a barrel, and the financial projects you see here are based on $60 oil.

Financial Highlights, Fiscal Year 2017

The recovery in energy prices gained momentum in 2017, with oil prices closing the year near $60, up from the mid-40s for most of 2016. Revenues advanced 14 percent while a few remaining asset disposals cut into reported profits, which did move back into positive territory. Projections call for a 4 percent revenue gain in 2018, which seems almost surely understated, since oil prices have now reached $70 and the company has achieved a 16 percent production gain; at that level they're still projecting a near doubling of net profit. For 2019, projected revenues are to rise somewhere around 10 percent (again with no price increase baked in) with earnings up 11–13 percent. In mid-2018 the company raised the dividend for the first time in three years after two years of cuts and announced its first buyback program in years—$1 billion—and another $1 billion for debt reduction on some fairly high-interest debt.

Reasons to Buy

After a sudden departure from the *100 Best* list in 2016, welcome back, Devon. The company regains its spot on the list as an innovative and efficient energy exploration and production machine right in our own backyard, devoid of the international political risks that face most producers. They have made more of both "fracking" and conventional methods than most. We like their balanced mix of oil, natural gas, and natural gas liquids. The company seems well poised to deliver excellent results well ahead of forecast if energy prices continue firm, and to deliver the fruits of their efforts to shareholders. As a side note, we applaud their clean and informative website, presentations, and annual report materials.

Reasons for Caution

Energy prices continue to be the wild card. Devon does well and better than most when prices are firm or higher and can generate red ink (although very little of it in this last go around) when energy prices falter.

As Devon and other producers become more efficient, the glut of oil and gas can not only drive down prices and drive up storage costs; it can also cause transportation bottlenecks in getting crude and gas to refiners and to market. The transport issue is currently driving down the price of delivered crude, as supply has been backed up waiting to go to its destination—taking as much as $10 off the price of a barrel of oil. This is but one ripple from the supply/demand disruption a few years back; there will be others.

Finally, we'd like to see a bit more cash flow go to shareholders, but we think there's a good chance of that in coming years.

SECTOR: Energy ◻ BETA COEFFICIENT: 2.16 ◻ 10-YEAR COMPOUND EARNINGS PER-SHARE GROWTH: -8.5% ◻ 10-YEAR COMPOUND DIVIDENDS PER-SHARE GROWTH: 9.0%

	2010	2011	2012	2013	2014	2015	2016	2017
Revenues (mil)	9,940	11,494	9,502	10,407	19,566	13,145	12,197	11,3949
Net income (mil)	2,543	2,485	1,285	1,727	2,014	1,044	(38)	835
Earnings per share	5.75	5.94	3.26	4.29	4.91	2.52	(0.13)	1.59
Dividends per share	0.64	0.67	0.80	0.86	0.94	0.96	0.42	0.24
Cash flow per share	10.02	11.71	10.09	11.15	13.04	9.95	3.35	5.54
Price: high	78.9	93.6	76.3	66.9	80.6	70.6	50.7	49.4
low	58.6	50.7	50.9	50.8	41.8	28.0	18.1	28.8

Website: www.devonenergy.com

GROWTH AND INCOME

DowDuPont

Ticker symbol: DWDP (NYSE) ❑ Large Cap ❑ Value Line financial strength rating: A+ ❑ Current yield: 2.4% ❑ Dividend raises, past 10 years: NM

Company Profile

We don't normally stick around when companies do what DowDuPont did—and still plans to do. When a company goes through the kinds of structural changes that the new DowDuPont has gone through and is planning for the future, we normally take a back seat until the dust settles. If we like the resulting business, we're back in. We've gone to the sidelines with Abbott Laboratories and others as they have split and reorganized. It is usually too difficult to size up the outcome.

We could have very easily adopted the same stance with DuPont—now DowDuPont as a result of the 2017 merger of the two chemical giants. We had faithfully maintained predecessor E.I. du Pont de Nemours ("DuPont") on the *100 Best* list for many fairly quiet but successful years. DuPont first came into change in 2015 as a proxy fight led to the spin-off first of a coatings business, then of the lower-margined commodity chemical businesses into "Chemours," which makes mainly pigments and refrigerants. That was followed with the 2016 blockbuster mega merger announcement between two large equals—DuPont and Dow Chemical. As if that wasn't enough, the merger plan includes a split of the combined company into three separate businesses: a materials science business centered on plastics, an agriculture business, and a specialty chemicals business—all now expected to occur in mid-2019. "When in doubt, reorganize." This popular satire about Corporate America has enjoyed no finer hour than with DuPont. But in this case, we like the direction and think the ultimate outcome could be worth the wait and uncertainty. Meanwhile, the current DowDuPont business has also fared pretty well after the Chemours spin-off; that's what most of the rest of this narrative is about as we enter the fourth, and hopefully final, transition year. Owners of DowDuPont shares should own shares in three companies by the end of 2019 with combined annual sales in the $90 billion range.

"Global Leaders in Agriculture, Materials Science and Specialty Products" touts the first page of the current DowDuPont website. Although the company is still known to many as a cyclical diversified chemical company making a host of lifeless chemical products and ingredients, many by the tank car–load, with recent changes today's DowDuPont continues to take the lead in science and technology with important end-product ingredients in a range of disciplines within the three categories noted earlier. "Market driven science" is still the principal banner, and previous innovation icons—such as Nylon and Rayon in earlier years and Teflon and Kevlar more recently—bear out that vision, and there are many, many others inside and outside the materials and plastics space.

Today's transitional DowDuPont operates in the three fields noted previously:

- The Agriculture Division delivers a portfolio of conventional and digital products and services specifically targeted to achieve gains in crop yields and productivity, such as Pioneer brand seed products and well-established brands in crop protection, including insecticides, fungicides, and herbicides. Pioneer develops, produces, and markets corn hybrid and soybean varieties and sells wheat, rice, sunflower, canola, and other seeds under the Pioneer and other brand names. DowDuPont also sells a line of crop protection products for field and orchard agriculture. The company describes itself as the global leader in "production agriculture" with a presence in 130 countries. FY2017 sales were $14.7 billion, about 18 percent of DowDuPont's total.
- The Materials Science unit, largely the former Dow (and will become Dow again after adding some former DuPont businesses), makes and markets polymers (translation: plastics for the most part) for packaging, infrastructure, and consumer markets. It also includes DuPont's former Industrial Intermediates & Infrastructure and Performance Materials & Coatings businesses—both of which bring numerous specialty chemicals and coatings to a variety of markets. FY2017 sales were $43.8 billion, or 55 percent of the combined business.
- The Specialty Products segment is made up of Electronics and Imaging, which makes a line of high-tech materials for the semiconductor industry, including ceramic packages and LCD materials. E&C supplies differentiated materials and systems for photovoltaics (solar), consumer electronics, displays, and advanced printing. The Transportation & Advanced Polymers unit supplies high-performance polymers, films, plastics, adhesives, and substrates to a variety of industries from automotive to aerospace and consumer durable goods manufacturers and many others. The Safety & Construction unit makes protective fibers

and clothing, including bulletproof apparel; disinfectants; and protective building surfaces—Tyvek house wrap is one of the bigger brands here. Finally, the Nutrition & Biosciences unit uses naturally sourced ingredients and bioscience to bring enzymes, antimicrobial technologies, pharmaceutical intermediaries, and other biomaterials to market. The Specialty Products business brought in $21 billion in 2017, about 28 percent of the total business.

According to company documents, plans are to split (tax-free) into the three aforementioned companies by mid-2019: "Dow" will assume the materials science business; specialty chemicals and products will be made, marketed, and distributed by "New DuPont" (or just DuPont); and the agriculture business will become "Corteva." The details are still being worked out at the time of this writing.

Financial Highlights, Fiscal Year 2017

Once again the organizational dynamics make a full financial review somewhat pointless; meaningful comparisons with previous years, growth measures, and forward-looking projections are difficult to come by. The following table reflects only DowDuPont history, which is assembled just for the 2017 year. What we do know is that the Materials Science and Specialty Products segments are doing fairly well, while Agriculture lags in sympathy with crop price and world agriculture weakness. Despite that weakness, total sales are projected to grow for the DowDuPont configuration as much as 9 percent for the 2018 year and another 7 percent in 2019. Earnings growth is projected in the 25 percent range in 2018 and 15 percent for 2019 for the combined company, reflecting new efficiencies, a focus on higher margined businesses, and lower tax rates. Share buyback and dividend growth were projected at fairly aggressive levels but it's hard to say how that's going to work out with the upcoming split.

Reasons to Buy

The transformation, long waiting in the wings, looks anything but tentative and should allow DuPont (and its brother Dow) to unlock value and settle into an effective alignment for the long term. The product pipeline continues to be full, individual product margins remain strong, the product mix is improving, and the company's biggest moneymakers still dominate their markets. Exits from commodity businesses, lower commodity costs, and a large slate of cost cuts, totaling $3 billion annually according to current projections, should help the bottom line.

The company—and its descendants—will continue to capitalize on "global megatrends": population growth, alternative energy production, and so forth, and should also get a boost from Trump administration "made in America" initiatives. The improvement of worldwide food production is at the center of the all-important agricultural products business. The combined businesses have brand leadership in many important categories and have been committed to total shareholder returns with a good dividend track record and an aggressive share buyback program. It remains to be seen how and how much value will be unlocked going forward; it will certainly be an interesting ride.

Reasons for Caution

Mergers and reorganizations are complex, and DuPont is taking on both in a big way. Things could change or fall apart, and the list of possible distractions is long—there is some risk here. DuPont is no longer a "quiet" stock suitable for buying and putting away for the long term. While we do think there is unrealized value down the road, new and existing shareholders will have to keep track of the situation as it develops. It's way too soon to declare "success."

SECTOR: Materials ▢ **BETA COEFFICIENT: NM** ▢ **10-YEAR COMPOUND EARNINGS PER-SHARE GROWTH: NM** ▢ **10-YEAR COMPOUND DIVIDENDS PER-SHARE GROWTH: NM**

	2010	2011	2012	2013	2014	2015	2016	2017
Revenues (mil)	—	—	—	—	—	—	—	79,535
Net income (mil)	—	—	—	—	—	—	—	3,969
Earnings per share	—	—	—	—	—	—	—	3.07
Dividends per share	—	—	—	—	—	—	—	1.52
Cash flow per share	—	—	—	—	—	—	—	4.81
Price: high	—	—	—	—	—	—	—	73.9
low	—	—	—	—	—	—	—	61.3

Website: www.dow-dupont.com

Eastman Chemical Company

Ticker symbol: EMN (NYSE) ◻ Large Cap ◻ Value Line financial strength rating: A ◻ Current yield: 2.2% ◻ Dividend raises, past 10 years: 8

Company Profile

Spun off in 1993 from the now-bankrupt Eastman Kodak, Eastman Chemical is one of those "better living through chemistry" companies with a history of solving problems and providing standard, high-tech, and high-precision materials to industries ranging from food and beverage to toys to medical equipment to computers and electronics. The Eastman mission could almost be refined into "better living through *polymer* chemistry"—the chemical building blocks, mostly sourced from petroleum and other feedstocks known as hydrocarbons, that turn into all things useful such as plastics, paints, coatings, inks, and the like. Many of their products are "intermediaries," used to manufacture *other* chemicals and products. When speaking the language of the company you quickly pick up expressions like "olefin cycle" and "phthalate," among the more difficult concepts and spelling challenges, like "ophthalmology." We aren't chemists but have enough understanding of basic chemistry to feel comfortable reading their reports; if you don't, you may want to look elsewhere.

The company is organized into four product segments, all of which have something more or less to do with petrochemicals:

- Additives & Functional Products (35 percent) produces chemical products for the coatings industry and for tires, paints, inks, building materials, durable goods, and consumables markets. Key technology platforms include rubber additives, cellulosic polymers, ketones, coalescents, polyester polymers olefins, and hydrocarbon resins.
- Advanced Materials (27 percent of 2017 sales) produces and markets specialty plastics, interlayers, and films, including copolyesters, cellulose esters, and safety glass, plastic, and solar-protecting window film products for the automotive, building, and transportation industries, building materials, LCD and display manufacturing, health and wellness, and durable goods industries.
- Chemical Intermediates (27 percent) is a catchall for other chemical products that don't fall into the other segments, including new or

custom-made polymer-based products for key customers. Acetic acid, ethylene, paint and building materials intermediaries, agrichemicals, adhesive resins, plasticizers, and aviation hydraulic fluid are among the many products in this group.

- Fibers (9 percent) produces acetate tow, triacetin, and solution-dyed acetate yarns for the apparel, filtration, tobacco (filters), fabric, home furnishings, medical tape, and other industries.

Obviously, there could be considerably more detail in these descriptions, but it would only engage those with a strong chemistry or materials background. A trip through their "Products" page on their website is fascinating. Bottom line: Eastman makes a lot of strategically important materials that support a lot of manufacturing processes for common and fairly high-volume items, such as beer bottles, automotive glass, and LCD displays. By end-use market, sales divide into Transportation (20 percent), Consumables (17 percent), Building & Construction (14 percent), Industrial Chemicals & Processing (11 percent), Filter Media (8 percent), Consumer Durables (7 percent), Food, Feed, and Agriculture (7 percent), Personal Care/Health (6 percent), Energy, Fuels, & Water (5 percent), Electronics (3 percent), and Other (2 percent). Additionally, these materials are used in considerable amounts in overseas manufacturing. Eastman has adapted by setting up plants in 16 countries and driving foreign sales to 56 percent of the total. By region, sales are 44 percent from North America, 24 percent Asia-Pacific, 27 percent EMEA, and 5 percent Latin America.

Acquisitions of adjacent or related technologies are an important part of Eastman's strategy. More recently the company has divulged a new strategy to become a leader in innovation, to become known as a "materials innovation" company introducing new, more specialized, higher-margin and sometimes branded products into the mix, such as Impera performance resins for tires and Saflex windshield coatings to enable non-glare "heads-up displays" projected on windshields.

Financial Highlights, Fiscal Year 2017

Strength across the board and particularly in the higher-margined Advanced Materials and Additives and Functional Products segments led the way to a good 2017 performance; net income was up 17.2 percent on a 6 percent rise in revenues. Net profit margins rose to over 10 percent for only the second time in ten years. Continued mix and margin improvements will lead the way to another 20 percent profit gain in 2018 on another 6 percent revenue rise, slowing to about an 8–9 percent net income gain in 2019 on a 2–4 percent sales rise. Strong cash flows came back to investors in the form of an 11 percent dividend raise this year; 10 percent raises going forward look likely, with another $2 billion earmarked for share buybacks as well.

Reasons to Buy

Although Eastman lies on the edge of the "buy businesses you understand" test, this well-managed company really does produce things vitally important to manufacturing mainstream and advanced products. Successful product development has always been a key strength for Eastman, and now that gains more emphasis. Eastman will benefit from the continued strength in domestic manufacturing, although its international operations, particularly in Asia, are also a source of strength. Eastman continues to position itself for continued moderate organic growth with a strong base of repeat business, a more favorable cost structure, and excellent cash flow.

Reasons for Caution

Eastman's fortunes will follow those of the larger manufacturing sector in general and, to a lesser extent, the feedstock (petroleum) market more specifically. Feedstock costs are starting to increase. The recent DowDuPont merger (another *100 Best* stock) brings a stronger competitor and perhaps a more focused one after their proposed split. It's a competitive industry to begin with.

There is always headline risk with chemical companies. Environmental and health risks can pop up in the headlines any time, as well as production risks such as a 2017 explosion in a coal gasification plant. Another example: there is some concern about the health effects of phthalates, one of their key plasticizer products, although they do sell a line of non-phthalate plasticizers.

The prospect of acquisitions, particularly a large one to keep up with DowDuPont, does add some risk. That all said, Eastman has all the earmarks of a well-managed and well-positioned company.

SECTOR: **Materials** ❑ BETA COEFFICIENT: **1.27** ❑ 10-YEAR COMPOUND EARNINGS PER-SHARE GROWTH: **9.0%** ❑ 10-YEAR COMPOUND DIVIDENDS PER-SHARE GROWTH: **7.5%**

	2010	2011	2012	2013	2014	2015	2016	2017
Revenues (mil)	5,842	7,178	8,102	9,350	9,527	9,648	9,008	9,549
Net income (mil)	514	653	802	1,008	751	848	854	1,001
Earnings per share	3.48	4.56	5.38	6.45	4.95	5.66	5.75	7.22
Dividends per share	0.90	0.99	1.08	1.25	1.40	1.60	1.84	2.04
Cash flow per share	5.62	6.76	7.55	9.45	8.08	9.60	9.79	11.11
Price: high	42.3	55.4	68.2	83.0	90.6	83.9	78.8	95.0
low	25.9	32.4	39.2	63.5	70.4	62.8	56.0	74.8

Website: www.eastman.com

GROWTH AND INCOME

Empire State Realty Trust

Ticker symbol: ESRT (NYSE) ❑ Large Cap ❑ Value Line financial strength rating: NR ❑ Current yield: 2.5% ❑ Dividend raises, past 10 years: 2

Company Profile

Nobody would dispute that the Empire State Building is a national treasure. Beautifully designed, it is an emblem of New York business well known to the world. It is such an emblem that more than 4 million people came to visit it last year, just to go up to the observation deck; 65 percent of them were from overseas. That observation deck is a $127 million annual icing on the cake for what we still think is an exciting and relatively new REIT built around the Empire State Building. But is this REIT just the Empire State Building? No—it has diversified to hold 14 office buildings in key locations across the New York area, nine in Manhattan and five others in or near major transportation hubs in White Plains, NY, and Stamford and Norwalk, CT. ESRT also owns six standalone retail properties, four in Manhattan and two in Connecticut. The Empire State Realty Trust is a pure play on real estate in the most dynamic and sought-after real estate market in the world.

The Empire State Realty Trust was formed in 2011 and went public in October 2013. As a REIT, ESRT is relatively small in comparison to other real estate trusts, but they make up for that in their strengths, which they call out quite clearly in their presentations:

- *Unique, irreplaceable properties.* ESRT is a pure play in the New York area, one of the world's most prized office markets; the cornerstone of their base, the Empire State Building, is one of the most recognized icons in the world. Another concentration of office properties is in the revitalizing 34th Street and Broadway area, home of the Macy's flagship store.
- *Expertise in reconditioning such properties.* The Empire State Building is beautiful, particularly for you fans of classic Art Deco architecture. But it needed a facelift—and got a big one from ESRT. In addition to managing properties, ESRT has a construction arm specializing in reconditioning and repurposing buildings and spaces for tenant use. The Empire State Building got a major energy retrofit; it is a showcase project and is estimated to save some tenants 38 percent and as much as 57 percent on energy costs (check out www.esbsustainability.com for details); it got a new fitness center for tenants also. ESRT will lease you "white box" space—or spaces tailored to your needs. ESRT is performing energy and functionality upgrades to other vintage buildings as well. It is part of their strategy to increase attractiveness...and of course, rents.

In area, ESRT owns and manages about ten million rentable square feet; 75 percent of that is Manhattan office space, 18 percent is Greater New York space, and 7 percent is dedicated retail, mostly in Manhattan. The Empire State Building itself is about 2.7 million square feet, or about 27 percent of the rentable space in the trust. The client list is a corporate who's who, with older companies like Macy's, Bank of America, Johnson Controls, and Thomson Reuters, and Bulova mixed in with latter-day names like LinkedIn, Expedia, and Shutterstock. The client base is diverse, with just 18 percent being the "typical" New York financial industry names. About 89 percent of current office space is leased; 92 percent of retail is also rented. Most clients sign long-term leases of ten years or so, and the company is trying to move to large block or entire floor leases.

For 2017, the roughly $712 million in annual revenue breaks down as follows: 65 percent Manhattan office, 14 percent Greater New York Metro office, and 3 percent standalone retail. *What about the other 18 percent?* you may ask. Look up, please. It's from the Observatory, split between the 86th and 102nd floor of the Empire State Building. We mentioned it at the beginning of this narrative—the Observatory brought in $127 million in FY2017, a nice "kicker" business, one that most REITs don't have.

Financially, ESRT touts what they refer to as "embedded, derisked growth." The "embedded" part refers to loyal tenants and a carefully managed "laddering" of lease expirations; the company attempts to have 5–10 percent of its lease base expire each year. Those expirations will be renewed at higher rates, to include not just inflation but also to cover improvements. ESRT estimates that rents will grow overall 8 percent to as much as 12 percent per year through 2021 as leases expire. "Derisked" refers to this smooth steady upward path but also to the location and desirability of the properties they own. They also present "best in class" financial fundamentals, with Manhattan leasing spreads (roughly comparable to gross margin—lease less mortgage obligations) of 29 percent versus 3.9 percent for their peer group. The "debt to enterprise value" ratio is 17 percent versus 40 percent for peers. Only about 41 percent of the portfolio is encumbered by mortgages—down from 99 percent at IPO. Less debt, less leverage, greater profitability.

As investments REITs are typically good income producers, since they are required by law to pay a substantial portion of their cash flow to investors. The accounting rules are different, and REIT investors should focus on Funds from Operations (FFO), which is analogous to operating income; net income figures have depreciation expenses deducted, which can vary in timing and not always be realistic. FFO support the dividends paid to investors.

Financial Highlights, Fiscal Year 2017

As ESRT only went public in the fall of 2013, we still do not have a well-developed financial presentation for the company or its financial history. Revenues increased 5 percent and total FFO increased 7 percent driven by a slight improvement in occupancy and a more substantial increase in rents. ESRT signed 167 leases across the portfolio with a 30.8 percent mark-to-market rent increase. Observatory revenue slowed to a 1.8 percent growth over 2016. The REIT says that it has "substantially" completed its $802 million spending plan to redevelop and restore its Manhattan buildings (the largest, of course, being the Empire State Building). The completion of that spend should enhance reported net income going forward—and in turn, shareholder payouts, since REITs are legally required to pay out 90 percent of reported income.

As yet, we have not been able to obtain projections into FY2018 and FY2019.

Reasons to Buy

ESRT exhibits most of the traits we like to see when we consider buying a real estate investment trust. It has good real estate, yes, but it isn't just the real estate—it's a good business too. It adds value in the form of redevelopment services, and the observation deck is a nice bonus. We don't depend solely on the rising value of the underlying real estate, and we don't depend too much on increasing the rent. That said, the prime locations they own and the exclusive focus on the New York area make for an excellent opportunity to raise rents—which is, in fact, happening at a good pace.

Who wouldn't want to own a piece of the Empire State Building? The energy and whole-building retrofit of the Empire State Building has won considerable acclaim with green building advocates and others; a search on "empire state building energy retrofit" gives several angles to this story. The building was once felt to be in an irreversible decline; the retrofit, energy, and publicity around it have returned it to its classic status as a prestige address. ESRT is using it wisely as a brand centerpiece for events, social media, and general marketing—even as a centerpiece for a recent Gwen Stefani Christmas show.

In short, not only do we like the fundamentals; we also admire the overall value creation strategy. As retrofits and other investments in the portfolio are now mostly paid for, ESRT will become a much stronger cash machine, and with REIT distribution rules, that cash will end up in the pockets of shareholders—we think—in the not too distant future.

Reasons for Caution

ESRT is new and less proven than most of our choices, although it has a seasoned management team from its roots as a private equity trust. We can't give you as much historical analysis as we would with most *100 Best Stocks* investments. As well, the short-term future of retail real estate in general is not too bright, as many major tenants are reviewing their space commitments—that said, we don't think this concern affects New York real estate so much. All in all, ESRT still appears to be an opportunity to "get in on the ground floor" of what we think will be a strong investment for years to come.

SECTOR: **Real Estate** ◻ BETA COEFFICIENT: **0.95** ◻ 10-YEAR COMPOUND FFO PER-SHARE
GROWTH: **NM** ◻ 10-YEAR COMPOUND DIVIDENDS PER-SHARE GROWTH: **NM**

	2010	2011	2012	2013	2014	2015	2016	2017
Revenues (mil)	—	—	—	—	635.3	657.6	677.7	712.4
Net income (mil)	—	—	—	—	70.0	73.8	51.5	62.6
Funds from operations per share	—	—	—	0.84	0.97	0.97	0.94	0.93
Real estate owned per share	—	—	—	—	8.42	8.55	6.55	8.95
Dividends per share	—	—	—	—	0.34	0.34	0.42	0.42
Price: high	—	—	—	15.6	18.1	19.0	22.3	21.72
low	—	—	—	12.6	14.1	14.6	17.2	16.26

Website: www.empirestaterealtytrust.com

GROWTH AND INCOME   NEW FOR 2019

Enterprise Products Partners, L.P.

Ticker symbol: EPD (NYSE) ◻ Large Cap ◻ Value Line financial strength rating: B+ ◻ Current yield: 6.8% ◻ Dividend raises, past 10 years: 10

Company Profile

It's no secret that our nation uses enormous amounts of petroleum products—oil and natural gas—for everything from transportation fuels to plastics to feedstocks to pharmaceuticals. But when's the last time you actually physically saw a gallon of gasoline? A cubic foot of natural gas? Other than inside rail tank cars or trucks, when have you seen these vast quantities move from Point A to Point B?

The simple fact is that most of it moves underground, out of sight and largely out of mind. The US consumption of barrels of oil is somewhere around 20 million *a day*; one of those big black rail tank cars you often see carries about 800 barrels, so it would take almost 25,000 cars to carry a day's consumption of oil, and this doesn't even include natural gas or other chemicals and liquids. Put simply: pipelines are vital to moving today's energy needs.

That's where Enterprise Products Partners comes in as one of the leading "midstream" networks of pipelines, natural gas–processing plants, and storage facilities vital to moving today's energy needs from "upstream" (production or in many cases import) to "downstream" (filling stations, natural gas utilities, airports, chemical plants) the end user.

Since being formed in 1998, Enterprise has assembled, through construction and acquisition, a network of 50,000 miles of pipelines carrying crude oil, raw natural gas, natural gas liquids ("NGL"), which is essentially compressed natural gas ready for delivery to utilities and the end customer, refined products, and petrochemicals. It has salt dome storage facilities for 260 million barrels of liquid capacity and 14 billion cubic feet of natural gas. The company also operates 26 natural gas–processing plants and 22 NGL and propylene fractionators, which refine NGL into basic petrochemical substrates. Enterprise also runs a large import and export terminal in the Houston Ship Channel.

Much of Enterprise's network is where you might expect it to be. Crude oil and natural gas sourcing pipelines crisscross Texas, Oklahoma, and Louisiana, while NGL, petrochemical, and refined product pipelines head north into the Northeast, Midwest, and Rocky Mountain states. Most gas processing plants are in Texas and Louisiana but there are several in Colorado, New Mexico, and Wyoming. Typically, the larger the pipeline network, the stronger the offering to petroleum products shippers, because they can reach a destination from a source location without transfer, delays, or additional costs. The combination of transport, storage, and some processing also provides an advantage.

Enterprise Products Partners, like many others in the pipeline business, is technically a limited partnership, which is run by a corporate general partner called Enterprise GP; you don't buy shares but rather limited partnership units. There are no taxes at the corporate level, so all profits are passed on to partnership holders as "distributions," not dividends, and certain other expenses like depreciation are allocated among the partners as well. This can cause some headaches at tax time, so we advise using this type of security in a tax-deferred retirement account if feasible.

Financial Highlights, Fiscal Year 2017

The resurgence of the US shale resource industry in 2017 spearheaded a very successful year. Revenues rose almost 28 percent while net income rose a more modest 11 percent as more construction projects were taken on. The forecast for 2018 calls for a further 5–7 percent revenue gain with a more respectable 22–25 percent income gain as some of those construction projects wind up. For 2019, forecasts call for a 10 percent profit gain on a

7–8 percent gain in the top line. The distribution should grow in the 5–10 percent range annually through 2019.

Reasons to Buy

Pipeline and processing systems typically represent a high fixed-cost structure, and with Enterprise, most of that infrastructure is already in place, so throughput is relatively profitable and is getting more so as more of the network is finished. Profit margins increase as more of the infrastructure is completed and get better yet if there is volume growth. EPD's margins have increased from the mid-single digits to over 11 percent recently.

Enterprise's network serves many of the key shale resource–producing areas in the southern US and is well positioned to tap the growth in store for this particular source.

Pipeline systems, while affected by energy price fluctuations, are relatively less affected than most other parts of the industry—the stuff still has to get to market, regardless of price. That said, volatility can cause demand and supply shifts, which can destabilize flows and create periods of excess capacity and undercapacity in certain pipeline lanes. Pipeline businesses bring in relatively steady income, and because of the limited partnership setup and no taxes at the corporate level, they pay relatively high and consistent dividends. Enterprise is basically a cross between an unregulated utility and a transportation company, with the steady base and modest growth potential one might expect from such a combination.

Finally, the yield is enticing and—we think—relatively safe, and the share price is relatively steady.

Reasons for Caution

High fixed-cost businesses are vulnerable to slowdowns and shifts in the geography of production and consumption. These systems are funded with large amounts of debt, which can get expensive in times of higher interest rates—although EPD is thought to be capitalized at largely favorable interest rates. All pipelines are susceptible to safety hazards and fires. The limited partnership structure is difficult to understand, especially at tax time if you use these investments in non-tax-deferred accounts.

SECTOR: **Energy** ❑ BETA COEFFICIENT: **0.86** ❑ 10-YEAR COMPOUND EARNINGS PER-SHARE
GROWTH: **10.5%** ❑ 10-YEAR COMPOUND DIVIDENDS PER-SHARE GROWTH: **6.0%**

	2010	2011	2012	2013	2014	2015	2016	2017
Revenues (mil)	33,739	44,313	42,583	47,727	47,951	27,028	23,022	29,242
Net income (mil)	1,380	2,047	2,419	2,597	2,787	2,521	2,513	2,799
Earnings per unit	0.88	1.19	1.36	1.41	1.47	1.26	1.20	1.30
Distributions per unit	1.15	1.21	1.27	1.35	1.43	1.51	1.59	1.67
Cash flow per unit	1.40	1.73	1.96	2.00	2.14	2.01	1.92	2.02
Price: high	22.2	23.3	27.7	33.5	41.4	37.0	30.1	30.3
low	14.5	13.9	22.8	25.5	30.7	20.8	19.0	23.6

Website: www.enterpriseproducts.com

AGGRESSIVE GROWTH

Fair Isaac Corporation

Ticker symbol: FICO (NYSE) ❑ Mid Cap ❑ Value Line financial strength rating: B++ ❑ Current yield: 0.1% ❑ Dividend raises, past 10 years: 0

Company Profile

Ordinarily when a share price quadruples in five years and outpaces sales and earnings growth by a considerable margin, we take a very hard look at whether there's any room to run despite the excellence of the company. Fair Isaac is a clear case, having run from the low 40s in 2013 to the 170s in early 2018. But can we run from such an 800-pound gorilla in today's most valuable space of "big data" and analytics? Fair Isaac continues to be the Apple, the Google, the Amazon of this key space, a pure play in this ever-expanding and lucrative niche. We think the compounded growth of the company's native market—analytics—plus the growth of the company's business *within* the market will continue to make this company stand out. FICO once again stays on the list for 2019—not because it's a bargain, but because it continues to dominate its healthy niche—and we couldn't find anything better to buy.

"Expanding Credit Access Responsibly" is one motto of the Fair Isaac Corporation, which provides decision support analytics, software, and solutions to help businesses improve and automate decision making and risk management. "Artificial Intelligence × Human Intelligence" is another. The most well-known and best example of these solutions is the FICO score—an analytic single-figure estimate of a consumer's creditworthiness used mainly in the credit industry but also for other purposes such as employment and insurance. More recently, the FICO score has been more widely distributed to consumers free of charge by financial institutions wishing to give customers insight into their own credit and, by proxy, financial health.

FICO provides its analytic solutions and services to a variety of financial and other service organizations, including banks, credit-reporting agencies, credit card–processing agencies, insurers, telecommunications providers, retailers, marketers, and healthcare organizations. It operates in three segments: Applications, Scores, and Decision Management Software. The Applications segment provides decision and risk management tools, market targeting and customer analytics tools, and fraud detection tools and associated professional services, all now under an umbrella called Enterprise Fraud Management. (If you've had a credit card fraud alert recently, it probably came from FICO's "Falcon" suite of fraud prediction and protection services, which are currently deployed to protect some 2.5 billion credit cards.) The Scores segment includes the business-to-business scoring solutions; myFICO solutions, delivering FICO scores for consumers; and associated professional services. The Decision Management Software segment provides software products and consulting services to help organizations build their own analytic tools. Many of these analytics and scores are now delivered through their "Analytic Cloud" as "SaaS"—Software as a Service—applications, providing an ongoing revenue stream tied to their use.

The company actively works with customers in a variety of vertical markets to identify and apply their tools and applications; these analytics go beyond traditional financial applications into marketing and operational optimization. FICO's analytics are not only used to manage risk and fraud but also to build more profitable customer relationships, optimize operations, and meet government regulations. The company promotes its vertical applications in the grocery, retail, pharmaceutical and life sciences, insurance, financial services, consumer packaged goods industries, and in education and public sector applications as well.

Financial Highlights, Fiscal Year 2017

Led by the Scores segment, total revenues advanced 5.8 percent in FY2017. The largest segment, Applications (at 57 percent of the business) grew 4 percent. The Scores segment, which now contributes 29 percent of the business, grew 10 percent, while the Decision Management Software business, accounting for 13 percent of the business, moved forward at a 5 percent rate. Earnings jumped ahead 17 percent after a 26 percent gain in FY2016 on higher margins related to an improved mix and efficiencies. Expectations call for a 13 percent rise in FY2018 earnings on a 6 percent rise in revenues as the company profits from a broadening base of applications outside the financial services industry, and as the transformation to a cloud-based SaaS model becomes more complete.

We should note that the company has had a very modest dividend policy and in fact intends to cut it altogether in 2019 moving forward. However, this is offset by aggressive share buybacks; the company bought back 700K shares in FY2017 of the 31 million outstanding; more importantly it has reduced share counts some 50 percent since 2005. Plans call for another 10–15 percent reduction over the next few years—a very deliberate approach to returning cash to shareholders.

Reasons to Buy

"Big data" and related analytics are gaining strength right now as more vertical industries (banking, retail, utilities, pharma, medical devices, health insurers, etc.) learn how to use them more efficiently and effectively to manage different parts of their business. The market is growing both deeper (more analytics being used) and wider (more companies in more industries using them)—a very good scenario as pointed out previously.

There are a number of companies, large and small, in the analytics business, but few have the brand reputation, product packaging, and leadership enjoyed by FICO, which serves more than 95 percent of the largest financial institutions in the US. The company is a pure play and is considered to be the gold standard for this type of product. It is more turnkey and easy for customers who don't have advanced mathematicians and software engineering staffs. As a consequence, and with the brand recognition of the FICO score, the company has attained a large moat on its brand and is a good example of how packaging and market definition can be as important as the product.

FICO's modeling approaches are now being used to analyze customer behavior and provide decision support for insurability, employability, acceptance into schools, and even customer behaviors in stores or online, other areas well beyond a consumer's ability to repay extended credit. Its analytics predict risks of insurance fraud, cyber security debt default and resolution potential, and a host of other very abstract but also very real risks. As mentioned before, the FICO "score" is more and more becoming a household term and feature. International demand for FICO's products continues to grow, too, notably in China, where fraud protection continues to be a big business.

The dividend is history, but the company provides shareholder returns in the form of share buybacks.

Reasons for Caution

There continues to be some competition on the scoring front, but the forefront FICO brand keeps serious competition at bay. Software companies always run a certain amount of technology risk. The ability to sell in a "cloud" environment and to maintain or increase margins by selling the right mix of products and channels will be key. There is some public concern that scoring models oversimplify lending and insurability decisions and should not be used or relied on so heavily.

But mainly we're concerned about how much investors have already loved this stock and have priced FICO's excellent market position to perfection. This not only creates downside price risk but also makes the company's share buybacks expensive. "Score" your purchases carefully—buy when the price is right.

SECTOR: **Business Services** ❑ BETA COEFFICIENT: **1.30** ❑ 10-YEAR COMPOUND EARNINGS PER-SHARE GROWTH: **6.5%** ❑ 10-YEAR COMPOUND DIVIDENDS PER-SHARE GROWTH: **NM**

		2010	2011	2012	2013	2014	2015	2016	2017
Revenues (mil)		605.6	619.7	676.4	743.4	789.0	839.0	881.4	932.2
Net income (mil)		64.5	71.6	92.0	90.1	94.9	86.5	109.4	128.3
Earnings per share		1.42	1.79	2.55	2.48	2.72	2.65	3.39	3.98
Dividends per share		0.08	0.08	0.08	0.08	0.08	0.08	0.08	0.04
Cash flow per share		2.36	2.58	3.20	3.54	3.98	3.85	4.56	5.44
Price:	high	27.0	38.5	47.9	63.5	74.4	97.6	133.0	159.9
	low	19.5	20.0	34.6	41.3	50.3	69.4	80.2	118.9

Website: www.fico.com

AGGRESSIVE GROWTH

FedEx Corporation

Ticker symbol: FDX (NYSE) ❑ Large Cap ❑ Value Line financial strength rating: A++ ❑ Current yield: 0.8% ❑ Dividend raises, past 10 years: 9

Company Profile

FedEx Corporation is the world's leading provider of guaranteed express delivery services and a major player in the overall small shipment and small-package logistics market. The corporation is organized as a holding company, with four individual businesses that compete collectively and operate independently under the FedEx brand, offering a wide range of express delivery services for the time-definite transportation of documents, packages, and freight: these services, as a whole, reach 60,000 drop-off locations in 220 countries, operating 660 aircraft through ten air express hubs and approximately 170,000 ground vehicles, operates in some 375 airports and 5,000 facilities overall, sorts and processes some 14 million shipments a day, and estimates that it reaches markets that comprise about 99 percent of global GDP. The four businesses include:

- FedEx Express (57 percent of FY2017 revenues) offers the familiar overnight and deferred air service through hubs to the 375 airports mentioned earlier, with customs clearance services, critical delivery services from centralized "banks," e.g., "Partsbank" and other express logistics services. The 2016 acquisition of TNT Worldwide provided a major step function upward in revenues overall (12 percent) and especially into international markets; the integration won't be 100 percent complete until 2020.
- FedEx Ground (30 percent of revenues) offers overnight service from 575 pickup/delivery terminals for up to 400 miles anywhere in the US for packages weighing up to 150 pounds. Ground serves 100 percent of US residences and now features the so-called "SmartPost" operation, where small and less urgent packages are delivered "last mile" to local addresses by the US Postal Service and newly acquired reverse logistics provider GENCO—both key offerings for the e-commerce business. The unit now includes ground services of TNT mainly in Europe and has gained revenue share with double-digit margins—the latter especially notable in the relatively low-margin ground transport business.
- FedEx Freight (10 percent of revenues) offers standard and priority LTL (less than truckload) service across North America mainly for business supply-chain operations with 370 terminals and service centers.
- FedEx Services (3 percent of revenues), which includes 1,800 former Kinko's copy and office centers, now operates under the FedEx/Office brand, and FedEx TechConnect provides solutions to integrate supply-chain management IT tools with FedEx's systems.

A key part of FedEx's strategy is to provide integrated logistics solutions, that is, encourage customers to use all services (Express, Ground, Freight) according to need rather than just a single service. The company estimates that over 95 percent of its customers use two or more of these services; 77

percent use all three, attesting to the fact that FedEx's business is increasingly tuned to providing a total and flexible logistics solution.

The company recently arranged to offer pickup and drop-off services at all Walgreens store locations and many Kroger, Albertsons, and Office Depot/Office Max locations, pickup being especially important in this modern era of "porch piracy" of e-commerce shipments. To accommodate higher e-commerce volumes (which the company projects to grow at 15 percent annually for the foreseeable future) FedEx recently opened four major hubs and 19 new sorting centers in the Ground network. Recently the company has been focused on its competitive advantages, promoting its Ground service as faster than UPS in 29 percent of major shipping lanes and its flexible but more time-definite home delivery services with heavier allowed weights as compared to UPS.

Financial Highlights, Fiscal Year 2017

Stronger e-commerce, the integration of TNT, and strong global commerce in general fueled an overall 20 percent growth in revenues, or about 8 percent without TNT. Net profit rose about 10 percent hemmed in somewhat by fuel costs, TNT integration, and some one-time costs from a cyberattack involving TNT. The rise in home-delivered e-commerce has also hurt margins somewhat (it takes more resources to deliver many one-off small packages to individual residential addresses). Price increases, scale in home e-commerce delivery, and TNT integration should bring a rise in margins beyond pre-TNT levels in 2019 following another soft year in 2018; current forecasts call for net income to rise 10 percent in 2018 and a heftier 20–25 percent in 2019 on revenue gains of 6–7 percent and 5–6 percent respectively. Cash flows continue strong, making moderate buybacks and dividend hikes likely. The company raised the dividend 60 percent in 2017.

Reasons to Buy

FedEx has several tailwinds now—a broad product offering, best-in-class cost structure, customer-driven logistics fine-tuning, and the growth of e-commerce.

The growing e-commerce business and greater need for a complete, economical, and partially time-sensitive logistics mix makes FedEx the right place to be as American manufacturing activity and local sourcing increase— although this could dampen international shipments. With SmartPost and other business expansions, the Ground segment has reached a 30 percent market share for such services, a position from which it can start to call the shots in the marketplace for lucrative e-commerce and time-sensitive ground business. Indeed, of late, the company has been able to raise prices while also gaining market share.

Volumes will clearly benefit from the rise in e-commerce and from the economy in general, while profitability will benefit from scale and innovation—a solid success story.

Reasons for Caution

The company is always vulnerable to economic downturns and fuel price increases, particularly if cost increases come faster than they can be recovered in rates and fuel surcharges—as is often the case. It remains to be seen how much the Trump administration's trade policies will affect international trade, which could hurt international volumes and pricing with some offsetting gains in domestic business. Rumors of an Amazon entry into the shipping business (for its own account) seem to be overblown and wouldn't make much of a dent in the overall FDX business—no single customer, including Amazon, accounts for more than 3 percent of the business. While the company has done a good job of carving out its "full service" niche, it is always vulnerable to competition in both domestic and overseas markets; that said, its size, scale, and innovation give it advantage.

While we applaud recent dividend increases, we still think they could do more given the strong cash flow.

SECTOR: **Transportation** ▫ BETA COEFFICIENT: **1.30** ▫ 10-YEAR COMPOUND EARNINGS PER-SHARE GROWTH: **6.5%** ▫ 10-YEAR COMPOUND DIVIDENDS PER-SHARE GROWTH: **13.0%**

	2010	2011	2012	2013	2014	2015	2016	2017
Revenues (mil)	34,734	39,204	42,680	44,287	45,567	47,453	50,365	60,319
Net income (mil)	1,184	1,452	2,032	1,561	2,097	2,572	3,016	3,330
Earnings per share	3.76	4.90	6.41	6.23	6.75	8.95	10.80	12.30
Dividends per share	0.44	0.48	0.52	0.56	0.60	0.80	1.00	1.60
Cash flow per share	10.01	11.13	13.08	12.41	16.32	18.35	21.27	23.58
Price: high	97.8	98.7	97.2	144.1	183.5	185.2	201.6	255.1
low	69.8	64.1	82.8	90.6	128.2	130.0	119.7	182.9

Website: www.fedex.com

First Solar, Inc.

Ticker symbol: FSLR (NASDAQ) ❑ Mid Cap ❑ Value Line financial strength rating: A ❑ Current yield: Nil ❑ Dividend raises, past 10 years: NA

Company Profile

First Solar is the largest US-based provider of photovoltaic (solar) energy solutions. It is a vertically integrated business, producing the core building-block solar panels as well as large-scale generation systems that utilize these same panels. They also provide Operations and Management (OM) services for utility-scale installations and sell these OM services for any installation worldwide. They are the world's largest OM provider, with over 4 percent of the global market under their management. They develop, finance, engineer, build, and operate many of the world's largest grid-connected photovoltaic power plants. These plants are built to customer specifications and then turned over when complete or are managed and run by FSLR. In short, FSLR is much more than just another solar panel company.

The company's panels employ a proprietary thin-film cadmium-telluride chemistry, which, while less efficient than the highest-grade mono-crystalline silicon, is competitive with polycrystalline, the most commonly used crystalline material for energy generation. First Solar's technology also has certain other advantages in production and application that make it very attractive in terms of its cost and longevity.

Founded in 1990 as an R&D-focused endeavor and renamed in 1999, FSLR began commercial operations in 2002 and now designs, manufactures, operates, and maintains all elements of the solar power chain across residential, commercial, and utility-scale applications. They continue to be the industry leader in R&D spend.

Financial Highlights, Fiscal Year 2017

After an "interesting" 2016 in which the company recorded its first non-profitable year, FY2017 delivered on expectations, generating a sunny net margin more closely in line with years past. The company shipped 2.3GW of modules (a 26 percent decrease compared to FY2016) but completed the sale of several large-scale turnkey projects and turned in net sales of $2.9 billion, matching FY2016's numbers. Expectations for FY2018 are for 3.1GW of panels shipped, including 1.0GW of System 6 panels. Gross margins fell 3.3 percentage points due to pricing pressure on panels sold to third parties.

Revenues for FY2018 are expected to be flat, with improved operating margins, while FY2019 should bring a 10 percent improvement in revenues and significant improvement in margins, with System 6 transition costs in the rearview mirror.

Reasons to Buy

Last year we cautioned that the new political administration may not be big fans of renewable energy. As it turns out, the investment tax credit schedule for renewable sources agreed to by Congress in 2015 remains in place, providing some welcome stability to the industry. The last two years have been a good environment for renewable energy projects in general, and solar in particular: US electricity generation from photovoltaics has risen from 0.5 percent in 2015 to 1.3 percent in 2017. Continued support from regulatory agencies, the tax code, and low interest rates should provide for a healthy business (and breathing) climate.

In April 2018 the US Federal Trade Commission placed tariffs of 30 percent on imported solar panels in what seems to be an attempt to support (or revive) domestic solar panel production. These tariffs have been widely denounced by the US solar industry as a whole, as the bulk of revenues in the US are generated not by the manufacturing of panels but by the configuration, installation, and management of complete solar systems, and the tariffs will serve to raise costs to large domestic operators in this business. In any case, FSLR has applied for and received an exemption from these tariffs, as their technology is unique in the industry (explained later in this section) and not a focus of the government's ire. Domestic production of silicon-based panels may or may not be invigorated by the tariffs, but First Solar's panel sales will clearly benefit from the increased costs of competitive products.

FSLR's proprietary photovoltaic cell technology requires very little silicon; instead of polysilicon or monocrystalline silicon as a photoelectric core it uses a thin cadmium-telluride film over glass. FSLR is thus not exposed to the vagaries of the worldwide market for polycrystalline silicon. The volatility of this "poly" market played a large role in the unpredictable pricing for panels in the late 2000s and was a major factor in the elimination of many of FSLR's early competitors.

From a business-management perspective, First Solar shines, particularly when compared to some of their "wildcat" competitors. Rather than living on the edge of thin margins and low capitalization, First Solar's balance sheet is very strong. Despite operating in a very dynamic environment last year, the company ran its manufacturing facilities at 99 percent capacity utilization, a year-over-year improvement of 2 percentage points.

The big story for First Solar in 2018 will be the performance of their latest Series 6 panel technology. The company will continue to ship its older Series 4 product while the Series 6 product ramps up, but the cost and performance of the Series 6 modules is so far very encouraging. Early data indicates a 35 percent reduction in cost per watt and an efficiency improvement from 17–18 percent when compared to Series 4 product. Series 6 production tooling will come online at the Perrysburg, OH, manufacturing facility in early 2018. First Solar's higher-volume facility (in Malaysia) has begun its retooling for Series 6 production.

Finally, First Solar is the largest provider of OM services for the solar industry. This is an attractive business, as most traditional utilities have little experience and/or expertise with the technology and welcome a turnkey solution for their state-mandated renewable energy quotas. The global OM market is expected to triple by 2020, and it serves to steady the revenue and profit stream, which would otherwise be more volatile if the company simply built and sold photovoltaic products.

Reasons for Caution

Offshore producers of silicon-based panels have historically been extremely aggressive in their pricing for panels, and we anticipate the downward trend will continue. FSLR brings several cost-of-ownership advantages to the table, but pricing pressure on panels is expected to be a factor, even with tariffs in place.

The tariff development underlines the sensitivity of the solar business as an object of political, as much as economic, interest. With tax rebates and incentives comes scrutiny, and many suppliers, undercapitalized and/or just guessing incorrectly, have been whipsawed into bankruptcy. Obviously, we don't see that happening with FSLR, but the back and forth between the US and China will demand attention. International projects, of course, should be unaffected by the tariffs.

SECTOR: **Energy** ❏ BETA COEFFICIENT: **1.40** ❏ 10-YEAR COMPOUND EARNINGS PER-SHARE
GROWTH: **NA** ❏ 10-YEAR COMPOUND DIVIDENDS PER-SHARE GROWTH: **NA**

	2010	2011	2012	2013	2014	2015	2016	2017
Revenues (mil)	2,564	2,766	3,369	3,309	3,392	3,579	2,951	2,941
Net income (mil)	664	484	430	353	397	546	(358)	241
Earnings per share	7.68	5.55	4.90	3.70	3.91	5.37	(3.48)	2.31
Dividends per share	—	—	—	—	—	—	—	—
Cash flow per share	9.56	8.31	7.95	5.90	6.40	7.90	(1.22)	3.40
Price: high	153.3	175.4	50.2	66.0	74.8	67.8	74.3	71.8
low	98.7	29.9	11.4	24.5	40.5	39.2	28.6	25.6

Website: www.firstsolar.com

CONSERVATIVE GROWTH

Fresh Del Monte Produce, Inc.

Ticker symbol: FDP (NYSE) ❏ Mid Cap ❏ Value Line financial strength rating: B++ ❏ Current
yield: 1.2% ❏ Dividend raises, past 10 years: 6

Company Profile

Founded in 1892, Del Monte originated as a brand for coffee packaged
for the prestigious Del Monte hotel in Monterey, CA. The original firm
expanded its business and selected Del Monte as the brand for a new line
of canned peaches, and the rest, as they say, is history. The company has
grown—in a large part based on acquisitions particularly of tropical fruits
and food producers—into one of the largest vertically integrated producers and distributors of fresh and fresh-cut fruits and vegetables, as well as
prepared fruits and vegetables, juices, beverages, and snacks, in the world.

The company has 90,000 acres in production, and its products are
available in 100-plus countries through 40-plus distribution centers and 18
"fresh-cut" centers. Products include bananas (the largest product line at 43
percent of 2017 sales), an all-important "other fresh produce" category (48
percent of sales), and prepared food (8 percent). The "other fresh produce"
category deserves further breakout, and in some cases, description:

- Fresh-cut produce (15 percent)—this is the fastest-growing segment
  and the category we're most excited about (it was 13 percent last year
  and 10 percent in 2015). It offers fresh-cut fruits—pineapples, melons,
  grapes, citrus, apples, mangos, kiwis, and others—and vegetables for

salads packed in convenient, safe, and branded plastic containers; so far sold only in the US, Canada, UK, Japan, and the Middle East. These products are gaining traction in foodservice and convenience store end markets.

- Gold pineapples (12 percent)—the branding is "Del Monte Gold Extra Sweet."
- Nontropical fruit (6 percent)—includes grapes, apples, pears, peaches, plums, nectarines, cherries, citrus, and kiwis.
- Avocados (8 percent).
- Melons (3 percent).
- Tomatoes (2 percent).
- Vegetables (1 percent).
- Other fruit, products, and services (2 percent).

A big part of why we like Fresh Del Monte is that it's not just a producer but is also a logistics company specializing in fresh packaging and transport, really for all parts of the fresh-food supply chain. It runs from farm to store shelf, including sophisticated refrigerated storage and transport, all the way to helping end-store operators with market research, promotion, display, stocking decisions, and other logistical support. The company owns a fleet of 20 ocean-going refrigerated vessels and manages a network including 4,500 refrigerated containers, refrigerated port facilities, and the aforementioned distribution and "fresh-cut" centers. The company has also innovated in such areas as Controlled Ripening Technology for bananas, which it licenses to other producers.

By geography, 58 percent of sales are in North America, 16 percent in Europe, 11 percent in Asia, and 13 percent are in the Middle East and North Africa. This supply-chain leadership gives the company a distinct advantage and a laboratory within which they can produce and distribute all sorts of new products and packages to a large part of the world, a big advantage over the world's many, many small producers. See a market for fresh fruit snacks in special packages in Japan? Fresh Del Monte can produce it and get it there.

Fresh Del Monte acquired Mann Packing, a fresh packer of vegetables and vegetable products, a good complement to the fresh-cut fruit business.

Financial Highlights, Fiscal Year 2017

Softness in the banana market (sorry!) and the prepared foods market (mostly canned food) and higher distribution costs were offset by an 8 percent rise in the "fresh-cut" segment; however, the net of it was a 1 percent sales gain and a steep 46 percent decline in net income for FY2017. Pricing pressure on bananas dropped operating margins some 3 percent, from 8.8 percent to 5.8 percent. A new focus on revenue diversification (away from bananas) and operational efficiencies are projected to raise income levels slowly, 7–8 percent in 2018 on a 12–13 percent sales gain, then another 7–8 percent on a 4–5 percent sales gain. We think new product innovations in the fresh-cut space will strengthen that component of the business and bring overall gains higher; we hope we're right. After 2017, the projected 10 percent shift from bananas to other products will help the company considerably.

Reasons to Buy

What brought us to Fresh Del Monte three years ago wasn't just the pineapple, or even the bananas. It is their emerging leadership in healthful and especially innovative and modern fresh packaged foods, items we think will play well with today's demographic, who demand fresh, convenient, natural, unique, and customizable foods and "fresh-cut" food packages. More fundamentally, we're attracted to the brand, the logistics network, "fresh-cut" opportunities, increased scale, and operating efficiency. The company claims that "Del Monte" is one of the two top-of-mind brands in the fresh produce space with over 90 percent awareness; that not only supports higher prices but also makes it easier to enter new markets.

We like the vertical integration, which gives it control of its supply chain, and most of all, we like Fresh Del Monte's competitive advantage in distribution, and we see this playing well with what we expect to be a growing demand for smartly packaged fresh and fresh-cut food offerings, which are currently only 13 percent of the business. This category is starting to take off, and combined with packaged salads and such, become a major category in groceries and mass distributors of food products. People want convenience and variety, and these prepackaged items fit in—and when you take into account storage and spoilage, they actually become cheaper than their unpackaged equivalents. They can be mixed any way the markets want, as we've seen with prepackaged salads. Like pineapples, blueberries, and mangos together? Fresh Del Monte can produce and distribute just such a medley. You don't have to buy a pineapple, cut it up, buy a bag of blueberries; you get the idea.

All of that, plus a helping of financial strength (debt is only 17 percent of total capital) and a bias toward shareholder returns, makes this Mid Cap offering a worthwhile recipe to play emerging trends in the food industry.

Reasons for Caution

Past results have been volatile, and the still-thin margins reflect a company that is more of a "commodity" producer than anything else. We think the "fresh-cut" offerings will continue to help grow Fresh Del Monte out of this low-margin category. As a logistics company, particularly one with a moderate amount of air cargo in its mix, it is vulnerable to fuel price shocks. There is also strong competition in most parts of this industry.

SECTOR: **Consumer Staples** ❑ BETA COEFFICIENT: **0.44** ❑ 10-YEAR COMPOUND EARNINGS PER-SHARE GROWTH: **6.0%** ❑ 10-YEAR COMPOUND DIVIDENDS PER-SHARE GROWTH: **2.5**

	2010	2011	2012	2013	2014	2015	2016	2017
Revenues (mil)	3,552	3,590	3,421	3,684	3,928	4,057	4,012	4,066
Net income (mil)	62	93	143	87	144	132	222	121
Earnings per share	1.02	1.56	2.46	1.54	2.73	2.49	4.33	2.39
Dividends per share	0.05	0.30	0.40	0.50	0.50	0.50	0.55	0.60
Cash flow per share	2.40	2.87	3.69	2.79	4.12	3.89	5.85	4.12
Price: high	25.2	28.6	26.9	30.8	35.0	47.5	66.9	62.8
low	19.2	21.3	21.8	24.7	24.0	32.0	36.7	43.0

Website: www.freshdelmonte.com

AGGRESSIVE GROWTH   NEW FOR **2019**

Home Depot

Ticker symbol: HD (NYSE) ❑ Large Cap ❑ Value Line financial strength rating: A++ ❑ Current yield: 2.4% ❑ Dividend raises, past 10 years: 8

Company Profile

There are many pitfalls over the course of long-term investing that can cause you to lose money or to miss out on substantial gains. One we'll call "stigmatization" is well in play here: a company goes through a bad stretch, seems strategically lost often in the face of new competition, and can languish for up to several years. As an investor, you may take this bad stretch as evidence that the business itself is broken or outmoded; you conclude its best days are in the past, and you never really overcome that fear. That's basically what your friendly authors did with Home Depot some years ago—languishing performance in the face of new competition in a bad economy with a high stock valuation, and throwing in a few bad service experiences of our own to boot—we gave Home Depot up for dead. That was then, when the stock was in the 20s; this is now, and the stock is in the 170s. Clearly a lot happened to right the ship, and it sailed on without us. We apologize for letting so many years go by before adding this stock but still think it's a very strong investment.

Founded in 1978, Home Depot overlaid a big-box retail format on lumber yards and other specialty building materials stores essentially set up to sell to the trades, not to end customers. It brought in one-stop shopping, low prices, and a wide assortment of merchandise covering all facets of mostly residential building materials, all with convenient suburban locations and extended retail hours. The formula gained traction, first with an ever-growing base of consumer do-it-yourselfers, then with the contractors that serve the consumer base.

Today's Home Depot operates 2,284 retail stores across the US, with stores in Canada, Guam, Mexico, and Puerto Rico as well. The stores average 104,000 square feet with about 24,000 square feet of additional garden area. In addition to consumer-accessible merchandising in a warehouse environment, the stores have customer service representatives throughout the store to give advice and help shoppers, many of whom are former contractors themselves. Most have a contractor service "PRO" desk for handling contractor business. The stores carry 35,000 SKUs of lumber, floor and wall coverings, plumbing, electrical, paint, furniture, storage and seasonal items. The primary market has been consumer, but more recently stores are catering to the "MRO"—maintenance, repair, and operations facilities in business, government, and others.

Financial Highlights, Fiscal Year 2017

A strong 6.5 percent increase in same store sales, combined with a 4.5 percent average ticket increase (both figures the best in years) drove a 7 percent overall increase in sales, although some of that was driven by late fall 2017 hurricanes. Higher revenues and a lower SG&A expense rate led to an 11 percent gain in net profits, and a 4 percent share buyback led to a 16 percent increase in per-share earnings. Sales are projected to grow in the 4–6 percent range annually through 2019, with net earnings, boosted by tax savings, growing in the 20–25 percent range in 2018 and 4–5 percent in 2019.

Reasons to Buy

Home Depot has been on a roll for about eight years. Sales and profits have risen steadily—while share counts have fallen dramatically at the same time.

Over that time, dating back to 2011, sales are up 50 percent, and net profit margins have almost doubled to a retail nirvana of 10 percent, thanks to scale and other efficiencies and the new tax code; annual net profits in total have doubled. While all that was happening, the company was busy buying back shares—some 600 million, or 38 percent of the float. In fact, it has bought back half of its 2.1 billion shares outstanding since 2005.

Clearly, beyond these stellar financial results—or more to the point, in advance of them—Home Depot has found a retail sweet spot as more consumers are able and willing to take on do-it-yourself projects (which itself can be attributed in part to HD's existence), and more contractors rely on it as a primary material source. Perhaps most to the point is that Amazon cannot match or duplicate its offering—4 by 8 sheets of plywood just don't go well with Amazon Prime. While Amazon does sell some of the same items, it cannot offer HD's depth, breadth, and convenience. The company has achieved scale sufficient to become a powerful buyer in its markets, often dictating or heavily influencing supplier prices. With that size and scale, it can pretty much set the selling price for many of its products. The resulting 10 percent net profit margins are exceptional for a large retailer. Finally, while the stock price has risen almost relentlessly, one can take comfort in the fact that much of that results from share buybacks and past earnings gains, rather than relying on future expectations.

Reasons for Caution

The big fly in the ointment for Home Depot over the years has been economic downturns, which slow the building supply market both for new and remodel home materials. Rising interest rates as we move toward 2019 give us some concern, and less favorable property tax and interest deduction treatment may attenuate demand in some markets, but we think the overall strength in the economy and a greater "stay-at-home" tendency among today's population will make home—and Home Depot—where the improvements will be.

SECTOR: **Retail** ❑ BETA COEFFICIENT: **1.14** ❑ 10-YEAR COMPOUND EARNINGS PER-SHARE
GROWTH: **7.5%** ❑ 10-YEAR COMPOUND DIVIDENDS PER-SHARE GROWTH: **17.5%**

	2010	2011	2012	2013	2014	2015	2016	2017
Revenues (bil)	68.0	70.4	74.8	78.8	83.2	88.5	94.6]	100.9
Net income (bil)	2.8	3.4	3.9	4.7	5.4	6.1	6.8	8.0
Earnings per share	2.03	2.47	3.10	3.76	4.56	5.34	6.45	7.49
Dividends per share	0.95	1.04	1.16	1.56	1.88	2.36	2.76	3.56
Cash flow per share	3.07	3.55	4.21	5.08	5.96	6.82	8.07	9.25
Price: high	37.0	42.5	65.9	82.5	106.0	135.5	139.0	191.5
low	26.6	28.1	41.9	62.4	74.0	92.2	109.6	133.0

Website: www.homedepot.com

AGGRESSIVE GROWTH

Honeywell International

Ticker symbol: HON (NYSE) ❑ Large Cap ❑ Value Line financial strength rating: A++ ❑ Current
yield: 2.1% ❑ Dividend raises, past 10 years: 9

Company Profile

Honeywell is a diversified international technology and manufacturing
company engaged in the development, manufacturing, and marketing of
aerospace products and services; control technologies for buildings, homes,
and industry; and specialty and safety materials. For many years the company grouped these activities into four segments: Aerospace (36 percent of
FY2017 sales), Home and Building Technologies (24 percent), Performance
Materials and Technologies (26 percent), and Safety and Productivity (14
percent). By 2019 the company will divest itself of most or all of the homes
and transportation systems business, following the previous disposal of the
automotive business. We're not exactly sure what the new organizational
alignment will be, but the action is clearly one of "deconglomeratization" to
look less like a conglomerate of unrelated businesses and more like a focused
business—a trend started in the wake of the GE blowup. The Aerospace
businesses produce and market products, software, and services including
avionics, cockpit controls, power-generation equipment, satellite and space
components, and wheels and brakes for commercial and military aircraft and
for airports and ground operations. It also makes jet engines for regional and
business jet manufacturers. Products include avionics, auxiliary power units
(APUs), aircraft lighting, and landing systems. The remaining automotive

business includes parts and supplies for the automotive, railroad, and other industries such as cooling system components and turbochargers. In 2014 the company sold its "friction materials" business (mainly brake components) and had previously sold its retail consumer automotive brands to focus on OEM components.

The Performance Materials and Technologies operation makes a wide assortment of specialty chemicals and fibers, plastics, coatings, and semiconductor and electronics materials, which are sold primarily to the food, pharmaceutical, petroleum-refining, and electronic packaging industries. Carbon fiber materials are among the more important and fastest-growing products in this segment. Safety and Productivity Solutions markets supply-chain and warehouse automation equipment, portable data collection devices, gas detection equipment, and an assortment of other solutions and components.

The Safety and Productivity Solutions segment is a leading global provider of products, software and connected solutions that improve productivity, workplace safety, and asset performance. Safety products include personal protection equipment and footwear designed for work, play, and outdoor activities. Productivity Solutions products and services include gas detection technology; mobile devices and software for computing, data collection, and thermal printing; supply chain and warehouse automation equipment; software and solutions; custom-engineered sensors, switches and controls for sensing and productivity solutions; and software-based data and asset management productivity solutions.

The former Home and Building Technologies segment was best known for its home and office climate-control equipment and home automation systems; thermostats; sensing and combustion controls for heating, A/C, and other environmental controls; lighting controls; security systems and sensing products; metering and measuring products; and fire alarms. This segment produced most of the components of what is known in the trade and advertising lingo as a "smart building," along with devices that play well with the new "connected" homes, data analytics, and "Internet of Things" concepts. We elaborate on this exited business only because it is what a lot of us knew Honeywell best for.

The company has a considerable international footprint, with technology and manufacturing centers located outside the US; five such centers are located in China along with a similar number in India. Before the homes divestiture, about 56 percent of its business came from outside the US. US government sales, mainly from the Aerospace segment, account for about 9 percent of total sales.

Financial Highlights, Fiscal Year 2017

FY2017 sales were pretty healthy on all fronts, with a 3.1 percent reported overall gain but a 4 percent "organic" gain—reflecting business strength reduced by divestitures. Backlogs are strong, and net income rose 7.6 percent. For 2018, several new product introductions will lead the way to a 4–5 percent top-line gain, while cost efficiencies will grow gross margins about 0.7 percent and thus net earnings 9–10 percent. For 2019, the company expects another 9–10 percent earnings gain, on a 3–5 percent sales gain; these figures may be different when the divestitures are complete. Annual dividend increases should run in the 10 percent range, while share buybacks are on hold for the moment.

Reasons to Buy

A bet on Honeywell is a bet on a well-managed "best in class" producer of a wide variety of business and consumer products with an underlying technology theme—not really "high tech" but using advanced technologies to deliver a solution. The company shows many of the traditional signs of being well managed, with a strong and strategic focus on profitability, cash flow, and operational efficiency and a healthy respect for transparency, as evidenced by its informative annual reports, investor presentations, and other corporate materials. The company's profit margins are notably higher than others in this type of business—and growing—in this case, one doesn't care so much about anemic revenue growth. In the grand scheme, Honeywell has clearly outperformed GE, Siemens, and other rivals—but is not content to rest on its laurels as it seeks to reposition itself in the wake of GEs problems. We approve of their efforts to focus the business.

Like GE, however, the company is investing more in providing software products to complete the automation cycle started by its hardware products. It is now expanding its focus to complete solutions through "connectivity" and "adjacency" opportunities, many being software driven, within many of their platforms; software sales are expected to grow by a factor of four over the next five years. Honeywell has a solid balance sheet and participates almost exclusively in high-margin businesses.

Reasons for Caution

Big changes such as what are occurring here can be painful; in addition, if you get rid of too much too fast cost efficiencies can disappear—it becomes difficult to absorb costs with remaining revenue and cash flow streams. Many of the industries Honeywell sells to can be cyclical and/or low-growth businesses. However, as we've seen, the focus on efficiency and profitability will make the most of cyclically sensitive businesses.

SECTOR: **Industrials** ❑ BETA COEFFICIENT: **0.97** ❑ 10-YEAR COMPOUND EARNINGS PER-SHARE GROWTH: **10.0%** ❑ 10-YEAR COMPOUND DIVIDENDS PER-SHARE GROWTH: **10.5%**

		2010	**2011**	**2012**	**2013**	**2014**	**2015**	**2016**	**2017**
Revenues (mil)		33,370	36,500	37,665	39,055	40,306	38,581	39,302	40,634
Net income (mil)		2,342	2,998	3,552	3,965	4,422	4,768	5,104	5,492
Earnings per share		3.00	3.79	4.48	4.97	5.56	6.04	6.59	7.11
Dividends per share		1.21	1.37	1.53	1.68	1.87	2.15	2.45	2.74
Cash flow per share		4.27	5.11	5.72	6.32	6.83	7.34	8.06	8.80
Price:	high	53.7	62.3	64.5	91.6	102.4	107.4	120.0	158.7
	low	36.7	41.2	52.2	64.2	82.9	87.0	93.7	113.6

Website: www.honeywell.com

CONSERVATIVE GROWTH

Illinois Tool Works, Inc.

Ticker symbol: ITW (NYSE) ❑ Large Cap ❑ Value Line financial strength rating: A++ ❑ Current yield: 2.0% ❑ Dividend raises, past 10 years: 10

Company Profile

Illinois Tool Works is a multinational conglomerate involved in the manufacture of a diversified range of mostly industrial intermediary and end products. Customers include the automotive, machinery, construction, food and beverage, and general industrial markets. The company currently operates some 85 businesses in seven segments in 57 countries, employing approximately 50,000 people. Some of the products are branded and familiar, like Wolf and Hobart kitchen equipment and Paslode air power tools; most are obscure and only known to others in their industries. Sales outside North America account for 56 percent of the total. The seven segments are presented here with approximate revenue percentages:

- Automotive OEM (23 percent of 2017 revenues) includes transportation-related components, fasteners, and polymers, as well as truck remanufacturing and related parts and service for the automotive manufacturer market. Important brands include Drawform ("high volume, highly toleranced deep drawn metal stampings") and Deltar Interior Components, which makes things like interior door handles.

- Test & Measurement/Electronics (15 percent) supplies equipment and software for testing and measuring of materials and structures, solder, and other materials for PC board manufacturing and microelectronics assembly. Brands include Brooks Instrument, Buehler, Chemtronics, Instron, Magnaflux, and Speedline Technologies.

- Food Equipment (15 percent) produces commercial food equipment and related services, including professional kitchen ovens, refrigeration, mixers, and exhaust and ventilation systems. Major brands include Hobart, Traulsen, Vulcan, and Wolf.

- Polymers & Fluids (12 percent) businesses produce adhesives, sealants, lubrication and cutting fluids, and hygiene products for an assortment of markets. Their primary brands include Futura, Krafft, Devcon, Rocol, and Permatex and such brands as Rain-X and Wynn's for the automotive aftermarket.

- Construction Products (12 percent) concentrates on tools, fasteners, and other products for construction applications. Their major end markets are residential, commercial, and renovation construction. Brands include Ramset, Paslode, Buildex, Proline, and others.

- The Welding segment (11 percent of revenues) produces equipment and consumables associated with specialty power conversion, metallurgy, and electronics. Their primary products include arc-welding equipment and consumables, solder materials, equipment and services for electronics assembly, and airport ground support equipment. Primary brands include AXA Power, Hobart, and Weldcraft.

- Specialty Products (13 percent) is a hodgepodge of brands and businesses that includes Diagraph (industrial marking and coding systems), Fastex (engineered components for the appliance industry), and ZipPak reclosable plastic packaging.

In 2012, the company embarked on a five-year "Enterprise Strategy" program aimed at simplifying the business and applying sound customer-driven operating principles to fine-tune its base of customers, markets, products, facilities, and supply chains. Emphasis is placed on removing customer pain points, reducing complexity by applying the "80–20" rule (focusing on the 20 percent of customers, products, and processes that deliver 80 percent of the results), and by fine-tuning the relationships between headquarters and the operating entities. Growing organically (instead of by acquisition) and improving margins are the chief business objectives; the main strategy is to focus on businesses with strong sustainable differentiation. The company closely monitors operating margin improvements in each of its seven segments. We normally don't bring too many such strategic initiatives to light, but we will in this case because (1) it's working, as company-wide operating margins have improved from the 19–21 percent range to 27 percent in FY2017 (which is 3–5 percent better than the average of competitors across its industries); and (2) such focus is needed in a company with such size and operating complexity; otherwise, it quickly becomes an uncoordinated conglomerate jumble, as many others before it have. ITW has divested 30-plus businesses and two segments, simplified the rest from 800 business units to 85 businesses ("divisions"), and identified specific growth drivers in each of the seven segments.

These efficiency measures and "80–20" thinking have not only improved profitability of continuing operations but have also guided the company's thinking in terms of acquiring and selling businesses and in strategically managing the fundamentals within those businesses. The net result can be no better demonstrated than by the fact that in the five years since 2012, per-share earnings have increased 62 percent while revenues have *decreased* 31 percent in that time. We continue to appreciate ITW's efforts and look forward to the ongoing benefits of this initiative into 2019.

Financial Highlights, Fiscal Year 2017

FY2017 was another year of solid profit gains exceeding revenue gains: net earnings rose almost 16 percent on a 5 percent rise in revenues. Operating margins rose 1.2 percent to 27.2 percent, exactly what was forecast in the multiyear Enterprise Strategy noted earlier—for 2018! This year the Automotive OEM and Test & Measurement and Electronics segments stood out with organic growth in the 5 percent range compared to 3 percent for the company overall. Projections call for organic sales gains in the 3–4 percent range and total sales gains in the 5–6 percent range through 2019, with per-share earnings rising in the 15–18 percent range in 2018 driven by margin improvements and tax law changes, dropping a bit to 11–12 percent in 2019. The company commits half its profits each year to shareholder returns through dividends and buybacks and plans to increase its payout ratio (dividends to free cash flow) from 43 to 50 percent in the coming years.

Reasons to Buy

Buying shares of ITW continues to be like buying a fund of medium-sized manufacturing businesses you've probably never heard of but would definitely like to own. Indeed, think of it as the Berkshire Hathaway of manufacturing companies if you will—we do. We much admire this management team, with its solid strategic focus and drive to benefit shareholders. Headquarters prescribes the strategies such as margin focus and the 80–20 mindset; managers of the subsidiary businesses have the autonomy to figure out how to deliver results. The model works. We enjoy doing this presentation every year; it's a good tour through how to run a modern conglomerate effectively, and the company presents itself well to investors.

ITW is well diversified and serves many markets, some with end products, some with components, some in cyclical industries such as automotive and construction, some in steady-state industries like food processing. The businesses balance each other out. The company has solid models for making acquisitions and seems to do better than most conglomerates historically in choosing candidates and then managing them once they're in the fold. The new "Enterprise" initiative is turning opportunity into cash flow and using that cash flow to enhance shareholder returns.

Reasons for Caution

ITW is by nature tied to some of the more volatile elements of the business cycle, so it may not be the best pick for investors living in fear of the next downturn. In particular, we worry a bit about the Automotive segment going forward, although recently the unit has been gaining share in the automotive market. Conglomerates are notoriously difficult to manage (it's hard enough to manage one business, let alone 85 of them); that said, the company has made a conscious decision to downshift its acquisitions for now. Finally, shares have reached all-time highs recently—not undeserved but priced to perfection going forward.

SECTOR: **Industrials** ◻ BETA COEFFICIENT: **1.21** ◻ 10-YEAR COMPOUND EARNINGS PER-SHARE GROWTH: **7.0%** ◻ 10-YEAR COMPOUND DIVIDENDS PER-SHARE GROWTH: **13.0%**

	2010	2011	2012	2013	2014	2015	2016	2017
Revenues (mil)	15,870	17,787	17,924	14,135	14,484	13,405	13,599	14,314
Net income (mil)	1,527	1,852	1,921	1,629	1,890	1,886	2,036	2,302
Earnings per share	3.03	3.74	4.06	3.63	4.67	5.13	5.70	6.64
Dividends per share	1.27	1.38	1.46	1.60	1.75	2.07	2.40	2.73
Cash flow per share	4.17	5.06	5.55	5.20	6.25	7.17	7.22	8.09
Price: high	52.7	59.3	63.3	84.3	97.8	100.1	128.0	169.7
low	40.3	39.1	47.4	59.7	76.3	78.8	79.1	120.1

Website: **www.itwinc.com**

AGGRESSIVE GROWTH

International Flavors & Fragrances, Inc.

Ticker symbol: IFF (NYSE) ❑ Large Cap ❑ Value Line financial strength rating: A+ ❑ Current yield: 1.9% ❑ Dividend raises, past 10 years: 10

Company Profile

"Pioneering sensorial experiences that move the world" crows the well-crafted website for International Flavors & Fragrances—a company that continues to pass our smell and taste tests. IFF is a leading manufacturer of such "sensorial experiences"—natural and artificial flavoring and fragrance chemicals for the food and beverage and consumer products industry, including cosmetics, perfumes, soap and detergents, hair care, pharmaceuticals, and a wide variety of other products. Fragrances accounted for about 53 percent of 2017 sales; flavorings the other 47 percent. Not surprisingly, the company's value proposition and strategy are to create a differentiated and high value add for its customers by providing critical, unique, and highly researched ingredients. Many of the thousands of flavorings and fragrances are custom made for clients. For the food and beverage industry, the company estimates that its flavorings cost only 1–5 percent of the product's total cost but generate 45 percent of the motivation to purchase it and to purchase it repeatedly.

IFF is truly "international," with 75 percent of sales originating outside North America; in fact, nearly 50 percent of sales originate in emerging markets. Recognizing that flavor and fragrance preferences are very local in nature, the company has established an operational presence in 32 countries and lab facilities in 13 of them, including the US. Still, it estimates only a 16 percent share of the global flavorings and fragrances market and holds the number two position behind Swiss flavorings maker Givaudan. For US investors, it is by far the largest pure play available in this niche.

Research and development—at 8.2 percent of sales—is a big part of what IFF does. The company does extensive research on consumer tastes and preferences, how flavors and aromas work and hold up in different environments, and how to manufacture their products and develop the best delivery system to make them work over the desired life cycle. Research includes things like study of the "psychophysics of sensory perception" and the genetic basis for preferences in flavor and fragrance. Among successful new products are recently introduced encapsulation technologies that coat fragrance droplets with polymeric shells to enhance life cycle performance and shelf life, and "PolyIFF" embedding scent into molded plastic. Through acquisitions the company now offers "PowderPure" natural food drying and powdering technology and a new "Tastepoint" line of middle market products as a subbrand—with another clever slogan "the perfect blend of heart and science." The strategy: grow business with small and mid-tier clients by providing a small-company look and feel when working with these clients, and Tastepoint. The company collaborates regularly with chefs, fashion designers, filmmakers, and other trendsetters to evolve new ideas.

Financial Highlights, Fiscal Year 2017

IFF projects that the $20 billion market for flavors and fragrances will grow about 2–3 percent annually, with fully 75 percent of the growth coming from emerging markets, as taste and aroma become more important as product components in China, Latin America, Africa, and the Middle East. Net sales rose 9 percent in FY2017, 5 percent of that due to acquisitions. Net and per-share earnings were up almost 7 percent, trailing sales just a bit due to acquisition costs. Forecasts anticipate revenue growth of 5–6 percent in 2018 and 2019, while earnings should rise in the 6–8 percent range annually. Dividend growth should approach 10 percent with modest steady share buybacks.

Reasons to Buy

Things are smelling pretty good at IFF these days with new products, new product packages, and new ways to approach markets—a good and strategically thought out combination. That, with a continued emphasis on flavor and smell as an important value add, may cause our current forecasts to prove conservative.

IFF has a strong niche and produces elements critical in differentiating products in the fairly undifferentiated food and consumer products businesses. That should play better over time as people's tastes become more trained and more demanding—both in the rich world and especially in developing nations, which is an important trend right now. Not only does the company produce many of the world's leading flavorings and fragrances; it also has the market research and know-how to give it a competitive advantage—a moat—both with its customer insights and knowing how to make and deliver the stuff. We also like the relatively recession-proof nature of this business; we doubt that they will take the flavoring out of your favorite foods any time soon. Flavorings only account for 1–5 percent of the cost of your favorite beverage, but we Coke drinkers all know what happens when a company monkeys with that.

Reasons for Caution

The cost and availability of key ingredients like vanilla (a large portion of which comes from unstable regions in West Africa) can affect IFF adversely. The strong overseas footprint is probably an advantage most of the time, but strong dollar environments and volatile emerging markets like China and Brazil attenuate that advantage; also, it's hard to keep up with changing consumer tastes in so many places. At 2–3 percent growth, the flavorings and fragrances business is low growth; growth has to come from market share gains and acquisitions, always a challenge. Intellectual property protection is also a challenge; many try and some succeed in reverse engineering key ingredients.

SECTOR: **Consumer Staples** ◻ BETA COEFFICIENT: **1.11** ◻ 10-YEAR COMPOUND EARNINGS PER-SHARE GROWTH: **9.5%** ◻ 10-YEAR COMPOUND DIVIDENDS PER-SHARE GROWTH: **11.0%**

	2010	2011	2012	2013	2014	2015	2016	2017
Revenues (mil)	2,623	2,788	2,821	2,953	3,089	3,023	3,116	3,399
Net income (mil)	264	306	328	368	416	427	441	468.3
Earnings per share	3.26	3.74	3.98	4.47	5.08	5.25	5.51	5.89
Dividends per share	1.04	1.16	1.30	1.46	1.72	2.06	2.40	2.61
Cash flow per share	4.27	4.71	4.95	5.54	6.25	6.45	6.70	7.40
Price: high	56.1	66.3	67.8	90.3	105.8	123.1	143.6	156.6
low	39.3	51.2	52.1	67.5	82.9	97.6	97.2	113.2

Website: www.iff.com

AGGRESSIVE GROWTH

NEW FOR 2019

Intuitive Surgical, Inc.

Ticker symbol: ISRG (NASDAQ) ◻ Large Cap ◻ Value Line financial strength rating: A+ ◻ Current yield: Nil ◻ Dividend raises, past 10 years: NA

Company Profile

Intuitive Surgical designs, manufactures, and markets da Vinci surgical systems and their related instruments and accessories, and provides training and support in their use. The da Vinci system combines the benefits of minimally invasive surgery with the precision and ease-of-use of traditional open surgery. Confused?

Have you ever had to replace the timing belt on your car? You probably didn't do it yourself, since the belt is buried in the innards of your engine and just getting to it is a major production. You might need special model-specific tools, you will need a lot of time, and if you set the timing cogs incorrectly when reassembling the thing, you just might destroy your engine the first time you turn the key.

Such was the state of abdominal and thoracic surgeries before the development of endoscopic surgical techniques. Even though the actual area or object of surgical interest in a procedure might have been very small and the surgical act itself trivial, getting in there meant the hole you had to make in the patient was anything but. Why? Because even a small surgical tool had to be in the hands of a skilled surgeon, and the surgeon's hands were (comparatively) huge. The hands had to be deep in the patient, and so did all of the tools that were there just to make access possible. Like the timing belt procedure, removing a gall bladder meant moving aside lots of other stuff—abdominal wall, stomach, pancreas—and holding it all in place during the procedure.

Endoscopic surgical techniques, on the other hand, eliminate nearly all of these complications by putting the surgical tool on the business end of a narrow rod or rods, which are inserted through *small* holes in the patient. The surgeon then manipulates these tools from outside the patient's body cavity.

Intuitive Surgical did not invent what has come to be known as "minimally invasive" surgery. Rather, it has refined the methods by using electromechanical devices (the "robot" in "robotic surgery") that perform most of the required movements under the control of a trained surgeon. Benefits (over what is referred to as "open" surgery) include reduced risk of infection, reduced blood loss, reduced time spent in the hospital, and generally faster recovery periods. A faster surgical process also means more patients can be attended to with reduced waiting periods. And, in some cases, patients for whom open surgical procedures might not be practical at all can be treated effectively using Intuitive's products.

The big story when it comes to the da Vinci system is, of course, its ability to work in a remote surgical theater. The surgeon's console, with its controls and imaging systems, and the patient-side cart, with its cameras and robotic arms, can be far apart, allowing the surgeon to perform procedures on patients thousands of miles away, requiring only a solid data link and a local support staff for patient interactions and technical support. Healthcare providers can (theoretically) have a patient-side cart positioned as needed and a surgeon's console located at a single facility with a staff of experienced surgeons, and thus provide expert surgical care in a plurality of locations without the need to staff surgical theaters at every facility.

The company was founded in 1995 after acquiring the associated intellectual property of SRI International, which had done much of the early research into what would eventually become the da Vinci system. The company went public in June 2000, and in 2003 acquired its principal competitor (and a litigant in a patent dispute) Computer Motion. They are now the world leader in robotic-assisted surgery and have been approved for use in abdominal, thoracic, cardiac, urological, gynecological, pediatric, and other procedures.

Financial Highlights, Fiscal Year 2017

Total revenue was up 16 percent for the year, with 73 percent of that generated in the US. Sales outside the US have been holding steady at approximately 28 percent each of the past three years, though management have indicated they expect that figure to rise as a percentage going forward. Instrument and accessories revenue grew at very close to the same pace as systems. Service revenue increased by 13 percent and has been rising fairly steadily over the past three years as the installed base has increased significantly over the same period. Looking forward through 2019, estimates are for a 30 percent increase in revenues and a 33 percent increase in earnings on steady net margins of 32 percent.

Reasons to Buy

Intuitive's Q1 2017 results included a note that da Vinci procedures were up 15 percent year-over-year. The stock jumped over $50/share in the next trading session. In the assisted surgical market, customers vote with their hands, and every time a da Vinci–assisted process displaces an open surgery process, it's a sign of acceptance and growing reliance on these machines.

Along those lines, the da Vinci system is proving to be not only a boon for experienced operators but also a powerful training tool for those learning new procedures. The da Vinci system has shown to be successful in reducing the time required to achieve competence in complicated procedures. It is rapidly becoming the preferred surgical treatment for localized prostate cancer and allows surgical procedures to be offered to high-BMI (obese) patients for whom open surgery may not have been an option.

The disciplines of medicine are, often appropriately, slow to change. In light of this philosophy, it's safe to say that the da Vinci system has made surprising progress in the last decade in advancing the state of the art in surgical technique, safety, and availability. The development of new techniques takes time and the support of the surgical community, but Intuitive has made believers of their users, and the company continues to develop procedures and new hardware for the current platform.

Finally, Intuitive is far and away the leader in the market and has been able to operate (pun intended!) over the past decade with little in the way of pricing pressure. Management indicated some concern over competition at the end of 2017, but the Q1 2018 results showed a 60 percent increase in per-share earnings. This may simply be a case of under-promising with a plan to over-deliver.

Reasons for Caution

Even with revenues of over $3 billion last year, Intuitive is, in a way, a young company and the hardware equivalent of a pharmaceutical business: massive R&D costs and a long wait for uncertain success. The platform holds great promise, but many of the da Vinci's potential applications are yet to be developed, tested, and approved. Any new procedures will take time to perfect, and their final approvals are not guaranteed. There's no question that the company is an exciting prospect, but it's also trading at forty-five times earnings, so bear that in mind when deciding if this is the right stock for your portfolio. No matter where you buy in, this is going to be a bumpy ride. Over time, however, we think the operation will be a success.

SECTOR: **Healthcare** ◻ BETA COEFFICIENT: **0.8** ◻ 10-YEAR COMPOUND EARNINGS PER-SHARE GROWTH: **24.5%** ◻ 10-YEAR COMPOUND DIVIDENDS PER-SHARE GROWTH: **NA**

	2010	2011	2012	2013	2014	2015	2016	2017
Revenues (mil)	1,413	1,757	2,179	2,265	2,132	2,384	2,704	3,129
Net income (mil)	382	495	657	671	419	589	736	978
Earnings per share	3.16	4.11	5.33	5.58	3.70	5.18	6.24	8.50
Dividends per share	—	—	—	—	—	—	—	—
Cash flow per share	3.62	4.44	5.73	6.26	4.29	5.83	6.96	9.48
Price: high	131.3	156.4	198.3	195.2	180.4	188.3	242.4	405,0
low	82.0	87.3	143.1	117.0	115.5	149.0	167.3	208.2

Website: www.intuitivesurgical.com

Itron, Inc.

Ticker symbol: ITRI (NASDAQ) ❑ Mid Cap ❑ Value Line financial strength rating: B+ ❑ Current yield: Nil ❑ Dividend raises, past 10 years: NA

Company Profile

The winning streak continues. After five years of writing about the virtue of patience in love, marriage, business, and investing, using the moribund Itron as a premier example (it was our worst pick in 2014), the company has now given us a sustained winner. It morphed from a sleepy unloved provider of utility metering systems—some wireless—into an exciting player in the Internet of Things ("IoT") space. Things didn't really change that much—but they gained traction through persistence, patience, technology evolution, visibility, and now a pretty big acquisition. After another year of strong gains, we're going to stick with this horse for at least one more race.

"Creating a more resourceful world" is the main webpage slogan of Itron, the world's largest provider of standard and intelligent metering systems, mainly to utility companies, for residential and commercial gas, electric, and water usage. Intelligent meters, in addition to tracking raw usage over time, can also measure at the point of use operating parameters such as pressure, temperature, voltage, phase, etc. This information can be extremely valuable to the supplying utility but has in the past been difficult and expensive to obtain.

Itron supplies a range of products from basic meters that are read manually to meters that act as network devices and transmit their data in real time to the managing utility and/or to the consuming customer. Electric, gas, and water meters are sold; the meters come in three groupings:

- Standard metering—basic meters that measure electricity, gas, or water flow by electrical or mechanical means, with displays but no built-in remote reading or transmission capability.
- Advanced metering—these units, depending on the country and the communications technologies available, transmit usage data remotely through telephone, cellular, radio frequency (RF), Ethernet, or power line carrier paths. Among other value adds, these meters transmit usage data for billing, thereby eliminating the need for onsite meter reading— a big savings for utility companies.

- Smart metering—smart meters collect and store interval data and other detailed info, receive commands, and interface with other devices through assorted communication paths to thermostats, smart appliances, and home network and other advanced control systems.

Itron also sells a range of software platforms for utilities and building managers for the management of the installed base and the analysis and optimization of usage. The company also markets advanced metering initiative (AMI) contracts to utilities, where it installs devices and monitors and optimizes power usage for a utility.

At present, electric meters represent about 50 percent of the business, gas meters and water meters about 25 percent each. The company has about 8,000 customers in 100 countries, and about 43 percent of the business comes from outside the US and Canada. Itron has become a major player in the emerging "Smart City" energy use concept, where utility grids manage themselves in real time, and sees long-term benefit from the growing electrification of transport. Itron products are also frequently mentioned in "Internet of Things" circles. It's "OpenWay Riva" product family puts computing power in local meters to analyze data and feed it back into the grid for a real-time systemic management. Itron notes a migration from AMI, which avoids on-site meter reads and more effectively captures history to improve the revenue cycle and detect theft to a Smart Grid and beyond to an Active Grid, where faults and emerging needs within the grid can be anticipated and fixed or delivered in real time.

The biggest news for 2017 and the early part of 2018 is the acquisition of Silver Spring, a sizeable industry rival providing much the same set of products and services with a stronger emphasis on software and system or grid management solutions. This acquisition should strengthen and somewhat modernize Itron's position in this now rapidly growing market.

Financial Highlights, Fiscal Year 2017

Prior to 2016 Itron struggled with soft demand and the lack of critical mass—that is, the lack of enough demand and throughput to keep its facilities running at full efficiency—also referred to as *operating leverage*. Now new technologies—and an increased adoption of the old ones as utilities see the virtues of, and budget for, these new technologies—has led to several major deals for existing and new products. International markets are gaining strength as well.

Revenues were actually flat in 2017, but the bigger story continued to be sales mix and capacity utilization, which led to another 2 percent–plus expansion in operating margin. Net profit grew 270 percent, a second huge jump in a row. The lights don't appear to dim any time soon: FY2018 revenue projections call for a 20 percent gain; with 6–8 percent to follow in 2019. With a much better cost structure, earnings should increase 10–15 percent in 2018 and again in 2019.

Reasons to Buy

Can you picture a day when you might manage your energy consumption, device by device, in your home using your smartphone? Even if you're away from home? Or the day when utilities can monitor usage in real time to shift supply of a resource such as electricity that cannot be easily stored? A day when you (or your apps) work together with your utility to optimize energy use from all sources at all times of the day? A day when solar energy generated from one locale on a sunny day is moved to another with clouds and rain?

If you believe that the need for managed energy efficiency will continue to catch on, and if you believe in the IoT concept in general, Itron is a good place to be. As utilities modernize, reduce costs, and replace infrastructure, Itron products and networks are in the sweet spot. Internationally, utilities are adding infrastructure, as well as replacing it, and Itron is positioned well for that too. Public policy will provide some tailwinds too. Recent droughts bode well for water conservation and smart metering. Worldwide, only about 20 percent of 2.5 billion meters are "smart" or "advanced," while in the US that figure is approaching 60 percent. Smarter, more advanced meters—all part of an expanding IoT network—are where the puck is going, and Itron has a commanding share of this market.

Reasons for Caution

Companies that sell good ideas don't always grow, particularly if the size of their markets is limited or they are particularly conservative about spending money. For these past few years, we thought we were a victim of this mantra but held out hope, and we were right. That said, an economic downturn or some other disruption to Itron's recent success in its marketplace could put us right back in the penalty box. The next few years will be a test of Itron's sustained ability to execute. We also forgive Itron for not paying a dividend for the moment—there are good opportunities for this company to put its cash to work on its own—but we would like to see some of this success come through the pipe to investors eventually.

SECTOR: **Information Technology** ◻ BETA COEFFICIENT: **1.02** ◻ 10-YEAR COMPOUND EARNINGS PER-SHARE GROWTH: **1.5%** ◻ 10-YEAR COMPOUND DIVIDENDS PER-SHARE GROWTH: **NA**

	2010	2011	2012	2013	2014	2015	2016	2017
Revenues (mil)	2,259	2,434	2,178	1,949	1,971	1,883	2,013	2,000
Net income (mil)	133.9	156.3	128.5	15.0	13.7	12.7	31.5	84.5
Earnings per share	3.27	3.85	2.71	0.36	0.35	0.33	0.82	2.15
Dividends per share	—	—	—	—	—	—	—	—
Cash flow per share	4.85	5.56	4.84	2.60	2.93	2.34	2.81	3.85
Price: high	81.9	64.4	50.3	48.4	43.7	42.7	66.1	79.9
low	52.0	26.9	33.3	37.0	32.3	27.9	29.0	57.8

Website: www.itron.com

GROWTH AND INCOME

Johnson & Johnson

Ticker symbol: JNJ (NYSE) ◻ Large Cap ◻ Value Line financial strength rating: A++ ◻ Current yield: 2.6% ◻ Dividend raises, past 10 years: 10

Company Profile

"Caring for the world, one person at a time" is the apt slogan of Johnson & Johnson, one of the largest and most comprehensive healthcare "family of companies" in the world. JNJ offers a broad line of consumer products, over-the-counter drugs, prescription drugs, and various other medical devices and diagnostic equipment. It is—or at least has been—one of the most solid and steady names in an ever-changing medical and pharmaceutical field.

With total FY2017 sales of over $76 billion, the company has three reporting segments: Pharmaceuticals (about 47 percent of revenues), Medical Devices and Diagnostics (about 35 percent), and Consumer Healthcare (surprisingly, since it is so recognizable, only about 18 percent). Across those segments, Johnson & Johnson has more than 250 operating companies in 60 countries, selling some 50,000 products in more than 175 countries. Among Johnson & Johnson's premier assets are its well-entrenched brand names, which are widely known in the US as well as abroad. As a marketer, JNJ's reputation for quality has enabled it to build strong ties to commercial healthcare providers. About 64 percent of sales come from overseas.

In the Consumer segment, the company's vast portfolio of well-known trade names includes Band-Aid adhesive bandages; Tylenol; Stayfree,

Carefree, and Sure & Natural feminine hygiene products; Mylanta; Pep-cid AC; Motrin; Sudafed; Zyrtec; Neosporin; Neutrogena; Johnson's baby powder, shampoo, and oil; Listerine; and Reach toothbrushes. Names in the Pharmaceutical segment are less well-known but include major entries in the areas of antiseptics, antipsychotics, gastroenterology, immunology, neurol-ogy, hematology, contraceptives, oncology, pain management, metabolics, and many others distributed both through consumer and healthcare profes-sional channels. Leading diseases addressed include rheumatoid and psori-atic arthritis, inflammatory bowel disease, Alzheimer's, HIV, schizophrenia, prostate cancer, diabetes, and many others. XARELTO (vascular health), STELARA (inflammatory diseases), and the recently approved JULUCA (HIV-1 infection) are among the more prominent pharmaceutical names.

Medical Devices and Diagnostics products include professionally used cardiovascular, orthopedic, diabetic, neurologic, and surgical products, ACUVUE contact lenses and other vision care products and others.

The company is typically fairly active with acquisitions, picking up mostly small niche players to strengthen its overall product offering. Acqui-sitions accounted for about 2 percent of the company's 6.3 percent revenue growth reported in 2017 and include Abbott Medical Optics and Actelion, a Swiss maker of pulmonary arterial hypertension drugs.

Financial Highlights, Fiscal Year 2017

Johnson & Johnson continues to own a dominant and stable franchise in a secure and lucrative industry. The basic model is to have steady, recurring income from solid consumer brands such as Tylenol combined with more aggressive and profitable ventures into pharmaceuticals and surgical prod-ucts. Recently the company has become more aggressive in the pharma seg-ment. FY2017 saw an acceleration in revenue to a 6.3 percent gain, helped along by slightly favorable currency conversion and small acquisitions. The Pharmaceutical segment weighed in with an 8 percent gain, while the Con-sumer segment lagged with a 2.2 percent gain, which would have been nega-tive without currency and acquisitions—softness in oral care and baby care products were cited as causes. Net income as reported rose about 1 percent after some one-time items; we should note that there was a $13.6 billion write-off due to the new federal tax law enacted in late 2017. Per-share earnings, helped by buybacks, rose 8.5 percent. For FY2018 the company projects a 4–5 percent top-line gain, and the greater emphasis on pharma and new approvals in the pipeline will bring higher net margins and a pro-jected 20 percent gain in net income. FY2019 gains are projected in the 5–6 percent range for revenue and in the 8 percent range for net income Buy-backs may attenuate as the company becomes a more aggressive acquirer, while dividend increases should continue in the 5–7 percent range annually. The company has raised its dividend for 55 straight years.

Reasons to Buy

JNJ continues to be a conservatively run company whose growth prospects have traditionally been on the lower end of this book's scale, but clearly the company has entered a bit of a growth phase. That said, JNJ still retains great appeal in the investment community especially in periods of market volatility. We still like JNJ's slow steady business model mixing reliable, branded performers with more lucrative pharma and medical device products bringing steady earnings and cash flow combined with healthy dividend growth. The 23–25 percent *net* profit margins are enviable. It's a "sleep at night" stock with a decent growth component and track record for shareholder "raises."

Reasons for Caution

While we still think JNJ is a good, steady horse for a relatively long race, it has picked up some speed of late through increased emphasis on pharma, the recent Actelion acquisition, and others that may be pending, increasing the chance of getting winded somewhere along the way. The P/E, a figure we don't rely on heavily but do look at, has expanded from 14–15 to the 17–18 range, adding a bit of downside risk to the mix. We wouldn't like to see JNJ take too much risk just to achieve growth; they have a market position and high profit margins—don't monkey with what works!

SECTOR: **Healthcare** ❑ BETA COEFFICIENT: **0.74** ❑ 10-YEAR COMPOUND EARNINGS PER-SHARE GROWTH: **6.0%** ❑ 10-YEAR COMPOUND DIVIDENDS PER-SHARE GROWTH: **9.5%**

	2010	2011	2012	2013	2014	2015	2016	2017
Revenues (mil)	61,587	65,030	67,224	71,312	74,311	70,074	71,890	76,450
Net income (mil)	13,279	13,867	14,345	15,576	16,323	15,409	16,540	16,680
Earnings per share	4.76	5.00	5.10	5.52	5.70	5.50	5.93	6.20
Dividends per share	2.11	2.25	2.40	2.59	2.76	2.97	3.15	3.32
Cash flow per share	5.90	6.25	6.45	7.10	7.26	6.90	7.45	7.95
Price: high	66.2	66.3	72.7	96.0	109.5	106.5	126.1	144.4
low	56.9	64.3	61.7	70.3	86.1	81.8	94.3	110.8

Website: www.jnj.com

CONSERVATIVE GROWTH

The Kroger Company

Ticker symbol: KR (NYSE) ❑ Large Cap ❑ Value Line financial strength rating: A ❑ Current yield: 2.1% ❑ Dividend raises, past 10 years: 10

Company Profile

Those of you who follow our fortunes year in and year out know that our fortunes took a hit two years ago with Retail in general. Target and Macy's came off the list as they seemed to be enveloped by the advance of Amazon Prime and other Internet shopping venues. But they bounced back on the strength of the economy in general, the loyalty of their customers, and some of the strategies they put in place to deliver a better experience and compete more effectively with the titans of e-commerce. With a little more patience, we could have ridden that recovery, but it seemed to be risky at the time.

As we eliminated Target and Macy's, we faced a similar situation with Kroger. Kroger, too, seemed vulnerable to shifts in the shopping space, not just online but also to competitive shifts as Walmart and others continue to challenge the traditional grocery store with more warehouse-y discount formats. Then along came Amazon itself—buying Whole Foods. Competition was heating up faster than fried chicken in hot oil, margins were declining, and so was the stock price.

So here we sit, wondering whether Kroger, through no mistake of its own, is strategically lost in its own wilderness? Or will it adapt and flourish in its giant full-service grocery niche? We're going to bet on the latter, and bet that Kroger, like Target, like Macy's, will avoid the rush to check out with an empty basket. Kroger is the nation's largest retail grocery store operator, with about 2,782 supermarkets and multi-department stores, 782 convenience stores, and 274 specialty jewelry stores operated around the country. Supermarket operations account for about 94 percent of total revenue and are located in 35 states with a concentration in the Midwest (where it was founded) and in the South and West, where it grew mostly by acquisition. The company is dominant in the markets it serves, with a number one or two market share position in 42 of its 49 major markets. Kroger operates through a series of store brands many of you will be familiar with but probably did not associate with the Kroger name, including King Soopers, City Market, Fred Meyer, Fry's, Ralphs, Dillons, Smith's, Baker's, Food 4 Less, Harris Teeter, and an assortment of others totaling about two dozen business names. There are five convenience store chains:

Kwik Shop, Loaf 'N Jug, Quik Stop, Tom Thumb, and Turkey Hill located in 18 states.

In late 2015 Kroger acquired Roundy's, parent company of the urban upscale supermarket chain Mariano's, which operates 34 stores in the Chicago area and 117 other stores mainly in Wisconsin. The Mariano's footprint is urban and somewhere between a traditional grocery and Whole Foods—an interesting new style of store that should play well with urban and millennial consumers and naturally could be expanded elsewhere.

The typical Kroger supermarket is full service and well appointed with higher-margin specialty departments such as health foods, seafood, floral, and other perishables. The Fred Meyer stores carry a large assortment of general merchandise in addition to groceries, turning them into modern-era big-box department stores; the company has 132 stores in all that meet this format, mostly in the West. There are also 130 "price impact warehouse" stores under the Food 4 Less, Foods Co., and Ruler Foods brands and 153 "marketplace" stores—"Kroger Marketplace," "Fry's Marketplace," "King Soopers Marketplace," and so forth—with expanded offerings similar to Fred Meyer to complement the supermarkets. About 1,489 "supermarket fuel centers" and 1,950 pharmacies round out the supermarket picture. Finally, the company has a considerable presence in manufacturing its own store-branded food items, with 38 such plants located around the country and estimates that 26 percent of revenues and 30 percent of unit volumes come from in-house brands. On the innovation front a new online and mobile "ClickList" tool allows customers to shop online and pick up at the store. Other initiatives focus on loyalty and data-driven promotion to valued customers.

Financial Highlights, Fiscal Year 2017

Prior to 2017 Kroger had boasted that same-store supermarket sales had grown for 45 consecutive quarters—a good track record in light of the Great Recession and heightened competition from the likes of Walmart, Target, and others. However, this streak came to an end in early 2017 on a combination of competition, food price deflation, and lower gas prices. But, while 2017 was fairly soft, Kroger did post a same-store sales gain of 1.1 percent (0.7 percent excluding fuel) for the year. In total, revenues were up a bit over 6 percent, but price competition did take a bite out of net margins (1.5 percent versus 1.8 percent in 2016), and net profit declined accordingly almost 9 percent. FY2018 looks like a consolidation year where the company invests and grows its e-commerce business (which was up 90 percent in 2017) and fine-tunes its stores and store network; earnings may drop another 3 percent on a slight revenue gain. The payoff starts in 2019 with a 5 percent earnings gain on a 3–4 percent rise in sales, and initiatives currently underway bode well for business performance in 2020 and beyond. Steady buybacks and high-single-digit dividend increases should continue. Kroger's own shares continue to top its own shopping list; they have now retired more than 30 percent of their float since 2010.

Reasons to Buy

We're taking a bit of a risk here in this increasingly competitive industry, but we think Kroger continues to do a good job in a tough market, gaining market share for the thirteenth consecutive year. Major discount retailers such as Walmart and Target have stepped into the grocery business with a fairly significant price advantage, yet so far Kroger has been able to fend them off by focusing on product breadth, the shopping experience, and strategic price reductions. Here's the kicker: while we see price competition taking away some share on typical mostly commoditized grocery products, we see full-line grocers like Kroger taking away share on higher-margined organic and natural products at the expense of Whole Foods, Sprouts, and other "natural" retailers—even with Amazon behind Whole Foods. About 14 percent of Kroger's sales are natural or organic today. Kroger loses some share on "ordinary" groceries to Walmart but gets some from the specialty direction, which should help margins and overall results going forward. Kroger will also expand the reach of its "ClickList" digital seamless shopping and pickup and delivery experience to a wider geographic area. We're still not convinced that Amazon/Whole Foods can deliver enough fast enough and with a complete assortment people would desire—and think Kroger and potentially other partners can answer this online challenge anyway.

We also like the Fred Meyer quality grocery-plus-department-store format, a more pleasant and balanced shopping experience than either Walmart or Target and a format that Kroger would do well to roll out nationwide. We also see the recently acquired Mariano's as a good expansion model.

All told, Kroger is a well-managed company that continues to dominate its niches, and its shares have been on the discount endcap of late.

Reasons for Caution

You can't think "full-service grocer" without raising the fear of competition from discounters—and now Amazon. If the conventional grocery store format is condemned to the dustbin of retail history, Kroger could be vulnerable, but we feel it has the direction and wherewithal to adapt and upgrade both the shopping experience and the food basket to please today's choosier millennial shoppers. But the razor-thin 1.5 percent profit margins characteristic of this industry leave little room for error. We continue to believe that differentiated bricks-and-mortar retail can still succeed in today's world, and we hope we're right that Kroger remains a category winner. But if we see them trying to compete broadly on price rather than selection, convenience, healthfulness, and so forth, it will be time to find another checkout line.

SECTOR: Retail ▫ **BETA COEFFICIENT: 1.04** ▫ **10-YEAR COMPOUND EARNINGS PER-SHARE GROWTH: 10.5%** ▫ **10-YEAR COMPOUND DIVIDENDS PER-SHARE GROWTH: 17.0%**

	2010	2011	2012	2013	2014	2015	2016	2017
Revenues (bil)	82.1	90.4	96.7	98.5	108.5	109.8	115.3	122.7
Net income (mil)	1,118	1,192	1,423	1,445	1,757	2,039	2,046	1,858
Earnings per share	0.87	1.00	1.32	1.43	1.76	2.06	2.12	2.04
Dividends per share	0.20	0.22	0.27	0.32	0.35	0.41	0.47	0.50
Cash flow per share	2.19	2.52	2.99	3.15	3.81	4.27	4.75	4.96
Price: high	12.1	12.9	13.5	21.9	32.5	42.8	35.0	19.7
low	9.7	9.5	10.5	10.5	12.6	17.8	27.3	28.3

Website: www.kroger.com

CONSERVATIVE GROWTH

McCormick & Company, Inc.

Ticker symbol: MKC (NYSE) ▫ Large Cap ▫ Value Line financial strength rating: A+ ▫ Current yield: 1.9% ▫ Dividend raises, past 10 years: 10

Company Profile

"To Make Every Meal and Moment Better" is spice maker and marketer McCormick & Co.'s tasty slogan. The company manufactures, markets, and distributes spices, herbs, condiments, seasonings, flavors, and flavor enhancers to consumers and to the global food industry. It is the largest such supplier in the world. Customers range from retail outlets and food manufacturers to foodservice businesses.

McCormick's Consumer business (about 61 percent of sales), its oldest and largest, manufactures consumer spices, herbs, extracts, proprietary seasoning blends, sauces, and marinades. Spices are sold under an assortment of recognizable brand names: McCormick, Lawry's, Zatarain's, Thai Kitchen, Simply Asia, Club House, Billy Bee, Produce Partners, Golden Dipt, Old Bay, Mojave, and now, with the largest acquisition in its history, French's mustard and Frank's RedHot sauces. The company estimates its retail market share to be four times the nearest competitor.

Industrial customers include foodservice, food-processing businesses, and retail outlets. The Industrial segment was responsible for 39 percent of sales.

Many of the spices and herbs purchased by the company, such as black pepper, vanilla beans, cinnamon, and herbs and seeds, must be imported from countries such as India, Indonesia, Malaysia, Brazil, and the Malagasy Republic. Other ingredients such as paprika, dehydrated vegetables, onion, garlic, and food ingredients other than spices and herbs originate in the US.

The company was founded in 1889 and has approximately 11,700 full-time employees in facilities located around the world. The company has brands for sale in about 150 countries, and tapping into local tastes is a priority—there are innovation centers in 14 countries. The biggest sales components are Americas Consumer (42 percent), Americas Industrial (26 percent), EMEA Consumer (12 percent), EMEA Industrial (6 percent), and Asia-Pacific Consumer (8 percent). McCormick has been innovating both on the product and on web and media fronts, including more informative print and web content with recipes and other information to spur cooking with spices. Product innovations included the conversion of 75 percent of their premium spice line to organic; the company is now number one in the US for organic spices and seasonings, and major US retail chains have expanded the presence of these lines in response. New gluten-free and non-GMO products and relabelings have entered the market. Overall, 9 percent of 2017 sales came from products introduced in the past three years.

As well, for the past three years, the company has been ranked in the Top 5 out of 114 food brands in the US market for its "Digital IQ" index. In 2017 it achieved a number 3 brand ranking. A new marketing campaign emphasized the importance of flavor and quality of McCormick's spices and seasonings—the company estimated a 2 percent rise in millennial household penetration as a result. More examples of innovative brand and Internet marketing include an initiative to map your spice tastes by giving you a personalized "FlavorPrint"—then emailing you weekly recipes with spice recommendations tailored to that map. Flavor and flavor trend innovations include a new packaging initiative—called Recipe Inspirations—to sell prepackaged spices set to cook a particular meal. As well, they have a place on their website to enter in a singular spice, one that you might like and/or have an abundance of in your pantry; they shoot back recipes for that spice (something we amateur hash slingers have longed for in cookbooks; give me a selection of recipes that use allspice, for instance). All of these initiatives broaden the market to reach the millions of plain folks like us who weren't born with a wooden spoon in our mouths. For those who were born with such a spoon, or who acquired one through years of training and experience, there is also a "McCormick for Chefs" page. In short, we like this recipe: dominant brand, effective digital marketing to spice it up. McCormick continues to be one of the best examples we've seen.

Financial Highlights, Fiscal Year 2017

Overall, business continues to respond nicely to new trends for more interesting foods and a stronger preponderance to stay at home for meals. That, the RB Foods acquisition (French's and Frank's) and realizing results of a long-term "continuous improvement initiative" led to a pretty spicy 2017; sales were up almost 10 percent while net earnings were up over 13 percent on a full percentage point increase in operating margin. Effective marketing, a fine-tuning of the product mix toward higher-margined offerings and moderate productivity improvements should bring another 12–13 percent sales gain and an 18–20 percent net income gain in 2019, slowing to a 5–7 percent income gain in 2019 on a 3 percent top-line gain. Dividend increases, which have occurred for 32 straight years now, should continue, while buybacks have stopped for the moment as the company invests in innovation and product marketing.

Reasons to Buy

Simply put, McCormick dominates its food business niche and it's an important one—some 90 percent of food flavor is delivered with 10 percent of its cost, and flavor is the biggest determinant of choice. As a strong pure play in the seasonings business, McCormick is the largest branded producer of seasonings in North America and one of the largest in the world. McCormick is not just a producer, it is also an innovator and a marketer, and we feel they've done the right things to build interest in their products and in their brand. They also do well in specialized niche markets such as Mexico and China. We think they're in the right place as new, fresher, and more tailored, customized, interesting, and international food trends all emerge. We also think they're in a pretty good place with millennials, who want new, different, healthy, and customizable approaches to almost everything—including food—and who want to source their information about food and culinary excellence from the Internet.

On the consumer side, as amateur cooks ourselves we continue to feel that people would use more spices if they only knew how to use them. The website and its recipe offerings and the prepackaged Recipe Inspirations meal kits will get the less-experienced cooks using spices more effectively in their own cooking. In our view, these initiatives, combined with continuing growth in the health-conscious segment by learning to replace fat flavoring with spice flavoring, will add to a solid business base for the company.

McCormick estimates the spice market to be growing at 6 percent annually, and with its 22 percent share of the global market, there is plenty of opportunity; market share expansion is a key strategy. That all mixes well with the profitability, stability, and defensive nature of the company; it's an attractive combination for investors.

Reasons for Caution
Downsides include the rising cost of ingredients and the sourcing of many of these ingredients in geopolitically unstable regions. There is also increasing competition from private-label products. While earnings and share-price growth have been steady, the price of the stock has been spiced up a bit by its success. All that said, we don't see people's tastes in taste diminishing any time soon.

SECTOR: **Consumer Staples** ▫ BETA COEFFICIENT: **0.56** ▫ 10-YEAR COMPOUND EARNINGS PER-SHARE GROWTH: **8.0%** ▫ 10-YEAR COMPOUND DIVIDENDS PER-SHARE GROWTH: **9.0%**

		2010	**2011**	**2012**	**2013**	**2014**	**2015**	**2016**	**2017**
Revenues (mil)		3,339	3,650	4,014	4,123	4,243	4,396	4,411	4,834
Net income (mil)		356.3	380	408	418	442	450	479	547
Earnings per share		2.65	2.80	3.04	3.13	3.37	3.48	3.78	4.26
Dividends per share		1.04	1.12	1.24	1.36	1.48	1.60	1.72	1.88
Cash flow per share		3.39	3.55	3.85	4.00	4.24	4.36	4.64	5.13
Price:	high	47.8	51.3	66.4	75.3	77.1	87.5	107.8	106.5
	low	35.4	43.4	49.9	60.8	52.6	70.7	78.4	89.6

Website: **www.mccormick.com**

McKesson Corporation

Ticker symbol: MCK (NYSE) ❑ Large Cap ❑ Value Line financial strength rating: A++ ❑ Current yield: 0.9% ❑ Dividend raises, past 10 years: 8

Company Profile

Sometimes even your surest bets—like our bets on healthcare—hit a rough patch. Such is the case with McKesson, one of our steadiest healthcare performers, and winners, over the years. We wrote about this each of the last two years, and to our surprise, it continues. The business hasn't changed much, but the valuation did, with a P/E ratio falling from the low 20s to—what, 11?—where it has remained for almost two years—on some pricing weakness in generic and prescription lines, weakness in the international sector, and uncertainty about the Affordable Care Act. Add to that the new consortium formed by Amazon, Berkshire Hathaway, and JPMorgan Chase to address the healthcare infrastructure, delivery models, and costs—and a few mergers such as CVS–Aetna—and you can see how a little more uncertainty has crept into this staid business. But we think this business and McKesson's market leadership will remain largely intact. Remember that in emotional markets, often the business is just fine; the pricing of the stock gets out of whack. McKesson stays on the 2019 *100 Best* list.

McKesson Corporation is America's oldest and largest healthcare services company and engages in two distinct businesses to support the healthcare industry. Pharmaceutical and medical-surgical supply distribution is the first and by far the biggest business: the company is the largest such distributor in North America, delivering about a third of all medications used daily to 50 percent of US hospitals and all but one of the top 25 health plans. The company delivers to approximately 40,000 pharmaceutical outlets as well as hospitals and clinics throughout North America from 27 domestic and 13 Canadian distribution facilities, and recently added a major distribution stronghold for Europe from which it serves 13 countries. The company has also been adding company-owned pharmacies and has about 4,800 Health Mart outlets in the US with 470 more in Canada from the acquisition of Rexall Health in that country. The distribution business, known as McKesson Distribution Solutions, accounts for about 99 percent of sales.

Second, and not to be ignored though only accounting for 1 percent of the business, is a technology solutions business, McKesson Technology Solutions, which provides clinical systems, analytics, clinical decision support, medical necessity and utilization management tools, electronic medical records, physical and financial supply-chain management, and connectivity solutions to hospitals, pharmacies, and an assortment of healthcare providers. "We build essential connections that make health care smarter" is their apt slogan. The strategically important information technology business is a $2.6 billion business all by itself. McKesson's software and hardware IT solutions are installed in some 76 percent of the nation's hospitals with more than 200 beds and 52 percent of hospitals overall. In 2017 the company reported that it is looking at strategic options for this business.

The company offers products and services covering most aspects of pharmacy and drug distribution, including not only physical distribution and supply-chain services but also a line of proprietary generics and automated dispensing systems, record-keeping systems, and outsourcing services used in retail and hospital pharmacy operations. The central strategies are to provide a one-stop distribution solution for pharmaceuticals, generics, and surgical supplies, and to provide technology solutions to deliver higher-quality and more cost-effective care at the hospital and clinical levels.

Financial Highlights, Fiscal Year 2017

Once again you'd think that with a 30 percent drop in the share price since the 2015 peak, revenues and earnings would be marching backward at a rapid rate. But for the most part revenue and earnings have advanced steadily and appear to be accelerating as we move into 2019. FY2017 revenues were up about 7 percent; earnings were up a more modest 3 percent, but per-share earnings were up a healthier 10 percent. FY2018 revenues are projected to rise in the 9–10 percent range, with earnings jumping ahead at a 15 percent rate or better; FY2019 appears to be on track to generate another 10 percent top-line growth with 6–8 percent on the bottom line. The company will continue with moderate dividend increases; share buybacks appear to be on hold (we'd like to see them buy back more at today's depressed share prices), but some cash has been deployed to pay off long-term debt from recent acquisitions.

Reasons to Buy

Although price reductions do hurt in such a low-margin business, the distribution business continues to be solid and relatively recession-proof. Demographics and the addition of millions to the insured healthcare rolls have kept demand moving in the right direction, and acquisitions have strengthened that position in domestic and especially international markets. McKesson dominates its niches and is a go-to provider of much of what hospitals and clinics need to operate. It holds market leader position in several important market categories, including number one in pharmaceutical distribution in the United States and Canada, number one in generic pharmaceutical distribution, number one in medical management software and services to payers…you get the idea.

Additionally, hospitals and other healthcare providers are starting to get the memo that it is time to improve utilization and operational efficiency, and McKesson's technology solutions are hard to ignore, although many might do so at first glance, as they are only 1 percent of the business. As most distributors do, McKesson operates on very thin margins; the expansion of technology services and generic-equivalent drugs should eventually become a growth driver as efficiency measures continue to catch on.

The company has a strong track record of stability and operational excellence and is well managed; for long-term investors, the recent share-price weakness would seem to signal a buying opportunity; a recent P/E of 11.1 seems too low for a company of this strength and track record, especially with solid earnings growth projected ahead.

Reasons for Caution

McKesson does operate on thin margins and as such has a low tolerance for mistakes or major changes in the healthcare space, changes that could be brought on by legislation, regulation, or competition including the afore-mentioned Amazon/Berkshire/Morgan effort. Hospital censuses are low these days as patients and payers find other ways to get things done and to shorten visits. Amazon itself may turn up the competitive pressure as they have announced their intent to get into the hospital supply distribution business. Changes in the ACA could hurt some, as well as new efforts to reduce drug pricing, and other healthcare changes present more of a wild card than the company has faced in the past. We'd like to see a bit more return to shareholders in the form of cash dividends; that said, the company has quintupled the indicated dividend since 2007 and appears to be poised to continue on that path.

SECTOR: **Healthcare** ❑ BETA COEFFICIENT:**1.22** ❑ 10-YEAR COMPOUND EARNINGS PER-SHARE GROWTH: **16.0%** ❑ 10-YEAR COMPOUND DIVIDENDS PER-SHARE GROWTH: **16.0%**

	2010	2011	2012	2013	2014	2015	2016	2017
Revenues (bil)	112.1	122.7	122.5	137.6	179.5	190.1	198.5	212.0
Net income (mil)	1,316	1,463	1,516	1,947	2,614	2,290	2,589	2,675
Earnings per share	5.00	6.05	6.33	8.35	11.11	9.84	11.61	12.75
Dividends per share	0.72	0.76	0.80	0.88	1.04	1.08	1.28	1.40
Cash flow per share	7.18	8.40	9.30	11.50	15.68	14.11	16.58	17.50
Price: high	71.5	87.3	100.0	166.6	214.4	243.6	199.4	169.3
low	57.2	66.6	74.9	96.7	96.7	160.1	114.5	133.8

Website: www.mckesson.com

AGGRESSIVE GROWTH

Medtronic, PLC

Ticker symbol: MDT (NYSE) ❑ Large Cap ❑ Value Line financial strength rating: A++ ❑ Current yield: 2.2% ❑ Dividend raises, past 10 years: 10

Company Profile

Medtronic is the world's largest manufacturer of implantable medical devices and is a leading medical technology company, providing lifelong solutions to "alleviate pain, restore health, and extend life," primarily for people with chronic diseases. FY2015 was a year of major change for the company, as it completed a $50 billion acquisition of "rival" device maker Covidien, expanding sales by almost 40 percent mostly by gaining market share internationally and in three key segments: Surgical Solutions, Vascular Therapies, and Respiratory and Monitoring Solutions. Through the acquisition of Covidien, Medtronic also acquired an offshore headquarters in Dublin, Ireland, reducing tax rates and increasing net profit margins in the process— although with the passage of the 2017 Tax Cuts and Jobs Act, much of this saving would have occurred anyway.

Since that acquisition, and the more recent divestiture of certain patient care, deep vein thrombosis and nutritional supplements businesses to Cardinal Health, a more focused Medtronic continues to operate mainly in the areas of cardiovascular, neurological, and other surgeries and therapies and in diabetes management. There are four business segments:

- Cardiac and Vascular Group (35 percent of FY2017 sales). Businesses include Cardiac Rhythm & Heart Failure, Coronary & Structural Heart, and Aortic & Peripheral Vascular. This group as a whole develops products that restore and regulate a patient's heart rhythm as well as improve the heart's pumping function. This segment markets implantable pacemakers, defibrillators, Internet- and non-Internet–based monitoring and diagnostic devices, and cardiac resynchronization devices. Micra, a new implantable cardiac monitor about a third the size of an AAA battery and 80 percent smaller than competing products—about the size of a medicine capsule—exemplifies the company's R&D leadership in this industry, as do new efforts to automate remote monitoring and management of heart rhythm patients, a promising expansion of the "Internet of Things" concept into healthcare. Products also include therapies to treat coronary artery disease and hypertension, including balloon angioplasty catheters, guide catheters, diagnostic catheters, guidewires, and accessories. Another line of products and therapies treats heart valve disorders and repairs/replaces heart valves, some through catheters without chest incisions. The unit also markets tools to assist heart surgeons during surgery, including circulatory support systems, heart positioners and tissue stabilizers, ablation tools, stent graft, and angioplasty solutions.
- The Minimally Invasive Therapies Group (33 percent of sales) produces an assortment of products under its Surgical Solutions and Patient Monitoring and Recovery business units. The majority of Covidien's products fell into this group.
- The Restorative Therapies Group (25 percent of sales) includes Spine, Biologics, Neuromodulation, Surgical Technologies, and Neurovascular business units. The Spine unit develops and manufactures products that treat a variety of disorders of the cranium and spine, including traumatically induced conditions, deformities, herniated discs and other disc diseases, osteoporosis, and tumors. This unit recently rolled out "Intellis"—the world's smallest implantable spinal cord stimulator for chronic pain. The Biologics business is the global leader in biologics regeneration and pain therapies across a variety of musculoskeletal applications including spine, orthopedic trauma, and dental. The Neuromodulation unit employs many technologies used in heart electrical stimulation to treat diseases of the central nervous system. It offers therapies for movement disorders; chronic pain; urological and

gastroenterological disorders, including incontinence, benign prostatic hyperplasia (BPH), enlarged prostate, and gastroesophageal reflux disease (GERD); and psychological diseases. The Surgical Technologies unit develops and markets products and therapies for ear, nose, and throat–related diseases and certain neurological disorders; among them are precision image-guided surgical systems.

- The Diabetes Group (6 percent of sales—but still totaling $1.9 billion, a good-sized business) offers advanced diabetes management solutions, including insulin pump therapy, glucose monitoring systems, and treatment management software.

Overseas sales represent about 40 percent of the total; R&D is 7.5 percent of sales.

Financial Highlights, Fiscal Year 2017

The Covidien acquisition, completed in early 2015, created a steep step up in sales, profits, and margins, which Medtronic continued to enjoy into FY2017 with some $600 million in synergy savings. Overall revenue and profits were largely flat mostly due to the divestitures noted previously; the company reports a 5 percent constant currency "organic" increase for the year. Revenue growth and cost savings will really kick in in FY2018 with a projected 5 percent growth once again and a stronger 8–9 percent growth in net income; the growth story is expected to be largely the same in FY2019. Steady dividend raises and modest share buybacks will continue to be part of the shareholder picture.

Reasons to Buy

The name Medtronic continues to be synonymous with medical technology; the company remains one of the pure plays in the healthcare technology space. The company was already a "best in class" player in the markets and technologies it was engaged in, and over time its technologies have become more mainstream. We are also big supporters of its investments in remote medicine, its investments in emerging markets, and its involvement with new products and breakthroughs, especially in neuromodulation and diabetes management. The Covidien merger appears to be working both as a product line expansion and as an entry ticket into overseas markets. Finally, while the merger adds some acquisition risk and long-term debt, we expect the company to gradually retire the 400 million shares issued for the acquisition and to continue its steady track record of dividend increases.

Reasons for Caution

Having an overseas headquarters in Ireland and a large manufacturing plant in Puerto Rico looked like a good idea until the Trump administration took over; now that strategy may backfire. The healthcare landscape is changing, with new emphasis on reducing hospital stays, cutting costs, and managing and rewarding patient outcomes. As a consequence, the healthcare "food chain" is changing with new mergers, alliances, and agreements—and where Medtronic fits into this all remains to be seen. Some might find the company's growth rates to be a little shy of the mark, which of course suggests more acquisitions may be forthcoming—another risk factor. Still, that all said, Medtronic continues to be a strong, entrenched leader in medical technology, and well positioned to get stronger still.

SECTOR: **Healthcare** ◻ BETA COEFFICIENT: **0.93** ◻ 10-YEAR COMPOUND EARNINGS PER-SHARE GROWTH: **9.0%** ◻ 10-YEAR COMPOUND DIVIDENDS PER-SHARE GROWTH: **15.0%**

		2010	2011	2012	2013	2014	2015	2016	2017
Revenues (mil)		15,933	16,184	16,590	17,005	20,261	26,833	29,715	29,500
Net income (mil)		3,647	3,447	3,857	3,878	4,937	8,750	7,359	7,535
Earnings per share		3.22	3.46	3.75	3.82	4.45	5.16	5.40	5.50
Dividends per share		0.90	0.97	1.04	1.12	1.22	1.52	1.72	1.84
Cash flow per share		4.16	4.13	4.60	4.73	5.15	7.28	7.55	7.75
Price:	high	46.7	43.3	44.6	58.8	75.7	79.5	89.3	89.7
	low	30.8	30.2	35.7	41.2	53.3	55.5	71.0	69.4

Website: www.medtronic.com

AGGRESSIVE GROWTH

Microchip Technology, Inc.

Ticker symbol: MCHP (NASDAQ) ◻ Large Cap ◻ Value Line financial strength rating: A ◻ Current yield: 1.5% ◻ Dividend raises, past 10 years: 9

Company Profile

Your washing machine senses the load, adjusts the wash time and temperature accordingly, and texts you when it's done. Your refrigerator expands or contracts its power cycle according to outside temperature and the time of day to save on peak power costs. You tell your Alexa-enabled device to play a song, record a shopping list, or tell you the weather in St. Louis in advance of a business trip. Security systems show you what's happening in all parts of your home—and in other homes, such as that of your aging elders. Asset monitors keep track of inventory and key business equipment. It's all connected, always on, all the time.

The "Internet of Things" describes a world in which the devices we rely on for some pretty mundane tasks (making coffee, for example) can be connected to other devices in clever ways to compound their utility. We like the fact that when we do finally stumble into the kitchen in the morning, the coffee is brewed, the lights are dimmed a bit, the temperature is appropriate for the hour, and the morning news briefing is playing with our selected feeds. The prospect of all of our stuff connected to all our other stuff and doing our thinking for us opens up a world of possibilities, and this "bolt-on" intelligence, making "dumb" devices into "smart" tools, is a large part of what Microchip Technology is about.

Interestingly, this "local intelligence" concept is nothing new to MCHP. They've been building low-power microcontrollers (and the tools to integrate them) for over thirty years. The advent of zippy wireless local networking and other enabling technologies has played right into MCHP's strengths as a known quantity in the processor business.

Microchip Technology is a leading manufacturer and supplier of specialized semiconductor products primarily embedded as controllers, processors, or memory products other than what are generally thought of as computers. The company's devices, many of which are customizable, custom-made, or programmable, sense motion, temperature, touch, proximity, and other environmental conditions, process the information, and control the device accordingly. Applications number literally in the thousands but are concentrated in automotive, communications, consumer product, appliance, lighting, medical, safety and security, and power and energy management products. The March 2018 acquisition of chipmaker Microsemi has expanded their markets considerably to include defense, aerospace, and communications applications. The company offers a full suite of design assistance, tools, and consulting services to help customers, usually OEMs, develop the best applications. They position these services as "low-risk product development" resources for their customers.

Microchip owns most of its manufacturing capability in five plants: two in Arizona, one in Oregon, one in California, and one in Thailand, as part of a deliberate strategy to increase process yields and shorten cycle times (about 60 percent of their sales derive from internal wafer fabs). Most but not all products are shipped "off the shelf" with short cycle times or as a scheduled production. R&D accounts for about 17 percent of revenues. As the company sells primarily to other OEM electronic product manufacturers, about 81 percent of sales are to international customers; about 30 percent are to China. Technology licensing accounts for about 4 percent of revenues.

Microchip has more clearly aligned itself and its branding behind the concept of embedded control solutions and now calls itself "The Embedded Control Solutions Company"—a clear and well-defined business position. The company continues to be an active acquirer as the semiconductor industry consolidates; the two most recent acquisitions include the 2016 purchase of microcontroller and touch technology supplier Atmel for $3.4 billion and the $8.4 billion acquisition of broadly diversified chipmaker Microsemi.

Financial Highlights, Fiscal Year 2017

FY2017 was the first full year of wholly organic growth for MCHP in some time, and so we have a chance to see how well the Atmel integration is going. The results are pretty clear: operating margins have improved by eight percentage points over the past two years while revenue has grown nearly 70 percent. Of that sales increase, approximately 9 percent was organic in FY2017. Earnings grew a healthy 42 percent. There were charges associated with the closure of a redundant Atmel fabrication facility, and capital spending is up significantly but is well in line with what is considered normal for a semiconductor manufacturer with in-house silicon processing capability. It should be noted that MCHP does not require "bleeding-edge" process facilities for its products and is well-served by 6- and 8-inch wafer fabs running older, higher-yield geometries and processes and standard, non-exotic packaging.

Looking forward, revenue gains from the Microsemi acquisition should provide a $2 billion bump in 2018/2019, with organic growth rates in the 5–7 percent range for FY2018 and FY2019, with per-share earnings growing in the 10–15 percent range annually. Microsemi was an all-cash deal, so share counts are steady, but debt service will rise significantly.

Reasons to Buy

We like companies that make the things that make things work, and Microchip seems well positioned as a leading supplier of all this intelligence as "smart" moves far beyond the "smartphone." We tend to keep a closer eye on the fundamentals of semiconductor companies in general; development and manufacturing costs are high, especially if a company owns its own "fabs" (manufacturing facilities) and product cycles are short. There is plenty of competition everywhere for most products, much of it from lower-cost producers in Asia. Inventory cycles can also play havoc with semiconductor producers, who do best by producing in large quantities. Microchip, in our view, has overcome a lot of that by playing in high-value-add niches and by offering plenty of design and technical support "value add" to go along with the product—and now with its acquisitions, by becoming a more dominant player in its niche.

Another differentiator employed by Microchip is a long-standing policy of keeping older parts in their catalog. The nature of their customers' markets (and thus, Microchip's market) often calls for the development of a pervasive architecture over time. Industrial users rarely need the latest in CPU speeds and features, but they do have a large investment in software that's been developed and customized for their application over perhaps decades. If Microchip were to discontinue a line of older, low-volume products, their customers would have to undergo an expensive redesign just to keep their existing product line going. MCHP probably doesn't make a lot of money selling 20-year-old controllers, but their customers do, and keeping their customers in the money makes for a loyal customer base, and a loyal customer base has been very good for business.

Recent consumer technology trends include the concept of the "throwaway" device; smartphones become obsolete, memory requirements grow exponentially, and everything shrinks. MCHP certainly participates in this space, and the addition of Microsemi gives them significant new inroads there, but MCHP, with its tremendous product line breadth and unique customer base, might be the most conservative play in a very nonconservative industry.

It has become a tradition for capital-intensive semiconductor companies not to pay dividends or much else in the way of cash returns to shareholders. Capital is gobbled up internally for what seems to be endless new investments in fab capacity, design tools, and ever more expensive materials and supplies. Microchip has also bucked *that* trend with their approach to shareholder value—how many semiconductor firms have paid a dividend, let alone raised it, for nine consecutive years? Even with the recent run-up in price, the stock is clearly undervalued by the market. This is a very profitable, rapidly growing semiconductor manufacturer at the heart of some very hot markets trading at less than 18 times earnings—less than the S&P multiple at the time of writing.

Reasons for Caution

There's nothing about $8 billion in new debt that makes you scream, "Yay!" No doubt, the Microsemi purchase is a big deal and will eat up resources for at least a couple of years. On the other hand, there's very little overlap between the product lines of MCHP and Microsemi, and Microsemi brings a broad and deep catalog of parts and an extensive customer base. If we were to advise caution here it would only be in the area of future acquisitions. Semiconductor firms can sometimes end up paying a premium for markets, and so having pulled $1.6 billion out of the balance sheet for this acquisition, we'd like to see MCHP take it easy for a while.

SECTOR: **Information Technology** ❑ BETA COEFFICIENT: **1.15** ❑ 10-YEAR COMPOUND EARNINGS PER-SHARE GROWTH: **9.5%** ❑ 10-YEAR COMPOUND DIVIDENDS PER-SHARE GROWTH: **9.5%**

		2010	2011	2012	2013	2014	2015	2016	2017
Revenues (mil)		1,487	1,383	1,606	1,920	2,150	2,180	3,401	3,965
Net income (mil)		430	337	389	531	594	590	910	1,340
Earnings per share		2.21	1.65	1.89	2.45	2.65	2.65	3.90	5.42
Dividends per share		1.37	1.39	1.41	1.42	1.43	1.43	1.44	1.45
Cash flow per share		2.83	2.26	3.02	3.60	4.32	4.25	6.30	8.30
Price:	high	36.4	41.5	38.9	44.9	50.0	52.4	66.8	95.9
	low	25.5	29.3	28.9	32.4	36.9	37.8	39.0	62.2

Website: www.microchip.com

AGGRESSIVE GROWTH

The Mosaic Company

Ticker symbol: MOS (NYSE) ❑ Large Cap ❑ Value Line financial strength rating: B+ ❑ Current yield: 0.4% ❑ Dividend raises, past 10 years: 4

Company Profile

Despite a modest recovery, Mosaic remains one of our "stubborn" stocks—stocks where short-term performance and shareholder returns are just north of abysmal, but where we think we see long-term value. Indeed, there appears to be a light at the end of the tunnel for Mosaic in the form of a long-delayed cyclical recovery in farm commodities and materials in general, and in the form of a major deployment in the Brazil market at what appears to be a bargain price.

As value-oriented investors, such stubbornness has often served us well, as it has with Itron, Schnitzer Steel, Microchip Technologies, and many others on our current list. True, sometimes we hang on too long in the face of major strategic or market or business shifts, as we did perhaps in the past two years with Macy's and General Electric. Sometimes we don't hang on *long enough*, as happened with Tiffany's or Target, both of which we bailed on too soon. In the case of Mosaic, which has been beaten up by the commodity bust and some competitive shifts inside the industry, we still think we see value—first, at a macro level, because of long-term trends and dependence on agriculture, and on a micro level because it's a well-run business and market leader. So, we'll be stubborn and take the plunge—despite a recent plunge in sales, earnings, and the dividend—into Mosaic once again. There are new signs of life, and you should at least consider the buying opportunity. We hope we're right…and if not, we've just offered up another big bag of fertilizer.

"Helping the World Grow the Food It Needs" is the website headline for plant nutrient miner and producer Mosaic Company. Formed in 2004 through a merger of Cargill's fertilizer operations with IMC Global, Mosaic is the dominant world producer in the so-called "P+K" market—that's phosphorus and potassium, for those of you who shied away from high school chemistry. In case you're not clear on why P and K are important, they are vital fertilizer ingredients and hence essential to most of the world's agriculture production. Plants require more potassium than any other nutrient besides nitrogen, and it is important to root-system development and many processes that form plant starch and proteins. Potassium is mined and sold in its oxide form known more popularly as potash. Phosphorus is a vital component of photosynthesis for plant metabolism and growth.

Mosaic is the largest combined—and among the most efficient—P+K producers in the world. About two-thirds of the business is phosphorus and a third potash. Both minerals are produced commercially in a limited number of places in the world. Mosaic has interests in the important locations in North and South America, notably Florida phosphorus mines and potash mines in Saskatchewan, Michigan, New Mexico, and Peru. Through a network of processing and packaging plants in several countries, the company sells its products to wholesale distributors, retail chains, cooperatives, independent retailers, and national accounts in approximately 40 countries, and international sales account for about a third of the total.

In January 2018 the company completed the $1.9 billion acquisition of Vale Fertilizantes of Brazil, bringing five phosphate mines, one potash mine, four chemical plants, and a distribution business into the portfolio.

Financial Highlights, Fiscal Year 2017

Phosphate and potash prices have finally ticked up; that plus greater production efficiency led FY2017 revenues higher for the first time in five years, albeit only 3.4 percent. Margins stayed flat though are expected to improve dramatically as prices and volumes increase; the price and volume improvement didn't happen until late in the year. Net earnings were up almost 18 percent. Better pricing, balanced inventory, Brazil, and a better supply/demand balance are now projected to bring 2018 sales growth in the 12–15 percent range, with another 7–8 percent in 2019 and for most years after that. Improved margins will bring earnings growth somewhere in the 40 percent range in 2018 and the 25–30 percent range in 2019—a strong recovery in a relatively short time frame, which should also spawn a dividend recovery. We're betting that most of the bad news is in the rearview mirror now; that said, the company cut its dividend 90 percent—we were obviously disappointed in this move. In the meantime, buybacks continue at bargain prices.

Reasons to Buy

Obviously, a lot depends on what happens from here, as the markets balance, Vale is integrated, and prices and production recover. We're betting on Mosaic's long-term industry leadership in a long-term strategic industry. Demand for food will only increase over time—as much as 70 percent by 2050 according to company projections, and 90 percent of that will have to come from land already in production, which means it must be made more effective and efficient through induced nutrients—which of course are supplied by Mosaic, the largest of ten world producers of P+K. The combination of prime mining sites, size, and operational efficiency in its processing and distribution operations should lead to at least maintaining, if not expanding, market share. Another $275 million in cost savings will accrue from Vale in addition to dominance in a lucrative market. In sum, we see good, "resilient" management and a leaner meaner company emerging in a better sales and marketing environment.

Reasons for Caution

A lot of negatives have piled up for this company, and how they sort out over time will matter, although the company has enough financial strength and management savvy to deal with them in the best way possible. Commodity markets and commodity producers are inherently volatile, and any reduction in planting or backup in inventory, not to mention overall global economic weakness or short-term droughts, can drive prices down in a heartbeat. These days, we have to think about trade wars too—not just for nutrients but also for the crops they support. Commodity volume and price wars can be a race to the bottom, for if one company gains an advantage it doesn't usually last for long; we typically prefer companies that have paths other than cost and price to gain and sustain advantage. For Mosaic, we think the natural economics of world food demand and supply will carry the day. Mosaic continues to be a long-term story as well as a buying opportunity as market conditions begin to improve.

SECTOR: Materials ❑ BETA COEFFICIENT: **1.28** ❑ 10-YEAR COMPOUND EARNINGS PER-SHARE GROWTH: **12.5%** ❑ 10-YEAR COMPOUND DIVIDENDS PER-SHARE GROWTH: **NM**

	2010	2011	2012	2013	2014	2015	2016	2017
Revenues (mil)	6,759	9,937	11,108	9,974	9,056	8,895	7,163	7,410
Net income (mil)	863	1,942	1,930	1,744	1,029	1,000	298	351
Earnings per share	1.93	4.34	4.42	4.09	2.68	2.78	0.85	0.99
Dividends per share	0.20	0.20	0.28	1.00	1.00	1.08	1.10	0.35
Cash flow per share	2.94	5.35	5.73	5.51	4.64	4.94	2.86	2.90
Price: high	76.9	59.5	62.0	64.6	51.3	53.8	31.5	34.4
low	37.7	44.9	44.4	39.8	40.3	27.0	22.0	19.2

Website: www.mosaicco.com

AGGRESSIVE GROWTH   NEW FOR
2019

Myriad Genetics

Ticker symbol: MYGN (NASDAQ) ❑ Mid Cap ❑ Value Line financial strength rating: B++ ❑ Current yield: Nil ❑ Dividend raises, past 10 years: NA

Company Profile

Molecular diagnostics. That's the intriguing and somewhat scary-sounding phrase appearing prominently in the website and marketing materials of genetic testing pioneer Myriad Genetics. And we don't use the word "pioneer" loosely—much of their genetic and hereditary analysis comes from the well-developed genetic and genealogical databases of the Mormon community in northern Utah, where Myriad is based.

What are these "molecular diagnostics"? What do they do for us, and what products and services does Myriad provide? Put simply (and there's a lot of science behind it), Myriad develops and markets tests that predict predispositions to certain diseases and syndromes—originally hereditary cancers such as breast, uterine, colon, prostate, and others—by examining biomarkers on DNA, RNA, and other proteins. Patients who may suspect a high risk of certain cancers based on their family history can have a test run to see if in fact these markers exist, leading to increased scrutiny or even a removal of a uterus or similar procedure in such patients.

The company is now moving toward other kinds of biomarkers to (1) detect a wider variety of diseases beyond cancer, such as immune system deficiencies, rheumatoid arthritis, neurological and urological disorders, and depression, and (2) evaluate whether certain treatments will work before they are administered, saving lives but also thousands of dollars in treatment costs. It is known in the trade as *personalized medicine*, where treatments are specific to one's genetic and biological makeup. Generally speaking, these diagnostics and treatments, while pricey, are thought to reduce overall healthcare costs.

Myriad's stated goal is to provide physicians with critical information to guide patient healthcare management by addressing four key questions:

- What is my likelihood of getting a disease?
- Do I have a disease?
- How aggressively should my disease be treated?
- Which therapy will work best to treat my disease?

Products include the legacy myRisk Hereditary Cancer testing kit for testing for overall cancer risk and BRACAnalysis for assessing the risk of breast and ovarian cancer; with more recent releases of GeneSight for psychotropic health and depression, COLARIS and COLARIS AP for colorectal cancer, Prolaris for prostate cancer, Vectra DA for rheumatoid arthritis, myPath Melanoma for melanoma, and EndoPredict, which assesses the aggressiveness of breast cancer. The myRisk Hereditary Cancer test accounted for some 74 percent of the business in 2017 and is declining as other more specific tests take over.

Financial Highlights, Fiscal Year 2017

Myriad has gone through something of a product shift from the declining legacy myRisk Hereditary Cancer test to the more specific tests that are gaining traction today. The company is working to grow international markets, broaden insurance coverage, sign long-term contracts with insurers, and take other measures to build volume and strengthen realized prices.

Revenues have been somewhat stuck in the $750 million annual range, with a 2.5 percent growth reported in 2017. Lower margins were the rule as well in 2017 as the company was forced to lower prices in many markets. Improved volume and pricing are expected to lift revenues 4–5 percent in 2018 with a recovery of profits to near previous levels; 2019 should see a stronger 6–8 percent revenue growth and a 10–11 percent increase in profits. We think these figures could be low as the cost savings benefits of these products become more visible to providers and payers in the healthcare space.

Reasons to Buy

There is plenty of wisdom to the idea of personalized medicine, where treatments can be handcrafted to the individual to have the most effect for the least cost. Myriad is an early mover in this space, has broadened their product line into an "industry-leading portfolio" of molecular diagnostic tests—and, importantly and unlike many others in the biotech and this "avant-garde" medical space, they *make money* doing it. These tests are becoming more of a standard procedure, which is good, but they have a long way to go before truly becoming mainstream providing a good "runway" for long-term growth. The concept and products are just now gaining traction in the international space. We don't usually like to make this kind of prediction, but Myriad would seem ripe as a takeover candidate for a larger pharma or medical supplier.

Reasons for Caution

Although Myriad has an early mover advantage, this space is becoming more crowded, especially as consumer genetic analysis provider 23andMe has announced some direct-to-consumer cancer detection products in the breast cancer space. Myriad's success depends on adoption by both provider and payer at price points that bring profitability, success against competition, and the successful defense of patents. These factors have caused some distress in the form of relatively weak 20 percent operating margins of late (which are predicted to improve to 30 percent by the next decade). The transition from the more generalized legacy myRisk Hereditary Cancer product to the more specific newer products has been a bit painful and has led to fluctuations in financial performance, but as these new products gain traction and as more are developed and released, that performance should level out and eventually move higher.

SECTOR: **Healthcare** ❑ BETA COEFFICIENT: **0.44** ❑ 10-YEAR COMPOUND EARNINGS PER-SHARE GROWTH: **NA** ❑ 10-YEAR COMPOUND DIVIDENDS PER-SHARE GROWTH: **NA**

	2010	2011	2012	2013	2014	2015	2016	2017
Revenues (mil)	363	402	496	613	778	723	754	771
Net income (mil)	152	101	112	147	176	80	125	59
Earnings per share	1.54	1.10	1.30	1.77	2.25	1.08	1.71	0.87
Dividends per share	—	—	—	—	—	—	—	—
Cash flow per share	1.54	1.10	1.47	1.94	2.59	1.53	2.20	1.57
Price: high	27.1	25.9	31.8	38.3	42.5	46.2	43.7	37.3
low	14.1	17.5	20.0	20.0	20.5	30.3	15.9	15.1

Website: www.myriad.com

GROWTH AND INCOME

NextEra Energy, Inc.

Ticker symbol: NEE (NYSE) ❑ Large Cap ❑ Value Line financial strength rating: A+ ❑ Current yield: 2.6% ❑ Dividend raises, past 10 years: 10

Company Profile

NextEra is a full-service retail utility, wholesale power-generating operation, and utility services holding company. It is built around the utility stalwart Florida Power & Light; the name "NextEra" was adopted in 2010 telling us how the company sees itself now and in the future. NextEra is the world's leading user and innovator in clean and large-scale alternative energy for its own use and for the power market.

Headquartered in Juno Beach, FL, NextEra Energy's principal operating subsidiaries are NextEra Energy Resources, LLC, and the original Florida Power & Light Company, the third-largest rate-regulated electric utility in the country. FP&L serves 8.9 million people and 4.9 million customer accounts in eastern and southern Florida. FP&L accounts for about two-thirds of NEE's total revenues. Through its subsidiaries, NextEra collectively operates the third-largest US nuclear power generation fleet and is the world's largest user of wind and sun resources to generate electricity. As proof that such leadership works, customer electricity rates in its operating territories are 30 percent below the national average.

As a nonregulated subsidiary, NextEra Energy Resources, LLC (or "NEER"), is a wholesale energy provider and is the world's largest generator of electricity from the wind and the sun. Unlike many other alternative energy-driven businesses, it is a viable standalone business entity. About 95 percent of NEER's generation comes from clean or renewable fuels—wind (52 percent), natural gas (2 percent), nuclear (30 percent), solar (5 percent), and oil (4 percent).

NEER has 117 wind farm facilities in 20 US states and Canada, with 14 solar and 3 nuclear energy facilities, and gas infrastructure operations in most of those locations. NEER's energy-producing portfolio includes 9,300 wind turbines on 110 farms in 19 states and four Canadian provinces, which is estimated to comprise 16 percent of the entire wind power–generating capacity in the US, 11 percent of utility-scale solar power production, and 6 percent of total US nuclear power production. All told, the combined fuel mix of alternative energy and natural gas not only reduces NEE's overall fuel costs (25 percent of revenues, compared to 40s and 50s in much of the industry); it also produces levels of sulfur dioxide (the cause of acid rain) some 97 percent below the average for the US electric industry, a nitrous oxide emission rate 79 percent below the industry, and a carbon dioxide (CO_2) emission rate 55 percent below industry averages—these numbers are still improving. The NEER subsidiary accounts for nearly a third of NextEra's total revenue—and nearly half of its profits—a healthy return for an alternative energy–based operation.

The company has a few small but promising nonregulated subsidiaries, offering design and consulting services for other alternative and conventional utility providers, and it also operates a fiber-optic network. NextEra is a regular winner of awards for most green, most ethical, and most admired companies—in fact, it made a Top 10 position on 2018 *Fortune*'s list of World's Most Admired Companies and was number one in the Utility industry category for the eleventh year out of the last twelve.

Financial Highlights, Fiscal Year 2017

In late 2017 Hurricane Irma did about $1.3 billion in damage to the FP&L system in central and south Florida. Normally that might wipe out half of NEE's profits for a given year, but not this time. Why? Because the new tax law will bring that much (and then some, about $1.7 billion) to NEE's coffers. The company can repair the damage and, in a gesture of good corporate citizenship, forgo a rate relief request it had filed earlier. Bravo.

FY2017 revenues and earnings ended up basically flat, although up from the down year of 2016, which was dinged by mild weather and Hurricane Matthew. Population growth of 1 percent annually, expansion and scale in renewables, a rate increase already in place, and continued lower taxes will combine in a "perfect storm" to nearly double earnings in FY2018 going forward into 2019 as revenues rise in the 4–5 percent range annually. Notably, the dividend was raised 14 percent in 2017 with similar raises likely through 2019.

Reasons to Buy

Every year we look forward to evaluating and writing about NextEra; they are leading so many initiatives in what's otherwise a pretty boring industry, and their website and presentation materials do a good job describing them.

For those who believe that alternative energy is the future for large-scale power generation (as we do), NextEra continues to be the best play available. The company continues to grow alternative energy capacity on all fronts, particularly wind and solar, and, importantly, continues to make good money on these efforts. All of this adds to the solid and traditional FP&L regulated utility base; this company has the steady feel of a traditional utility blended with a leading-edge alternative energy platform and leading-edge power utility technology. NextEra will lead the way into figuring out the grid of the future, utilizing an optimized mix of centralized and distributed (as in "rooftop") alternative and conventional generating resources. Cash flow is very strong and supports both hearty dividend increases and continued investments in alternative energy production but hasn't been used to reduce share counts (much has been used to reduce debt instead).

Reasons for Caution

The company's FP&L subsidiary is still a regulated utility and may not always receive the most accommodating treatment. Additionally, alternative energy tax credits may diminish over time. Alternative energy innovations and nuclear power carry some risk, and there are those pesky hurricanes. In addition, the low price of natural gas makes some of the alternative energy offerings less attractive in the short run. Growth prospects lead to a relatively high share price and low yield for the industry—this is not your Grandma's utility stock—but NEE also is a clear leader in the industry, a trendsetter, a model utility for others to follow.

SECTOR: **Utilities** ❏ BETA COEFFICIENT: **0.28** ❏ 10-YEAR COMPOUND EARNINGS PER-SHARE
GROWTH: **8.0%** ❏ 10-YEAR COMPOUND DIVIDENDS PER-SHARE GROWTH: **8.5%**

	2010	2011	2012	2013	2014	2015	2016	2017
Revenues (mil)	15,317	15,341	14,256	15,136	17,021	17,465	16,155	17,195
Net income (mil)	1,957	2,021	1,911	2,062	2,469	2,761	2,687	4,893
Earnings per share	4.74	4.82	4.56	4.83	5.60	6.06	5.78	10.47
Dividends per share	2.00	2.20	2.40	2.64	2.90	3.08	3.48	3.93
Cash flow per share	9.60	9.29	8.70	10.65	12.10	12.90	12.60	16.10
Price: high	56.3	61.2	72.2	89.8	110.8	112.6	132.0	159.4
low	45.3	49.0	58.6	69.8	84.0	93.7	102.2	117.3

Website: www.nexteraenergy.com

AGGRESSIVE GROWTH

Nike, Inc.

Ticker symbol: NKE (NYSE) ❏ Large Cap ❏ Value Line financial strength rating: A++ ❏ Current yield: 1.2% ❏ Dividend raises, past 10 years: 10

Company Profile

Nike is the world's largest designer, developer, and marketer of athletic footwear, apparel, and related equipment and accessory products. Products are sold through a mix of traditional and direct retail, including Nike-owned retail outlets (of which there are 384 in the US and 758 overseas), its website, and a mix of independent distributors and licensees in more than 190 countries around the world. Recently, the company has added specialized destination "Running Stores" and has expanded reach with more "Direct-to-Consumer," or DTC or "factory" outlets, carrying its traditionally strong product innovation to the channel and retail marketplace. DTC sales now account for 28 percent of Nike brand revenues, up from 26 percent last year.

Nike does no manufacturing—virtually all of its footwear and apparel items are fashioned by independent contractors outside the United States, while equipment products are produced both in the United States and abroad. In total, there are 127 footwear and 363 apparel factories in 37 countries.

Nike's shoes are designed primarily for athletic use, although a large percentage of them are worn for casual or leisure purposes. Shoes are designed for men, women, and children for running, training, basketball, and soccer use, although the company also carries brands for casual wear. The company has been very successful with its offerings for the women's market.

Nike sells apparel and accessories for most of the sports addressed by its shoe lines, as well as athletic bags and accessory items. Nike apparel and accessories are designed to complement its athletic footwear products, feature the same trademarks, and are sold through the same marketing and distribution channels. The new buzzword is "athleisure," and Nike is there front and center. All Nike-branded products are marketed with the familiar "swoosh" logo, one of the most recognized and successful branding images in history.

Nike has a number of wholly owned subsidiaries, or "affiliate brands," including Converse, Hurley, Jordan, and Nike Golf, which variously design, distribute, and license dress, athletic, and casual footwear, sports apparel, and accessories, some targeted to specific audiences, such as Hurley to a youth audience.

Nike-branded products account for about 94 percent of 2017 revenues. Of the total $32.3 billion in Nike-branded revenues (excluding subsidiaries), about 65 percent of it comes from footwear, 30 percent from apparel, and the remainder from equipment. Footwear remains the fastest-growing segment of the business at 8 percent; the much smaller Converse subsidiary accounts for the remaining 6 percent of the total business and was up about 6 percent for the year.

In total, 54 percent of FY2017 sales came from outside the US. Approximately 46 percent of sales come from North America, 19 percent from Western Europe, 13 percent from China, 5 percent from central and eastern Europe, 3 percent from Japan, and 12 percent from other emerging markets. FY2016 growth came from China (12 percent), Japan (17 percent), and emerging markets (8 percent).

Finally, while Nike has always been known for innovation in this space, it's worth pointing out one new direction: personalized shoes. In early 2018 the company acquired a computer vision company called Invertex; it has also been experimenting with 3D-printed shoe uppers. Soon will come the day when shoes can be built to your unique fit and spec right in front of you in a Nike store. It's all part of an initiative and new organizational alignment called Consumer Direct Offense, designed to focus innovation and product creation in a digital direct-to-consumer format.

Financial Highlights, Fiscal Year 2017

FY2017 revenues slowed to a fast jog but were up despite currency effects, disruptions in the retail channel, and soft emerging markets. Sales rose 6–8 percent on a constant currency basis. Gross margins decreased due to higher material and manufacturing costs, but with a 3 percent average selling price increase, the DTC business, and tax cuts, net margins increased, and total earnings jumped almost 13 percent. That and another 2.3 percent share buyback combined to strengthen per-share earnings by 16 percent.

Extreme competition and some lag in reaching the millennial market in North America are tempering forward forecasts, and particularly earnings forecasts, in 2018. Total sales are expected to rise about 5 percent, but net earnings may take as much as a 10 percent hit as taxes on repatriated cash, more competitive pricing and investments in technology hit the bottom line. Nike expects recovery and then some in 2019 with a 13–15 percent earnings rise on a 7–8 percent gain in sales. The forecast really gets into gear in the early 2020s as more digital and direct sales penetrate the mix. Double-digit dividend increases and 1–3 percent share buybacks should continue through the period.

Reasons to Buy

The Nike brand and its corresponding swoosh continue to be one of the most recognized—and sought after—brands in the world. It is a lesson in simplicity and image congruence with the product behind it. Nike doesn't sit still with it; rather, the company is learning to leverage it into more products outside the traditional athletic wear circuit even to a new line of GPS watches and apps to find, say, a new route for your run and to track your performance on your phone. The company continues to invest in innovation in all of its segments, including new fabrics, colors, uniform materials, and digital design linkages to make active lifestyles more individual, productive, and fun—and it is now extending this innovation further into marketing and retail. Today's "fast fashion" context requires rapid time-to-market, and the innovation cycle at Nike has been turned into more of a sprint in response. As well, Nike doesn't just limit the brand appeal to athletes: slogans such as "Just Do It" and "If you have a body, you're an athlete" emphasize the appeal and lifestyle across all segments of the population. We continue to think this is drop-dead smart.

We also think it's drop-dead smart to be investing in the DTC channel now, as traditional retail struggles. Nike is in the front of the pack in this regard, a good thing as the retail shift accelerates. Improved manufacturing efficiencies, strong channel relationships, and international exposure all keep the company moving faster in the right direction. Despite its size, the company continues to deliver double-digit per-share earnings, cash flow, and dividend growth. We continue to like the combination of protected profitability through brand excellence, operational excellence, and a clean conservative balance sheet, all providing a good combination of safety and growth potential. Finally, the recent slowdown to a fast jog has enabled some of us looking for good entry points to finally get onto the track.

Reasons for Caution

Our biggest source of caution last year and again this year, as sales growth slowed somewhat, was whether the Nike brand resonates as well with the upcoming millennial generation as it did with us for so many years since the company's inception in the early eighties. The jury is still out on whether Nike is losing market share or is simply suffering from market maturity, but it appears that competitors like Adidas and Under Armour are encountering some of the same difficulties. It may take some tweaks—and some digitally based personalization as Nike is already developing—to win the millennials over. We think, but can't be sure, that Nike will remain the best pair of shoes in this race. Other risks come from the rollout of the DTC channel in keeping the right balance between DTC and traditional wholesale and in avoiding channel conflicts. Risks also include higher labor and commodity input prices.

SECTOR: **Consumer Discretionary** ❑ BETA COEFFICIENT: **0.65** ❑ 10-YEAR COMPOUND EARNINGS PER-SHARE GROWTH: **13.0%** ❑ 10-YEAR COMPOUND DIVIDENDS PER-SHARE GROWTH: **15.5%**

	2010	2011	2012	2013	2014	2015	2016	2017
Revenues (mil)	19,014	20,862	24,128	25,313	27,799	30,601	32,376	34,350
Net income (mil)	1,907	2,133	2,223	2,464	2,693	3,273	3,750	4,240
Earnings per share	0.97	1.10	1.18	1.35	1.49	1.85	2.16	2.51
Dividends per share	0.27	0.30	0.35	0.41	0.47	0.52	0.62	0.70
Cash flow per share	1.15	1.30	1.42	1.62	1.85	2.26	2.62	3.01
Price: high	23.1	24.6	28.7	40.1	49.9	68.2	65.4	65.2
low	15.2	17.4	21.3	25.7	34.9	45.3	49.0	50.3

Website: www.nikeinc.com

CONSERVATIVE GROWTH

Norfolk Southern Corporation

Ticker symbol: NSC (NYSE) ❑ Large Cap ❑ Value Line financial strength rating: A ❑ Current yield: 2.1% ❑ Dividend raises, past 10 years: 9

Company Profile

Norfolk Southern Corporation was formed in 1982 as a holding company when the Norfolk & Western Railway merged with the Southern Railway. Including lines received in the split takeover (with CSX) of Conrail, the current railroad operates 19,500 route-miles of track in 22 eastern and southern states. It serves every major port on the East Coast of the United States and has the most extensive intermodal network in the east.

Company business in FY2016 was about 15 percent coal (down from the high teens and low 20s in previous years), 63 percent carload industrial, agricultural, chemical, automotive, and basic materials products, and 22 percent intermodal. Major gateways include ports in the eastern half of the US, Great Lakes ports, and major interchange points with the two major Western systems: Union Pacific (another *100 Best Stock*) and Burlington Northern Santa Fe. The company estimates that its networks reach 65 percent of US manufacturing and 55 percent of US energy consumption. In the late 1990s, the company split the acquisition of northeastern rail heavyweight Conrail with rival CSX Corporation, so it has considerable operations in the Northeast and Midwest in addition to its traditional southern base; it currently owns 58 percent of the old Conrail. The heaviest traffic corridors are New York–Chicago; Chicago–Atlanta; and Cleveland–Kansas City. The company has a diverse base of large Midwestern factories and large and smaller southern factories and basic materials producers in the coal, chemical, automotive, and lumber industry, giving a well-diversified traffic base.

The company provides a number of logistics services and has substantial traffic to and from ports and overseas destinations. The opening of the widened Panama Canal is giving some lift to southern and East Coast ports, which NSC serves well. The company has an active program to attract lineside customers to build freight volumes.

Financial Highlights, Fiscal Year 2017

Continued shifts in the energy market, which first reduced coal and now oil shipments, are still affecting NSC. Coal revenues, which had been sequentially down for years, finally rose slightly mainly due to exports, while intermodal traffic was up, reflecting a generally stronger economy and shortages in the trucking industry. Oil, which had made up some of the coal shortfall, continues to be soft as the recent oversupply has cut into domestic production, but increased prices and production recently may stem this downward trend. Overall, 2017 freight volumes were up 5 percent and revenues were up 7 percent, reflecting rate increases and some shift in traffic from rival CSX, which has encountered recent challenges. Net income was up 13.7 percent percent due to efficiency savings and some tax effects; however, higher fuel costs and incentive compensation somewhat offset these improvements.

Per-share earnings rose a solid 16.4 percent. As the US industrial economy strengthens and commodity markets improve, the company now projects revenue gains in the 4–5 percent range through FY2019, with continued productivity gains and share buybacks giving a green light to per-share earnings gains in the low 20 percent range in 2018 and 10–12 percent in 2019. The key "operating ratio" measure—the ratio of variable to total costs—dropped to a solid 67.4 following 68.9 in 2016, and 72.6 in 2015.

Reasons to Buy

For the last few years NSC and its competitors had all been hurt by slowdowns in coal and exports due to the strong dollar and by slow oil shipments and fracking supplies necessary to support oil production. But we appear to be at the end of the cycle for all three of these, as commodities demand and exports are recovering. In the meantime, NSC, like other companies, became more efficient in the interim and is well positioned to perform even better as freight volumes recover. It remains to be seen how much the trade policies of the Trump administration will affect domestic business, but a renewed emphasis on US manufacturing will help NSC, as is the Panama Canal widening. We should note that the new tax law should benefit NSC and other such capital-intensive domestic industries more than most.

Additionally, NSC serves some of the more dynamic and up-and-coming manufacturing markets in the United States, namely, Asian and other foreign-owned manufacturing facilities found particularly in the Southeast. We like the strength and diversity coming from serving the domestic and especially the foreign-owned auto industry—the company serves plants for (in alphabetical order) BMW, Chrysler, Ford, General Motors, Honda, Isuzu, Mazda, Mercedes-Benz, Mitsubishi, Nissan, Subaru, Suzuki, and Toyota.

Finally, cash flow continues to be strong. The company decided against a dividend raise in 2016 due to soft business. But it will more than make up for that with a high-double-digit increase in 2018, and otherwise the track record of raises and share buybacks is excellent.

Reasons for Caution

The decline in coal traffic, which mostly supports electric utilities, also exposed the company more to general economic downturns as the remaining mix is more economically sensitive. Oil-related traffic may take a while to come back if energy prices stay low and if pipeline building resumes at full speed ahead due to Trump administration policies. In addition, oil shipments expose the company to headline risk and accidents.

There were some service issues in late 2017, as volumes exceeded capacity in certain segments. This points to a bugaboo typical of the railroad industry, as in other capital-intensive, high–fixed-cost industries: it's hard to have just the right amount of capacity. Too much volume can actually be a bad thing as it overtaxes the physical plant and causes service disruptions. For the most part we think NSC has made the right investments and has proven agile overall in managing business cycles, but there may have been some miscalculations affecting 2017 performance, which may take a while to mend. As well, recent derailments attract public scrutiny and cries to accelerate expensive safety measures such as Positive Train Control. Finally, the stock price has once again risen sharply in view of the end of the down cycle; it would be wise to stop, look, and listen before investing.

SECTOR: **Transportation** ❑ BETA COEFFICIENT: **1.29** ❑ 10-YEAR COMPOUND EARNINGS PER-SHARE GROWTH: **7.0%** ❑ 10-YEAR COMPOUND DIVIDENDS PER-SHARE GROWTH: **16.5%**

		2010	2011	2012	2013	2014	2015	2016	2017
Revenues (mil)		9,516	11,172	11,040	11,245	11,624	10,513	9,888	10,551
Net income (mil)		1,498	1,853	1,749	1,850	2,000	1,556	1,668	1,896
Earnings per share		4.00	5.27	5.37	5.85	6.39	5.11	5.62	6.54
Dividends per share		1.40	1.68	1.94	2.04	2.22	2.36	2.36	2.44
Cash flow per share		6.48	8.22	8.49	8.96	9.57	8.76	9.25	10.15
Price:	high	63.7	78.4	78.5	93.2	117.6	112.1.	111.4	146.3
	low	46.2	57.6	56.1	62.7	87.1	72.1	64.5	105.9

Website: www.nscorp.com

Novo Nordisk A/S

Ticker symbol: NVO (NYSE) ❑ Large Cap ❑ Value Line financial strength rating: A++ ❑ Current yield: 1.9% ❑ Dividend raises, past 10 years: 8

Company Profile

Unfortunately, diabetes is a widespread and growing disease as more people around the world live to an older age and eat higher-calorie diets. Novo Nordisk, which started out in the early 1920s as two separate diabetes medicine producers, merged in 1989 and now garners almost 81 percent of its current $18 billion in revenues supplying diabetes medicine and care products. The company estimates that it owns 47 percent of the world market and 36 percent of the US market for insulin; and 45 percent of the world market for "modern" or "new generation" insulin, which is delivered using new technologies and delivery mechanisms.

Unfortunately, diabetes as a disease continues to grow. Although diabetes is a complex disease for which the many treatments aren't easy to understand, it does break down into two "types" (really, three, if you include the rarer gestational diabetes occurring only in pregnant women): type 1, in which the pancreas fails to produce enough insulin (and regular insulin supplements are required), and type 2, a condition whereby cells fail to absorb insulin properly, often called "adult onset" diabetes. NVO estimates that 425 million people (about 6 percent of the world population) have diabetes of one type or another, and that only about half of them have been diagnosed. That number is likely to grow to 629 million by 2045, according to the World Health Organization. On top of that, NVO estimates that 650 million live with obesity, which has a tendency to bring on diabetes. The company estimates that its products are used by about 25 million people worldwide today and plans to grow this to 40 million by 2020.

Major products include traditional human-based insulin and protein-related products for type 1 diabetes treatment, which are being replaced by higher-performance "modern" and "new generation" insulins. The company has reaped the benefits of several recently rolled out new-generation insulins. One is Tresiba, which lasts 42 hours or more and reduces the risk of hypoglycemia. Another treatment called Ryzodeg for both type 1 and type 2 diabetes is manufactured artificially. It is absorbed faster and lasts longer than traditional human insulin. Xultophy is another new type 2 diabetes and hypoglycemia treatment. Collectively these new products doubled their sales last year to about $1.4 billion, leading the way to the 14 percent sales gain for the 2017 year.

New for 2018 is Ozempic (semaglutide)—a once-weekly type 2 diabetes and obesity treatment; Fiasp, a fast-acting mealtime insulin, and N8-GP, a hemophilia treatment. The pipeline is full, with new treatments especially in the Obesity sector, which grew 60 percent last year. You can see the pattern and emphasis on new, more effective formulas and delivery systems (including new oral delivery systems) typically approved and rolled out in non-FDA-controlled markets first. By the time they hit the US, they are both proven and more profitable. These new therapies now comprise over half of the overall diabetes care revenue stream, are growing at a 20–35 percent clip annually, and deliver both sales growth and higher margins.

We shouldn't ignore the 19 percent of Novo Nordisk devoted to diseases outside the diabetes space. The Biopharmaceuticals segment targets hemophilia and other bleeding disorders, hormone-replacement therapies, and human growth hormone markets. The model is similar: pioneering approvals outside the US, then migrating them into US markets. The company spends about 13 percent of revenues on R&D; about 52 percent of sales in total come from the US, which the company indicates is currently responsible for 37 percent of its top-line growth.

Financial Highlights, Fiscal Year 2017

The new product rollouts previously mentioned and a favorable currency environment led to a 13.7 percent increase in reported FY2017 sales; earnings followed suit with a similar 14.6 percent gain. New products and an expanding market, offset somewhat by generic and other competition, will lead the way to modest 2–4 percent sales gains in 2018 and 2019 with similar profit gains. Meanwhile, NVO has plans to retire about 10 percent of its shares over the next few years and grow the dividend at something around 10 percent. Also worth noting: the company has zero long-term debt and, since domiciled outside the US, enjoys a tax rate in the low 20s versus low 30s for most US-based corporations.

Reasons to Buy

Novo Nordisk continues to be an excellent long-term growth story. It is the closest thing to a "pure play" in the diabetes market, and it's an important player in obesity, growth disorder, coagulation (hemophilia), and hormone replacement markets as well. The overall and unfortunate growth in these chronic diseases, particularly diabetes and obesity, will provide tailwinds for years to come. There is a lot of interest in new medications such as Saxenda that address obesity and diabetes simultaneously.

Steady revenues and profits from a traditional insulin treatment base fund new research and releases of more effective, more tailored, easier-to-use diabetes treatments. Despite some recent pricing pressures, we still feel very comfortable with this course, and the strong international footprint allows them to gain regulatory and market acceptance long before they enter the prized US market. Financials, too, continue to be excellent.

Reasons for Caution

Once you're targeted as a "bad guy" in healthcare, it can take a long time to shake that notion. In 2016, NVO became a bit of a bad guy, being accused of predatory pricing—of course, the 32–35 percent net profit margins didn't help their cause. Some may see room for complaint, and a less aggressive stance on pricing and growth may rule for a while. Naturally, we are concerned about regulatory approvals, attempts to control prescription drug costs, and the potential aggressiveness of competitors, who could want their bigger slice of this lucrative market. Some regulatory bodies outside the US are holding prices to less-than-acceptable levels—the blockbuster Tresiba was taken off the market in Germany for a while as an example. Finally, even though Novo presents itself well, it is in a complex business on a complex international stage; it continues to push our "buy businesses you understand" mantra to its limits.

SECTOR: **Healthcare** ❑ BETA COEFFICIENT: **0.67** ❑ 10-YEAR COMPOUND EARNINGS PER-SHARE GROWTH: **20.0%** ❑ 10-YEAR COMPOUND DIVIDENDS PER-SHARE GROWTH: **28.0%**

	2010	2011	2012	2013	2014	2015	2016	2017
Revenues (mil)	10,814	11,559	13,384	15,435	14,511	15,779	15,832	17,988
Net income (mil)	2,563	2,979	3,800	4,651	4,326	5,093	5,356	6,147
Earnings per share	0.88	1.04	1.38	1.73	1.65	1.98	2.11	2.48
Dividends per share	0.27	0.38	0.50	0.62	0.83	0.73	1.41	1.14
Cash flow per share	1.05	1.24	1.58	1.95	1.88	2.19	2.32	2.66
Price: high	22.8	26.6	34.1	38.9	49.1	60.3	58.2	54.1
low	12.8	18.9	22.8	29.9	36.6	41.7	30.9	32.8

Website: www.novonordisk.com

AGGRESSIVE GROWTH

Oracle Corporation

Ticker symbol: ORCL (NYSE) ❑ Large Cap ❑ Value Line financial strength rating: A++ ❑ Current yield: 1.6% ❑ Dividend raises, past 10 years: 8

Company Profile

Founded in 1978 as the rather blandly named Software Development Laboratories, Oracle Corporation has since grown to become the second-largest software company in the world (by revenue) only behind Microsoft. The company's early entry into the then-new relational database market eventually led to an extended period of dominance for that flagship product (the Oracle Database) in the enterprise market. The company successfully leveraged this position with associated software and hardware products through acquisitions and internal development and now has a strong presence in both the middleware and applications space.

Oracle was one of the early proponents of cloud architecture before the name "cloud" became a catchall for any remotely run and managed software. As a consequence, today some of the company's strongest growth vectors are in what are becoming widely adopted IaaS, PaaS, and SaaS architectures (Infrastructure/Platform/Software as a Service). In this space, the customer doesn't own the tool or application but rather pays a fee to use it on a remote server. Increasingly, customers use a "hybrid" model, where some software resides in the cloud and other platform components reside on premises.

The company owes its current product breadth to both internal development and an aggressive acquisition strategy, most significantly with the purchases of applications software provider PeopleSoft in 2004, hardware supplier Sun Microsystems in 2010, and e-commerce software specialist NetSuite in 2016. Acquisitions continue to be a focus for Oracle, with over $70 billion spent since 2006 and $12 billion spent in 2016 alone, mostly on small firms in the tool, applications, and security spaces.

Financial Highlights, Fiscal Year 2017

Revenues in FY2017 (ending June 1) were up a bit over 2 percent, as currency headwinds subsided (53 percent of sales are overseas), SaaS sales advanced 55 percent, and cloud services grew 44 percent. As you can tell, these are relatively small though rapidly growing business components: overall traditional new software licenses accounted for 17 percent of revenue; software updates and support 51 percent; SaaS, PaaS, and IaaS 12 percent; hardware systems and support (from the acquired Sun Microsystems) 11 percent; and Services 9 percent. The bottom line for FY2017 inched up about 3 percent as cloud-based products and services carry slightly lower margins. A further transition to SaaS and improved scale will get those margins up in 2018, giving a projected 8–9 percent increase in net profits on a 5 percent revenue rise. Increased corporate spending due to recent tax cuts could make these forecasts appear low. Finally, the company continues to buy back 1–3 percent of its shares annually and raise its dividend gradually.

Reasons to Buy

Oracle is one of those rare beasts: a mature technology company that has pretty much become an industry standard. At the ripe old age of 40 years, Oracle is clearly in select company. The fact that they've been able to grow and remain at the head of the pack in an industry where it is commonplace for technological tidal shifts to eliminate entire classes of companies speaks to their robust market awareness, sound and aggressive acquisition strategy, and competent execution.

That said, this is a large company with a large presence in older, slow-growth businesses. For decades Oracle was a strong proponent of captive, in-house IT operations and sold software, hardware, and services into that segment quite successfully. As this model fades in favor of SaaS/PaaS and similar models that require less capital investment, Oracle is in the happy position of having a solid, high-margin revenue stream to fund the development of the replacement, all while retaining a loyal customer base reluctant to move to anything "too" new. Many of their competitors in this developing space are not as established or as well funded and so will need to be good, fast, and lucky, where Oracle really just has to be good. Displacing an existing Oracle "seat" (software installation) will require a long sales cycle and a compelling solution. Retaining an Oracle seat, however, simply requires a reasonable transition and a credible road map going forward. Oracle thus gains a helpful march on their competition during this critical period of transition to the new computing model.

A quick glance at Oracle's share price history does not stir the blood. But looking at Oracle's revenues and share price over the past five years (which have been basically flat) does not really inform the reader. The bigger part of the story here is what the company has been doing to prepare for the current transitional period in their major business. Having platforms and strategies in place to cannibalize your own businesses is far preferable to having others eat it for you.

Reasons for Caution

Oracle would never admit to overpaying for some of their acquisitions, but it's clear in retrospect that some of their purchases have been driven less by the numbers and perhaps more by exuberance. The Sun acquisition, which we actually defended previously as a move to sell a bundled software and platform solution, has not turned out as well as hoped. The numbers have not been a disaster, but Oracle has scaled back the scope of the Sun business more than most had expected.

In their cloud businesses, Oracle's IaaS infrastructure goes up against established IBM SoftLayer, Microsoft, and, more dauntingly, Amazon Web Service offerings. IaaS is inherently a lower-margin model, and the marketplace challenges will be significantly greater than in SaaS/PaaS. More broadly, the company must not become too complacent or play fast and loose with its existing installed base; its customer relationships are one of its chief advantages and "moats" against its rivals.

SECTOR: **Information Technology** ❑ BETA COEFFICIENT: **1.08** ❑ 10-YEAR COMPOUND EARNINGS
PER-SHARE GROWTH: **12.5%** ❑ 10-YEAR COMPOUND DIVIDENDS PER-SHARE GROWTH: **29.0%**

	2010	2011	2012	2013	2014	2015	2016	2017
Revenues (mil)	27,034	35,850	37,221	37,253	38,305	38,253	37,056	37,900
Net income (mil)	6,494	11,385	12,520	12,958	13,214	12,489	11,236	11,550
Earnings per share	1.67	2.22	2.46	2.68	2.87	2.77	2.61	2.74
Dividends per share	0.20	0.20	0.24	0.30	0.48	0.51	0.60	0.64
Cash flow per share	1.75	2.32	2.65	2.91	3.10	3.04	2.93	3.04
Price: high	32.3	36.5	34.3	38.3	46.7	45.3	42.0	53.1
low	21.2	24.7	25.3	29.9	35.4	35.1	33.1	38.3

Website: www.oracle.com

AGGRESSIVE GROWTH

Ormat Technologies

Ticker symbol: ORA (NYSE) ❑ Mid Cap ❑ Value Line financial strength rating: C++ ❑ Current
yield: 0.8% ❑ Dividend raises, past 10 years: 5

Company Profile

Ormat Technologies, a developer and operator of geothermal plants and
maker of thermal power recovery products, is the largest geothermal energy
pure play in North America. A renewed interest in baseline "green" power,
combined with a growing need for electrification far from traditional grid-
based solutions puts Ormat in a unique position as a provider of clean,
always-on baseline electricity at the lowest operating cost of any solution.
"Green energy you can rely on" is their apt slogan.

The company operates in two business segments. The Electricity segment builds, owns, and operates geothermal power plants, selling the electricity mostly into the grid as a wholesale power generator. The Product
segment sells power plant equipment utilizing their proprietary geothermal
technology to geothermal operators and to industrial users for use in remote
power generation and recovered energy applications.

Ormat's total worldwide installed capacity is 795 megawatts, concentrated in 19 sites mainly in the states of Nevada and California, but including Hawaii, Idaho, Oregon, and Utah. Their geothermal plants (68 percent
of 2017 revenue) top out at about 35MW each in the western United States,
the Pacific Rim, and the Mediterranean and east Africa.

The Product segment has sold and built 150 power plants producing 2,200 megawatts in installations located around the world, including far-off locations such as Turkey, Ethiopia, and Indonesia as supported by the local geology. The power generation products are particularly attractive for harsh, remote locations as the technology requires very little in the way of management or maintenance. The company also produces "REGs"—Recovered Energy Generation units, which produce electricity from nearly any form of waste heat. The vast majority of these units are currently sold outside of the United States and are commonly used in gas pipeline compressor stations but are suited to any process that generates significant waste heat, including oil refineries.

The company owns over 100 patents on its efficient "binary" geothermal energy conversion process and related technologies. Their products do not require exotic manufacturing processes or materials, and the company builds almost all of its own products at its plants in Nevada and Israel.

Financial Highlights, Fiscal Year 2017

For FY2017, Electricity segment revenues rose 7 percent while product revenues were basically flat. About 85 percent of Electricity revenues are from fixed purchased power agreements, with an increase in generated power of 1.7 percent. Earnings increased nearly 20 percent largely due to the retirement of high-interest debt, reduced income taxes, and a large one-time admin expense in the prior year. Orders and backlog remain strong in the Product segment, with $186 million in recognized revenue expected through the end of 2018. Forecasts call for high-single-digit revenue gains through FY2018, with greater operating leverage, higher and more consistent profit margins, and low- to mid-double-digit net income gains each year. Moderate dividend increases should continue and are well supported by the cash flow.

Ormat commenced operations at three new facilities in FY2017, including one of their largest to date, a 330MW plant in Indonesia. In January 2018, Ormat announced their acquisition of US Geothermal for $110 million. US Geothermal has three plants in operation totaling 45MW and four additional projects underway totaling 90MW.

Reasons to Buy

We've been watching Ormat for about eight years now and have seen the company transition from "green energy experiment" to an important niche player in the renewable energy market to the primary geothermal solution in the US and several other countries, with approximately 22 percent of the entire US market. This year the company has moved into the "smart grid" environment with the acquisition of Viridity Energy, a privately held provider of software and consulting expertise in the fields of Capacity Demand Response and energy management and storage solutions. Ormat plans to "leverage our technological capabilities over a variety of renewable energy platforms, including solar power generation and energy storage," which, on its face, would represent a large add to the company's current geothermal play. Based on the information made available to date, we believe the implementation strategy begins with Ormat using their existing technology in concert with Viridity's expertise to initially provide peak-contouring capability for traditional grids via geothermal sources and battery caches. The company anticipates that the BESS market (Battery Energy Storage Systems, typically used for grid stabilization) will grow to $160 billion over the next ten years and that the Viridity technology will provide them with an early presence there. We also see this acquisition as a positive step for increasing Ormat's viability in the developing "microgrid" market, whereby traditional grid customers continue to rely on incumbent electrical supply for their backup and bulk needs, but tailor a solution that also employs renewables and peak capacity to reduce their overall cost and improve uptime. Microgrids have been employed in universities, small municipalities, military bases, and large industrial facilities to good effect, and Ormat's technology is a very good fit in these scenarios.

Although Ormat is far less of a speculative play than it was when we first started covering its business, this sector still relies on governmental incentives for a significant chunk of its financial lifeblood. These incentives take the form of widely marketed long-term carbon credit swaps and carbon reduction mandates issued by both state and federal agencies. Global incentives are also taking shape, and now Australia, China, the EU, Germany, Japan, and the UK all have renewable portfolio standards of various types in place. Ormat sees these as the most important drivers for expansion of their existing power plants and new projects. The State of Nevada, long a friend of Ormat, may well lead the nation in clean energy implementation, recently passing legislation requiring the elimination of at least 800MW of coal-fired generating capacity by the end of 2019. Neighboring California has stringent renewable energy requirements as well.

These incentives are important for geothermal installations given their higher initial cost and their (often) remote locations. A geothermal plant will cost approximately $2,500 per kW of installed capacity versus $1,000 per kW for a gas turbine facility. Operating costs, however, are where the geothermal plant shines—generation costs are in the range of $0.01–$0.03 per kilowatt hour.

Coal, the next cheapest alternative, yields costs of $0.02–$0.04 per kilowatt hour. Geothermal plants are also extremely reliable, with 24/7 availability (a big differentiator from solar and wind power) and provide nearly 98 percent uptime, with very little maintenance and near zero environmental impact. Coal plants, on the other hand, average about 75 percent availability and come saddled with massive environmental costs that are rarely subsidized directly by ratepayers (for now). These geothermal plants are very good solutions for particular needs in particular locations, but they cannot be plopped down just anywhere, as they require a source of geothermal heat. Fortunately, the Department of Energy estimates a large number of potential sites in the western United States. Developing nations without access to coal or oil but with geothermal resources can create baseline electrical capacity with extremely low rates given appropriate levels of investment.

In all, Ormat remains well positioned with their geothermal business and has some exciting new opportunities in grid stabilization and microgrid developments.

Reasons for Caution

The most recent tax legislation in the US has brought a mix of changes to the renewables environment, many of them (unfortunately) geared toward placating the major players in the fossil fuel industries. Some of these changes may negatively impact the introduction of new geothermal generating capacity, while others may actually benefit the industry. Ormat has not yet made a full assessment of these changes and in fact delayed the release of their annual report so that they could offer at least preliminary guidance. Tax legislation is still in flux, and the EPA has also indicated that the previous administration's Clean Power Plan overstepped statutory authority and will likely be modified. The president and the EPA administrator have yet to provide clear statements of their intent.

Noxious gases of another sort are causing some minor concern in Hawaii as the Kilauea volcano is disrupting operations at Ormat's facility at Pune. The plant has been taken off-line, and it may be several months before operations can resume.

SECTOR: **Energy** ❑ BETA COEFFICIENT: **0.90** ❑ 10-YEAR COMPOUND EARNINGS PER-SHARE
GROWTH: **9.5%** ❑ 10-YEAR COMPOUND DIVIDENDS PER-SHARE GROWTH: **14.0%**

	2010	2011	2012	2013	2014	2015	2016	2017
Revenues (mil)	373.2	437.0	514.4	533.2	559.5	594.6	662.6	692.8
Net income	10.4	(43.1)	(51.1)	37.3	54.2	119.6	93.9	115
Earnings per share	0.22	(.95)	(1.12)	0.81	1.18	2.43	1.87	2.30
Dividends per share	0.27	0.13	0.08	0.08	0.21	0.26	0.52	0.41
Cash flow per share	2.14	1.17	1.13	2.87	3.40	4.62	4.02	4.45
Price: high	38.8	31.2	22.2	28.2	30.5	40.9	53.9	66.5
low	25.8	14.1	16.0	18.8	24.0	25.9	32.3	51.4

Website: **www.ormat.com**

AGGRESSIVE GROWTH

Paychex, Inc.

Ticker symbol: PAYX (NASDAQ) ❑ Large Cap ❑ Value Line financial strength rating: A ❑ Current
yield: 3.2% ❑ Dividend raises, past 10 years: 8

Company Profile

Paychex, Inc., provides payroll, human resources, and benefits outsourcing
solutions for small- to medium-sized businesses with 10–200 employees.
Founded in 1971, the company has more than 100 offices and serves over
605,000 clients in the United States as well as about 2,000 clients in Germany and a new base through a partnership in Brazil. Some 85 percent of
its customers are the small- to medium-sized businesses previously mentioned; the company estimates that it pays one out of every 12 employees
nationwide. The company has two sources of revenue: service revenue, paid
by clients for services, and interest income on the funds held by Paychex for
clients.

Paychex offers a one-stop shop portfolio of services and products
including:

- Payroll processing
- Payroll tax administration services
- Employee payment services, including expense reporting, reimburse-
  ments, etc.
- Regulatory compliance services (new-hire reporting and garnishment
  processing)

- Retirement services administration
- Workers' compensation insurance services
- Health and benefits services
- Time and attendance solutions
- Medical deduction, state unemployment, and other HR services and products

About 60 percent of Paychex's revenue originates from payroll (service revenue plus interest income); the remaining 40 percent comes from its human resource services offerings. In addition to its website and direct sales force, the company uses its relationships with existing clients, CPAs, and banks for new client referrals and to grow the base of services used by existing clients. Approximately half of its new clients come via these referral sources.

Larger clients can choose to outsource their payroll and HR functions or to run them in-house using a Paychex platform. For those clients, the company offers what it calls "Paychex Flex," which can be run locally or on a web-hosted, SaaS environment.

In addition to traditional payroll services, Paychex offers full-service HR outsourcing solutions; custom-built solutions including payroll, compliance, HR, and employee benefits sourcing and administration; outsourcing management; and even professionally trained onsite HR representatives. The company also manages retirement plans and other benefits, including pretax "cafeteria" plans, and has a subsidiary insurance agency offering property and casualty, workers' comp, health, and auto policies to an employer's employee base.

The company is the nation's number one provider of payroll services to small businesses (1–50 employees) and number two for midsized businesses (50–500 employees). The majority of these small business clients are in Professional Services, Health Care, and Construction. About 37,000 of the 605,000 Payroll clients use the full Human Resource Services offering, with a total employee count of about one million. The company has recently implemented web-based and mobile versions of its key products, adding to convenience and reducing paperwork for its clients, and has also added a suite of analytics to its HR offerings. Through the Retirement Services Group, the company administers 78,000 retirement plans, achieving the number one spot nationwide by number of plans.

Finally, as a payroll and benefits processor, the company holds significant short-term funds received from clients to pay out to employees—and earns interest on these funds while they are held. Low recent interest rates have held this revenue and profit source back, but as interest rates rise, this segment, while small, is expected to grow about 10 percent a year on a $50 million annual base.

Financial Highlights, Fiscal Year 2017

The economy appears healthy, and it appears that many of the policies of the Trump administration will help smaller domestic businesses, and this will help Paychex. The company should (1) add new clients, (2) sell more services to new and existing clients, and (3) sell more to each client as the employee base rises. This combination led to a 7 percent top-line gain and an 8 percent bottom-line gain in FY2017 as the mix and scale of the business improved. Favorable margin and mix trends should continue into FY2018 and beyond, with revenues continuing up 7 percent and net profit up in the 8–10 percent range. Interest income ("Interest on Funds Held for Clients" in company vernacular) could give a nice upside lift in 2018 and especially 2019.

Reasons to Buy

A bet on Paychex is a bet on four things: (1) strength in the economy and employment, (2) the continued rise of "small" and independent businesses and contractors, (3) continued adoption of broader "one-stop" platform services, and (4) an increase in interest rates (so they can make money on the float). In the meantime, you get a decent yield, steady gains, and little downside risk if you own the stock.

Paychex's primary market is companies with fewer than 100 employees. The all-important small business segment has been strong since the Great Recession (as companies outsourced formerly in-house services) and is likely to get stronger with Trump's domestic business–friendly approach. Beyond that, the cost of switching and good client relationships has made for a loyal client base. We continue to think the trend to outsource payroll and HR activities will not only continue but will accelerate as easier Internet-based solutions come more into favor.

The company has been a rock-steady performer—conservatively run, well managed, and well financed. It isn't just a "service" company, it is an IT company with a lot of innovation in its DNA. Margins are significantly higher than its closest competitor, Automated Data Processing (ADP). It carries no long-term debt—zero—and should have little difficulty funding the generous dividend, even at its current payout level of 80 percent of earnings. Fragmentation in the market and Paychex's extremely strong financial position will allow the company to continue to grow market share through acquisition. Finally, as short-term interest rates tick upward the company will once again be able to profit from the float (the company has $3–$4 billion of its customers' money held for payroll at any given time). This is one of the few stocks on our list that can tangibly benefit from *moderate* interest rate increases. We like that defensive characteristic.

Reasons for Caution

This company will always be vulnerable to economic swings, such as those brought on by *large* interest rate increases. The company's acquisitions of small payroll processors and human resource service providers make sense, as those acquisitions increase market share, but they do come with costs and risks.

SECTOR: **Information Technology** ❑ BETA COEFFICIENT: **0.95** ❑ 10-YEAR COMPOUND EARNINGS PER-SHARE GROWTH: **7.5%** ❑ 10-YEAR COMPOUND DIVIDENDS PER-SHARE GROWTH: **12.5%**

		2010	2011	2012	2013	2014	2015	2016	2017
Revenues (mil)		2,001	2,084	2,230	2,326	2,519	2,739	2,952	3,151
Net income (mil)		477	516	548	569	627	675	757	817
Earnings per share		1.32	1.42	1.51	1.56	1.71	1.85	2.09	2.25
Dividends per share		1.24	1.24	1.27	1.31	1.40	1.52	1.68	1.84
Cash flow per share		1.56	1.67	1.78	1.83	2.02	2.16	2.42	2.63
Price:	high	32.8	33.9	34.7	45.9	48.2	54.8	62.2	70.4
	low	24.7	25.1	29.1	31.5	39.8	41.6	45.8	54.2

Website: www.paychex.com

AGGRESSIVE GROWTH

Perrigo Company

Ticker symbol: PRGO (NASDAQ) ❑ Large Cap ❑ Value Line financial strength rating: A ❑ Current yield: 0.9% ❑ Dividend raises, past 10 years: 10

Company Profile

Perrigo is the world's largest manufacturer of over-the-counter pharmaceutical products for the store-brand market. They also manufacture generic prescription pharmaceuticals and nutritional products. The most familiar products are their over-the-counter products in cough, cold, allergy, sinus, analgesic, gastrointestinal, smoking cessation, infant formula, personal care, natural health, vitamins, and other similar categories.

Perrigo operates in three main segments: Consumer Healthcare Americas (CHCA), Consumer Healthcare International, and Rx Pharmaceuticals. The two Consumer Healthcare segments, which include generics and nutritionals such as baby formula and vitamins, together generated about 79 percent of Perrigo's FY2017 revenue. Rx Pharmaceuticals produces about 20 percent, and other specialty businesses, about 1 percent. In 2017 the company spun off most of its API business, which supplied pharmaceutical active ingredients to other manufacturers.

The company's success depends on its ability to manufacture and quickly market generic equivalents to branded products. It employs internal R&D resources—which run 3.4 percent of sales—to develop product formulations and manufacture in quantity for its customers. It also develops retail packaging specific to the customers' needs. The company expects a greater percentage of medicines to become available over the counter (versus Rx); this has been the case with Allegra and similar medications in recent years. The company estimates that 72 percent of educated consumers choose store brands, and 91 percent of them stay with them once chosen. They also estimate that they save consumers $7 billion a year with more favorably priced generics.

If you have bought a store-branded over-the-counter medication such as ibuprofen, acetaminophen, skin remedies, or cough medicine at a store like Target or Walmart in the past year, there's a good chance (a 75 percent chance, in fact) that it was made by Perrigo. The company's combined Consumer Healthcare business produces and markets more than 2,700 store-brand products in 26,000 individual SKUs of 11,000 formulations (the difference between the two is mainly different package sizes) to approximately 1,000 customers, including Walmart, CVS, Walgreens, Kroger, Target, Safeway, Dollar General, Costco, and other national and regional drugstores, supermarkets, and mass merchandisers. Walmart is its single largest customer and accounts for 13 percent of Perrigo's net sales (down from 19 percent a few years ago). It's a good deal, because it's a steady cash stream, and Perrigo doesn't really have to invest in marketing. The company estimates that population demographics, new store-branded products, and transitions of certain drugs from prescription to over-the-counter sales all contribute about equally to growth.

The Nutritionals business, part of Consumer Healthcare, distributes 900 store-brand products in 3,400 SKUs to more than 150 customers.

Enlarged by the 2014 Elan acquisition, the Rx Pharma operations produce generic prescription drugs (in contrast to the over-the-counter drugs produced in the Consumer Healthcare segment), obviously benefitting when key patented drugs run past their patent protection. Rx Pharma markets approximately 800 generic prescription products, many of them topicals and creams, with more than 1,300 SKUs, to approximately 350 customers, while the API division markets an assortment of active ingredients to other drug manufacturers as well as for the company's own products, including a number of active ingredients that we'd have trouble spelling correctly, so we won't even try.

In 2017 Perrigo completed the sale of the multiple sclerosis pharmaceutical TYSABRI for $2.85 billion to pay off debt (about 45 percent of outstanding debt) and focus on the mainline businesses.

Financial Highlights, Fiscal Year 2017

A complex crosscurrent of acquisitions and divestitures including the TYSABRI sale netted Perrigo a 5 percent revenue decrease and a 3.4 percent decrease in net income. Net profit margins, as expected, declined to the 13–15 percent range from 18–21 percent again due to TYSABRI, but are expected to rise gradually with efficiency measures and volumes. Revenues will tick modestly higher, in the 2–5 percent range annually, through 2019. Net income should rise in the 6–8 percent range through the period. Debt reduction continues to take priority over share buybacks for the moment, although the longer the share price languishes, the more likely increased buybacks will result.

Reasons to Buy

Perrigo has been a story of solid niche dominance (store-branded medications) with a couple of high-growth, high-margin businesses mixed in. While we don't like the margin deterioration, a stronger focus on over-the-counter and generic medicines seems to make sense, and the niche dominance should keep it moving forward. We like the slogan "Quality Affordable Healthcare Products." People are becoming more sensitive to their own healthcare costs and spending in general and are opting more often for the store brand; after all, 200 mg of ibuprofen is 200 mg of ibuprofen. This all sits on top of the demographic tailwind of the aging population and the institutional tailwind of doing what's necessary to rein in costs.

The stock as of this writing has lost more than two-thirds of its value and is priced at about 15 times earnings. We think it's a good value at a time when good values are particularly hard to find.

Reasons for Caution

Perrigo broke most of our rules in making a major acquisition of a complex business (Elan), then moving to another country where accounting standards make business evaluation more difficult. Normally we would have dropped the company right then and there, but again, we like its track record and niche dominance—and now, losing its most profitable product and all of this restructuring is not necessarily a good pill to swallow. There's a lot of change here for a *100 Best Stock*, and change can cause a lot of heartburn (fortunately, they sell the medication). True, it was probably overvalued three years ago; takeover fever will do that. Naturally, we're not too thrilled with the company's cash returns to investors and increasing share counts from the Elan acquisition. Behind all this fog sits a pretty good business in our opinion, one that has become more fairly valued to boot—albeit not without risk.

SECTOR: **Healthcare** ◻ BETA COEFFICIENT: **0.76** ◻ 10-YEAR COMPOUND EARNINGS PER-SHARE GROWTH: **24.0%** ◻ 10-YEAR COMPOUND DIVIDENDS PER-SHARE GROWTH: **12.0%**

	2010	2011	2012	2013	2014	2015	2016	2017
Revenues (mil)	2,269	2,765	3,173	3,540	4,061	4,604	5,521	4,925
Net income (mil)	263	341	411	442	739.5	1,001	726	703
Earnings per share	2.83	3.64	4.37	4.68	6.39	7.24	5.07	4.93
Dividends per share	0.25	0.27	0.32	0.35	0.39	0.46	0.58	0.64
Cash flow per share	3.69	4.78	5.84	6.41	8.21	10.60	8.20	8.15
Price: high	67.5	104.7	120.8	157.5	171.6	215.7	152.4	91.7
low	37.5	62.3	90.2	98.6	125.4	140.4	79.7	63.7

Website: www.perrigo.com

CONSERVATIVE GROWTH

Praxair, Inc.

Ticker symbol: PX (NYSE) ◻ Large Cap ◻ Value Line financial strength rating: A ◻ Current yield: 2.1% ◻ Dividend raises, past 10 years: 10

Company Profile

Praxair, Inc., is the second-largest supplier of industrial gases in the world. The company, which was spun off to Union Carbide shareholders in June 1992, supplies a broad range of atmospheric, process, and specialty gases; high-performance coatings; and related services and technologies.

Praxair has long been a staple on the *100 Best* list, and we thought 2017 was its last year in its current form. In late 2016 the company agreed to a 50–50 merger with German-based gas supplier The Linde Group. Ordinarily we remove companies from the list upon merger or acquisition at least until we get a better handle on the combined entity. In this case, the business will stay much the same as Linde is in much the same business—although the combined company (to be called Linde) will be three times the size ($31 billion in sales annually) with $1 billion in cost synergies. It appears the merger will be completed in late 2018, and we think the combined entity qualifies as a *100 Best Stock* without question. Since we don't have many facts and figures on the combined entity, we will write about Praxair for 2019 as it exists in 2018; just assume that the merged Linde will be a bigger, more profitable, more high-tech, and more international version of what we discuss in this narrative.

Praxair's primary products are atmospheric gases—oxygen, nitrogen, argon, and rare gases (produced when atmospheric air is purified, compressed, cooled, distilled, and condensed) and process and specialty gases—carbon dioxide, helium, hydrogen, and acetylene (produced as by-products of chemical production or recovered from natural gas). Customers include makers of primary metals, metal fabricators, petroleum refiners, and producers of chemicals, healthcare products, pharmaceuticals, biotech, food and beverage, electronics, glass, pulp and paper, and environmental products. By end market, manufacturing, metals, and energy producers account for 51 percent of 2017 sales (energy alone is 12 percent, up from 11 percent in 2016 but down from 13 percent in 2015); chemicals, electronics, and aerospace another 22 percent; and healthcare and food/beverage the next 17 percent; with the remaining 11 percent to "other" industries.

The gas products are sold into the packaged-gas market and the merchant market. In the packaged-gas market, bulk gases are packaged into high-pressure cylinders and either delivered to the customer or to distributors. In the merchant market, bulk gases are liquefied and transported by tanker truck to the customer's facility.

The company also designs, engineers, and constructs cryogenic and noncryogenic gas supply systems for customers who choose to produce their own atmospheric gases onsite. This is obviously a capital-intensive delivery solution for Praxair but results in lower delivered cost to the customer and higher returns for Praxair, as all operational costs are paid by the customer. Contracts for these installations can run to 20 years. About 28 percent of volume is packaged, 34 percent is "merchant," and 28 percent is generated on-site (8 percent is "other").

Praxair Surface Technologies is a subsidiary that applies wear-, corrosion-, and thermal-resistant metallic and ceramic coatings and powders to metal surfaces in order to resist wear, high temperatures, and corrosion.

Aircraft engines are a primary market, but it serves others, including the printing, textile, chemical, and primary metals markets, and provides aircraft engine and airframe component overhaul services. About 48 percent of Praxair's sales come from outside North America. Once combined with Linde, that number is expected to rise to 62 percent.

Financial Highlights, Fiscal Year 2017

A modest recovery in the energy, strength in manufacturing across most sectors, operating leverage, and the ability to pass on price increases to cover input cost increases led to a solid 2017 performance. Revenues rose 9 percent; net and per-share earnings followed suit after a soft 2016. Without the merger, the company projects revenue gains in the 5–7 percent range annually through 2019; with a stronger 15 percent rise in earnings for 2018 as price increases and tax changes take effect, slowing to a 5–6 percent gain in 2019. Notable again is the substantial cost savings likely at the consolidated company, which should start having effect in 2019. Dividend increases appear healthy in the 8–10 percent annual range and modest share buybacks, although what happens with the combined company remains to be seen.

Reasons to Buy

The big story is the Linde merger, and the outcome should be in place as 2019 commences. (For those who read this narrative last year, we said the same thing for 2018—regulatory paperwork takes time to complete although all systems appear "go.") There's a lot we don't know, but we do know that the combined company will be much larger, more diversified, and more cost efficient.

Aside from soft years in 2015 and 2016 due to energy and manufacturing weakness and a strong dollar, Praxair has had a steady history of high margins, growth, and few to no surprises. It has a strong franchise, likely to get stronger especially on the international front with the merger. Tailwinds in energy, metals, electronics manufacturing, emerging markets, and currency will help. Much of its business is delivered on a contract basis, providing a bit of extra stability. The company is a big player in the re-emergence of US manufacturing, and that could be important as new Trump administration policies take hold.

Reasons for Caution

As hydrocarbon energy products are feedstock for many of Praxair's products, the company has enjoyed recent trends but could take a minor hit as energy prices recover—although at least for now it has been able to pass on those increases. The strong international presence means that results are sensitive to currency fluctuations. In addition, the merger could produce some short-term disruptions and costs.

SECTOR: **Materials** ❑ BETA COEFFICIENT: **1.03** ❑ 10-YEAR COMPOUND EARNINGS PER-SHARE
GROWTH: **8.0%** ❑ 10-YEAR COMPOUND DIVIDENDS PER-SHARE GROWTH: **14.0%**

	2010	**2011**	**2012**	**2013**	**2014**	**2015**	**2016**	**2017**
Revenues (mil)	10,118	11,252	11,224	11,925	12,273	10,776	10,534	11,437
Net income (mil)	1,195	1,672	1,692	1,755	1,694	1,547	1,500	1,641
Earnings per share	3.84	5.45	5.61	5.87	5.73	5.35	5.21	5.68
Dividends per share	1.80	2.00	2.20	2.40	2.60	2.86	3.00	3.15
Cash flow per share	6.95	8.95	9.10	9.70	9.90	9.45	9.20	9.90
Price: high	96.3	111.7	116.9	130.5	135.2	130.4	125.0	156.4
low	72.7	88.6	100.0	107.7	117.3	98.6	95.6	115.0

Website: www.praxair.com

CONSERVATIVE GROWTH

The Procter & Gamble Company

Ticker symbol: PG (NYSE) ❑ Large Cap ❑ Value Line financial strength rating: A++ ❑ Current
yield: 3.5% ❑ Dividend raises, past 10 years: 10

Company Profile

We thought this would never happen, given our defensive, dividend-oriented stance in stock selection: the legendary Procter & Gamble has become the sole remaining broadline consumer home staples company on our *100 Best* list. Last year we eliminated Clorox; this year we cut Colgate-Palmolive and Kimberly-Clark in an effort to make our list more nimble and reflective of the times. Procter stands the lone winner in this race because of its relatively stronger brands, more profitable operations, and greater presence of adaptation and change both recently and in the near future.

Procter & Gamble dates back to 1837, when William Procter and James Gamble began making soap and candles from surplus animal fat from the stockyards in Cincinnati, OH. The company's first major product introduction took place in 1879 when it launched Ivory soap. Since then, P&G has continually created a host of blockbuster products, added some key acquisitions, exited the food business and now downsized its brand list by over

100 brands—but still in total has some of the strongest, most recognizable consumer brands in the world.

P&G is a uniquely diversified consumer products company with a strong global presence. P&G markets its broad line of products to nearly 5 billion consumers in more than 180 countries.

The company is a recognized leader in the development, manufacturing, and marketing of quality laundry, cleaning, paper, personal care, and healthcare products.

To understand Procter, it's worth a look at how the company is organized:

- Beauty (18 percent of FY2017 sales, 15 percent of pretax profits) includes shampoo, skin care, deodorant, hair care and color, and bar soap products, including such traditional brands as Head & Shoulders, Ivory soap, Safeguard, Secret, Pantene, Vidal Sassoon, Olay, and Old Spice.
- Grooming (10 percent, 14 percent) includes razors, blades, pre- and post-shave products, and other shaving products, including Braun, Gillette, Gillette Fusion, Gillette MACH3, and Prestobarba brands.
- Health Care (11 percent, 13 percent) is made up of two subunits, Personal Health Care and Oral Care. Personal Health Care in turn includes gastrointestinal, respiratory, rapid diagnostics, and vitamins/minerals/supplements, and includes such brands as Vicks, Metamucil, Prilosec, and Pepto-Bismol. Oral Care includes the familiar Crest, Scope, and Oral-B brands among others.
- Fabric and Home Care (32 percent, 29 percent) covers many of the familiar laundry and cleaning brands—Tide, Dawn, Febreze, Downy, Bounce, Mr. Clean, Swiffer, and a handful created for international markets.
- Baby, Feminine, and Family Care (29 percent, 26 percent) markets mostly paper products like Puffs, Charmin, Pampers, Luvs, Bounty, Always, and Tampax into baby care, feminine care, adult incontinence, and family care markets.

Procter has always been a hallmark example of brand management and building intrinsic brand strength—that is, strength not from the company name but through the brand's own name and reputation. It is described as a "house of brands," not a "branded house," although we're starting to see the "P&G" name more prominently in its marketing and advertising. The company tells us that its 50 "Leadership Brands" are some of the world's most well-known household names, that 90 percent of its business comes from these 50 brands, and that 25 of them are billion-dollar businesses.

The company has a strong and growing international presence, with 55 percent of sales originating outside the US and Canada. The company also manufactures locally in its largest international markets, with on-the-ground operations in approximately 70 countries.

In an effort to become a "much simpler company," Procter has now completed its brand realignment, which entailed shrinking the portfolio from 166 brands down to just 65 by the end of 2017. Additional savings will result from everything from reducing manufacturing sites to organizational units to the number of legal entities and invoices produced. The remaining 65 brands account for approximately 85 percent of earlier FY2015 sales and 95 percent of pre-tax profit. The number of country/category combinations will drop from 140 to 50, with new focus on everything from innovation to a reconfigured supply chain. In beauty parlance, it's a total makeover.

As if this wasn't enough change, the company endured an expensive proxy fight with Nelson Peltz and his Trian Investors fund. While the vote was almost too close to call, Procter capitulated and got a seat on the board and an opportunity to showcase its top-line expansion plans; whether this works out is a wait-and-see, but it is likely to have more good effect than bad.

Financial Highlights, Fiscal Year 2017

FY2017 sales dropped a fraction from 2016, which had in turn dropped some 15 percent from 2015; these "ugly" compares had mostly to do with the aforementioned product line shakedown. Profits rose about 3 percent on the decreased revenue—more evidence of a successful "right-sizing" and trimming of dead branches. For 2018, the first year in a while with reasonably good comparisons, revenues are projected to rise about 3 percent with profits remaining relatively flat as streamlining efficiencies kick in; 2019 looks to produce a 4–5 percent earnings gain on 3–4 percent revenue increase. Modest dividend increases and share buybacks should give way to stronger increases as the simplified business moves forward.

Reasons to Buy

Regardless of developments in the world economy, people will continue to shave, bathe, do laundry, and care for their babies, and P&G is the global leader in baby care, feminine care, fabric care, and shaving products. Everyone should consider at least one defensive play in their portfolio, and P&G continues to deserve a spot at the top of the list.

We like the company's new position on brand proliferation. More is not always better, particularly when each brand carries with it a not-insignificant

SG&A and Marketing overhead. Also, does a company like P&G bring anything special to the battery business? We didn't think so, and we're glad they agreed. As the company continues to evolve its organizational structure, it has departed from its traditional model of managing brands as wholly separate businesses with brand-specific advertising budgets, product research labs, and so forth. Synergies from combining ads and ad strategies alone should reduce total costs across the company's many portfolios (to that point, they estimate a 50 percent reduction in advertising, PR, and other agencies). While we will miss some of the brands they are likely to cut, the business won't miss them all that much; focus, critical mass, simplicity, and profitability appear to be their strategic mainstays moving forward—and the Peltz involvement is likely to strengthen that direction.

In short, we continue to like the brand, marketplace, and financial strength; sure and steady dividend growth (the company has raised its dividend 62 straight years); and short- and long-term prospects.

Reasons for Caution

So much change so fast can be disruptive, and there's been a lot of it. The brand simplification has worked; it remains to be seen what influence Trian has, and there's always the chance that some bitter after effects of the proxy struggle might linger and poison the well with management and employees—but things seem okay so far. Competition is fierce in P&G's markets, and operational and marketing missteps can be painful.

Finally, rising commodity costs can negatively affect P&G, as it is hard to pass them on through price increases.

SECTOR: **Consumer Staples** ❏ BETA COEFFICIENT: **0.58** ❏ 10-YEAR COMPOUND EARNINGS PER-SHARE GROWTH: **3.5%** ❏ 10-YEAR COMPOUND DIVIDENDS PER-SHARE GROWTH: **8.5%**

	2010	2011	2012	2013	2014	2015	2016	2017
Revenues (mil)	78,938	82,559	83,680	85,500	83,062	76,279	65,299	65,058
Net income (mil)	10,946	11,797	11,344	11,869	12,220	11,535	10,441	10,733
Earnings per share	3.53	3.93	3.85	4.05	4.22	4.02	3.67	3.92
Dividends per share	1.80	1.97	2.14	2.29	2.45	2.59	2.66	2.70
Cash flow per share	4.87	5.21	5.20	5.33	5.57	5.31	4.97	5.21
Price: high	65.3	67.7	71.0	85.8	93.9	91.8	90.3	94.7
low	39.4	57.6	59.1	68.4	75.3	65.0	74.5	83.2

Website: www.pg.com

GROWTH AND INCOME

Prologis, Inc.

Ticker symbol: PLD (NYSE) ❑ Large Cap ❑ Value Line financial strength rating: B+ ❑ Current yield: 3.1% ❑ Dividend raises, past 10 years: 4

Company Profile

We like ordinary stocks: shares of prosperous, growing businesses. In addition to ordinary shares, we've come to like REITs—or real estate investment trusts—shares of specialized income-producing real estate portfolios. These specialized investments allow you to become a landlord and to collect (usually rising) rents. Beyond rents, at least with the REITs we prefer and choose, there is a good business sitting on top of the real estate that adds a measure of growth to the base rental income produced by the real estate.

Long averse to investment "products," we first dipped our toes into the REIT pool by adding Welltower to the *100 Best* list five years ago. Good business (senior living) on top of a strong real estate asset core (high-end senior living properties). Then we added Public Storage four years ago, again a good business (self-storage units) despite a slowdown two years ago. Then we added the cream-of-the-office-space crop, Empire State Realty Trust, three years ago. Two years ago, we went to the well one more time with a logistics business and real estate core called Prologis. With Prologis, we rounded out our REIT portfolio at four of the *100 Best Stocks*, a number that we probably won't exceed so as not to have to change the book title! We feel pretty good with four REIT choices—and we feel good with *these* choices. Prologis is the global leader in industrial logistics real estate across the Americas, Europe, and Asia. "Industrial logistics real estate" is mainly distribution warehouses and specialized facilities that store goods and prepare them for shipment, sometimes with some final assembly or value-add, and are an integral component of the supply chain for many types of organizations. Major clients include third-party logistics providers, transportation companies, retail (including online), and manufacturers.

Prologis operates 3,232 properties all across 19 countries on four continents, with about 64 percent of the square footage in the US, 23 percent in Europe, 7 percent in "other" Americas, and 3 percent in Asia. The company owns and operates most of these properties mainly as standard warehouses in industrial parks or near port or airport facilities, leasing them to large and small companies either in whole or in sections according to need. Prologis also develops custom partner solutions through their "Global Customer

Solutions" business, which designs, builds, and operates custom distribution facilities for major accounts like Amazon, DHL, and others. In fact, their top ten customers accounted for 12.4 percent of the business; Amazon is the largest customer at 4.7 percent of "net effective rent"; Home Depot is second at 1.8 percent; and FedEx is third at 1.3 percent. Overall, however, the customer base is quite diverse with 5,200 customers in all, and the top 23 customers account for 21.6 percent of the revenue.

Financial Highlights, Fiscal Year 2017

FY2017 was a decent year for the business, with demand exceeding supply for such kinds of facilities—a statement borne out in the numbers. Occupancy rates rose to another record 97.2 percent, and average rent increases on property rollovers (rentals to new tenants) increased 15.4 percent. Core Funds From Operations (FFO—a standard measure of true income for REITs) was up 8 percent for the year on a relatively light 3.4 percent increase in net revenue.

Forward projections call for a stabilization of net income on relatively small revenue increases of 3–5 percent going forward into 2019—we think this is conservative.

Reasons to Buy

The value proposition of modern, flexible logistics sites for today's organizations is strong, and particularly strong for e-commerce businesses—such as Amazon, as previously noted. More generally, the state of the art in supply-chain management has advanced significantly in just a few years, driven by e-commerce and just-in-time production management. As supply chains become more global, and as products become more customized and have shorter life cycles, as shipments get smaller, more numerous, and more likely to have an assembly and a "reverse" component, flexible logistics solutions become far more important. Also, e-commerce, because of its high shipment "granularity," requires about three times the space per dollar of revenue as bricks-and-mortar warehouse operations. In short, current trends toward e-commerce and urbanization have driven changes in consumption and supply chain management, and Prologis is at the heart of that change. The company projects a 162 percent increase in e-commerce volumes over the five-year period 2015–2020.

Equally important is today's current business climate, with companies relying on back-end productivity rather than top-line growth to increase profits. Prologis sits right in the middle of this trend, with a solid base of real estate, skills to manage it, and skills to partner with major clients to deliver the right and often customized solution.

All major financial metrics are on a strong upward advance, occupancy levels are at an all-time high, pricing power is apparent, and steady dividend increases appear likely. We think, given the favorable supply/demand picture in this business, that Prologis's financial forecasts could be too conservative going forward; there is more upside than downside assuming continuing strong global e-commerce growth. Consistent with much of the REIT industry, share counts are on the rise as Prologis replaces debt with equity or uses equity to finance acquisitions. The current debt-to-equity ratio of 25 percent is very healthy for the industry and getting healthier.

Reasons for Caution

We've picked four REITs—in senior living, self-storage, New York real estate, and now, logistics and warehousing: Prologis. Guess which one is most vulnerable to economic downturns. Prologis? Right. A protracted economic downturn would hurt this business more than many REITs (we have avoided shopping center and hospitality REITs altogether because in our view they're even more vulnerable). We should also note that e-commerce, the strongest growth vector, currently accounts for only about 13 percent of the business. As millennials shift their focus from goods to experiences, and as most sought-after goods get smaller (such as smartphones), the future global economy could simply require less physical space to operate.

SECTOR: Real Estate ❑ BETA COEFFICIENT: **0.83** ❑ 10-YEAR COMPOUND EARNINGS PER-SHARE GROWTH: **NM** ❑ 10-YEAR COMPOUND DIVIDENDS PER-SHARE GROWTH: **NM**

	2010	2011	2012	2013	2014	2015	2016	2017
Revenues (mil)	—	1,533	2,006	1,750	1,761	2,197	2,533	2,618
Net income (mil)	—	(153.4)	(102.4)	219.4	636.2	869.4	1,210	1,652
Funds from operations per share	—	1.10	1.19	1.65	1.88	2.23	2.57	3.06
Real estate owned per share	—	57.25	55.74	45.67	47.63	52.47	51.30	51.96
Dividends per share	—	1.12	1.12	1.12	1.32	1.52	1.68	1.76
Price: high	—	37.5	37.6	45.5	44.1	47.6	54.9	67.5
low	—	21.7	28.2	34.6	36.3	36.3	35.3	48.3

Website: www.prologis.com

Prudential Financial

Ticker symbol: PRU (NYSE) ◻ Large Cap ◻ Value Line financial strength rating: B++ ◻ Current yield: 3.5% ◻ Dividend raises, past 10 years: 9

Company Profile

"Own a Piece of the Rock" is one of the classic slogans of corporate America. We've all heard it so many times it's like a song you can't get out of your head; yet it's so familiar that you might well have forgotten the company it stands for. Oh yeah. Prudential. The Rock of Gibraltar in the picture. A trademarked symbol. Does it ring a bell? In choosing stocks for our *100 Best* list, we look for stability and safety. Yes, we look for a piece of the rock in every choice we make. But we also look for innovation and the sort of market leadership that leads to profitable growth. We usually do not look for financial stocks, as they are hard to understand and can be fickle as we all learned in 2008. But due to a rock-solid base plus an innovative growth vector we'll share in a moment, we replaced the ailing Wells Fargo with "Pru" last year.

Prudential began selling life insurance 141 years ago, and has evolved this rather unsexy business into an insurance, asset management, and retirement powerhouse well positioned to handle not only your retirement planning needs but also those of major corporations—that's where the innovation we hinted at previously comes in. The company operates in four Divisions in the wake of a late 2017 reorganization:

- Workplace Solutions (50 percent of 2017 operating income) is comprised of two segments: Retirement and Group Insurance. The Retirement segment provides administrative services and products including group annuities, structured investment products, and the pension risk transfer products (the innovation cited several times in this narrative).
- Individual Solutions contains Individual Annuities and Individual Life. The Annuities business "manufactures" and distributes individual variable, fixed, and fixed indexed annuities primarily to the "mass affluent" market for retirement income stabilization and supplement.
- The Investment Management segment provides portfolio management and specific investment products such as mutual funds, which are both publicly and privately available.
- International Insurance creates, modifies, and distributes life insurance, retirement, and related products outside the US through various

channels. Important developed markets include Japan and Korea while emerging markets include Brazil and Chile.

The company has $1.2 trillion in assets under management and currently operates in 47 countries. Unlike many such companies, international expansion is a major strategy.

The innovation we're really excited about is a new initiative to sell packaged corporate pension plans to employers of all types. When a company takes on a pension obligation, either willfully or as a consequence of a union negotiation or some such, it takes on a risk. The pension is a promise to pay a defined amount (hence "defined benefit"), and it's up to the company to pay this amount come whatever happens to its own resources and investments. Bottom line: the employer company takes on a lot of risk when it creates a pension program. Here's where Prudential comes in: companies can transfer this risk to Prudential by paying Prudential a fee to take over, essentially buying an annuity to cover future pension obligations. Prudential takes on the risk of the employer for a fee. That's what insurers do. It's a new business that Prudential knows how to do and will realize economies from as it takes over in larger volumes from employer customers.

Financial Highlights, Fiscal Year 2017

Lower fees and pricing in some segments were offset by a favorable product mix, improved market conditions, higher interest rates, expense controls, and a strong performance from the new pension risk transfer business leading to a pretty good year for PRU. Revenues (Premium plus Investment plus Other) advanced less than 1 percent; however, net income advanced almost 19 percent. Modest revenue gains in the 2–4 percent range should continue through 2019, while net earnings, helped along by a lower tax rate, should advance 5–10 percent annually. Healthy buyback activity will take per-share earnings 15 percent higher in 2018 and 8–10 percent in 2019. Two to 3 percent buybacks are likely going forward with dividend increases in the high single digits typically—although management raised it a full 20 percent in early 2018.

Reasons to Buy

Prudential, long a stalwart of the sleepy life insurance business, has witnessed an accelerating transition toward the ever-greater need for retirement planning solutions both on the part of individuals and employer organizations. Annuities, long another fairly sleepy part of the business, are enjoying a resurgence as corporate and public pensions evolve away from full-coverage defined benefit plans; annuities are also becoming more acceptable and more easily used by financial advisors to round out financial plans as their roles and features are better tailored and better understood. The new pension risk transfer product "innovation" offers an exciting path to growth as more employers with traditional pension obligations come on board; Prudential is the market leader in this new growth opportunity. The international expansion also bodes well particularly as the dollar stabilizes. All of the businesses should fare well in a higher interest rate and less regulated environment. Finally, investor cash returns have been on the rise for years and should continue along that path.

Reasons for Caution

Hats off to you if you can understand this business! We found this company's investor materials profoundly difficult to understand. Like most financials it is hard to sort through the terminology and nuances of each business—and this year we had to deal with a major organizational realignment to boot. It seems as if managers of a financial business speak in financial terms; it took quite a bit of research to understand exactly what products Prudential supplies to what markets! We're still not sure we got it.

There are some other risks here too: longevity (people living longer makes annuities less profitable) and general risks associated with the financial industry, mostly risks of complexity and greed we fell into back in 2008 and regulatory actions that can result from such events. We're breaking the "invest in things you understand" rule a bit here, but we do understand the idea of pension risk transfer and of annuities becoming a more important and more trusted retirement planning vehicle as pensions continue to go away and people become more responsible for their own retirement destinies.

SECTOR: **Financials** ❑ BETA COEFFICIENT: **1.52** ❑ 10-YEAR COMPOUND EARNINGS PER-SHARE GROWTH: **8.0%** ❑ 10-YEAR COMPOUND DIVIDENDS PER-SHARE GROWTH: **12.0%**

		2010	2011	2012	2013	2014	2015	2016	2017
Premium income (bil)		15.3	21.4	62.1	23.1	25.1	25.5	28.0	29.2
Total income (bil)		31.0	39.4	81.1	45.3	49.8	48.6	51.6	53.6
Net profit (bil)		3.0	3.1	3.0	4.8	4.2	4.5	3.9	4.7
Earnings per share		6.27	6.41	6.27	9.67	9.21	10.04	9.13	10.58
Dividends per share		1.15	1.45	1.60	1.73	2.17	2.44	2.80	3.00
Price:	high	66.8	67.5	65.2	92.7	94.3	92.6	108.3	118.2
	low	46.3	42.4	44.5	53.4	75.9	73.2	57.2	97.9

Website: www.prudential.com

Public Storage

Ticker symbol: PSA (NYSE) ❑ Large Cap ❑ Value Line financial strength rating: A+ ❑ Current yield: 4.0% ❑ Dividend raises, past 10 years: 8

Company Profile

You have stuff. We have stuff. We all have stuff. Stuff to store somewhere. Stuff from our families, stuff from our kids, stuff from our past. Boats, RVs, and extra vehicles. Boxes, boxes, and more boxes. And we all need to store that stuff somewhere. But where? As more of us live in houses with smaller yards and devoid of basements, where? As more of us choose to rent rather than buy, where? As more of us, especially the younger "millennials" among us, choose to live closer to the centers of larger cities, where? As the retirees among us downsize, where? As the elderly give up their primary residences, where?

You get the idea. There is more personal stuff for most of us to store, and less space to do it. That's where Public Storage becomes a pretty good investment idea.

Public Storage is a real estate investment trust (REIT) owning and operating 2,386 self-storage properties (2,348 in 2016) in 38 states and another 221 facilities in seven countries in Europe. The company has a 49 percent interest in Europe's "Shurgard," and also owns a 42 percent interest in another trust called PS Business Parks, which owns 103 rentable properties in six states. The company points out that, based on the number of tenants, it is one of the world's largest landlords. The slogan "We're in your neighborhood" also tells you something.

Most are probably familiar with the format—small, unfinished, generally not-climate-controlled lockers rentable on a month-to-month basis for personal and business use. They range in size from 25–400 square feet, and there are typically 350–750 storage spaces in each facility. Some include covered parking for vehicle, boat, and RV storage. On average the company nets a little over $1 per square foot per month—a rather handsome sum considering these units do not come with any of the finish or comfort of an apartment or even a home, which may rent for something similar per square foot depending on the market.

Not surprisingly, the largest concentrations are in California, Texas, and Florida (since these are centers for retirees and homes with no basements), and most are near a major US or European city. The three largest markets are New York, San Francisco, and Los Angeles. Branding in the US is "Public

Storage"; in Europe it is "Shurgard." US self-storage revenues account for about 75 percent of the total; European self-storage accounts for about 7 percent, and the commercial business park business accounts for about 12 percent. The remaining "ancillary businesses" include selling supplies like locks for storage units and storage unit insurance.

The key strategies continue to be revenue and cost optimization, market-share growth in major markets, achieving scale to lower operating costs, and building brand recognition. The company has a centralized call center and a website to help market its product and facilitate transactions. Acquisitions are also an important part of the strategy; the current market is fragmented with PSA only owning 10–20 percent of the market at most, and good properties come up regularly. The company expects to grow its property base a steady 1–2 percent annually.

Our principle in owning REITs remains the same; we're not looking for just real estate, we want to own a good business that *just happens* to own a lot of real estate. REITs are typically good income producers, as they are required by law to pay a substantial portion of their cash flow to investors. The accounting rules are different, and REIT investors should focus on Funds From Operations (FFO), which is analogous to operating income; net income figures have depreciation expenses deducted, which can vary in timing and not always be realistic. FFO supports the dividends paid to investors.

Financial Highlights, Fiscal Year 2017

Higher rents were the primary driver of a moderate 4 percent increase in FY2017 revenues; however, damage and insurance losses and higher interest expense resulted in a modest 1 percent decrease in net income. Occupancy rates ended 2017 at 93.8 percent, down a tick from 94.5 percent in 2016 but still strong given the relatively high turnover in this type of business. Realized rents rose 3.0 percent compared to 4.9 percent in 2016. Per-share FFO as a consequence of all these factors remained unchanged at $9.70. Forecasts call largely for more of the same, with revenues advancing 3–5 percent in each of the next two years. Per-share FFO and dividend increases should also be in the 3–5 percent range through 2019. Debt is a mere 14 percent of total capital, and while this is up from 5 percent, it reflects a strong and conservative capital structure.

Reasons to Buy

With REITs, our emphasis continues to be more on the business and less on real estate, and with Public Storage, we feel we've found a good business that happens to be based on real estate. PSA has the best brand and highest operating efficiency and profitability in the business, and the core business model and need for its product is sustained and growing—albeit more slowly of late. No matter how easy it is to sell stuff on Craigslist, it's also too easy to acquire stuff, and although millennials are more about "experiences" than "things," there will still be plenty of people in the habit of acquiring "stuff." At the same time, real estate is trending away from large suburban McMansions with extra space and more toward city digs, patio homes, cluster homes, and the like. All point to strong, steady business prospects for providers of flexible storage solutions, and as PSA strengthens its brand and market-share foothold, more of that business will go its way.

Reasons for Caution

There is growing evidence that millennials and others are simply less about collecting "stuff" than their predecessors—ask any antique dealer and they'll tell you. Occupancy and rent growth are starting to slow. Also, any profitable business will attract competitors, and there is some evidence of overbuilding and competition in markets like Houston, Chicago, DC, and Denver. That said, PSA has a pretty good lock on the tighter, more lucrative markets like Los Angeles, San Francisco, Seattle, and Portland with three to ten times the market share of the next competitor. This is a good, steady, profitable real estate business with 43 percent profit margins; that said, investors may have to become more patient about growth prospects.

SECTOR: **Real Estate** ◻ BETA COEFFICIENT: **0.28** ◻ 10-YEAR COMPOUND FFO PER-SHARE GROWTH: **6.5%** ◻ 10-YEAR COMPOUND DIVIDENDS PER-SHARE GROWTH: **14.0%**

	2010	2011	2012	2013	2014	2015	2016	2017
Revenues (mil)	1,647	1,752	1,826	1,982	2,195	2,382	2,561	2,669
Net income (mil)	672	824	670	845	908	1,053	1,184	1,172
Funds from operations per share	5.22	5.93	6.31	7.53	7.98	8.79	9.70	9.70
Real estate owned per share	44.51	43.35	42.71	47.97	49.20	49.49	51.49	53.09
Dividends per share	3.05	3.65	4.40	5.15	5.60	6.50	7.30	8.00
Price: high	106.1	136.7	152.7	176.7	190.2	253.9	277.6	232.2
low	74.7	100.0	129.0	144.4	148.0	192.1	200.9	192.1

Website: **www.publicstorage.com**

Quest Diagnostics, Inc.

Ticker symbol: DGX (NYSE) ❏ Large Cap ❏ Value Line financial strength rating: B++ ❏ Current yield: 1.9% ❏ Dividend raises, past 10 years: 7

Company Profile

If you have gone for any kind of medical test, either at the recommendation of a doctor or as required by an employer or insurance company, chances are you got that test in a lab operated by Quest Diagnostics. Quest is the world's leading provider of diagnostic testing, information, and services to support doctors, hospitals, and the care-giving process.

The company operates more than 2,200 labs and patient service centers including about 150 smaller "rapid-response" labs in the US and has facilities in India, Mexico, the UK, Ireland, and Sweden. It provides about 150 million lab test results a year and serves physicians, hospitals, employers, life and healthcare insurers, and other health facilities. The company has a logistics network including 3,700 courier vehicles and 23 aircraft and has some 20 *billion* test results from the past decade in its databases, a rich source for medical research data. Quest estimates that it serves more than half the hospitals and physicians in the United States and estimates that it "touches the lives" of 30 percent of all US adults each year.

The company offers diagnostic testing services covering pretty much the gamut of medical necessity in its testing facilities. It also offers a line of diagnostic kits, reagents, and devices to support its own labs, home and remote testing, and other labs. Employer drug testing is a big business. The company offers a series of "wellness and risk management services," including tests, exams, and record services for the insurance industry. The company also does tests and provides other support for clinical research and trials, and finally, through its information technology segment, it offers a Care360 platform to help physicians maintain charts and access data through its network, which has about 200,000 physicians enrolled. Mobile technology is another innovation front; the company has developed a mobile patient portal within Care360 known as "MyQuest" to help patients keep track of test results, schedule appointments and medications, and share information with physicians and other care providers.

Other innovations include a new initiative called "Data Diagnostics," a tool delivering real-time analytics to the point of care suggesting possible conditions and additional tests to perform "to achieve better clinical and financial outcomes" in diagnosis, treatment, and utilization management. The company has also been a leader in developing so-called "moderate complexity" direct molecular testing procedures, where more complex diagnostic tests can be performed in "moderate complexity" environments—i.e., a "retail" lab format such as Quest operates. The company is a leader in "gene-based" and "esoteric" testing and has launched an assortment of molecular genetics tests supporting new trends in the health industry toward individualized medicine—medicine based on a patient's own unique gene makeup and characteristics. A new "ImmunoCAP" allergy test can identify hundreds of allergens with a single blood sample. And, in a bit of good news for all of us and especially our kids, the new "Quiggles" phlebotomy device uses an ice pack and vibration to make those blood draws more comfortable and less stressful.

Financial Highlights, Fiscal Year 2017

What would seem like a pretty steady industry has gone through some crosscurrents recently; first the attempted takedown of the Affordable Care Act, which caused some apprehension but no damage, followed by a lesser-known initiative called the Protecting Access to Medicare Act, which decreased the Medicare reimbursement rates for a majority of lab tests. Despite the bad news, Quest logged a 3 percent revenue and a 7.6 percent earnings increase for FY2017. The diminished reimbursement may end up causing some smaller mom-and-pop lab competitors to leave the business, so that some of the innovations highlighted earlier and the new tax law have the company forecasting a robust 12–13 percent earnings gain on nearly flat revenue in 2018 and a 4–5 percent earnings rise on a 3–5 percent revenue gain in 2019. Dividends should rise in the 8–10 percent range annually with relatively steady share counts. We think these forecasts could be conservative as new tests and test packages become mainstream.

Reasons to Buy

People are becoming more health conscious, and an ever-greater emphasis on wellness and preventative care is likely to send more people for routine checkups, particularly if insurance carriers offer benefits (like free tests or lower coinsurance) to motivate such preventative care.

Even more, we're excited about the innovative new tests performed at the retail lab level for molecular-level and gene-based diagnostics, which bode well for the future; the company is advancing to higher, more profitable levels of the diagnostic food chain.

We're also fans of the "package" tests and of Quest's ancillary businesses— clinical trials, insurance qualifications, employer testing, and IT services—

which all should do well in an environment favoring greater cost control and outsourcing of distinct services such as Quest provides. The company is a leader in its industry and has a beta of 0.68 indicating relative safety. Finally, Quest has retired 30 percent of its shares in the past ten years.

Reasons for Caution

Continued pressure to contain healthcare costs will likely bring some additional malaise over the next few years. Offsetting that is the placement of more emphasis on preventative care, a Quest sweet spot. The path to sustained revenue growth seems to be the big question, and the company continues to work on answers. The competitive landscape continues to change as the healthcare industry evolves and new combinations are formed. In addition, the high share price could bring some high blood pressure; there are many moving parts here in a formerly staid industry.

SECTOR: **Healthcare** ❑ BETA COEFFICIENT: **0.68** ❑ 10-YEAR COMPOUND EARNINGS PER-SHARE GROWTH: **5.5%** ❑ 10-YEAR COMPOUND DIVIDENDS PER-SHARE GROWTH: **15.5%**

	2010	2011	2012	2013	2014	2015	2016	2017
Revenues (mil)	7,400	7,511	7,468	7,146	7,435	7,493	7,515	7,709
Net income (mil)	720	728	700	612	587	695	737	792
Earnings per share	4.05	4.53	4.43	4.00	4.10	4.77	5.15	5.67
Dividends per share	0.40	0.47	0.81	1.20	1.29	1.52	1.65	1.80
Cash flow per share	5.00	6.42	6.23	6.22	6.21	6.99	7.19	7.75
Price: high	61.7	61.2	64.9	64.1	68.5	89.0	93.6	113.0
low	40.8	45.1	53.3	52.5	50.5	60.1	59.7	90.1

Website: www.questdiagnostics.com

AGGRESSIVE GROWTH

ResMed, Inc.

Ticker symbol: RMD (NYSE) ❑ Large Cap ❑ Value Line financial strength rating: A ❑ Current yield: 1.4% ❑ Dividend raises, past 10 years: 5

Company Profile

Sleep disorders are a big deal among adult populations. Reading the clinical description of sleep disorders and their myriad causes could for some be a cure for such disorders, but suffice it to say (as ResMed does in its market analysis) that 26 percent of US adults age 30–70, or about 46 million people, have some form of sleep apnea. That's where the story of ResMed begins, and it continues around the world: a recent study estimated that one in four adults worldwide has some form of sleep apnea.

Perhaps you know someone using a "CPAP" (Continuous Positive Airway Pressure) machine to alleviate "SDB" (sleep-disordered breathing) or "OSA" (obstructive sleep apnea). As we age and tend to gain weight, these devices are becoming a more mainstream way for folks (and their partners) to get some much-needed sleep.

Formed in 1989, ResMed develops, manufactures, and distributes medical equipment for treating, diagnosing, and managing sleep-disordered breathing and other respiratory disorders. Products include diagnostic products, airflow generators, headgear, and other accessories. The original and still largest product line of CPAP machines delivers pressurized air through a mask during sleep, to prevent collapse of tissue in the upper airway, a condition common in people with narrow upper airways and poor muscle tone—in many cases, people who are older and overweight. A great many of the estimated 46 million with sleep apnea, who exhibit the typical symptoms of daytime sleepiness, snoring, hypertension, and irritability, have yet to be diagnosed.

CPAP machines and their cousins VPAP (variable positive airway pressure) and others were at one time massive, clunky machines restricting movement and very difficult to travel with. No more: the new machines are smaller, lighter, cheaper, and easier to use. We don't like solutions that are worse than the problem, and ResMed has turned the corner on that with the new machines; they're becoming more acceptable, less expensive, and more mainstream. We think the company's four-pronged strategy is a good one:

- Make the machines easier to deal with (and afford). This includes smaller, lighter machines, more comfortable masks, including pediatric and other special needs masks, humidifiers, and other enhancements. The new AirMini CPAP machine, the smallest on the market, fits in the palm of your hand and brings CPAP to people who travel a lot.
- Increase clinical awareness and the rate of diagnosis. Get doctors and other clinicians to understand and recommend the solution.
- Expand into new applications including stroke, congestive heart failure and COPD (Chronic Obstructive Pulmonary Disease) treatment.
- Expand internationally. The 2016 acquisition of Curative Medical gives ResMed access to the China market.

The company has executed effectively on all fronts.

The company markets its products in 120 countries, makes them in six countries outside the US, and invests about 7 percent of revenues in R&D. About 40 percent of sales come from outside the US.

ResMed continues to develop a holistic sleep management offering; a new "S+" noncontact sleep tracker is one new product example. A new line of airflow diagnostic machines known as AirFit is a good example and is expected to give a good boost to the business. The "AirMini" line of traveling CPAP machines described previously is another breakthrough. The company continues to make small acquisitions to broaden its product line particularly into disease treatment and into new international markets. The 2016 acquisition of cloud software provider Brightree entered the company into the teleconnected post-acute home sleep disorder care market. A new cloud-connected platform known as AirView now has more than 4 million cloud-connected diagnostic and monitoring devices with more than 2 million of those receiving home monitoring. Predictive analytics are now making diagnostic use of the one billion nights of sleep data gathered by these cloud tools. Finally, consumables—mainly sleep masks—add a strong repeatable sales base and today comprise about 37 percent of sales.

Financial Highlights, Fiscal Year 2017

FY2017 sales rose 12 percent on robust sales of both devices and software. This year the effects of the Brightree acquisition were positive: earnings rose 13 percent. For 2018 and especially 2019, an improved product mix and operating leverage will bring net margin improvement and earnings gains in the 16–19 percent range in 2018 and 14–16 percent in 2019 on 10 percent revenue gains each year. Dividends should grow steadily through the period, but significant buybacks are not in the plans.

Reasons to Buy

We believe that the company's four-pronged strategy, previously outlined, is right on. As these machines, and the diagnosis of the condition they're designed for, become more mainstream, we expect more people in the market, lower prices, and reduced inconvenience. Software, size, and improved comfort technologies will all play a role in growing this market. All these things should open up larger and larger slices of the market for the company. We like the robust application of teleconnected medicine; it really makes sense in this space and can go a long way to reduce hospital admissions and overall healthcare costs.

Demographics are a plus, too—as people get older and heavier, these machines will find more potential users. It's a niche business, and ResMed dominates the niche and is the only company solely focused on this market. While we tend not to rely on this in our selections, we feel the company has the earmarks of a good acquisition candidate for a larger provider of health-care technology products.

Reasons for Caution

One of the bigger issues facing CPAP and related technologies is the eligibility for reimbursement or coverage through Medicare/Medicaid and through private insurers. The current landscape is a mixed bag: many non-Medicare health insurance plans do not cover the machines (which range from about $600–$1,900 in price), and Medicare has driven payment rates down through competitive bidding and across-the-board cuts. That all said, this treatment is becoming more mainstream, and payer resistance is less than it used to be.

In addition, the market is becoming more competitive, and there have been a few legal contests on intellectual property—most of which have gone ResMed's way so far. We continue to feel that ResMed's technology leadership, full-line offering, and experience in this market will prevail.

Finally, shares are up some 50 percent in the last 12 months—take a deep breath and choose entry points carefully.

SECTOR: **Healthcare** ❑ BETA COEFFICIENT: **0.92** ❑ 10-YEAR COMPOUND EARNINGS PER-SHARE GROWTH: **15.5%** ❑ 10-YEAR COMPOUND DIVIDENDS PER-SHARE GROWTH: **NM**

		2010	2011	2012	2013	2014	2015	2016	2017
Revenues (mil)		1,092	1,243	1,368	1,514	1,555	1,679	1,839	2,067
Net income (mil)		190.1	227.0	254.9	307.1	345.4	352.9	352.4	366.0
Earnings per share		1.23	1.44	1.71	2.10	2.39	2.47	2.49	2.57
Dividends per share		—	—	—	0.68	1.00	1.12	1.20	1.32
Cash flow per share		1.66	1.96	2.40	2.71	2.99	3.03	3.12	3.36
Price:	high	35.9	35.4	42.9	57.3	57.6	75.3	70.9	87.8
	low	25.0	23.4	24.4	42.0	41.5	49.0	50.8	61.2

Website: www.resmed.com

C.H. Robinson Worldwide, Inc.

Ticker symbol: CHRW (NASDAQ) ❏ Large Cap ❏ Value Line financial strength rating: A ❏ Current yield: 2.0% ❏ Dividend raises, past 10 years: 9

Company Profile

"We're the Original 3PL" proclaims the company website. "What's a 3PL?" "A third-party logistics provider." "Oh, good to know. Now what's *that*?"

The best way to explain is by original example: C.H. Robinson Worldwide. C.H. Robinson Worldwide, Inc., is one of the largest third-party logistics ("3PL") providers in North America. The company provides bundled and "turnkey" freight transportation services and logistics solutions to companies of all sizes, in a variety of industries. These customers are looking to outsource all or part of their logistics and supply chain activities to gain expertise, efficient capacity utilization, and better pricing—hence the "third-party" logistics provider moniker.

C.H. Robinson is a non-asset-based provider, meaning it contracts with a network of 73,000 transportation carriers (mostly trucking firms but also railroads, intermodal operators, ship and air lines) and a network of warehousing, customs clearance operations, and other supply-chain components to provide a complete, flexible, and tailored solution to customers across and around the world. In addition to transportation, the company has a division called Robinson Fresh that provides sourcing services in the perishable food industry buying, selling, and marketing fresh fruits, vegetables, and other perishable items and transporting them to market—120 million cases annually for 2,000 growers. The fresh produce division accounts for about 16 percent of revenues, while "North American Surface Transportation" accounts for 66 percent of gross revenues and Global Forwarding (mostly ship and air) accounts for 15 percent. Other services, including consulting and other "Managed Services," account for the remaining 4 percent of revenues. About 70 percent of net revenues (gross less carrier payment) comes from trucking services.

In 2017, C.H. Robinson handled approximately 16.9 million shipments and worked with over 120,000 active customers. The customer base is diverse—manufacturing, food and beverage, retail, chemical, and automotive are the largest customer segments. The company has 285 offices across North and South America, Europe, and Asia.

The company has invested heavily in technology; its "Navisphere" single global technology "ecosystem" connects 150,000 customers, carriers, and suppliers and covers the entire "life cycle" of a shipment from notification to scheduling to delivery. Customers can track their shipments down to a single item; about 70 percent of Robinson's customer contacts come through this platform. The 2015 acquisition of electronic freight broker Freightquote added significant revenues and customer convenience especially in the LTL ("less than truckload") shipping market for smaller customers. A new TMC division applies analytics and predictive modeling to a supply chain as a consulting service.

Financial Highlights, Fiscal Year 2017

A strengthening economy and continuing marketplace emphasis on logistics as a competitive advantage helped to drive revenues up 13 percent in 2017. But much of that did not get to the bottom line, as a mandated shift to onboard electronic logging devices, fuel prices, and a generally strong economy led to supply constraints and higher prices in the trucking industry, from whom Robinson buys services. Older fixed-price contracts didn't figure in these cost increases; net income actually dropped about 3 percent as a result. The trucking market should straighten out in 2018 and especially 2019; a lower tax rate should help too in generating a 25 percent net income increase on a 6–8 percent revenue gain in 2018 and a 10–12 percent net income increase on a 4–6 percent revenue gain in 2019. Operating margins should improve from 6 percent to about 7 percent in part due to new efficiencies and revenue streams garnered through technology, i.e., Freightquote, while net margins will also be helped along by the new tax law. The company reiterated a stated goal to return 90 percent of net income to shareholders annually, foreshadowing continued dividend increases and capturing the fact that the company has bought back about 22 percent of its shares since 2011.

Reasons to Buy

The main idea behind C.H. Robinson is to provide businesses, large and small, with a flexible and scalable way to outsource their logistics operations, thus reducing poorly matched capacities and risks. (Do you, as operator of a private trucking fleet, ever have the right number of trucks? Nope—always too few or too many!)

A 3PL firm can also achieve efficiencies by combining loads for different customers. The company's value proposition for customers, in fact, is to "drive costs down," "improve efficiency," "mitigate risk," and "manage change." In today's fast-moving business world, products and supply chains change quickly, and companies have an increasing mandate to find ways to control costs and create supply-chain advantages. ("Accelerate your Advantage" is one of their apt slogans.) As top-line improvements are hard to come by, services such as those offered by C.H. Robinson continue to make sense for an ever-increasing customer base. We like the way they do this with a minimal asset base—no trucks, ships, or trains of their own!

Traditionally, the company operated as a procurement, or forwarding, service for transportation services for its customers; today as much as anything else, it is a technology company deploying technology solutions to not only procure but also to manage and optimize the network. We like companies that deploy technology to create an advantage, particularly when it's an advantage for their customers. The strategy seems to be to become a fully integrated, technology-connected solution for firms shipping big stuff, just as FedEx and UPS have for firms shipping small stuff. The strong commitment to shareholder returns and the steady price related to the market (beta = 0.46) add to the list of attractions.

Reasons for Caution

Shipping and transportation services are always cyclical and often volatile; in addition, large changes in fuel costs can be difficult to adjust to. Changes in transportation economics—such as those caused by fuel prices, shortages of truck drivers, environmental regulations, and the like—can disrupt supply-chain networks and be costly to comply with. Competition in the industry is fierce, but C.H. Robinson has a pretty strong lead in integrating its suppliers and customers, and even the 73,000 transportation suppliers stand to gain from the Robinson intermediary even if it crimps their own margins. The company is a "win-win" in the transportation and logistics market.

SECTOR: **Transportation** ❑ BETA COEFFICIENT: **0.46** ❑ 10-YEAR COMPOUND EARNINGS PER-SHARE GROWTH: **11.5%** ❑ 10-YEAR COMPOUND DIVIDENDS PER-SHARE GROWTH: **15.0%**

		2010	2011	2012	2013	2014	2015	2016	2017
Revenues (mil)		9,274	10,336	11,369	12,752	13,470	13,476	13,144	14,689
Net income (mil)		387	432	594	416	450	510	515	505
Earnings per share		2.33	2.82	3.67	2.65	3.05	3.51	3.59	3.57
Dividends per share		1.04	1.20	1.67	1.40	1.43	1.57	1.74	1.81
Cash flow per share		2.51	2.62	3.92	3.18	3.46	4.00	4.15	4.25
Price:	high	81.0	82.8	71.8	67.9	77.5	76.2	77.9	89.9
	low	51.2	62.3	50.8	53.7	50.2	59.7	60.3	63.4

Website: www.chrobinson.com

AGGRESSIVE GROWTH

Ross Stores, Inc.

Ticker symbol: ROST (NASDAQ) ❑ Large Cap ❑ Value Line financial strength rating: A ❑ Current yield: 1.2% ❑ Dividend raises, past 10 years: 10

Company Profile

The current retail transition to more of an online, "from the couch" approach has claimed a lot of retail victims recently, including Macy's and Target from our *100 Best* list, and has forced us to evaluate whether the others have sufficient defenses against the Amazon Prime threat. We examined Ross carefully, and once again it passes the test; it is unique enough and its stores are enough of a destination for its current loyal shopper base that we think it can keep people coming to its bargain bins and largely fend off the change. "There's Always a Bargain in Store" is the apt and timely motto of Ross Stores, the second-largest off-price retailer in the United States. Ross and its subsidiaries operate two chains of apparel and home accessories stores. As of 2017 the company operated a total of 1,622 stores, up from 1,553 in 2016, 1,446 in 2015, and 1,125 in 2011. Of that total, 1,409 were Ross Dress for Less locations in 37 states, DC, and Guam, and 213 were dd's DISCOUNTS stores in 16 states. Just under half the company's stores are located in three states—California, Florida, and Texas—although the bulk of 2016 new store additions were in the Midwest.

Both chains target value-conscious women and men between the ages of 18 and 54. Ross's target customers are primarily from middle-income households, while dd's DISCOUNTS target customers are typically from lower- to middle-income households. Merchandising, purchasing, pricing, and the locations of the stores are all aimed at these customer bases. Ross and dd's DISCOUNTS both offer first-quality, in-season, name-brand and designer apparel, accessories, and footwear for the family at savings typically in the 20–60 percent range off department store prices (at Ross) or 20–70 percent off (at dd's DISCOUNTS). The stores also offer discounted home fashions and housewares, educational toys and games, furniture and furniture accents, luggage, cookware, and at some stores jewelry.

Sales break down by category roughly as follows: 27 percent Ladies', 26 percent Home Accents, Bed, and Bath, 13 percent each for Men's and for Accessories, Lingerie, Jewelry, and Fragrances, 13 percent for Shoes, and 8 percent Children's. The shopping demographic is 75–80 percent female, shopping for herself or other family members; the core customer averages about three store visits per month. Their market research also suggests that the average customer "wants"—not "needs"—a bargain; there are a number of frugal but fairly well-heeled customers looking for a brand at a price.

Ross's strategy is to offer competitive values to target customers by offering a well-managed mix of inventory with a strong percentage of department store name brands and items of local and seasonal interest at attractive prices. The company plans to add 75 more Ross stores and 25 dd's DISCOUNTS stores for 2018 while closing or relocating about ten stores, and it plans to ultimately grow to about 2,000 Ross and 500 dd's DISCOUNTS stores although probably not by the end of the decade as once thought.

Financial Highlights, Fiscal Year 2017

Store expansion, same-store sales gains, and a 53-week retail year all combined to produce a 10 percent revenue gain for FY2017. Ross added 89 new stores in FY2017 onto a 1,533-store base, and a 4 percent increase in same-store sales, same as the past two years, also contributed. Both pricing and average size of sale in turn drove the comp increase. Operating margins grew sequentially another 0.3 percent on top of a 0.5 percent gain last year (significant for a retailer) mostly on supply-chain efficiencies to 16.7 percent; net income rang up a nice 15 percent gain. A 3.1 percent share buyback rounded out the picture, helping per-share earnings to an 18 percent gain for the year—fairly familiar figures to you regular readers.

FY2018 forecasts call for roughly 5 percent revenue gains annually through FY2019 as comparable store sales growth slows somewhat to 1–2 percent. Margin expansion should likewise slow as wages rise (the company raised its minimum wage to $11/hour) and transportation costs rise, but this will be offset by lower tax rates. Net earnings are expected to increase 16–18 percent in 2018, then in an 8–10 percent range in 2019. Healthy share buybacks should continue, keeping per-share earnings growth humming along in the 10–20 percent range.

Reasons to Buy

We had become a little tired of this story, which really got a boost from the now-faded Great Recession years. We saw revenue growth being driven mainly by store expansion, and profit growth attenuating. Did we also see that, with more disposable income, consumers may wander away? Did we see signs of too many stores? All might be warning signs of future trouble, and these give us a bit of fright every year. But we've stayed on this horse year after year for one big reason: profitability. Net profit margins—after taxes and everything else—run in the 8–9 percent range. They've been steadily improving over the years to a figure over 10 percent in 2018, helped along by tax cuts. Where else can you find that in the retail world? It's not easy.

The recession apparently helped Ross gain mainstream appeal across a wider set of customers. While some of those customers defected back to full-price retail stores as things improved, a greater number have shown that they will continue to shop at the stores. At the same time, the company was successful with operational changes begun years ago to improve merchandising and inventory management, which led to better stocking of a more favorable mix of goods and better inventory turnover. The higher store count has increased operating leverage as well—more volume through the same infrastructure and cost base. Nothing is mentioned about international expansion, but we wonder if there too lies an opportunity.

Strong, defensible niche, moderate expansion, operational excellence, sustained shareholder returns; it's an attractive formula and the results speak for themselves as well as pointing to good management. And one more thing: we like how they present all of this to shareholders; their Investor Relations materials are better than average.

Reasons for Caution

E-commerce doesn't seem to have taken a bite out of Ross yet, but there's always that possibility, particularly with the advance of online promotional and coupon portals like Groupon. We still think the typical Ross shopper actually likes the "hunt" and is less likely to transition to couch-based shopping than most other shoppers. Another concern is that the company is dependent on the actions of others—mainly first-line apparel retailers—for its success. The availability of surplus inventories is high now as first-line retailers struggle…but who knows what lies ahead? We also remain concerned that the company still depends to a degree on store expansion, which carries its own risks, and could make supply bubbles and constraints hurt even more.

Finally, while Ross may be synonymous with bargains for shoppers, its share price has not followed suit for investors—the stock has been on a steady upward march for ten years. Look for "off price" bargains when picking up this one.

SECTOR: Retail ❑ BETA COEFFICIENT: 1.08 ❑ 10-YEAR COMPOUND EARNINGS PER-SHARE
GROWTH: 21.5% ❑ 10-YEAR COMPOUND DIVIDENDS PER-SHARE GROWTH: 24.0%

	2010	2011	2012	2013	2014	2015	2016	2017
Revenues (mil)	7,866	8,608	9,721	10,230	11,042	11,940	12,867	14,135
Net income (mil)	555	657	787	837	925	1,021	1,118	1,282
Earnings per share	1.16	1.43	1.77	1.94	2.21	2.51	2.83	3.34
Dividends per share	0.18	0.24	0.30	0.36	0.40	0.47	0.54	0.64
Cash flow per share	1.52	1.81	2.21	2.44	2.79	3.22	3.62	4.20
Price: high	16.8	24.6	35.4	41.0	48.1	56.7	69.6	81.5
low	10.6	15.0	23.5	26.5	30.9	43.5	50.4	52.8

Website: www.rossstores.com

AGGRESSIVE GROWTH

RPM International, Inc.

Ticker symbol: RPM (NYSE) ❑ Large Cap ❑ Value Line financial strength rating: B+ ❑ Current
yield: 2.5% ❑ Dividend raises, past 10 years: 10

Company Profile

Have you ever finished a piece of furniture or a wood floor with Varathane?
Stained it with Watco? Caulked a bathtub or sink with DAP? Spray-painted
a rusty gate with Rust-Oleum? Primed bathroom walls with Zinsser primers
before painting them? Glued a model airplane together with Testors? We
have—and it seems like every time we do those little weekend warrior tasks
around the house, we're using one of these products.

We wondered, who makes and markets this stuff? Where do these well-
established brands that seem to show up in every hardware store and home
improvement center we go into come from? How did they become household names, even category-defining names like Kleenex? After a little dig-
ging, we came up with a company we'd never heard of. Sometimes, that's a
really good sign. A "house of brands," each with its own strength, image, and
loyal following, can have more staying and growing power than a "branded
house." Just ask anyone on the marketing team at Procter & Gamble.

Anyway, the company we found is in all likelihood one you've never
heard of, based in Medina, OH—a town you've probably never heard of,
either. "The Brands You Know and Trust" is their slogan, and the company
is RPM International. RPM International makes and markets an assortment

of specialty chemicals and coatings, targeted mostly to repair, maintenance, and replacement, for consumer and industrial markets.

Industrial markets? Indeed, only about a third (34 percent, actually) of RPM's sales come from the aforementioned "consumer" brands found in Home Depot and the like. The company also makes and markets a vast line of brands for industrial and construction use—sealants, chemicals, roofing systems, corrosion control coatings, marine paints and coatings, fluorescent pigments (you've probably heard of DayGlo, their line of fluorescent paints), powder coatings, fire coatings, and concrete waterproofing and repair products.

There are now 37 "Industrial" brands in all including brands such as Increte Systems, a maker of textured stamped concrete systems, or USL BridgeCare solutions, or Carboline corrosion control coatings; you get the idea. The Industrial segment makes many products aimed at the preservation and corrosion protection of existing structures, which makes the company a strong play in the infrastructure reinvestment market. About 85 percent of the company's business comes from repair and maintenance, and about 15 percent comes from new construction. The Industrial segment accounts for 52 percent of the business, and many of its brands are made and sold in foreign markets. In fact, about 50 percent of Industrial business is overseas, while 85 percent of the consumer business originates in North America.

The "Specialty" segment produces DayGlo as well as other specialty coatings for specialty powder and marine coatings, edible coatings, insulation, and concrete repair, with 18 brands and about 15 percent of RPM's business.

Not to beat the brand thing to death, but Rust-Oleum, Varathane, DAP, and Zinsser on the consumer side own number one positions in their respective markets, while eight industrial and specialty brands, including DayGlo, of course, but also Tremco in roofing, Stonhard in polymer flooring, and Carboline in corrosion control own number one positions in their US markets.

The company has accumulated most of these brands through acquisitions of small specialty companies making single products or product lines in the "small chemical" space. Many of these small operators seek to be acquired by RPM; the resulting "conglomerate" has a bit of a Berkshire Hathaway feel with its stable of small, independently managed businesses. RPM has acquired 170+ companies in the past 30 years, 70 in the past decade, and 9 in 2017.

Financial Highlights, Fiscal Year 2017

When you own and run a large stable of diverse companies, every now and then one or two will fail miserably to meet expectations, thus taking down the whole. That is the story of FY2017; otherwise it was a fairly good year. Revenues advanced 3 percent, but net earnings declined about 6 percent due to a goodwill impairment charge at a failed subsidiary that made nail enamel coatings and a closing of a Flowcrete manufacturing facility in the Middle East. Overall economic strength, strength in Europe, currency tailwinds, and continued acquisitions bring an optimistic view of 2018 and 2019, with revenue growth in the 7–9 percent range in 2018 and 2–4 percent in 2019. Cost reductions and operating leverage are projected to grow margins and thus net income in the 20–25 percent range (albeit on a weak 2017) in 2018 followed by a 10–12 percent rise in 2019. Dividends should increase in the mid-single-digit range.

Reasons to Buy

We always like premier brands in relatively simple, well-managed businesses, and RPM International seems to fit the model. The company presents itself well: its website and investor materials are among the best and most informative we've encountered. From what we see, we like the straightforward qualities of the management team; it's one we'd want to work for. These factors alone wouldn't be enough to land RPM on our *100 Best* list; however, we also take notice of good businesses with good brands, marketplace position, and fundamentals. We also take notice of a company that has raised its dividend 44 straight years (and is proud of it), and we like the defensive nature of its repeat-purchase, mainly maintenance and repair, product lines. Finally, RPM should do well as new Trump administration infrastructure improvements take hold—this factor is still not really included in the forecasts.

Reasons for Caution

Clearly this has not been one of our best performers, and while we think patience may prevail, we do wonder how big the growth opportunity really is. We also wonder if the business is stretched a bit too thin and if consolidating some of those brands to make stronger brands might make sense. With so many acquisitions the chances of a failure grow—although the Berkshire model in place here does more good than bad in that respect. RPM would also be somewhat exposed to cost increases in petrochemical inputs. Is this a great company in a not-so-good business? It remains to be seen.

SECTOR: **Materials** ❑ BETA COEFFICIENT: **1.46** ❑ 10-YEAR COMPOUND EARNINGS PER-SHARE
GROWTH: **6.0%** ❑ 10-YEAR COMPOUND DIVIDENDS PER-SHARE GROWTH: **5.5%**

	2010	2011	2012	2013	2014	2015	2016	2017
Revenues (mil)	3,413	3,382	3,777	4,081	4,376	4,595	4,814	4,958
Net income (mil)	188	189	215	241	292	323	355	331
Earnings per share	1.45	1.45	1.65	1.83	2.18	2.38	2.63	2.47
Dividends per share	0.82	0.84	0.86	0.89	0.95	1.02	1.09	1.18
Cash flow per share	2.10	2.01	2.20	2.45	2.86	3.17	3.50	3.37
Price: high	22.9	26.0	29.6	41.6	52.0	51.4	55.9	56.5
low	16.1	17.2	23.0	29.1	37.6	40.1	36.8	47.9

Website: www.rpminc.com

AGGRESSIVE GROWTH

Schlumberger Limited

Ticker symbol: SLB (NYSE) ❑ Large Cap ❑ Value Line financial strength rating: A++ ❑ Current
yield: 2.9% ❑ Dividend raises, past 10 years: 7

Company Profile

Patience is a major investing thesis every year as we build out our list of
The 100 Best Stocks to Buy. In few places has that thesis been tested more of
late than in the energy industry, and in particular, in the competitive and
crowded energy *services* industry, where we find industry leader Schlumberger Ltd. Services are hit harder than energy companies in general, for
energy companies can sell existing inventories and production from existing wells if demand and prices drop, but are they motivated to drill new
ones? Emphatically not, and that's where we must see the forest through
the trees for a company like Schlumberger. Will we come out of the down
cycle? Almost assuredly yes, given the fundamental long-term demand and
supply features of the energy market. Or has the services business changed
forever, perhaps a victim of its own past success in delivering efficient, high-
volume energy production, now responsible for a lasting market glut? We
think probably not. Bottom line: we think patience will pay off once again.
Schlumberger Limited is the world's leading oil field services company. It
provides technology, information solutions, and integrated project management services with the goal of optimizing reservoir performance for its customers in the oil and gas industry. Founded in 1926, today the company has
a large international footprint, employing 100,000 people in 85 countries,

with 69 percent of revenue generated outside of North America. The company currently operates in four primary business segments:

- The Reservoir Characterization Group (22 percent of FY2017 revenues, 31 percent of pretax income) is mostly a consulting service, applying many digital and other technologies toward finding, defining, and characterizing hydrocarbon deposits. Interestingly, the company compares the electronic characterization of a hydrocarbon-producing zone to the imaging of a human body, using an assortment of technologies (for example, a technology referred to as a "Saturn 3D radial fluid sampling probe") to identify what you can't see directly.
- Not surprisingly, the Drilling Group (27 percent of revenues, 28 percent of pretax income) does the actual drilling and creation of wells for production, both in onshore and offshore environments. Again, a number of new drilling, drill bit, and drilling fluid technologies are in play, and naturally, so-called "fracking" is an important part of the product offering.
- The Reservoir Production Group (34 percent of revenues, 23 percent of pretax income) completes and services the well for production, maintaining and enhancing productivity through its life. The business mix has shifted a few percentage points in this direction as new drilling activity has slowed.
- The Cameron Group (17 percent of revenues, 18 percent of pretax income) is newly formed with the 2016 acquisition; Cameron specializes in pressure and flow control systems of onshore and offshore wellhead management.

Throughout the petroleum production process, the company provides not only physical onsite services but also substantial consulting, modeling, information management, total cost, yield, and general project management around these activities. In short, SLB offers a fully outsourced supply chain for oil and gas field development and production.

Schlumberger manages its business through 28 GeoMarket regions, which are grouped into four geographic areas: North America (31 percent, up from 25 percent in 2016)); Latin America (13 percent); Europe, Commonwealth of Independent States, and Africa (23 percent, down from 26 percent); and Middle East and Asia (31 percent). The company continues to position itself as a technology leader in the industry. As an example, the recent partnership with Weatherford called "OneStim" announced in March 2017 targets "unconventional resource development"—high-tech fracking, essentially. The company has implemented new software-driven processes and services for optimizing discovery, well construction, and life cycle management; SLB now estimates that technology sales make up 24 percent of all sales.

The slump has served to both shake out weak competitors and drive down the cost of acquiring others (the purchase of Cameron International in 2016 is an example), and led to efficiency measures within the company, both of which bode well during an eventual recovery. Being the biggest and best in the business helps a lot in these situations.

Bottom line, as the company itself suggests: US producers will have to lower costs, and thus apply SLB technologies and knowhow to producing shale oil and gas at a cost economical to a $50 or $60 oil price. In the company's view, the shakeout, the need to produce more cheaply, and the inevitable long-term growth in world oil consumption, will all. lead to a strong recovery, which has started in 2018 and will strengthen by the end of the decade.

Financial Highlights, Fiscal Year 2017

"Oil Market Rebalancing has Accelerated" starts off this year's company slide presentation, which is far more optimistic than "Better decrementals than the competition" from two years ago. North American revenues were up almost 80 percent as rig counts recovered, although international revenues ticked downward once again. That and the addition of some Cameron revenue led to an overall 9 percent increase in the FY2017 top line, while the bottom line advanced some 35 percent on scale and operational improvements. Diminishing stocks and stronger oil prices bode well for the next several years; current company forecasts call for revenue gains in the 10–12 percent range yearly through 2019, while net profits could as much as *double* through the two-year period. Chairman and CEO Paal Kibsgaard once again noted that depletion rates are now far outpacing reserve replacement, which in the long term bodes well for Schlumberger as eventually E&P producers will be forced to catch up. Share buybacks and dividend increases will resume when this scenario plays out.

The company projects a return to full health and then some in the 2020 to 2023 timeframe as the E&P cycle progresses and weaker hands in the industry decline.

Reasons to Buy

The cycle of supply and demand is the key here. It isn't lost on us—nor on SLB—that major producers *still* have to replace depleted reserves, and that world oil demand will continue to grow, albeit slowly, in the longer term. The most efficient producers in the US and abroad will prosper, and SLB is well positioned, with its size, present geography, and expertise, to move with them. The company is applying its competitive advantages in technology and size strategically.

In the long term, we agree that SLB could come out of this shift stronger than ever as the oil service industry and the US producer landscape both consolidate. But as an investor, you'll have to be patient and view current events as a buying opportunity. Remember too, that most stocks recover in advance of the actual business recovery; we expect that the stock price recovery, if not the business recovery, will be well underway by 2019.

Reasons for Caution

The overstocks and overproduction of past years could return depending on OPEC and other producers' policies, causing further market disruptions; that plus cutthroat competition could put a bigger dent in the oil service industry. The fortunes of SLB are inevitably tied to the price of oil and gas, which appear to be on the mend at least in the short term, but who knows? Anything above $60 for oil is generally good for SLB. The company will always face the traditional risks of oil drilling—particularly offshore drilling—that culminated in the BP disaster of 2010.

SECTOR: **Energy** ▫ BETA COEFFICIENT: **1.05** ▫ 10-YEAR COMPOUND EARNINGS PER-SHARE GROWTH: **-7.0%** ▫ 10-YEAR COMPOUND DIVIDENDS PER-SHARE GROWTH: **14.0%**

	2010	2011	2012	2013	2014	2015	2016	2017
Revenues (mil)	27,447	39,540	42,149	45,266	48,580	35,475	27,810	30,440
Net income (mil)	3,408	3,954	5,439	6,210	5,643	2,072	1,550	2,085
Earnings per share	2.70	3.51	4.06	4.70	4.32	1.63	1.14	1.50
Dividends per share	0.84	0.96	1.06	1.25	1.60	2.00	2.00	2.00
Cash flow per share	4.55	6.05	6.73	7.55	7.64	4.90	4.06	4.28
Price: high	84.1	95.6	80.8	94.9	118.8	92.1	87.0	87.8
low	54.7	54.8	59.1	69.1	78.5	66.6	59.8	61.0

Website: www.slb.com

AGGRESSIVE GROWTH

Schnitzer Steel Industries, Inc.

Ticker symbol: SCHN (NASDAQ) □ Small Cap □ Value Line financial strength rating: B □ Current yield: 2.2% □ Dividend raises, past 10 years: 2

Company Profile

One more year. That did it. We stuck with you, Schnitzer, for five years. You made sense as a business, and you paid a healthy dividend north of 3 percent while we waited. But you were stuck in the mud of the commodity bust, slack China demand, and a strong dollar. We saw the legs knocked out from under the price of your primary products: scrap metal and finished steel. We stuck with you one more year, and guess what? Metals prices firmed. Overseas demand firmed. The economy firmed. You came out of a multi-year exercise to cut costs, as all good companies do when times are tough, and the US government moved to protect the steel industry from below-cost exports. Suddenly, Schnitzer, you're back in the game. We're glad we waited, and we'll stay in the game, one of our four Small Cap picks, for the 2019 list.

Founded in 1946, Schnitzer Steel is mainly a collector and recycler of ferrous and nonferrous scrap, with smaller operations that collect, dismantle, and market auto and truck parts and a steel mill "mini mill" finished steel product business. There are two business segments: Auto and Metals Recycling (AMR) and Cascade Steel and Scrap (CSS).

The "AMR" business, which accounts for about 80 percent of Schnitzer's 2017 revenues, includes the Metals Recycling business (about 91 percent of AMR), which collects, recycles, processes, and brokers scrap steel and nonferrous metals to domestic and foreign markets—3.3 million tons of ferrous scrap metal and 510 million pounds of nonferrous metal in all. By revenues, 68 percent of 2017 revenues were ferrous (iron and steel), and 32 percent were nonferrous (dominated by copper and aluminum but also including stainless steel, nickel, brass, titanium, and lead among others).

Larger scrap mills are located in Oregon; Washington; Oakland, CA; and Massachusetts, with smaller mills in Rhode Island, Puerto Rico, Hawaii, and Alaska, all with adjacent deepwater ports, correctly suggesting an orientation toward international export of scrap metal for foreign mills. Indeed, that is true—some 70 percent of ferrous and 55 percent of nonferrous scrap shipments go overseas (which means that it doesn't much matter who wins the current trade wars in steel). The company operates 60 metals recycling facilities ("scrapyards," in popular vernacular) in 23 states, mostly on the coasts and in the south, seven in Canada, and five in Puerto Rico. The operation adds value in part by sorting and shredding input scrap into homogenous materials well suited to the needs of downstream customers.

The Auto Parts business portion of the AMR segment (9 percent of that segment's revenues) operates 53 self-serve locations and remarketing centers, some co-located with Metals Recycling facilities, in 16 states with a concentration in California under the "Pick-n-Pull" name. This operation processed 411,000 cars in 2017. Inventories of scrapped autos and common parts from those autos are posted online and updated as new inventory is received.

The Cascade Steel and Scrap business (18 percent of total revenues) principally operates an electric arc furnace mini mill in McMinnville, OR, producing rebar, wire rod, merchant bar, and other specialty products, mainly for western US markets, of course from scrap steel available from the company's own Metals Recycling facilities. CSS operates the recycling facilities in Oregon and Washington that supply this mill while other recycling facilities operate under the AMR segment.

About 42 percent of revenue comes from North America, while the rest comes from Asia (44 percent), Europe (12 percent), and 1 percent each to Africa and South America.

Financial Highlights, Fiscal Year 2017

Average ferrous scrap selling prices finally surged ahead to $242 per ton in 2017, up from $196 in 2016 and $179 in 2015. Rises in the price of steel and nonferrous scrap, a 10 percent volume increase, and effective cost reduction initiatives ultimately gave us the sort of year we were waiting for. Revenues rose 25 percent; earnings recovered from an $18 million loss to a $45 million profit. Margins improved with greater volumes and with significant productivity improvements started earlier. Forecasts call for a further recovery with a 16–18 percent revenue gain in 2018 slowing to about 5 percent in 2019; net income should rise another 25 percent in 2018 and 6–9 percent in 2019. These figures should allow for modest dividend raises and share buybacks after years of no change.

Reasons to Buy

Clearly, we continue to bet on strengthening steel and scrap prices and this company's strong focus and productivity track record in this industry. Scrap as a source of supply is much more flexible and environmentally sound and should lead the way as metals recover. We should also note that today's modern electric-arc furnace mills such as those operated by Nucor are more cost-effective and flexible than traditional blast furnaces and tend to use scrap as the main input resource. Scrap is easier to source, more flexible, and more local than traditional iron ore inputs for these modern mills.

There are a lot of mom-and-pop scrap dealers around the world, but few have the size, operating leverage, and remarketing abilities of Schnitzer. The company is a strong and recognized brand in a fragmented and unbranded industry, offering advantages both on the sales and operational side. When prices and markets are soft, the company loses, but as we saw particularly in 2008, when markets are strong, the company does really, really well. Whether steel is made domestically or imported, Schnitzer wins as a universal supplier. Schnitzer is well managed, adds a lot of value in a relatively non-value-add industry, and keeps its shareholders in mind.

Reasons for Caution

Schnitzer is still very sensitive to global steel and nonferrous metals markets and the ups and downs of pricing. While its size and marketing advantages serve it well in tough times, inventory is inventory, and the company can get caught with a lot of it purchased at higher prices if the markets don't move to its advantage. It does okay in bad economic climates, but the company is really a bet on recycling value add and on good times in global manufacturing. If you buy in, you'll want to watch global steel and other metals prices. Also, while the company has a good track record, there are always some environmental risks and costs in this sort of business.

SECTOR: **Industrials** ◻ BETA COEFFICIENT: **1.34** ◻ 10-YEAR COMPOUND EARNINGS PER-SHARE GROWTH: **NM** ◻ 10-YEAR COMPOUND DIVIDENDS PER-SHARE GROWTH: **27.0%**

	2010	2011	2012	2013	2014	2015	2016	2017
Revenues (mil)	2,301	3,459	3,341	2,621	2,544	1,915	1,352	1,688
Net income (mil)	67	119	30	(2.0)	5.1	(58.8)	(19.4)	44.9
Earnings per share	2.86	4.24	1.10	(0.07)	0.19	(2.25)	(0.66)	1.60
Dividends per share	0.20	0.20	0.41	0.75	0.75	0.75	0.75	0.75
Cash flow per share	4.75	7.08	4.28	3.05	3.19	0.23	1.32	3.50
Price: high	66.9	69.4	47.4	33.0	33.3	22.8	30.6	35.2
low	37.0	32.8	22.8	23.1	21.4	12.6	11.7	17.5

Website: www.schnitzersteel.com

The Scotts Miracle-Gro Company

Ticker symbol: SMG (NYSE) ◻ Mid Cap ◻ Value Line financial strength rating: B++ ◻ Current yield: 2.3% ◻ Dividend raises, past 10 years: 8

Company Profile

Scotts Miracle-Gro, formerly Scotts Co., formerly O.M. Scott & Sons, is a 150-year-old provider of mostly packaged lawn- and garden-care products for consumer markets. Over the past two years the company has entered into the hydroponics business through a series of small, targeted acquisitions. The new foray currently represents about 10 percent of revenues. Originally a seed company, today SMG's lawn-care products include packaged, pre-mixed fertilizers and combination fertilizer and weed/pest-control products marketed mainly under the Scotts and Turf Builder brand names. The company also markets packaged grass seed and a line of individually packaged pest/disease-control products mainly under the Ortho brand (acquired in 1997) and a line of specialty garden fertilizers and pest-control products under the Miracle-Gro name, acquired in 1995. The company also markets a line of consumer pest-control products and acts as the exclusive worldwide distributor (for Monsanto) for the Roundup brand of consumer weed-control products.

Scotts is a study in branding in an otherwise highly fragmented market. The attractive core brands of Scotts, Turf Builder, Miracle-Gro, and Ortho and Roundup take center stage in this business and in their respective markets. There are few nationally known brands in the lawn and garden maintenance sectors, and as such SMG's lines compete mainly with local and store brands for shelf space in regional chains like OSH and Tractor Supply. In the large national chains (Home Depot, Lowe's, etc.), SMG's best-known products are front and center.

Smaller but significant brands are Hyponex (bagged potting soil and manure), Weedol weed killers, Osmocote professional plant nutrients, and Fertilgene. The company's European and Australian brands were divested through sale in 2017 when SMG reorganized its International segment.

The vision is interesting: "To help people of all ages express themselves on their own piece of the earth." In addition to sounding pretty groovy, the message recognizes a demographic shift toward smaller, more-urban gardening environments. In support of this vision, the company over the past three years has made acquisitions of just over $500 million for brands targeting hydroponics for personal and commercial growing operations. Though it isn't mentioned anywhere on their websites or in their financial reports, these products are primarily used in the rapidly legitimizing cannabis industry— a high-growth business (no pun intended).

People are also seeking organic gardening products in consumer packages; Scotts' new line of organic Miracle-Gro products have begun to address this trend. Innovations also include new packaging to simplify the measurement and application and improve the safety of key products.

In 2016 the company spun off a nascent lawn-service business to a joint venture (TruGreen Holdings) in exchange for a 30 percent equity stake in the venture.

SMG has stated that it is far from finished in its acquisition strategy in the hydroponics market and has several undisclosed acquisitions in the works in the US and in Europe.

Financial Highlights, Fiscal Year 2017

In large part due to divestitures and in part due to delays in the development of the California cannabis market, revenues declined about 7 percent in 2017, mirroring the performance in the prior year and for largely the same reasons. The trend is not worrying, however, as cost-reduction efforts have paid off. Though revenues are at their lowest mark in ten years, earnings are at the second-highest level over the same period. Net sales from continuing operations were actually up 6 percent, with a 2 percent decline in US consumer, a 140 percent increase in Hawthorne (the hydroponics segment), and a 9 percent gain in Other (the remaining non-US geographies and commercial sales). Going forward, these are encouraging numbers, particularly with Hawthorne now accounting for some 11 percent of SMG's total sales. Growing like a weed, indeed.

Reasons to Buy

We continue to support SMG's re-focusing on the North American market as we feel their brand strength there is a significant differentiator. The early numbers strongly suggest that exiting the European market and the reinvestment of that capital in the Hawthorne segment was the right move at the right time. Interestingly, the company retains some exposure to the European market in that several of their recent acquisitions are based in the Netherlands and established suppliers to the Dutch cut-flower and hydroponics markets.

The company's lawn-care and gardening products business is much healthier as a result of the recent pruning. Net margins are 50–60 percent higher than just three years ago, and FY2018/2019 project to be the company's most profitable years ever.

The company's entry into the hydroponics market has an interesting genesis. The company's CEO was visiting retailers in Washington state and saw pretty much what he expected at one store: folks buying a bag or two of Turf Builder or potting soil and heading home. He then visited a second store in the same chain where the manager had invested in a large hydroponics display that was doing brisk sales. He asked the manager how the business was doing and was told the average purchase per visit was around $400, all cash. On the flight home (the CEO pilots his own plane), he considered the demographics of Washington, Oregon, Colorado, California, and the other states where the legalization of cannabis was being debated. Over the next few weeks at SMG headquarters in Ohio, he announced the plan for the company to expand into the hydroponics market and to support commercial growing operations with SMG products. Several members of the SMG board objected to the new business direction for non-business-related reasons. "It's just not something we do here," was one quote. Three of the board members resigned over the decision.

Based in California, we at *100 Best* have had a front-row seat to the back-and-forth political discussions attached to legalization. We would not presume to tell our readers what to think on this topic, but we do feel that a well-regulated, tax-paying cannabis industry is far preferable to what we've had in California over the past forty years. We think SMG is taking a business-savvy, prudent approach to an entry into what could be a tremendous market opportunity over the next decade.

Reasons for Caution

While big retailers have increasingly joined the Scotts bandwagon, they aren't the only brand in town, and the company does face some competition from less expensive house brands such as those sold at Ace Hardware, Home Depot, Lowe's, and elsewhere. Lawn and garden spend is naturally sensitive to sluggish economies, but we do think that there is a baseline level people will drop to and remain at; they want to maintain their lawns and provide pleasant stay-at-home environments if they can't do much else. Finally, the past decade of demographic shifts away from the suburbs, including downsizing and increases in renting versus owning, will continue to put pressure on the traditional bagged fertilizer and lawn goods business; Scotts' new products and services in new niches like hydroponics will keep the spreader moving forward here.

SECTOR: **Materials** ❑ BETA COEFFICIENT: **0.95** ❑ 10-YEAR COMPOUND EARNINGS
PER-SHARE GROWTH: **7.0%** ❑ 10-YEAR COMPOUND DIVIDENDS PER-SHARE GROWTH: **17.5%**

	2010	2011	2012	2013	2014	2015	2016	2017
Revenues (mil)	3,139	2,835	2,826	2,819	2,841	3,017	2,836	2,642
Net income (mil)	212.4	121.9	113.2	161.2	165.4	158.7	253.8	197.8
Earnings per share	3.14	1.84	1.62	2.58	2.64	2.57	4.09	3.29
Dividends per share	0.63	0.05	1.23	1.41	1.76	1.82	1.91	2.03
Cash flow per share	4.07	3.00	2.86	3.67	3.74	3.64	5.36	4.78
Price:　　high	55.0	60.8	55.9	62.6	64.0	72.3	98.8	108.0
low	37.5	40.0	35.5	42.0	52.4	58.1	62.2	81.5

Website: www.scottsmiraclegro.com

CONSERVATIVE GROWTH

Sealed Air

NEW FOR
2019

Ticker symbol: SEE (NYSE) ❑ Large Cap ❑ Value Line financial strength rating: B+ ❑ Current
yield: 1.4% ❑ Dividend raises, past 10 years: 4

Company Profile

According to digital market researcher eMarketer, e-commerce sales are
expected to grow almost 130 percent between 2015 and 2020—or about
20–25 percent annually—and are expected to top $4 trillion by 2020. And
every one of these shipments requires the proper product and shipment
packaging to make it work; the wrong package fails to protect the product,
gives the customer a poor experience, and/or costs too much to pack and/or
to ship—not to mention the environmental consequences. In short, packaging is becoming a key part of today's, and tomorrow's, never-leave-your-
couch e-commerce ecosystem. It's the reasoning behind our quest to pick a
product packaging specialist for the 2019 *100 Best Stocks* list.

Now the remaining question was: out of the six or seven large packaging
suppliers we could have chosen from, which one? We looked at several with
an eye to which company had a significant presence in e-commerce—and
more so, which company had the most innovative approach to improving
e-commerce packaging. We arrived at packaging producer Sealed Air as the
answer.

We all know Sealed Air as the original makers of Bubble Wrap, that
simple but effective cushioned wrapping material we all love to give to our
kids to pop on Christmas morning.

Actually, Bubble Wrap is part of the Product Care segment within Sealed Air, which represents about 37 percent of Sealed Air's 2017 total revenue, while the larger portion of the business is represented by the Food Care segment, which represents the other 63 percent of volume. The e-commerce business lies within Product Care; as a consequence, not surprisingly, Product Care revenues grew 8 percent in 2017 while Food Care grew only 5 percent.

So what's inside the package in each of these two segments? First, the Food Care division provides a broad range of products and integrated packaging systems to ship and store food products, minimizing contamination risk, improving shelf life, and improving merchandising and store display. These specialized packages, which you might see containing everything from your Thanksgiving turkey to packaged meats, vegetables, and pasta, are marketed under several brand names, "Cryovac" being the most prevalent. Focus is placed not just on the package but on the automation of the packaging process, bringing a complete solution for the producer supply chain.

Although we feel that the e-commerce boom will eventually spill over into this segment as better solutions are needed for the emerging food home delivery business, our e-commerce intrigue is really centered on the Product Care segment. The Product Care business exists to provide its customers with a "range of sustainable packaging solutions designed to reduce shipping and fulfillment costs, increase operational efficiency, reduce damage and enhance customer and brand experience." The largest customer sectors are e-commerce, general manufacturing, electronics, and transportation. Products include a range of packing materials and systems including the aforementioned Bubble Wrap but also AirCap cellular packaging, Cryovac shrink films, Instapak polyurethane foam systems, and others. More high-tech systems include "e-Cube," an automated high-velocity fulfillment solution that optimizes shipping box "cube" (to save shipping costs), and other bulk product packaging and storing systems that allow a shipper to pick and a pull product ready to ship in its own container, bypassing a pack-and-ship process in a logistics operation.

What really sealed the deal (sorry) for us with Sealed Air was the 2017 announcement of a joint Packaging Innovation Center with UPS (another *100 Best Stock*) in UPS's Louisville Supply Chain Solution's campus aimed specifically at "solving the packaging and shipping challenges of e-commerce retailers…by maximizing efficiency, minimizing waste, reducing shipping costs and increasing brand affinity." The joint effort, part of a larger strategic partnership between the two companies, puts specific focus on packaging innovation as part of supply chain innovation. In part the new effort recognizes the need for performance—and customer experience benefits—for not only the specific product package but also for the secondary and tertiary packages that products are shipped in. With the vast increase in package volume moving through e-commerce channels and delivery vehicles, it's not hard to see the importance of this focus. For us, this effort makes Sealed Air stand out among the many packaging manufacturers.

In 2017 the company completed the disposal of Diversey, another good-sized segment producing medical packaging, as well as cleaning and hygiene solutions, to focus more on its core businesses. This transition explains the large drop in financials reported in 2017 noted in the following section and will serve to increase not only margins but also research and operational focus going forward.

Financial Highlights, Fiscal Year 2017

The reported numbers for 2017 are fairly meaningless due to the Diversey disposal; it probably makes more sense to focus on the revenue performance of the remaining product segments, Food Care and Product Care, which reported 5 percent and 8 percent revenue gains respectively as noted previously. One-time adjustments gains and charges significantly cloud the net earnings picture, but pretax earnings (EBITDA) were up about 3 percent for the year. Going forward the company expects sales gains in the 7–9 percent range for 2018 and in the 4–5 percent range in 2019; earnings should recover beyond previous years' levels on higher margins by 2019 with per-share earnings in the $2.50 range. Share repurchases of about 2 percent annually will help per-share earnings; dividend raises are projected to be modest but could surprise to the upside as cash flows are strong.

Reasons to Buy

As mentioned at the outset there are a number of integrated packaging providers at the doorstep of e-commerce; we chose Sealed Air because of its track record and callout of e-commerce as a strategic priority. We also think the food packaging business, while fairly mundane at present, could be a hidden card to play as local and centralized home food delivery become more prevalent. Aside from e-commerce, we think the Diversey divestiture was the right move and approve of the efforts to bolster margins in this typically low-margin business.

Reasons for Caution

As a whole, the packaging industry is fairly mundane, as any employee of TV's Dunder Mifflin could tell you! It is competitive, and dynamic change and especially growth can be hard to come by. Second, while we're excited by the e-commerce opportunity, the entire Product Care group in which it lives still represents only a bit more than a third of the company. Input cost inflation could also pop Sealed Air's bubbles.

SECTOR: Industrials ❑ BETA COEFFICIENT: **1.15** ❑ 10-YEAR COMPOUND EARNINGS PER-SHARE GROWTH: **-1.0%** ❑ 10-YEAR COMPOUND DIVIDENDS PER-SHARE GROWTH: **9.5%**

		2010	2011	2012	2013	2014	2015	2016	2017
Revenues (mil)		4,490	5,641	7,648	7,691	7,750	7,031	6,778	4,461
Net income (mil)		256	243	200	263	258	335	486	63
Earnings per share		1.44	1.31	0.95	1.23	1.20	1.62	2.46	0.33
Dividends per share		0.50	0.52	0.52	0.52	0.52	0.52	0.61	0.64
Cash flow per share		2.58	2.25	2.59	2.77	2.49	2.80	3.62	1.25
Price:	high	25.7	28.8	21.5	34.4	43.7	55.8	52.8	50.8
	low	18.4	11.0	11.5	17.6	28.2	38.4	38.0	41.0

Website: www.sealedair.com

AGGRESSIVE GROWTH

Siemens AG (ADR)

Ticker symbol: SIEGY (OTC) ❑ Large Cap ❑ Value Line financial strength rating: A ❑ Current yield: 2.6% ❑ Dividend raises, past 10 years: 8

Company Profile

Setting the benchmark to "electrify, automate and digitize the world around us" is part of the clever mission statement of the $98 billion diversified industrial conglomerate known worldwide as Siemens. Siemens touches many industries and sectors of interest to us: infrastructure, healthcare, urban transportation, industrial automation, and alternative energy with an assortment of mostly technology-enhanced products and services. The company was founded in the late nineteenth century by Werner von Siemens, an early electrical engineering pioneer and inventor of the electric elevator.

Siemens operates in eight product segments:

- Power and Gas (18 percent of FY2017 revenues) supplies an assortment of products to the oil and gas, power, and industrial markets. Gas and steam turbines and other "heavy" power plant hardware of varying sizes are made by this operation.

- "Healthineers" (Healthcare—16 percent) is a leader in medical imaging, laboratory diagnostics, therapy systems, hearing instruments, and clinical IT. In early 2018, this unit was spun off in an initial public offering, so it is no longer an operating segment. However, Siemens as of this writing maintains ownership of 85 percent of the shares. The move was part of a larger strategy to "deconglomeratize"—that is, to go less wide and more deep in its core businesses, maintaining focus on digital manufacturing technologies, power and energy, and transport.

- Energy Management (15 percent) is a leading global supplier of electrical grid hardware, solutions, and services "for the economical, reliable, and intelligent transmission and distribution of electric power," including high- and low-voltage and smart-grid solutions.

- Digital Factory (13 percent) offers a portfolio of integrated hardware and software solutions to support product design processes worldwide and to reduce their time to market.

- Process Industries and Drives (11 percent) is the manufacturing and factory automation complement to the Digital Factory group.

- Mobility (10 percent) makes and sells various urban transportation infrastructure products, most notably so-called "light rail" transit cars; a large factory in Sacramento, CA, produces these vehicles for the US and certain global markets.

- Building Technologies (8 percent) is the "world market leader" for building automation technologies, HVAC controls, security, fire protection, and energy management products and services.

- Siemens Gamesa Renewable Energy, formerly Wind Power (9 percent), provides hardware, software, and services toward the creation of efficient onshore and offshore wind power generation facilities. The relative size and importance of this segment increased with the 2017 acquisition of Spanish wind turbine manufacturer Gamesa. In addition, the group has been awarded the world's largest onshore order to date from MidAmerican Energy (a Warren Buffett/Berkshire Hathaway company) in Iowa.

By region, revenues break down as follows: Americas (28 percent), EMEA (excluding Germany—39 percent), Asia/Australia (19 percent), and Germany (13 percent).

The company is stepping up and consolidating its software offerings particularly in its industrial businesses. In 2017 it released "MindSphere," a new operating system for the Internet of Things (IoT). The goal is to sell entire ecosystems of products linked together, as well as linked to machines and devices already in place. GE has marketed a similar platform called "Predix," but Siemens appears to be further ahead especially on the international front with these digitally enhanced manufacturing solutions.

Financial Highlights, Fiscal Year 2017

Currency translation effects are a major driver of the numbers shown here; the recent euro/US dollar conversion rate of 1.18 pales in comparison to the 1.46 rate back in 2009, hence results (and dividend payouts) look choppier than they really are. For 2017, acquisitions and strength in most international markets offset some weakness in the Power business worldwide and Mobility particularly in the US, altogether netting a revenue gain of almost 10 percent. A favorable product mix and efficiency measures raised margins, and this net profits up almost 20 percent. For 2018 and 2019, the company anticipates revenue gains in the 6–8 percent range and earnings gains in the 6–10 percent range, with steady moderate dividend increases and buybacks.

Reasons to Buy

"Digitalization, Globalization, and Urbanization" are the three stated marketplace themes of this progressive leader in the world of industrial design and infrastructure. We believe as Siemens does that the world will be a more integrated industrial and distribution arena, more connected, more processes will be created and managed digitally, and that new and modern urban infrastructure will become increasingly important as urban populations grow. To those trends, the company brings new focus on added value in "digitalization, automation, and electrification" of the industrial and infrastructure space worldwide. We think this is a solid and very progressive— not to mention more profitable—position in comparison to most of today's industrial and infrastructure suppliers. The strategy seems right, and we think Siemens has already achieved world leadership in these areas. In fact, we classified the company under "Industrials" as a sector but could have easily justified classifying it as a "Technology" company. The world's factories, energy grids, transportation, and other infrastructure are all ripe for a major refresh, and Siemens will be right in the middle of it.

The company has made great progress to build and optimize its product portfolio going forward with these markets and principles in mind. Although Siemens is notably global in its business footprint, a growing recovery in Europe should help. We also like their refocus on "core" businesses and technologies; as many conglomerates learned from rival GE this year, big is not always best. A more profitable business mix and cost efficiency measures are projected to increase gross and net margins moderately; as this occurs we expect moderately increasing shareholder returns over time.

Reasons for Caution

As the following numbers show, performance has been (and can be) choppy, not just because of currency but also exposure to economic cycles and slow-downs. Siemens makes capital equipment, and capital equipment is one of the first things to be cut out of customer budgets when the going gets tough. That said, recent Trump administration policies, cash repatriation, and a general sense that manufacturing and public infrastructure needs to be modernized should all help Siemens out. Finally—the usual warning about foreign-based companies—Siemens is harder to understand than a lot of US equivalents; it is complex, it operates differently, and it presents itself differently. That said, the company does a better-than-average job of explaining itself to potential investors on its website.

SECTOR: **Industrials** ❑ BETA COEFFICIENT: **1.49** ❑ 10-YEAR COMPOUND EARNINGS PER-SHARE GROWTH: **5.0%** ❑ 10-YEAR COMPOUND DIVIDENDS PER-SHARE GROWTH: **9.0%**

	2010	2011	2012	2013	2014	2015	2016	2017
Revenues (bil)	103.3	98.8	100.7	102.7	91.0	84.8	89.2	98.0
Net income (bil)	5.4	9.1	6.5	5.5	6.7	6.0	6.3	7.2
Earnings per share	3.09	5.19	3.67	3.26	3.91	3.53	3.60	4.27
Dividends per share	1.12	1.84	1.93	2.01	2.05	1.88	1.90	2.17
Cash flow per share	6.30	7.28	5.85	5.60	5.76	5.48	5.78	6.78
Price: high	62.6	73.4	55.4	69.6	69.0	57.5	62.1	79.4
low	41.4	42.4	38.9	49.3	51.6	43.9	43.3	60.1

Website: www.siemens.com

GROWTH AND INCOME

The J.M. Smucker Company

Ticker symbol: SJM (NYSE) ❑ Large Cap ❑ Value Line financial strength rating: A++ ❑ Current yield: 2.5% ❑ Dividend raises, past 10 years: 10

Company Profile

"With a name like Smucker's, it has to be good!" This ad copy says it all about this eastern Ohio–based firm, a leading manufacturer of jams, jellies, and other processed foods for years. Thanks in part to divestitures from the Procter & Gamble food division and other companies, it has grown itself into a premier player in the packaged food industry. The 2015 acquisition of Big Heart Pet Brands, a premier player in the pet food industry, signals further expansion into adjacent markets.

Smucker manufactures and markets products under its own name, as well as under a number of other household names such as Crisco, Folgers, Knudsen, Hungry Jack, Eagle, Carnation, Pillsbury, Jif (why not sell the peanut butter if they sell the jelly?), and naturally, Goober (a combination of peanut butter and jelly in a single jar), and Uncrustables (why not just sell the whole sandwich?). The company also produces and distributes Dunkin' Donuts coffee and produces an assortment of cooking oils, toppings, juices, and baking ingredients, and has recently acquired the Wesson cooking oil brand. The company has revitalized such brands as Folgers and Jif through improved marketing, channel relationships, and better focus on the packaging and delivery of these brands to the customer. In the coffee business, for example, Smucker's now offers custom blends, K-Cup offerings, etc., notably under the Dunkin' Donuts brand. The Café Bustelo brand targets Hispanic and millennial markets with edgy "experiential" marketing with pop-up cafés at music festivals and the like. "Coffee Served Your Way" is Smucker's motto, and there are new convenience packages for peanut butter, jelly, and other spreads as well—Jif To Go Dippers is but one example. Organic brands, most of which have been around for a while, include Santa Cruz Organic, Sahale Snacks, and truRoots brands, Smucker's Natural, Laura Scudder's, and a handful of others. New areas include fruit spreads, nut butters, and other organic baking materials, beverages, and snacks; they also produce a line of sugar-free, reduced-sugar, and sugar-alternative products. The Big Heart acquisition brought some top brands in the pet food business, including Meow Mix, 9Lives, Milk Bone, and others, and grew the total business by about a third. The company estimates that at least one of its products is found in 93 percent of all US households.

Overall, the company aims to sell the number one brand in the various markets it serves, and to develop on-trend or premium products in markets adjacent to these number one brands. An example is the "1850" series Folger coffee offering: an assortment of premium bagged coffees in retro classy 1850-style bags with bottled iced coffees and other products with the same look introduced in early 2018.

With the Big Heart acquisition, the company is currently organized into four evenly split reporting segments: Retail Coffee (29 percent of revenues), Retail Consumer Foods (28 percent), Retail Pet Foods (29 percent), and International and Foodservice (14 percent). Operations are centered in the US, Canada, and Europe, with about 10 percent of sales coming from outside the US with Canada representing more than 80 percent of that.

Even as a nearly $7.5 billion-a-year enterprise (in 2016), the company still retains the feel of a family business, with brothers Tim and Richard Smucker sharing the CEO responsibilities as chairman and president, respectively. The Company Store and Café located just outside of Orrville, OH, is a national treasure and a classic case study in branding and brand image.

Financial Highlights, Fiscal Year 2017

Unfavorable pricing and mix across all businesses hampered FY2017 performance as with many competitors, and coffee and pet foods were notably weak. Sales were flat, and operating earnings dropped on higher commodity costs, but net reported earnings enjoyed 8 percent gain on a one-time benefit. Aggressive cost cutting, lower tax rates, and improved sales especially in the coffee and pet foods segments should lead to sales gains in the 2–3 percent range annually through 2019 and net earnings gains in the 8–10 percent range in 2018, slowing to the 2–3 percent range in 2019. Dividend growth should be in the mid-single-digit range, with some fairly aggressive share buybacks in store.

Reasons to Buy

This is a very well-managed company with an excellent and lasting reputation in its markets. In recent years, it has a proven track record in buying and revitalizing key brands, the most prominent being former Procter & Gamble food brands, Sara Lee foodservice coffee and beverage brands, and a few International Multifoods brands. We expect this trend to continue. The company's aggressive moves into coffee and other beverages were well timed; it remains to be seen whether or when they can make the most of their Big Heart pet food acquisition, which was expected to bring a measure of stability, profitability, and growth to the table.

Overall growth and profitability figures are both among the best for the relatively staid food industry, with net profit margins exceeding 10 percent. The base for steady growth in cash flows and investor returns is well established over the long term. Steady and safe: Smucker is the ever-improving peanut butter and jelly sandwich of the investing landscape.

Reasons for Caution

The prepared-food business is very sensitive in the short term to competition as well as commodity costs. There is also the ever-present transition of the customer base to the millennial generation and tastes—do millennials eat peanut butter and jelly sandwiches? Smucker seems to have plenty on the drawing board in case they don't.

We do wonder if the company has strayed just a bit outside of its traditional feel-good, relatively healthy or at least wholesome, peanut butter and jelly base. While you can't grow a business much on peanut butter and jelly alone, ventures into donut-shop coffee, and now, pet food especially may not be such a good fit with what has made Smucker's taste so good up to now. Time will tell in the long run, but we still think that with a name like Smucker's, it has to be good.

SECTOR: **Consumer Staples** ❑ BETA COEFFICIENT: **0.62** ❑ 10-YEAR COMPOUND EARNINGS PER-SHARE GROWTH: **8.0%** ❑ 10-YEAR COMPOUND DIVIDENDS PER-SHARE GROWTH: **10.0%**

	2010	2011	2012	2013	2014	2015	2016	2017
Revenues (mil)	4,826	5,526	5,897	5,611	5,450	7,811	7,400	7,385
Net income (mil)	566.5	535.6	584	588	540	704	753	810
Earnings per share	4.79	4.73	5.37	5.64	5.30	5.89	6.45	7.15
Dividends per share	1.68	1.88	2.06	2.32	2.56	2.68	3.00	3.09
Cash flow per share	7.06	6.75	7.85	8.30	6.87	9.75	10.10	10.85
Price: high	66.3	80.3	89.4	114.7	107.1	125.3	157.3	143.7
low	53.3	61.2	70.5	86.5	87.1	97.3	117.4	99.6

Website: www.smuckers.com

Southwest Airlines Co.

Ticker symbol: LUV (NYSE) ❑ Large Cap ❑ Value Line financial strength rating: A ❑ Current yield: 0.9% ❑ Dividend raises, past 10 years: 6

Company Profile

For years we were critical of the airline industry for its inability to control prices because of intense competition and to control costs that are largely comprised of fuel, airport, and unionized labor. These factors—and persistent losses—made airlines into poster children for the kinds of stocks we tend to avoid.

Now most of that has changed. Fuel costs have dropped and, although slightly off their lows, look to stay down for a while. Most airlines have, by design or by default, rationalized their route structures and capacity. With this rationalized capacity, they are better able to control both prices and costs, and their outlooks are much brighter. So, for the sixth year in a row we've chosen the best of the best—Southwest Airlines—for our *100 Best* list.

Southwest Airlines provides passenger air transport mainly in the United States, all within North America. In early 2017 the company served 100 cities in 40 US states and serves all of the Top 50 US markets. With the acquisition of AirTran, it also serves Mexico, Cuba, and eight other countries in Central America and the Caribbean. Service to Hawaii may begin in 2018 or early 2019. The company serves these markets almost exclusively with 706 Boeing 737 aircraft, the largest Boeing aircraft fleet in the world. Southwest continues to be the largest domestic air carrier in the United States, as measured by the number of domestic originating passengers boarded. At 4,000 peak-season departures per day, the airline also originates the most flights. This should give an idea of their business model—low cost, shorter flights, and maximum passenger loads.

The business model is one of simplicity—no-frills aircraft, no first-class passenger cabin, limited interchange with other carriers, no onboard meals, simple boarding and seat assignment practices, direct sales over the Internet (over 80 percent of sales online), no baggage fees—all designed to provide steady and reliable transportation, with one of the best on-time performances in the industry, and to maximize asset utilization with minimal downtime, crew disruptions, and other upward influences on operating costs. The company has long used secondary airports—such as Providence, RI, and Manchester, NH, to serve Boston and the New England area; Allentown, PA, and East Islip, NY, to serve the New York/New Jersey area (though it now serves LaGuardia, too, if you want that choice); and Chicago Midway to reduce delays and costs. This strategy has worked well.

Southwest has successfully implemented initiatives to squeeze out some extra revenue without alienating the core passenger group, mostly business travelers. One such initiative is Business Select, which offers priority boarding, priority security, bonus frequent flyer credit, and a free beverage for a small upgrade fee. The company also sells early boarding as a standalone for a modest $15 fee. But they continue to offer the basic two-bag limit free for now, a move we strenuously applaud. Southwest also produces more than $600 million in revenue annually from its Rapid Rewards loyalty point program through partnerships and sales of points. The program routinely wins "best of" rewards in the industry.

New initiatives include a transition to newer Boeing 737 aircraft, including the Boeing 737-MAX, 40 of which are on order, which can fly

500 miles farther than existing models opening up more international markets, and more 143-seat 747-700s and 175-seat 737-800s (typical older 737 models range from 117 to 132 seats). Well over half the fleet is comprised of one of these newer models, and the company currently has 200 new aircraft on order, all Boeing 737 models.

Financial Highlights, Fiscal Year 2017

Southwest had already been taxiing into position with operational improvements, capacity rationalization, the AirTran acquisition, and other market and efficiency gains. The 50 percent drop in oil prices cleared Southwest for takeoff, and take off it did. By 2016, fuel costs as a percent of revenue dropped to 21.9 percent from the low- to mid-30s a few years ago reflecting three favorable trends—higher revenues, lower fuel prices, and greater fuel efficiency. They have ticked back up to 22.8 percent recently.

Wage increases from a new collective bargaining agreement and the 8 percent rise in fuel prices caused 2017 earnings to descend about 8 percent on a 3.7 percent revenue rise. A 3 percent share buyback held the per-share earnings drop at a far more level 4 percent. The load factor remained at 83.9, up from around 80 a few years ago (percentage of seats paid for and occupied—*that's* why their planes have been so crowded lately!), and that combined with more available seat miles, larger and more efficient aircraft, and longer average trips continued to help the top line and bodes well for the bottom line—other cost factors held constant. The rise in fares enjoyed through 2016, however, appears to have leveled off for now. Revenues should climb about 8 percent in 2018 and about 4–5 percent in 2019; more efficiencies and a leveling off in fuel price effects (some due to hedging) should land a jumbo 25 percent gain in 2018 (based on a soft 2017 comparison) and a steadier 4–6 percent gain in 2019. Annual share buybacks in the 2–4 percent range add to the story, as does (finally) a modernization of the dividend policy; while the yield is still very modest, it's getting better.

Reasons to Buy

The story remains much the same: Southwest continues to be the best player in an industry whose fundamentals have dramatically improved. The company continues to be the "envy" value proposition of the industry, and we continue to be surprised that no one else has been able to emulate it successfully—but at this point, even if they do, Southwest has a decades-long first mover advantage.

The airline "gets it" that what customers want is no-hassle transportation at best-possible prices—and yes, no bag fees—and has been able to do that better than anyone else for years and is now extending its value proposition further for business travelers, who increasingly book their own fares and respond well to $15 priority boarding upgrades and other offers. Good management, efficient operation, and excellent marketing make it all possible. Financially, the company has earned a profit for 45 consecutive years—in the volatile airline industry we know no greater testimonial to good marketing and good management.

Reasons for Caution

Fuel prices will always be a wild card. The company has shown in the past that it can use hedges to manage fuel price shocks, and they've been doing a lot of that lately. Generally, we fear anything that would move Southwest away from its core competencies—complacency in the short run, acquisitions in the longer term. The longer Southwest can stay Southwest, and avoid looking like other airlines, the better.

SECTOR: Transportation ❏ BETA COEFFICIENT: 1.17 ❏ 10-YEAR COMPOUND EARNINGS PER-SHARE GROWTH: 17.5% ❏ 10-YEAR COMPOUND DIVIDENDS PER-SHARE GROWTH: 32.0%

		2010	2011	2012	2013	2014	2015	2016	2017
Revenues (mil)		12,104	15,658	17,088	17,699	18,605	19,820	20,425	21,771
Net income (mil)		550	330	421	754	1,136	2,161	2,244	2,076
Earnings per share		0.73	0.42	0.58	1.05	1.64	3.27	3.55	3.41
Dividends per share		0.02	0.03	0.04	0.10	0.22	0.29	0.38	0.48
Cash flow per share		1.02	1.35	1.73	2.35	3.07	4.94	5.45	5.55
Price:	high	14.3	13.9	10.6	19.0	43.2	51.3	51.3	67.0
	low	10.4	7.1	7.8	10.4	18.8	31.4	34.0	48.7

Website: www.southwest.com

AGGRESSIVE GROWTH

NEW FOR 2019

Square, Inc.

Ticker symbol: SQ (NASDAQ) ❏ Large Cap ❏ Value Line financial strength rating: B ❏ Current yield: Nil ❏ Dividend raises, past 10 years: NA

Company Profile

Founded in 2009 and headquartered in San Francisco, Square, Inc., provides payment and point-of-sale solutions in the US, Canada, Japan, and Australia (so far). The company's aptly named "commerce ecosystem" includes point-of-sale hardware and software that enables sellers to turn iOS and Android mobile and computing devices into payment and point-of-sale solutions, which in turn connect to other business management platforms provided by Square and others. Hardware products include:

- Magstripe reader—the familiar white square-shaped attachment for mobile devices, which enables swiped transactions of magnetic stripe cards.
- Chip card reader—accepts "EMV" (Europay, MasterCard, Visa) chip cards and enables swiped transactions of magnetic stripe cards.
- Contactless and chip reader—accepts EMV chip cards and Near Field Communication payments from smartphones.
- Square Stand—enables an iPad to be used as a payment terminal or full point-of-sale solution.
- Square Register—a complete system combining hardware, point-of-sale software, and payments technology into a managed payment solution. Software products include:
  - Square Point of Sale software—operates inside the hardware to execute card- and smartphone-based transactions and allows merchants to use any of the hardware front ends or to enter a card number manually; also provides analytics, employee and facility management tools, and vertical-market specific tools such as for restaurants, retail, scheduling tools for service providers, etc. As an example, in mid-2018 Square launched "Square for Restaurants," a complete solution integrating point of sale throughout a restaurant with front-end and back-end processes including menu setup, ordering, tipping, tip and bill splitting, employee management, and performance tracking. It blends with the previously acquired "Caviar" app, which manages food pickup and delivery and carryout transactions.
  - Cash App—a peer-to-peer payments system that accesses the general banking and financial system, allowing customers to electronically send, store, and spend money.
  - Square Capital—a lending facility that provides loans to sellers based on real-time payment and point-of-sale data.

Additionally, the company provides an "Open Developer Platform": application programming interfaces ("APIs") allowing programmers of business-specific or market-specific software to integrate Square app features into their platforms.

This "commerce ecosystem" was originally designed to meet the commerce and transaction needs of small and often portable businesses, where the point of sale can be in a trade show, flea market, food court, or some other quasi-temporary setting in addition to most home-based businesses. Increasingly, Square products are being adopted by sellers of all sizes as a substitute for the traditional cash register and point-of-sale card reader even where portability isn't a requirement due to their ease of use and access to other parts of the Square ecosystem. Sellers with annualized Gross Payment Volume (transactions times selling price) of more than $500K per year have risen from 3 percent to 20 percent of the mix; sellers between $125K and $500K have risen from 16 percent to 27 percent of the mix, leaving only 53 percent of the payment base in small sellers selling less than $125K per year.

The business model is largely transaction-based, although the company does earn some income selling and renting equipment and through software subscriptions. Sellers are charged a per-transaction fee in the range of 3 percent (exact figures aren't disclosed in company documents); these transactions are then fed to an Acquiring Processor (usually associated with a bank) then to a Card Network (Visa, MasterCard, etc.) and its issuing bank. These entities charge fees, which essentially comprise cost of goods sold, totaling to about 2 percent of the transaction value; the resulting gross margin is about a third of the entire transaction revenue stream, or 1.06 percent of the total transaction value in 2017, up from 1.03 percent in 2016.

Financial Highlights, Fiscal Year 2017

Total net revenue for FY2017 rose almost 30 percent to $2.21 billion; of that almost 87 percent was transaction revenue, 11 percent was subscription- and services-based revenue, and 2 percent was hardware revenue (initial hardware is typically given for free to new app users). Cost of goods sold, 89 percent of which is transaction-based costs and fees as described before, totaled $1.374 billion, leaving an "adjusted revenue" of $983 million. Operating expenses, which included $322 million for product development, $253 million for sales and marketing, and $250 million for general and administrative expenses, led the way to a $54 million operating loss, down from $171 million in 2016 and $212 million in 2015. Square has never earned a profit but has finally turned cash-flow positive. The company expects a near breakeven performance in 2018 and to earn $65 million, or 15 cents a share in 2019, and to grow earnings well past that in 2020 and beyond. The play here is purely on scale; more users and more transaction volume will absorb fixed costs and drop in a large part to the bottom line once scale is achieved.

As Square customers use other parts of the ecosystem beyond the transaction capabilities, margins should increase as well.

Reasons to Buy

This is the first time in the history of *100 Best Stocks* that we've listed a company that has never made money and is still in the "cash burn" phase of its existence. To break that barrier must it be that we see something big in this company? Indeed we do.

Square and its commerce ecosystem fit right into the land of the millennials. Buy something where you want to, when you want to, using the latest technology. Square enables business to happen the way you want it to—whether for the seller or the buyer. We like the value proposition of simplicity, flexibility, and tie-in with customized business platforms. The brand is already strong, and their efforts to promote the product resonate; they've become the "go to" solution for small and many medium-sized businesses. International expansion is promising as well.

We've been conditioned by the success of Visa in its ability to live off of growing transaction volume and turning it into profit with a relatively minimal investment. We think Square will also reach critical mass and go far beyond, turning transaction fees into steadily increasing cash flows as volume builds. By 2019, it will have passed the critical breakeven point. When you mix in other parts of the ecosystem as revenue generators, the earning power grows further.

Reasons for Caution

Obviously there are inherent technology, marketplace, and financial risks in investing in a nascent business like Square. New competitors can emerge, taking the concept farther and faster; or an established player like Visa or Apple could enter the fray (or, on the flip side, could buy Square!). As we write this, the share price bakes in a lot of our favorable expectations already and is quite volatile to boot. Although Square ventures pretty far from our normal *100 Best* comfort zone, we think it's a great way to plug a little leading-edge technology into your portfolio. Swipe carefully.

SECTOR: **Information Technology** ❑ BETA COEFFICIENT: **4.24** ❑ 10-YEAR COMPOUND EARNINGS PER-SHARE GROWTH: **NA** ❑ 10-YEAR COMPOUND DIVIDENDS PER-SHARE GROWTH: **NA**

	2010	2011	2012	2013	2014	2015	2016	2017
Revenues (mil)	—	—	—	—	—	1,267	1,709	2,214
Net income (mil)	—	—	—	—	—	(179.8)	(171.6)	(62.8)
Earnings per share	—	—	—	—	—	(1.24)	(0.50)	(0.17)
Dividends per share	—	—	—	—	—	—	—	—
Cash flow per share	—	—	—	—	—	(0.45)	(0.35)	(0.06)
Price: high	—	—	—	—	—	14.8	15.9	49.6
low	—	—	—	—	—	9.0	8.1	13.7

Website: www.squareup.com

AGGRESSIVE GROWTH

Starbucks Corporation

Ticker symbol: SBUX (NASDAQ) ❑ Large Cap ❑ Value Line financial strength rating: A++ ❑ Current yield: 2.1% ❑ Dividend raises, past 10 years: 7

Company Profile

Starbucks Corporation, formed in 1985, is the leading retailer, roaster, and brand of specialty coffee in the world. The company sells whole-bean coffees through its retailers, its specialty sales group, and supermarkets. The Starbucks store footprint continues to expand. In the Americas there are now 9,413 company-owned stores (9,109 at the end of 2016) and 7,146 licensed stores (6,518 in 2016). In "CAP" (China Asia-Pacific) there are 3,070 (2,811) company-owned and 4,409 (3,632) licensee stores; in EMEA (Europe, Middle East, and Africa) there are 502 (523) and 2,472 (2,119) stores respectively; in "Other" there are 290 (358) company-owned stores and 37 licensees. In all it's a rich brew of 13,275 company-owned and 14,064 licensee stores worldwide. The company is currently moving to convert several hundred licensed stores to company owned in China. Retail coffee shop sales constitute about 89 percent of its revenue, unchanged from last year. About 79 percent of revenue originates in company-operated stores. Unlike many in the restaurant sector, the company does not franchise its stores—all are either company owned or operated by licensees in special venues such as airports, college campuses, and other places where access is restricted, and in foreign markets where it is necessary or advantageous.

The company continues to expand overseas, usually at first through partnerships and joint ventures; then sometimes through acquiring its partner. The FY2017 sales breakdown: 70 percent Americas, 5 percent Europe/Middle East/Africa, 14 percent China/Asia-Pacific, and 12 percent other segments and "channel development," which is largely made up of branded product sales through non-Starbucks retailers. The company now operates in 62 countries in total; with China and South Korea leading the way with 310 and 164 new stores opened, respectively.

The company continues to adjust its product portfolio beyond coffee. In 2017 Starbucks decided to sell its Tazo tea business and close its Teavana stores (Teavana premium teas will continue to be offered in Starbucks stores and sold into the grocery channel). Starbucks continues to offer Evolution Fresh juices, Ethos water products, numerous food items and specialty packages like "Via" and Keurig-compatible single-serve coffee packages and has added several "cold" beverages including Cold Brew and Iced Espresso to its menu. Finally, Starbucks has joint ventures with PepsiCo and Dreyer's to market bottled coffee drinks and coffee-flavored ice creams.

In 2017, the sum total revenue mix in company-operated stores was 73 percent beverages, 20 percent food, 3 percent packaged and single-serve coffees and teas, and 4 percent "other" including coffee-making equipment and other merchandise.

Starbucks continues to invest and expand its leadership in the deployment of technology. The company's "Mobile Order and Pay" app and platform, where users can order and pay for their drinks using smartphones, then subsequently arrive at locations to pick up their drinks, is growing. The company continues to add drive-thru locations as well. Speed of service remains a major objective. The company's retail goal continues to be the unique Starbucks experience, which the company defines as a third place beyond home and work. The "experience" is built upon superior customer service and a clean, well-maintained retail store that reflects the personality of the community in which it operates—all aimed at building loyalty and frequent repeat visits.

The company also gets high marks for citizenship, continuing to offer health coverage, equity participation, and even college assistance for its 277,000 employees ("partners"). Commitments to hire veterans, military spouses, and more recently, Syrian refugees, are notable among a list of other commitments to community service and social issues of the day.

Finally, founder and chairman Howard Schultz left his role as CEO to work on his "Reserve" high-end coffee bar concept. Both his departure and the new adventure bear watching; former operations chief Kevin Johnson has taken over.

Financial Highlights, Fiscal Year 2017

Technology improvements, brand, optimized store locations, and moderate expansion led to a 5 percent revenue gain on a 3 percent same store sales gain, most of which was based on a higher average ticket per visit rather than higher traffic. Margins remained largely unchanged; net profit was up 6 percent, and per-share earnings rose about 8 percent helped along by a 2 percent share buyback. Estimates call for an 11 percent top-line growth in 2018, mostly through International and especially China gains, tapering a bit to 8–9 percent in 2019. Continued operational improvements and improved international profitability will gradually widen margins and bring earnings growth in the mid to high teens. "Cream and sugar" comes in the form of dividend increases in the high double digits with a moderate amount of share buyback activity added in for good measure.

Reasons to Buy

After all these years, Starbucks is still a great story. The company's stores continue to be more than coffee shops and are really that "third place" where professionals, students, moms, and other prosperous folks will meet and dole out a few bucks for quality drinks. The "third place" aura creates a lot of the brand strength and, in our view, represents the company's *true* strength—well beyond the quality of the coffee itself and related products. The company has a steadily (and profitably) growing presence on the world stage. We believe the technology and experience improvements will be big both for customers and operations.

The company is well managed, has an extremely strong brand, has solid financials, and, once again, has a steady growth track record, and it is carving out an ever-stronger international footprint. Cash returns to investors are on the rise, and safety (as proxied by beta) has improved sharply from years ago. Starbucks offers both growth and, increasingly, cash returns and safety—a very nice brew for investors indeed. The recent flat share price in a surging market would appear to suggest that this is the time to start a grande half-caf caramel latte of your own.

Reasons for Caution

The biggest risk used to be overexpansion and cannibalization—which they've encountered and dealt with well in recent years but could reemerge as a trouble spot down the road. Competition from other mostly local premium coffee shops is growing. Despite operational and technology improvements, people still spend a lot of time in line at certain locations. Perhaps our biggest fear remains the temptation to expand too far into the foodservice business, which could reduce margins, dilute the experience, and make the stores smell like a sandwich shop, far less appealing for most than the aroma of coffee. It also brings operational complexities, so we score the experience with food so far as mostly a success but continue to keep our eyes (and noses) open for signs of stress.

SECTOR: Restaurant ❑ **BETA COEFFICIENT: 0.70** ❑ **10-YEAR COMPOUND EARNINGS PER-SHARE GROWTH: 17.5%** ❑ **10-YEAR COMPOUND DIVIDENDS PER-SHARE GROWTH: NM**

	2010	2011	2012	2013	2014	2015	2016	2017
Revenues (mil)	10,707	11,701	13,299	14,892	16,448	19,163	21,316	22,387
Net income (mil)	982	1,174	1,385	1,721	2,068	2,394	2,635	3,011
Earnings per share	0.64	0.76	0.90	1.13	1.36	1.58	1.91	2.06
Dividends per share	0.12	0.26	0.34	0.42	0.52	0.64	0.80	1.00
Cash flow per share	1.01	1.14	1.29	1.58	1.85	2.21	2.61	2.81
Price: high	16.6	23.3	31.0	41.3	42.1	64.0	61.8	64.9
low	10.6	15.4	21.5	26.3	34.0	39.3	50.8	52.6

Website: www.starbucks.com

CONSERVATIVE GROWTH

State Street Corporation

Ticker symbol: STT (NYSE) ❑ Large Cap ❑ Value Line financial strength rating: B++ ❑ Current yield: 1.7% ❑ Dividend raises, past 10 years: 7

Company Profile

Are you afraid of SPDRs? Not the eight-legged kind, but the original and one of three leading brands of exchange-traded funds (ETFs) out there rapidly gaining ground on the "traditional" fund industry? If you aren't afraid of SPDRs, and you aren't too afraid of financial stocks in general, you might think about investing in State Street. State Street continues to be, in our opinion, more than most, a safe and sane way to play the Financials sector, which, despite a more favorable regulatory and interest rate environment, we continue to hold generally out of favor—if nothing else because it is very hard to understand financial companies and to analyze their stocks.

Their slogan is simple: "We are the engine that powers the world's investments." State Street is a financial powerhouse like many others. But unlike many, its core products are concentrated on offering services to other financial services firms and on offering the relatively new and growing ETF investment package to individual and institutional investors. It is often analyzed as a bank, but it acts more like a company providing services to other financial institutions and the public, receiving a steady and growing stream of fees for those services. Only about 20 percent of their net income comes as interest income; the other 80 percent is "non-interest income"—mainly fees for investment services. Run a mutual fund, hedge fund, or private equity fund? You might well come to State Street for the "picks and shovels" you need to run the fund—and many have. The company estimates that it is involved in 10 percent of the world's investment wealth one way or another.

The company operates with three main lines of business:

- Investment Servicing (48 percent of 2017 revenues) provides fee-based administrative, custodial, analytic, and other value-add functions to investment companies—mainly mutual funds, hedge funds, and pension funds, including settlement and payment services, transaction management, foreign exchange trading and brokerage, and setting the NAV (net asset value, or price) of about 40 percent of US-based mutual funds on a daily basis. The company has $2.8 *trillion* in assets under its custody.
- Investment Management (about 15 percent of revenues) provides investment vehicles and products through its State Street Global Advisors, or SSGA, subsidiary, including the well-known SPDR ETFs and some of the analytic tools and indexes supporting these products.
- Trading Services (about 10 percent of revenues) provides research and market trading support for institutional clients including mutual funds, pension funds, and so forth, and acts as a broker/dealer in the market.

With these three fee-based business units accounting for 75 percent of total revenues, you might wonder where the rest of its $11 billion in revenues come from. The answer lies mainly in interest income—as mentioned earlier, roughly 20 (now closer to 25 percent) of revenues comes from the net interest generated on asset holdings.

State Street has operations in 29 countries, and about 64 percent of revenues come from assets managed in the US, 23 percent from the EMEA region, and 13 percent from Asia-Pacific.

Financial Highlights, Fiscal Year 2017

Relatively stable, nonvolatile markets hurt the trading business, but strength in the investment servicing and management businesses led to a 9.6 percent gain in fee-based revenues, and modestly higher interest rates led to a 10.6 percent gain in that segment, leading to a nearly 10 percent revenue gain overall. Investments in the business, particularly in a massive multiyear IT improvement project known as "Beacon" held profits flat in 2017, but higher interest rates, improved operating leverage, and ahead-of-schedule improvements from "Beacon" are projected to drive net profit ahead 24 percent in 2018 on a 6–8 percent revenue gain. Another aggressive 4 percent share buyback resulted in a 6 percent rise in per-share earnings in FY2017, and another similar buyback and projected stronger profit growth in FY2018 could increase per-share earnings as much as 30 percent. By the end of 2018, the company will have bought back all of its float issued to bolster finances during the Great Recession.

Reasons to Buy

When there's a gold rush, the people who sell picks, shovels, and maps usually win. That's the case with State Street. It makes a lot of steady money selling services to other financial services firms, and the investment climate has been good for the past several years. It's a steadier income stream absent some (but not all) of the risks facing its other financial brethren. We think that State Street has a steady business with an innovative growth path in the ETF business, and we like the SPDR brand. We also like the fact that, unlike most financial firms, the company's income is more driven by fees for services than interest margins and investment gains. That said, the prospect for increased interest rates bodes well for interest income; if interest rates rise moderately this income stream rises without dinging the other investment business, and we think this will be the case. The company continues to focus on operational efficiency through the ahead-of-schedule Beacon program and should be well positioned to respond to the more favorable economic and regulatory environment. State Street also continues to focus on investor returns, aggressively retiring shares and raising the dividend regularly.

Reasons for Caution

Despite the fact that State Street sells picks and shovels to other investment funds, many of its fees are based on asset valuations—which are in turn vulnerable to market downturns. The company estimates that every 10 percent drop in the markets reduces total equity-based revenues about 2 percent and total fixed income revenues about 1 percent. If the investment markets turn sour that would hurt results.

Like other financial firms, State Street is enormously complex and hard to understand. The company's 10-K detailed annual report has 27 pages of "Risk Factors"—neither an easy nor a pleasant read—and the "Business" section talks more about regulatory matters than the business itself. We almost gave up when we introduced this issue for 2014. If you insist on fully understanding how a business works, what it sells, how it delivers, and so forth, this one might not be for you. Although the business is different than most financials, it could be swept up in another financial crisis. That said, we think the risk of such a crisis has diminished.

SECTOR: **Financials** ❑ BETA COEFFICIENT: **1.31** ❑ 10-YEAR COMPOUND EARNINGS PER-SHARE GROWTH: **5.0%** ❑ 10-YEAR COMPOUND DIVIDENDS PER-SHARE GROWTH: **6.0%**

	2010	2011	2012	2013	2014	2015	2016	2017
Assets (bil)	160.5	216.8	222.6	243.3	274.9	245.2	242.7	238.4
Revenues (mil)	8,953	9,594	9,649	9,881	10,235	10,350	10,207	11,009
Net income (mil)	1,559	1,920	2,061	2,136	2,037	1,980	2,142	2,177
Earnings per share	3.09	3.79	4.20	4.62	4.57	4.47	4.97	5.24
Dividends per share	0.04	0.72	0.96	1.04	1.16	1.32	1.44	1.60
Price: high	48.8	50.3	47.3	73.6	80.9	81.3	81.9	100.9
low	32.5	29.9	38.2	47.7	62.7	64.0	50.6	74.4

Website: www.statestreet.com

AGGRESSIVE GROWTH

Stryker Corporation

Ticker symbol: SYK (NYSE) ❑ Large Cap ❑ Value Line financial strength rating: A++ ❑ Current yield: 1.2% ❑ Dividend raises, past 10 years: 9

Company Profile

Stryker Corporation was founded as the Orthopedic Frame Company in 1941 by Dr. Homer H. Stryker, a leading orthopedic surgeon and the inventor of several orthopedic products. The company now ranks as a dominant player in the global orthopedics industry with more than 59,000 products in its catalog and a strong innovation track record, with more than 6 percent of sales invested in R&D.

The Orthopaedics segment (that's how the company spells it) accounts for about 38 percent of 2017 sales and has a significant market share in such "spare parts" as artificial hips, prosthetic knees, implant products for other extremities, and trauma and recovery products. Within that group, knees are 13 percent of total Stryker 2017 sales, hips are 10 percent, and "Trauma & Extremities" are another 12 percent of sales. An "Other" category accounts for 3 percent.

The MedSurg unit, about 45 percent of sales, develops, manufactures, and markets worldwide powered and computer-assisted and robotic surgical instruments, endoscopic surgical systems, hospital beds, and other patient care and handling equipment. Instruments (14 percent of total sales), endoscopy (13 percent), and medical devices, including emergency devices (16 percent) are the largest contributors, and a new group called "Sustainability," which reprocesses and remanufactures certain medical devices, now contributes 2 percent.

The Neurotechnology & Spine segment, a large part of which was acquired from Boston Scientific in 2010, accounts for 17 percent of sales and sells spinal reconstructive and surgical equipment, neurovascular surgery equipment, and craniomaxillofacial products.

Stryker's revenue is split roughly 70/30 percent domestic and international. Stryker has been active on the acquisition front. After an active acquisition year in 2016, which brought in Sage Products (disposable intensive care products), Physio-Control (portable defibrillators and monitors) and Synergetics (neurotechnology products), two important 2017 acquisitions include NOVADAQ (fluorescence imaging and endoscopy technologies) and Entellus (sinusitis treatments). The company also invests in pioneering technologies such as 3D printing for orthopedic replacements.

Financial Highlights, Fiscal Year 2017

Helped along somewhat by acquisitions, FY2017 sales rose about 10 percent, with healthy sales gains in all three businesses. Net earnings grew about 13 percent as major acquisition costs have already been spent and with a better product mix and scale slightly improving margins. Going forward, Stryker projects an 8–10 percent revenue gain for FY2018 slowing a bit to 5–7 percent in 2019. Projections call for net earnings to grow 10–12 percent each year. Share buybacks have slowed due to acquisitions, but dividends should rise in the 5–10 percent range over the next few years.

Reasons to Buy

We continue to see Stryker as an innovative healthcare products ("med tech") company with relatively less-entrenched competition than many others and a strong presence in the orthopedic market and a growing presence in surgical and neurological markets. This should allow it to capitalize on aging trends and a general economic recovery, which will induce more elective surgeries. Emerging markets, particularly China, present a good opportunity, and recent acquisitions should strengthen the portfolio and brand worldwide. We also see steady dividend growth.

Reasons for Caution

Ongoing scrutiny of healthcare costs and a continuation of small acquisitions bring some risks to the company, but we don't think they are excessive. The future of the Affordable Care Act and its replacement, and new initiatives such as the Amazon/Berkshire/JPMorgan consortium to analyze healthcare cost and delivery models are other unknowns and concerns. While these bear watching, however, companies with stronger, more-dominated niches like Stryker stand to be relatively less affected. Another concern is today's reduced hospital census (that is, occupancy)—an industry-wide trend reflecting cost management and more effective outpatient treatments—the company makes a lot of hospital beds and similar products that might not do well in a major hospital shakeout.

Stryker makes fairly high-tech medical products and as such is exposed to legal, regulatory, manufacturing risks, warranty expenses and product recalls. While the dividend is increasing at a good pace, the yield could still be higher given the company's strong cash flow—obviously they think they can invest your cash in R&D and acquisitions better than you can—and they may be right for now given projected earnings increases.

SECTOR: Healthcare ❑ **BETA COEFFICIENT: 0.70** ❑ **10-YEAR COMPOUND EARNINGS PER-SHARE GROWTH: 7.0%** ❑ **10-YEAR COMPOUND DIVIDENDS PER-SHARE GROWTH: 26.0%**

		2010	2011	2012	2013	2014	2015	2016	2017
Revenues (mil)		7,320	8,307	8,656	9,021	9,675	9,946	11,325	12,144
Net income (mil)		1,330	1,448	1,298	1,006	960	1,439	1,647	1,853
Earnings per share		3.30	3.72	3.39	2.63	2.36	3.78	4.35	4.87
Dividends per share		0.63	0.72	0.85	1.10	1.26	1.42	1.52	1.70
Cash flow per share		4.40	5.08	4.69	4.01	3.94	5.44	6.15	6.65
Price:	high	59.7	65.2	64.1	75.8	96.2	105.3	123.6	160.8
	low	42.7	43.7	49.4	55.2	74.0	89.8	86.7	116.5

Website: www.stryker.com

CONSERVATIVE GROWTH

Sysco Corporation

Ticker symbol: SYY (NYSE) ❑ Large Cap ❑ Value Line financial strength rating: A+ ❑ Current yield: 2.4% ❑ Dividend raises, past 10 years: 10

Company Profile

Sysco is the leading marketer and distributor of food, food products, and related equipment and supplies to the US foodservice industry. The company distributes fresh and frozen meats, prepared entrées, vegetables, canned and dried foods, dairy products, beverages, and produce, as well as paper products, restaurant equipment and supplies, and cleaning supplies. The company might be familiar for its "institutional" number-ten-sized cans of food found in many high-volume kitchens, but the product line and customer base are much larger, including many specialty and chain restaurants, lodges, hotels, hospitals, schools, and other distribution centers across the country. Restaurants account for about 61 percent of the 2017 business; healthcare (mainly hospitals and nursing homes) about 9 percent, education (schools and colleges) and government about 9 percent, travel and leisure (hotels and motels) and retail about 9 percent, and "other" categories make up the rest—about 12 percent. You see their lift-gated "bobtail" delivery trucks continuously, but you may not notice them delivering and unloading a pallet or two of goods at a time for a broad assortment of foodservice venues in your area. If you eat out at all, you've most likely consumed Sysco-distributed products.

Sysco has more than 500,000 customer locations and distributes over 400,000 products, including 41,000 under its own label. The company operates 199 distribution facilities and conducts business in more than 90 countries through company-owned facilities and joint ventures. From these centers, Sysco distributes 1.4 billion cases of food annually using a fleet of 13,400 delivery vehicles. The facilities include its 95 "Broadline" facilities, which supply independent and chain restaurants and other food-preparation facilities with food and nonfood products. It has 11 hotel supply locations, 25 specialty produce facilities, 17 SYGMA distribution centers (specialized, high-volume centers supplying to chain restaurants), 27 custom-cutting meat locations, and two distributors specializing in the niche Asian foodservice market. There are 324 distribution facilities in all, 162 in the US (50 percent), 65 in the UK (20 percent), 38 in France, and 37 in Canada (11 percent each). The company has been adding non-GMO, sustainably sourced, and other such items into its menu, which should play well with foodservice customers expanding in this direction.

The company also supplies the hotel industry with guest amenities, equipment, housekeeping supplies, room accessories, and textiles. By product type, the top five products are: 19 percent meat and frozen meals, 16 percent canned/dry, 15 percent frozen, 11 percent dairy, and 11 percent poultry, with produce, paper goods, seafood, beverages, janitorial products, and others making up the rest.

Sysco is by far the largest company in the domestic foodservice distribution industry. It has grown mainly through small "bolt-on" acquisitions in specialty food companies (such as seafood) or new geographies. In mid-2016 Sysco acquired UK-based Brakes Group to become a leading foodservice provider in England, France, and Sweden. This move added about 10 percent to the top line and established a solid beachhead for growth in Europe.

Financial Highlights, Fiscal Year 2017

FY2017 was a pretty good year; revenues rose 10 percent with the full integration of Brakes Group and a strong economy; higher freight and food cost pressures were offset by volume increases and scale to deliver a 12 percent rise in net income. With Brakes, international revenues almost doubled to about 20 percent of the total. Revenues should move forward in the 4–6 percent range annually through 2019; net income, helped along by lower tax rates, scale, and international progress is forecast to rise in the 15–20 percent range in 2018 and the 11–15 percent range in 2019. Healthy share buybacks will continue to keep per-share earnings rising at a higher rate; per-share earnings are forecast 40–45 percent higher by the end of 2019. Dividend raises should continue at a steady pace.

Reasons to Buy

Sysco continues to be a dominant player in a niche that won't go away any time soon. The current foodservice environment is improving, and the company still has plenty to work on in the form of operational efficiencies, and now international expansion is added to the mix as a growth driver.

Sysco's recent investments in technology continue to bear fruit, and we like to see innovation in an industry not known for it. New analytics, routing optimization, and recycling initiatives are being applied to realize savings in people, fuel, and other costs; the effects are manifest in the profit margin improvement—from 2.0 percent to 2.7 percent since 2014—and should continue. New supply-chain tools—even a "My Sysco Truck" app—allow customers to view the location and status of the deliveries and more generally will expand efficiencies and extend the customer relationship. In sum, this is a steady and safe company with a pretty good track record for steady business, decent cash flow, and decent shareholder payouts.

Reasons for Caution

Although the trend is slowly reversing, the recession got many folks away from the habit of eating out, and many restaurants disappeared altogether during this period. Volatility in food and ingredient prices, and fuel costs too, can pressure margins; this is always a cause for concern especially as inflation appears ready to pick up a bit. We also now worry that new dining trends and tastes of the millennials and others will require more specialization in the restaurant market, something Sysco will need to adapt to at least to a degree (and has begun to).

As described previously, this is a low-margin business with not a lot of room for error. That said, Sysco, more than most, continues to be a "sleep at night" kind of investment.

SECTOR: **Consumer Staples** ❑ BETA COEFFICIENT: **0.55** ❑ 10-YEAR COMPOUND EARNINGS PER-SHARE GROWTH: **4.0%** ❑ 10-YEAR COMPOUND DIVIDENDS PER-SHARE GROWTH: **6.5%**

		2010	2011	2012	2013	2014	2015	2016	2017
Revenues (mil)		37,243	39,323	42,381	44,411	46,517	48,681	50,367	55,371
Net income (mil)		1,181	1,153	1,122	992	931	1,100	1,214	1,359
Earnings per share		1.99	1.96	1.90	1.67	1.58	1.84	2.10	2.48
Dividends per share		0.99	1.03	1.07	1.11	1.16	1.19	1.23	1.30
Cash flow per share		2.67	2.62	2.63	2.57	2.54	2.78	3.22	4.06
Price:	high	32.6	32.6	32.4	43.4	41.2	42.0	57.1	62.8
	low	27.0	25.1	27.0	30.5	34.1	35.4	38.8	48.8

Website: www.sysco.com

GROWTH AND INCOME

Target Corporation

Ticker symbol: TGT (NYSE) ❑ S&P rating: A ❑ Value Line financial strength rating: A ❑ Current yield: 3.4% ❑ Dividend raises, past 10 years: 10

Company Profile

You buy stock in a company, and it goes down. You sell stock in a company, and it goes up. As a disciplined investor, you take pause to try to understand what happened and why and to learn what you can from the experience.

You get up, dust yourself off, and move forward, never with emotion, always objectively.

Such is the case with Target. We took it off the *100 Best* list just last year. Why? It wasn't just the disruptive competitive threat, increased uncertainty, and loss of market share levied upon the "bricks and mortar" retail business by our old pal Amazon. We took it off because of their tepid initial response to the disruption. At first they said they would compete by lowering prices. Wrong song. You can't out-discount Amazon and Walmart and others; they are just too big and too vested in price leadership as their primary strategy. To go head to head with these competitors on price would have been nuts. When we read this announcement, during which the rest of the retail industry was getting hammered by the Amazon threat, we decided to head for the exits before the custodial staff locked the doors.

Shortly after the 2018 book was published, we learned of their current strategy, which now centers on a vast $7 billion reformatting and refinishing of their stores to refine the experience, a far better idea than investing billions in cutting prices. We'll describe the remodels in more detail; meanwhile as all investors should do, we hereby cast our emotions aside and admit our mistake. Welcome back, Target!

Target is the nation's second-largest general merchandise retailer and specializes in general merchandise at a discount in a large-store format. The company now operates 1,822 stores in 49 states (Vermont is the only state not represented), including 275 Super Targets with larger and more complete merchandise selections. The greatest concentration of Target stores is in California (15 percent), Texas (8 percent), and Florida (7 percent), with a combined total of about 30 percent of the stores. There is another concentration in the upper Midwest. Target positions itself against its main competitor, Walmart, as a more upscale and trend-conscious "cheap chic" alternative. The typical Target customer has a higher level of disposable income than that of Walmart, which the company courts by offering brand-name merchandise in addition to a series of 29 largely successful owned house brands such as Michael Graves, Market Pantry, Smith & Hawken, Fieldcrest, Room Essentials, and Archer Farms. These brands generate about a third of Target's sales. The company's revenues come from retail exclusively; it sold its credit card operations to TD Bank in 2013 and its pharmacy business to CVS in 2015. Digital sales accounted for 5.5 percent of the total, up from 3.4 percent in 2015 and enough to qualify as a meaningful portion of the business—not just a "me too" convenience factor for customers. The company dropped its money-losing Canadian operations in 2015 and bought local delivery provider Shipt in 2017.

The company is also investing domestically in its food lines, which now account for 20 percent of total 2017 sales. Food is sold in about 70 percent of stores. The total sales breakdown is: 23 percent beauty and household essentials, 20 percent food and pet supplies, 20 percent apparel and accessories, 18 percent hardlines, and 19 percent home furnishings and décor.

Among its peers, Target enjoys a loyal, somewhat upscale customer base, which shops at Target for basic household items, clothing, electronics, furniture, and seasonal items on a fairly regular basis, in addition to the food and beverage operations. They are known for good taste and design in the products they sell. The shopping experience is usually a plus—quiet, clean stores, good quality and attractive merchandising, and name brands with in-house brands sprinkled throughout.

When it came time to repulse the Amazon threat, Target management started with its "compete on price" strategy, then changed to capitalize on their core strengths: design, convenience, and experience. The outcome: a $7 billion "next generation" store design, which was piloted on its flagship Minneapolis and Houston area stores. Elements of the design include separate entrances for pick-up customers (often picking up what they ordered online) and for traditional "showroom" customers. The pick-up entrance will be staffed and have direct access to groceries and a beer and wine shop as well as merchandise pick-up for online customers. It will have dedicated parking spaces. A redesigned grocery department will sport wooden floors, new display cases, and a vastly expanded assortment of fresh produce as well as quick grab-n-go meals. They updated 110 stores during the year, and the goal is to bring about 600 stores—a third of the base—into this format by the end of 2019. The company also plans to open 100 "small-format" stores in urban areas and college towns by the end of 2021. To accompany this initiative, Target has added a redesigned app, mobile wallet technology, and network-tethered store floor employees who can look up items, place orders, and handle checkout right on the sales floor.

Financial Highlights, Fiscal Year 2017

After taking a 0.5 percent dip in 2015, same store sales started on the rise in 2017, up 1.3 percent for the year. In all, including new stores, revenues rose 3.4 percent—not a very exciting year as the economy recovers, but not awful, either. Earnings dipped mainly on store renovation, increased digital fulfillment costs, loss of pharmacy profits, and some store promotion activity; net income dropped about 11 percent for the year. However, on a per-share basis, earnings per share dropped only 6 percent after a 3 percent share buyback. Revenue increases through 2019 will be modest, in the 1–2 percent range. However, gross margin gains will help pave the way to about a 10 percent earnings gain in 2018 and another 2–4 percent in 2019. Share buybacks will continue strong (the company has retired more than 40 percent of its shares since 2003) producing per-share earnings gains exceeding 12 percent in 2018 and 4 percent in 2019. The dividend, which continued to grow in the darkest days of 2015–2016, looks to rise in the high single digits annually.

Reasons to Buy

After a 2013 credit card crisis, and now the online assault, we're pretty convinced this company can find its way through almost any storm. Target is well-managed and counts on its strengths in brand, customer loyalty, and its position in the marketplace.

In fact, Target remains a classic positioning success story. Customers understand and appreciate Target, and it has some of the highest customer satisfaction numbers in the industry. The company continues to take share away from specialty retailers in home lines, clothing, children's items, and other areas. People like the Target brand and associate it with well-managed stores and quality and good taste at a reasonable price with good locations. The strategy to transform a Target store into a "neighborhood fulfillment center"—a pickup and delivery point for goods in stock and goods ordered online—bodes well for store traffic and cross-selling opportunities, thus defusing the Amazon threat; Target wants its place in today's "from the couch" economy.

Better economic conditions and more spending on home and domestic goods should improve Target's market share. We still like the "roadmap"; the overall story remains solid and worthy of returning to the *100 Best* list now that the e-commerce "crisis" has been put in perspective. We admit our mistake in Target's hasty removal and welcome its return.

Reasons for Caution

Target is up against some very tough competitors: Walmart, Costco, and others, and one cannot ignore the Internet's destructive effects on "bricks and mortar" these days, even if the company operates one of the best online sites (www.target.com) out there. It looks like international expansion is off the table, at least for now. We still see some risk in the grocery business, as groceries are very low margin, and the company hasn't really figured out how to make the grocery offering complete with meats and fresh produce. From our personal observations, the grocery department seems pretty empty by comparison to other grocery stores and other parts of Target stores. Gross and operating margins may see some pressure from this business, depending on how valuable the generation of more frequent store visits turns out to be.

SECTOR: **Retail** ▫ BETA COEFFICIENT: **0.71** ▫ 10-YEAR COMPOUND EARNINGS PER-SHARE GROWTH: **4.5%** ▫ 10-YEAR COMPOUND DIVIDENDS PER-SHARE GROWTH: **19.0%**

		2010	2011	2012	2013	2014	2015	2016	2017
Revenues (mil)		67,390	69,865	73,301	72,596	72,618	73,785	69,496	71,879
Net income (mil)		2,830	2,829	2,925	2,060	2,734	2,978	2,920	2,592
Earnings per share		3.88	4.28	4.38	3.21	4.27	4.69	5.01	4.71
Dividends per share		0.84	1.10	1.32	1.58	1.90	2.16	2.32	2.48
Cash flow per share		6.98	7.46	7.82	6.77	7.60	8.62	9.38	8.84
Price:	high	60.7	61.0	65.5	73.5	76.6	85.8	84.1	74.2
	low	46.2	45.3	47.3	55.0	54.7	68.1	65.5	48.6

Website: www.target.com

AGGRESSIVE GROWTH

The Timken Company

Ticker symbol: TKR (NYSE) ▫ Mid Cap ▫ Value Line financial strength rating: B++ ▫ Current yield: 2.4% ▫ Dividend raises, past 10 years: 8

Company Profile

When you operate a 140-ton loaded railroad car, a giant windmill, or a rolling mill in a steel-fabricating plant, you have tremendous frictional forces to overcome, often in harsh environments, for long periods of operating time and with 100 percent reliability required. Without a dependable and efficient friction solution to these moving parts, they can overheat, fail, get out of alignment, and otherwise wreak havoc on your mobile system or stationary machine—not to mention make it cost more to operate. That's where premium-engineered, replaceable bearing assemblies come into play.

On rail cars, for instance, roller bearings—small, tapered, hardened steel bearings "rolling" between the rotating axle and the wheel housing—solved years of headaches (and fires and accidents) caused by oiled brass bearings. Years ago, roller bearings became mandatory for US railroad operation. Similar gains in performance, reliability, reduced friction, and cost came to other businesses and technologies; much the same sort of bearings are used in aircraft wheels, for instance. These specialized, high-value-add bearings—and now application-specific bearing assemblies and housings that hold them—are a critical manufactured and serviced component of most of today's mobile and many of today's stationary systems.

"Rolling Steady" is one apt slogan for Timken, the world's oldest, most established and focused, and largest producer of bearings and bearing products. Over time, they have evolved the product line from relatively simple tapered and ball bearings to a greater number of protected bearing assemblies, or "housed units," which enable solutions in harsher operating environments and create maintenance cost savings for the customer.

The company, after spinning off its steelmaking business in 2014, is made up of two business segments:

- *Mobile Industries* (55 percent of 2017 sales) offers bearings, bearing systems, seals, lubrication devices, and power transmission systems mainly to OEMs and operators of trucks, automobiles, rail cars and locomotives, rotor and fixed-wing aircraft, construction and mining machinery, and certain military items. There had been a separate Aerospace segment; it is now part of Mobile.
- *Process Industries* (45 percent of sales) supplies industrial bearings, bearing systems and assemblies, and power transmission components to OEMs and operators in metals, mining, cement, aggregates production, food processing, wind energy, turbine and oil drilling equipment, material handling equipment, and certain marine applications among many applications. These are stationary machines without wheels, whereas Mobile mainly supports things *with* wheels (or rotors or wings).

The company is still adding to its portfolio of adjacent machinery and mechanical power transmission parts, including chains, belts, gear drives, couplings, brakes, sprockets, clutches, including sales but also service and reconditioning businesses. Like bearings, these are relatively mission-critical, high-value-add components with serviceable lives requiring replacement. In 2017 the company made four small acquisitions to add power takeoff equipment, torsional bearings, lubrication solutions, and a bearing manufacturing operation in India. Timken's strategy is to position as a single-source, branded, full-service vendor for such components. The top five end-user markets are Industrial Machinery (21 percent), Automotive (14 percent), Heavy Truck (9 percent), Agriculture/Turf (9 percent), Rail (8 percent),

Energy (8 percent), and Defense (7 percent). About 57 percent of Timken's business originates in North America; EMEA (19 percent), Asia (17 percent), and Latin America (7 percent) make up the rest.

The product sales mix is about 74 percent bearings and related products, and 16 percent power transmission products and services. About half of total sales come from OEMs (manufacturers of new products) while the other half come from the Distribution and End User channel (mainly replacement and maintenance uses)—suggesting a steady revenue stream after the initial sale.

Financial Highlights, Fiscal Year 2017

After a fairly weak 2016, revenues rose a healthy 12.5 percent, about two-thirds organic and currency and a third from acquisitions. End-market demand was higher in almost all categories. Higher volumes drove higher margins although this was somewhat offset by higher raw material costs; net earnings were ahead a strong 54 percent. Favorable demand trends, especially in the previously soft rail and energy segments, currency tailwinds, and some price increases should produce another 20–25 percent earnings gain in 2018 on a 9–10 percent revenue rise; this growth will moderate a bit in 2019 with a forecasted 9–10 percent earnings on a 5–6 percent revenue increase. Moderate buybacks look to continue, and the company has been paying dividends since its IPO in 1922 and has been raising dividends albeit more moderately lately.

Reasons to Buy

While things have been slow of late, it appears that Timken will be "on a roll" the next couple of years as key customer industries recover and build volume. More generally, we like companies with strong brands and legacies that also happen to supply very key high-value-add components to a value chain. Timken offers such key components in several important value chains, and these components wear out and must be replaced periodically—they aren't just depending on new capital investment for business. In addition, they offer one-stop convenience on a variety of bearings and other "wear" components.

Timken's presentations drive this home—one highlights the rail car example (although the rail business has slowed recently), where a given rail car has a 35-year life and requires bearing replacement every five years bringing $800,000 in lifetime revenue to Timken for a 100-car train (or $8,000 per rail car for life for the million-and-a-half-plus of them out there if you'd prefer to look at it that way). Lifetime value calculations like this, spread across many industries, really bring Timken's value proposition home. The net profit margin of roughly 7–8 percent indicates a differentiated industry (not a commodity) and a strong market position.

Reasons for Caution

Economic cycles, of course, will affect Timken's fortunes, as will competition from foreign manufacturers mainly in China and other parts of Asia. We do like the spread of customers across many industries, however; they aren't overexposed to any one industry such as energy. Despite the recognized brand and market leadership position, the company still has only 5 percent of the overall bearing and 30 percent of the tapered bearing market; competitors are out there. This suggests both a challenge and an opportunity. Finally, higher input prices might become an issue, particularly if trade wars develop—such escalations could also hurt their export business as well.

SECTOR: **Industrials** ❑ BETA COEFFICIENT: **1.56** ❑ 10-YEAR COMPOUND EARNINGS PER-SHARE GROWTH: **0.5%** ❑ 10-YEAR COMPOUND DIVIDENDS PER-SHARE GROWTH: **6.0%**

		2010	2011	2012	2013	2014	2015	2016	2017
Revenues (mil)		4,056	5,170	4,987	4,341	3,076	2,872	2,670	3,003
Net income (mil)		289	457	456	263	234	189	156	208
Earnings per share		2.95	4.59	4.66	2.74	2.55	2.21	1.97	2.63
Dividends per share		0.53	0.78	0.92	0.92	1.00	1.03	1.04	1.06
Cash flow per share		4.89	6.65	6.81	4.93	4.19	3.98	3.70	4.50
Price:	high	49.3	57.8	57.9	64.4	69.5	43.6	41.2	53.1
	low	22.0	30.2	32.6	47.7	37.6	26.4	22.2	40.1

Website: www.timken.com

GROWTH AND INCOME

Total S.A. (ADR)

Ticker symbol: TOT (NYSE) ❑ Large Cap ❑ Value Line financial strength rating: A++ ❑ Current yield: 4.9% ❑ Dividend raises, past 10 years: 6

Company Profile

Total S.A. (S.A. is short for Société Anonyme, which is the French equivalent of "incorporated") is the fourth-largest international oil and gas company. Headquartered in France and primarily traded on the French CAC stock exchange, the company has operations in more than 130 countries. Total is vertically integrated with upstream operations engaged in oil and gas exploration and downstream operations engaged in refining and distribution of petroleum products; the company also has a chemicals and a solar subsidiary.

Upstream activities are geographically well diversified, with exploration occurring in 50 countries and production happening in 30 of them. As a deliberate strategy to spread risk, many of the E&P projects are done through partnerships—if you examine their major productive assets, in most cases they own a 20–50 percent share—not the whole operation.

The largest production regions are (in production-volume sequence for 2016): Europe and Central Asia, including the North Sea, Russia, and Azerbaijan (31 percent), Africa (26 percent), the Middle East and North Africa (21 percent), the Americas (11 percent), and Asia Pacific (10 percent). Liquids (oil) account for about 52 percent of production, while natural gas is 48 percent. The company is a leader in the emerging liquefied natural gas (LNG) market for export. Downstream operations are also worldwide and centered in Europe. Operations include interests in 20 refineries worldwide, with 8 refineries and 72 percent of total refining capacity in Europe. There are also 20 petrochemical plants. Total also operates 16,500 service stations in 65 countries, mainly under the Total, Elf, and Elan names, again weighted toward Europe and North Africa. The downstream presence is also growing in Asia-Pacific (including China), Latin America, and the Caribbean. The company now has a leading market presence in those regions.

Total also has ventures in alternative energy, notably solar. It owns a 57 percent interest in global solar leader SunPower, making it the number two solar operator in the world. Mainly through that venture it designs, manufactures, and distributes cells and solar panels ("upstream") and is active in designing, building, and operating large-scale solar plants ("downstream"). What is thought to be the world's largest solar plant, the Solar Star project, was brought online in the US in 2015; another large plant was brought on in Abu Dhabi in 2013. Long term, Total projects non-hydrocarbon energy sources to comprise 40 percent of total energy demand by the year 2035; the company is managing its energy portfolio accordingly.

By and large, Total used the recent cyclical low in energy prices as an opportunity to fine-tune, acquire, and produce from assets on several fronts. Production expanded holdings in the North Sea and Brazil and ramped up new operations in the Republic of the Congo and Kazakhstan, acquired an LNG business in Europe, expanded service station outlets in Mexico, and launched a new petrochemicals business in South Korea. Total is the first major company to return to production in Iran.

Financial Highlights, Fiscal Year 2017

Total S.A. dealt aggressively with the recent cyclical dip in energy prices, disposing of about $10 billion in nonstrategic assets and acquiring and ramping up a host of others (at a lower cost) as mentioned just previously. This repositioning and the recovery of oil prices put a lot of energy into both revenue and profits for FY2017; revenues jumped 17 percent and net earnings recovered some 33 percent—though neither figure is back to its $100-per-barrel 2014 days. These results are based on $54-per-barrel Brent Crude, up $10 from the previous year; going forward the company has worked to reduce breakeven prices to about $40 while actual prices appear headed higher; revenues are forecast to recover another 15 percent in 2018, 7–9 percent in 2019, and back to 2012–14 levels in the early part of the decade. Net earnings will advance faster; 25–30 percent in 2018, 10–15 percent in 2019, and beyond previous levels in the early 2020s. Investors should enjoy a moderate mix of dividend increases, share buybacks, and debt reduction.

Reasons to Buy

Due to advantageous geographic positioning and effective management during the downturn, Total's recovery appeared sooner and stronger than most. We like their branding and dominance in the key worldwide markets they serve. They seem to manage their business well both for the short and long term.

Reasons for Caution

The downsides are pretty much still the same. Risks still come from (1) oil prices, (2) dollar versus euro fluctuations, and (3) international tensions. More aggression on Russia's part, both militarily and economically, would add risk to a situation already destabilized by the usual Middle East tensions, European economic softness, and European Central Bank adventures. Finally, the company took on long-term debt to get it through the down cycle, albeit less than some of its competitors.

More generally, we remain cautious on investing in foreign companies because of differences in management style and accounting rules; they aren't necessarily bad but are difficult to understand and follow. Company information is hard to sift through; the website is mainly a collection of PR pieces and offers less in accessible concrete facts and information than most. Antiquated

European pension rules and other labor practices could also be a disadvantage, as could recent isolationist movements. Total has a bit more risk than some of the other majors; however, we still think the rewards outweigh the risks.

SECTOR: **Energy** ❑ BETA COEFFICIENT: **0.79** ❑ 10-YEAR COMPOUND EARNINGS PER-SHARE GROWTH: **-5.0%** ❑ 10-YEAR COMPOUND DIVIDENDS PER-SHARE GROWTH: **3.5%**

	2010	2011	2012	2013	2014	2015	2016	2017
Revenues (bil)	186	216	234	228	212	143	128	149
Net income (bil)	14.0	15.9	15.9	14.2	12.8	5.1	6.1	8.5
Earnings per share	6.24	7.05	7.01	6.28	5.63	2.19	2.52	3.36
Dividends per share	2.93	3.12	2.98	3.10	3.21	2.73	2.70	2.72
Cash flow per share	11.25	11.37	12.46	11.57	10.90	9.76	8.07	9.72
Price: high	67.5	64.4	57.1	62.4	74.2	55.9	51.4	57.1
low	43.1	40.0	41.8	45.9	48.4	40.9	39.1	48.2

Website: www.total.com

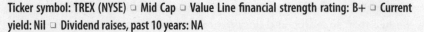

AGGRESSIVE GROWTH

NEW FOR 2019

Trex Company, Inc.

Ticker symbol: TREX (NYSE) ❑ Mid Cap ❑ Value Line financial strength rating: B+ ❑ Current yield: Nil ❑ Dividend raises, past 10 years: NA

Company Profile

We may be a year or two late with this new pick, but we were looking for an excellent company to follow in the footsteps of brand champ WD-40. We were looking for a company with a great brand, high and expanding margins, excellent management, low debt, strong focus, and growing possibilities in the marketplace. We landed on Trex, a dominant brand and a very successful play in the rapidly emerging non–wood decking and outdoor living products market.

"Engineering what's next in outdoor living" is the apt slogan of Trex, the world's largest manufacturer of composite wood decking. Composite deck boards and related materials are milled from a composite of mostly recycled sawdust and polyethylene, 95 percent recycled, in fact. Its "Wood-Polymer" lumber provides the appearance of wood (or better) and its benefits without the need of maintenance in the form of protective sealants—it is weatherproof and maintains its look for life. ("Twice the life of wood at half the cost.")

The products, all manufactured in the United States, include decking, fencing, railings, stairwell materials, trim, steel framing, outdoor furniture, and outdoor lighting materials, mainly for residential but increasingly for commercial and public sector (i.e., parks, etc.) use. The three decking product lines, roughly representing good, better, and best, include Trex Select, Trex Enhance, and Trex Transcend and provide several color and texture appearance options from gray weathered pine to Brazilian Ipe. Earlier versions of composite decking products tended to fade and stain over time; the more recent products do not.

Trex has traditionally been marketed through about 3,000 traditional lumber yards and building products dealers; over the years it has stepped up its presence, both in scale and brand presence, in the building products superstores, namely Home Depot, Lowe's, and similar retailers. It is now stocked in some 6,700 locations worldwide. The informative website helps not only with product selection but with deck design and dealer and contractor selection.

Financial Highlights, Fiscal Year 2017

Mix together brand recognition, market share growth, quality and process improvements, and wider distribution with a manufacturing process hungry for volume to make the most of fixed costs and you get what we call "scale" or "operating leverage" and thus significantly higher gross margins. Higher gross margins on higher sales is a powerful formula for success. So it is for Trex, which has grown volume 44 percent in the past three years and grown gross margins almost 9 points along the way, from 35.8 percent to 44.3 percent.

The year 2017 was an important stop on this journey. Sales rose 18 percent, operating margins rose a full 4 percent, and resulting net income rose a solid 40 percent. No complaints, and the increases and improvements look to continue, albeit perhaps at a slower rate: 2018 forecasts call for profits in the 20–25 percent range higher on a 10 percent sales increase; 2019 calls for a more modest 3–5 percent profit increase on a similar revenue rise. We think these figures could be conservative in light of the "macro" facts presented earlier. It does appear that dividends will be "nil" for some time, but the company okayed another $2.9 billion for buybacks, which would lower the share count more than 10 percent at today's prices.

Reasons to Buy

What attracts us to Trex is not only the beauty and resilience of these products for both new and replacement construction but also the fact that Trex is not only taking market share from other composite decking manufacturers (from 36 percent in 2012 to 45 percent in 2016); it is also taking share from the much larger traditional lumber market as appearance, maintenance, and now commodity pricing for lumber play a role in the choice. Yet it still only has 17 percent of the market versus wood, offering considerable opportunity.

Moreover, beyond the obvious consideration for outdoor living spaces on new construction, there were millions of decks built in the 1970s, 1980s, and 1990s well in need of replacement. According to the company, repair and remodeling projects are expected to grow 7.5 percent by the end of 2018. If that wasn't enough, the trend toward building attractive and useful outdoor living spaces continues to grow (again according to Trex, 34 percent of home improvement spending is on exterior improvements). These trends all provide substantial tailwinds for Trex. Finally, we like the transformation of inexpensive recycled materials into a high-value-add product with a strong brand—which by the way is becoming more prominent in the nation's large home improvement stores and is starting to gain traction overseas as well. Growing market, great brand, improved margins, cash flow and operating leverage, zero debt, recycled material: what's not to like?

Reasons for Caution

The main thing not to like is the price of the stock, which has been on a run commensurate to the business. A slowdown even to a more modest growth rate could hurt. The stock is a bit volatile and tends to pull back whenever there is bad news on the housing industry (which doesn't affect the company as much as one might think since a lot of its business is in replacement). We're only sorry we didn't bring this one to you sooner.

SECTOR: Materials ❑ **BETA COEFFICIENT: 2.30** ❑ **10-YEAR COMPOUND EARNINGS PER-SHARE GROWTH: 22.0%** ❑ **10-YEAR COMPOUND DIVIDENDS PER-SHARE GROWTH: NA**

		2010	2011	2012	2013	2014	2015	2016	2017
Revenues (mil)		318	267	307	344	392	441	480	565
Net income (mil)		10.1	(5.6)	26.6	48.2	41.5	48.1	67.8	95.1
Earnings per share		0.34	(0.14)	0.78	1.41	1.27	1.52	2.29	3.22
Dividends per share		—	—	—	—	—	—	—	—
Cash flow per share		1.00	0.40	1.28	1.93	1.94	2.02	2.80	3.61
Price:	high	13.3	17.0	20.4	41.5	44.8	57.7	72.2	118.6
	low	7.7	7.3	11.3	19.0	25.1	31.7	31.1	61.6

Website: www.trex.com

AGGRESSIVE GROWTH

Tupperware Brands, Inc.

Ticker symbol: TUP (NASDAQ) ❑ Mid Cap ❑ Value Line financial strength rating: A ❑ Current yield: 5.7% ❑ Dividend raises, past 10 years: 6

Company Profile

Every now and then you snap a lid off of one of our *100 Best Stocks* only to find a stinky, moldy mess. You may choose to throw out the whole container by discarding the stock forever, or you may choose to clean it and use it again—that is what we plan to do with Tupperware.

We added TUP last year as a known and high-prospect household products name to replace the unexciting, overpriced Clorox. This year we are doing some more housecleaning in the household products sector, and in looking at Tupperware's prospects *going forward* from a dismal 2017, we decided to keep it in the pantry.

We're all familiar with Tupperware. The famous lids that snap on with a solid click. The famous lids that, inevitably, somehow get separated from the rest of the container, giving us a drawer full of mismatched lids and containers. Tupperware kind of disappeared for a while as their direct sale "Tupperware Party" model languished in favor of the big-box discount shopping model. They went and hid overseas, in fact, and have done quite well there. But we think their brand and product quality are poised to reemerge in the domestic market—and you can't order Tupperware on Amazon Prime, or anywhere else for that matter. As bricks-and-mortar retail suffers, we think Tupperware and its sales model can prosper.

Tupperware Brands Corporation makes the familiar high-quality plastic household containers as regular products and distributes them almost exclusively through their vast direct-to-consumer model—a.k.a. Tupperware parties. They branched into the home-sale cosmetics business with the acquisition of Sara Lee beauty products in 2005; hence the recent renaming of the company to "Tupperware Brands," not just Tupperware. They have added several brands since, giving a total of five cosmetics brands including Avroy Schlain, Fuller Cosmetics, NatureCare, Nutrimetics, and Nuvo (they sold BeautiControl in 2017). These aren't exactly household brands (to us, anyway), but they come in nice packages, are relatively high end, and fit the Tupperware sales model well.

What's most interesting about Tupperware is its international presence. The 2017 breakdown of sales and profits (in order) is telling: Asia-Pacific

(33 percent of sales, 46 percent of profits), Europe (24 percent, 13 percent), South America (19 percent, 24 percent), and North America (24 percent, 17 percent). The company estimates that 69 percent of sales come from emerging markets, China and Brazil being the largest. Realizing that "North America" includes Mexico and Canada, the company in total has realized 90–92 percent of its total revenues from international markets over the past five years. Unfortunately, we don't get a clear breakout of the cosmetics business versus traditional housewares; segment reporting is on a geographic basis. In total, Tupperware is distributed in 100 countries worldwide by some 3.1 million Tupperware party hosts (dealers).

Financial Highlights, Fiscal Year 2017

When you open the lid on FY2017, do it carefully—it was a stinko year albeit not as bad as the reported numbers show. The company cleaned house with a restructuring and process reengineering exercise, a goodwill write-off for its Fuller Mexico business, the sale of BeautiControl, all offset by a gain on the sale of land near its headquarters. Sales were up 2 percent, and operating margins held pretty steady, but the roughly $100 million in write-offs spun reported earnings downward by about a third. These things happen, but we take umbrage with management for not putting these into last year's forecast. What kept this issue afloat for us was the forecast going forward: 2018 earnings 10 percent higher than 2016 on a 4 percent sales increase, and 13–15 percent higher again in 2019 on another 3–4 percent increase in revenues. Additionally, the generous dividend, while stuck in place for the last four years, is slated to rise in the mid to high single digits annually. This qualifies TUP for "Dividend Aggressor" status.

Reasons to Buy

Tupperware is a play on (1) international business, (2) a strong brand, (3) a sales model relatively immune to the shift to online buying, and (4) a high dividend and an attractive valuation at current prices. We like the rapid growth and acceptance in emerging markets, particularly the "BRIC"— Brazil, Russia, India, China—markets, an investing theme long out of favor but we feel ripe for recovery by 2019. We also think a domestic resurgence is likely. A weaker dollar will provide a tailwind. Put simply, the growth prospects exceed those of our replaced household products standbys by a wide margin—it just delayed its start by a year in our opinion. The business is well run and profitable with healthy cash flows and a focus on shareholder returns.

Reasons for Caution

With Tupperware's preponderance in international markets, obviously unfavorable trade policies can keep a lid snapped down tight on things. A backlash against a more isolationist US—and its companies—could hurt, especially in emerging markets. As noted earlier, management disappointed us with the poor visibility on 2017 results. We hope that doesn't become a pattern and that indeed they *have* truly cleaned house in 2017 (although there are some modest restructuring charges in the 2018 and 2019 forecasts). Put simply: guys (and gals) on the management team, you must regain our trust. As relatively frugal consumers, we find (and have always found) the plastic products to be a bit pricey, but they are appealing to rising emerging market middle classes. We'll admit that we don't really understand the cosmetics business; if you do, please write us at the email provided in the introduction.

SECTOR: **Consumer Staples**   ◻ BETA COEFFICIENT: **1.57**   ◻ 10-YEAR COMPOUND EARNINGS PER-SHARE GROWTH: **10.5%**   ◻ 10-YEAR COMPOUND DIVIDENDS PER-SHARE GROWTH: **12.0%**

	2010	2011	2012	2013	2014	2015	2016	2017
Revenues (mil)	2,300	2,585	2,584	2,672	2,606	2,834	2,213	2,256
Net income (mil)	226	218	193	274	214	186	224	145
Earnings per share	3.53	3.55	3.42	5.17	4.20	3.69	4.41	2.79
Dividends per share	1.00	1.20	1.44	2.48	2.72	2.72	2.72	2.72
Cash flow per share	4.39	4.74	4.49	6.54	5.60	4.92	5.55	3.95
Price: high	54.2	72.0	67.8	97.1	94.6	72.9	66.9	74.4
low	36.1	45.2	50.9	63.6	58.2	47.8	42.6	53.2

Website: www.tupperwarebrands.com

CONSERVATIVE GROWTH

Union Pacific Corporation

Ticker symbol: UNP (NYSE)   ◻ Large Cap   ◻ Value Line financial strength rating: A++   ◻ Current yield: 2.2%   ◻ Dividend raises, past 10 years: 10

Company Profile

Union Pacific has been a familiar name and logo in the railroad business since its inception during the Civil War. With about 32,000 miles of track covering 23 states in the western two-thirds of the US, today's Union Pacific Railroad, the primary subsidiary of the Union Pacific Corporation, describes itself as

"America's Premier Railroad Franchise." The route system is anchored by Gulf Coast and West Coast ports and areas in between and has coordinated schedules and gateways with other lines in the eastern US, Canada, and Mexico.

With 10,000 customers, a large number in today's era of trainload-sized shipments, UNP has a more diversified customer and revenue mix than the other rail companies, including the other three of the "big four" railroads: Burlington Northern Santa Fe, Norfolk Southern, and CSX. Energy (mainly Powder River Basin and Colorado coal) accounts for 13 percent of revenues (down from 16 percent in 2015 and 18 percent in 2014); Intermodal (trucks or containers on flatcars), 19 percent; Agricultural, 19 percent; Industrial, 21 percent; Chemicals, 18 percent; and Automotive, 10 percent of FY2017 revenues. As coal declines the company is putting more emphasis on diversifying the traffic base and recapturing smaller single-car shipments, mostly of manufactured goods, once given up to truckers. New trucking rules requiring time of service logging technology for trucks will put a tailwind behind this shift. Indeed, the "Industrial" segment rose from 18 percent in 2016 to 21 percent in 2017 as evidence of this change.

Union Pacific has long been an innovator in railroad technology, including motive power, communications and technology automation, physical plant, community relations, and marketing. Improved volumes and efficiencies dropped the operating ratio to an all-time best of 63.0 (that is, variable costs are 63 percent of revenues), the best in the industry and despite a 22 percent rise in fuel costs. By comparison, this closely watched ratio was 63.5 in 2016, 63.1 in 2015, 63.5 in 2014, 65.0 in 2013, 67.8 in 2012, and 70.6 in 2011—you get the idea. A low operating ratio allows a solid contribution to the substantial fixed costs of owning and running a railroad. This success has translated to continued strong operating margins, which of course have helped earnings and cash flows and in turn have funded physical plant improvements and shareholder returns over time.

The company also invests in marketing and community relations. One example is the steam-powered "Heritage Fleet" program, through which the company operates excursion trains with vintage equipment on selected lines. Literally thousands of people (and current and prospective customers) gather trackside in every town along the way as these beautiful trains roll through. The company recently began a five-year program to restore a "Big Boy" steam locomotive, the largest ever used in regular service (of course, for the UP originally) for a Golden Spike sesquicentennial rollout in 2019. Such public relations efforts show an extraordinary measure of pride and an appreciation for heritage and community. We continue to applaud this effort.

Financial Highlights, Fiscal Year 2017

After a relatively weak 2016, improved industrial shipments, coal and commodity volumes, import/export traffic, and selective rate increases all led to a 7 percent increase in 2017 revenues on a 2 percent rise in car loadings. Improved volume and efficiency led to the improved operating ratio mentioned before, which in turn led to a 9.6 percent net profit gain. Per-share earnings, helped along by a 4 percent buyback, chugged ahead 14 percent. Softness in auto and grain shipments in 2018 will keep revenue gains in the 4–5 percent range, with a similar figure forecast for 2019. The 2017 Tax Cut and Jobs Act will help UNP and other capital-intensive industries more than most; net earnings are expected to throttle up some 26 percent in 2018 followed by a more typical 7 percent gain in 2019.

Cash flows remain strong and should support persistent buybacks; the company has retired 22 percent of its shares since 2009 and has plans to retire 15 percent more by 2020. The dividend continues to enjoy regular increases.

Reasons to Buy

Put simply, whether or not you enjoy watching trains, this company has performed well even in bad times and has also returned plenty of cash to shareholders. After hitting some slow orders in 2016, it seems on track to emerge stronger than ever.

UNP is an extraordinarily well-managed company and has become more efficient and at the same time more user friendly to its customers and to the general public. The company continues to make gains at the expense of the trucking industry, and new short- and long-distance intermodal services move higher-valued goods more quickly and cost-effectively; we see a steady shift toward this business especially as the new trucking rules take effect. A continuing recovery in the energy and other commodity and basic materials industries will also help. The company has a solid and diverse traffic base and continues to have a good brand and reputation in the industry. The company got an early start expanding and modernizing its physical plant and technology base; that has paid off well and will continue to do so.

Reasons for Caution

No doubt, some of their coal traffic has shifted away forever. Railroads are chiefly a commodity-hauling business, and when commodities are down, they suffer. The company has had to adjust and execute well both in marketing and operations to backfill this lost volume; traffic once lost is hard to get back.

Railroads are and will always be economically sensitive because of commodity revenue and their high fixed-cost structure. They also have significant headline risk—a single event like a derailment or spill can put them in a bad public eye or worse, tangle them up in regulation, lawsuits, and unplanned costs. Regulation and mandates for Positive Train Control and other safety features are expensive. Longer-term factors also include effects from new Trump administration trade policies, which could hurt import traffic, and the widening of the Panama Canal, which has shifted some Asian import/export traffic to southern and eastern ports and away from the West Coast.

Railroads will always struggle to put the right amount of capacity on the ground—too little causes service problems and delays; too much eats into profits. After a soft year and some overcapacity in 2016, the pendulum has swung again toward some capacity constraints—2017 average train speeds were down 5 percent from 2016—but the company seems to have made the right capital improvements for the long term.

SECTOR: **Transportation** ▫ BETA COEFFICIENT: **0.84** ▫ 10-YEAR COMPOUND EARNINGS PER-SHARE GROWTH: **18.0%** ▫ 10-YEAR COMPOUND DIVIDENDS PER-SHARE GROWTH: **21.5%**

		2010	2011	2012	2013	2014	2015	2016	2017
Revenues (mil)		16,965	19,557	20,926	21,953	23,988	21,813	19,941	21,240
Net income (mil)		2,780	3,292	3,943	4,388	5,180	4,702	4,233	4,638
Earnings per share		2.77	3.36	4.14	4.71	5.75	5.41	5.07	5.80
Dividends per share		0.66	0.97	1.25	1.48	1.91	2.20	2.26	2.48
Cash flow per share		4.34	5.11	6.07	6.76	8.02	7.91	7.69	8.60
Price:	high	47.9	53.9	64.6	84.1	123.6	124.5	106.6	136.3
	low	30.2	38.9	52.0	63.7	82.5	74.8	67.1	101.1

Website: www.up.com

AGGRESSIVE GROWTH

UnitedHealth Group, Inc.

Ticker symbol: UNH (NYSE) ▫ Large Cap ▫ Value Line financial strength rating: A++ ▫ Current yield: 1.2% ▫ Dividend raises, past 10 years: 8

Company Profile

UnitedHealth Group is the parent company of a number of health insurers and service organizations. It is the largest publicly traded health insurance company in the United States, with $201 billion in revenue reported in 2017, a number six US company ranking on the *Fortune* 500 list, and a membership in the Dow Jones Industrial Average.

The company operates in two major business segments: UnitedHealthcare (health insurance and benefits) and Optum (health services), which, combined, touch about 78 million people worldwide in 50 US states and 125 countries globally.

UnitedHealthcare provides traditional and Medicare-based health benefit and insurance plans for individuals and employers, covering approximately 27 million individuals, with about 400 national employer accounts and 200,000 other smaller employer accounts. The company estimates that it serves more than half of the *Fortune* 100 companies list. The company, mainly through this unit, has been an active acquirer of other familiar healthcare and insurance brands over the years. The UnitedHealthcare insurance business in total accounts for 81 percent of FY2017 revenues and 56 percent of profits.

The UnitedHealthcare business unit actively markets traditional individual and employee health plans ("Employer & Individual"), which account for about 32 percent of the UnitedHealthcare branded insurance products. Even larger at 40 percent today is the senior and military market ("Medicare & Retirement"), with a growing assortment of Medicare Advantage, Medicare Part D, and Medicare supplement plans. The recently added TRICARE insurance program for active and retired military is a large contributor to this subsegment. The rest of the insurance unit is made up by Community & State (21 percent, programs for economically disadvantaged, mainly Medicaid) and Global (5 percent).

Beyond the insurance business lies the large and rapidly growing health services businesses, marketed under the Optum brand umbrella. This segment is far and away big enough to be a separate company and is a rapidly growing and increasingly important part of the overall UNH business offering.

Optum delivers these health services through three separate businesses. OptumHealth is an operating "information and technology–based health population management solution," deploying mostly remote telesupport for well care, mental health, ongoing disease management, and substance abuse programs to 91 million individuals. The OptumRx business is a pharmacy benefits provider serving 65 million customers and a network of 67,000 pharmacies and other outlets with about 600 million prescriptions annually, while OptumInsight is a management information, analytics, and process-improvement arm providing an assortment of services for health plans, physicians, hospitals, and life science research. Of the total Optum-branded business of $91 billion (43 percent of total company revenue and 9 percent ahead of FY2016), Rx accounts for the lion's share at $63 billion, while OptumHealth, which grew 22 percent again in FY2017, weighs in at $20 billion and OptumInsight at $83 billion with 10 percent annual growth. Although these numbers may seem small in the context of UNH's total $201 billion annual revenue footprint, they are sizeable businesses when looked at individually; all would be sizeable and significant standalone businesses. The Optum umbrella brand is gaining in prominence, and even has its own web presence at www.optum.com.

UnitedHealth Group has been a leader in process, delivery, and cost improvement and a recognized innovator in the industry. The company has moved aggressively to offer tools to manage and contain costs in the healthcare system, mostly through the Optum business. The company sits on top of a mountain of healthcare data and is putting it to good use and has emerged as a leader in developing remote and preventative care models.

UNH's experience and participation in the Affordable Care Act has been curtailed substantially—from 34 to three states in 2017—citing costs and mounting losses. It remains to be seen how the company participates in the ACA's future.

Financial Highlights, Fiscal Year 2017

Price increases, market share gains, membership gains and growth across the Optum business led to a 9 percent revenue gain for FY2017; this would have been higher if they hadn't exited most of the ACA business. Moderating healthcare costs, scale in the Optum businesses, and tax changes helped to ring up a substantial 28 percent gain in net income. Revenues are forecast ahead 10–12 percent in 2018 and another 8–10 percent in 2019; net earnings, again helped by tax changes, are expected to rise 20–22 percent in 2018; it slows but doesn't stop in 2019 with an 11–15 percent forecast gain as volumes and margins improve on all fronts. Dividend growth prospects are equally healthy, and share repurchase, while slowing some, should chip in as well.

Reasons to Buy

This bellwether company is one of the most solid, diverse, and innovative enterprises in the health insurance industry. Health insurers are doing a better job of understanding and managing their businesses through utilization management and other initiatives instead of just passing costs on; these initiatives are bearing fruit. As well, the scale of UNH's operation gives it tremendous leverage when negotiating for the services of healthcare providers.

Meanwhile, like Aetna, UNH brings a fair amount of innovation to the marketplace, primarily through its Optum offerings. We like its initiatives to make use of its own "big data" with analytics; the size of its database and the tools it possesses can deliver efficiency improvements, and even slight efficiency improvements can help the bottom line substantially.

Reasons for Caution

With the merger of Aetna and CVS, the healthcare cost investigation and consortium being launched by Amazon, Berkshire Hathaway, and JPMorgan Chase, and other possible mergers and acquisitions, the once-stable healthcare payer and provider landscape is suddenly starting to shift, and we don't know where this ends. UNH already has a pharmacy benefits operation (OptumRx) so isn't likely to grow in this direction—but who knows which way the winds blow; the company could still pull off a large acquisition somewhere in this space, and it's difficult to predict how these acquisitions will work out in the end. UNH may feel compelled to follow suit, and whether they do or not, competition is likely to strengthen. The company is vulnerable to shifts in public opinion and to new regulation (and pulling in almost $10 billion in annual profit doesn't help). Finally, while probably justified based on performance, the stock has made new highs in most of the last year and could correct on bad news or a large acquisition.

SECTOR: **Healthcare** ❑ BETA COEFFICIENT: **0.74** ❑ 10-YEAR COMPOUND EARNINGS PER-SHARE
GROWTH: **10.5%** ❑ 10-YEAR COMPOUND DIVIDENDS PER-SHARE GROWTH: **55.0%**

		2010	2011	2012	2013	2014	2015	2016	2017
Revenues (bil)		94.1	101.9	110.6	122.5	130.5	157.1	184.8	201.2
Net income (mil)		4,633	5,142	5,526	5,625	5,619	5,947	7,792	9,928
Earnings per share		4.10	4.73	5.28	5.50	5.70	6.15	8.05	10.07
Dividends per share		0.41	0.61	0.80	1.05	1.41	1.88	2.38	10.68
Cash flow per share		5.25	5.86	6.67	7.09	7.44	7.88	10.34	12.55
Price:	high	38.1	53.5	60.8	75.9	104.0	126.2	164.0	231.6
	low	27.1	36.4	49.8	51.4	69.6	95.0	107.5	156.1

Website: www.unitedhealthgroup.com

CONSERVATIVE GROWTH

United Parcel Service, Inc.

Ticker symbol: UPS (NYSE) ❑ Large Cap ❑ Value Line financial strength rating: A ❑ Current yield: 3.4% ❑ Dividend raises, past 10 years: 10

Company Profile

UPS is the world's largest integrated ground and air package delivery carrier. Over the years, UPS and rival FedEx have converged on the same business from different directions—FedEx being an air company getting ever more into the ground business; UPS being a ground business taking to the air. That convergence is now nearly complete. Both companies continue to build international capabilities, invest in technology to track shipments, and provide logistics services beyond a basic assortment of transportation services. UPS derives just over 62 percent of revenues from US package operations, 20 percent from international package operations, and 18 percent from Supply Chain & Freight, an assortment of bundled logistics and supply-chain services and solutions. Of the 63 percent US package operations, about 72 percent of that is ground, 18 percent is next-day air and the rest "deferred" (two days or longer) air.

The company operates 523 aircraft and 108,000 ground vehicles ("package cars"), most of the familiar brown variety. They serve more than ten million shipping customers in 220 countries with an assortment of priority to deferred services, with 154,000 domestic and international entry points including 39,000 drop boxes, 1,000 customer service centers, and 5,000 independently owned "UPS Store" (formerly "Mail Boxes Etc.") storefronts. The company delivered 19.1 million packages per day worldwide in 2016.

Once thought to be old-fashioned and averse to innovation, the company has invested in sophisticated package-tracking systems and links for customers to tie into them. An example is My Choice, which allows a customer to control the timing of deliveries mid-service—by smartphone if they choose—so no more waiting half a day at home for a delivery that might come any time (hallelujah!). The service, which is now used by over 30 million recipients, is a nice perk for a consumer waiting for an e-commerce shipment as well as a savings for the company, avoiding multiple delivery attempts and possible door-front theft. The company also offers specialized logistics services for vertical markets, such as the auto industry "Autogistics" and the healthcare industry, retail, high tech, and more. Other new services include UPS Worldwide Express Freight Midday, offering a 12 to 2 p.m.

delivery commit time from all 71 origin countries to 35 destination countries for urgent palletized shipments over 150 pounds, typically one to three days with customs clearance included.

The company has embarked on numerous revenue and cost-optimization campaigns, among them a detailed analysis of the cost drivers for their businesses. As an example, they found that one mile saved in their Small Package Pickup & Delivery business across all delivery routes saves $50 million per year; one minute saved would save $14.6 million per year, and one minute of idle time reduced would save $515K. The company continues to use analytics to predict and optimize route selection and other aspects of the delivery network. The first phase of "Orion," dubbed as the "world's largest operations research project," is now complete. Another project underway in 2018 calls for opening or remodeling 18 new US facilities including three new ground hubs. These initiatives, now all comprising the "UPS Smart Logistics Network" will be crucial to maintaining service and margins as the industry evolves to a higher percentage of single-package to single-address shipments with the e-commerce surge, while traditional users require ever more flexible logistics solutions.

Financial Highlights, Fiscal Year 2017

Despite the persistent shift toward e-commerce, which presents challenges to margins and thus profits, UPS rang up another good year in 2017. Rising volumes (just over 5 percent) and higher prices led to an 8.2 percent revenue gain; earnings, tempered by higher labor and fuel prices, delivered a 3 percent gain. Looking forward, e-commerce and other volume gains will keep revenue growth in the 5–6 percent range through 2019, with substantial tax benefits, price increases, and operational improvements leading to an 18–20 percent net profit gain in 2018 and an 8 percent rise in 2019. Dividend growth is healthy; the dividend has been raised 47 consecutive years—notable in the up-and-down transportation industry.

Reasons to Buy

The "fastest ship in the shipping business" continues to also be one of the most stable; UPS continues to position itself as the standard logistics provider of the world. The mainstay businesses are cyclical but sound; the emerging e-commerce business is gaining critical mass (volumes rising to the point of optimal efficiency) and will lead to better capacity utilization overall. In general, we applaud the use of technology to get "details" right on the operational front.

We are also fans of its logistics and supply-chain management businesses and the many innovations in that space, as the push for many customers to optimize this part of their business will lead them to UPS's front door.

Finally, the ability to raise prices enough not to just cover cost increases but also to boost profits tells us that demand is strong and getting stronger, and that UPS is positioned well to capitalize on that demand. "Big Brown" has many tailwinds at its back.

Reasons for Caution

Competition in this industry is fierce. The Postal Service is getting more aggressive in marketing its small-package and logistics services as it sees the writing on the wall for traditional mail services, and rival FedEx has made gains on UPS's traditional turf with their ground and Freight services and their SmartPost program (see FedEx, another *100 Best Stock*). Also of note is Amazon's saber rattling to get into the freight business itself—apparently, they have started acquiring aircraft and other assets. We think they would have far to go to displace the well-established supply-chain network of a UPS or a FedEx, but their actions (or threat) could force price concessions, and Amazon has been known to be surprisingly successful when attacking adjacent markets (like cloud computing). Labor relations and pension funding both bear watching. Of course, fuel prices are a wild card, and have already turned back upward a little.

SECTOR: **Transportation** ❑ BETA COEFFICIENT: **0.91** ❑ 10-YEAR COMPOUND EARNINGS PER-SHARE GROWTH: **4.5%** ❑ 10-YEAR COMPOUND DIVIDENDS PER-SHARE GROWTH: **8.0%**

	2010	2011	2012	2013	2014	2015	2016	2017
Revenues (mil)	49,545	53,105	54,127	55,438	58,232	58,363	60,906	65,872
Net income (mil)	3,570	4,213	4,389	4,372	4,389	4,923	5,104	5,259
Earnings per share	3.56	4.25	4.53	4.61	4.75	5.43	5.75	6.01
Dividends per share	1.88	2.08	2.28	2.48	2.68	2.92	3.12	3.32
Cash flow per share	5.43	6.60	6.90	6.75	6.97	7.81	8.36	8.65
Price: high	73.9	77.0	84.9	105.4	113.1	114.4	120.4	125.2
low	55.6	60.7	75.0	75.0	93.2	93.6	87.3	102.1

Website: www.ups.com

CONSERVATIVE GROWTH

United Technologies Corporation

Ticker symbol: UTX (NYSE) ❑ Large Cap ❑ Value Line financial strength rating: A++ ❑ Current yield: 2.3% ❑ Dividend raises, past 10 years: 10

Company Profile

"We do the BIG THINGS the right way" is the apt slogan of United Technologies, the large and diversified provider of mostly high-technology products to the aerospace and building systems industries throughout the world, which are sold to an assortment of mostly commercial and public sector customers. To many, it is an aerospace company, to others it is a producer of key pieces, parts, and systems for the building industry; to most investors it is a broadly diversified industrial conglomerate.

In 2015, the organizational sands shifted at UTX, with a management shakeup and the long-awaited sale of the Sikorsky helicopter unit. That turned out to be a good move as helicopter demand had crash-landed with the decline in offshore drilling and the necessary logistical support in the oil industry. That was followed by a fairly vast restructuring, reorganizing, and streamlining of existing assets, which has mostly concluded. Then Honeywell (another *100 Best Stock*) made a $90 billion merger offer for the company, which was turned down mostly citing "regulatory concerns." This offer underscored the underlying value of the company and stimulated management to continue its streamlining. Then the company made a bigger move, announcing the $30 billion acquisition of Rockwell Collins, a major aerospace technology supplier—a big bet on the core aerospace business. This merger should be completed by 2019 but is not included in the analysis presented here.

Currently UTX consists of four business units:

- UTC Aerospace Systems (25 percent of FY2017 revenues) produces aircraft electrical power generation and distribution systems; engine and flight controls; propulsion systems; environmental controls for aircraft, spacecraft, and submarines; auxiliary power units; space life-support systems; and industrial products including mechanical power transmissions, compressors, metering devices, and fluid handling equipment. It also provides product support and maintenance and offers repair services.
- Pratt & Whitney (27 percent) produces large and small commercial and military jet engines, spare parts, rocket engines, and space propulsion systems, and industrial gas turbines, and it performs product support,

specialized engine maintenance and overhaul, and repair services for airlines, air forces, and corporate fleets. P&W's commercial engines power about 25 percent of the world's passenger air fleet, and its military engines power fighters and transport aircraft for 29 world armed forces.

- UTC Climate (30 percent) produces heating, ventilating, and air conditioning (HVAC) equipment for commercial, industrial, and residential buildings; HVAC replacement parts and services; building controls; and commercial, industrial, and transport refrigeration equipment, much of it under the "Carrier" brand name. The group also includes the old UTC Fire & Security business, which provides security and fire protection systems; integration, installation, and servicing of intruder alarms, access control, and video surveillance and monitoring; response and security personnel services; and installation and servicing of fire detection and suppression systems.

- Otis (21 percent) is one of UTX's most recognizable brands. It designs and manufactures elevators, escalators, moving walkways, and shuttle systems, and performs related installation, maintenance, and repair services; it also provides modernization products and service for elevators and escalators, maintaining some 1.9 million elevators, escalators, and moving walkways worldwide.

Persistent rumors and the minitrend toward "deconglomeratization," a move toward shedding businesses away from the core business and concentrating on the important few raise speculation that UTX itself may split after the Rockwell Collins merger, spinning off the current aerospace business along with Rockwell into a new separate entity and perhaps splitting the remaining businesses as well. Stay tuned.

The company continues to provide useful breakdowns of their end markets to help understand its businesses:

- Commercial & Industrial: 50 percent
- Commercial Aerospace: 37 percent
- Military Aerospace & Space: 19 percent

These figures reveal that UTX is not as tied to military and government contracts as many think. About 61 percent of sales are outside the US, and about 46 percent of sales are for aftermarket purposes (rough translation: maintenance and repair).

Financial Highlights, Fiscal Year 2017

Stronger sales pretty much across the board and a steady currency led to a decent top-line gain for FY2017; total sales were up 4.5 percent and organic sales rose 4 percent. FY2018 and 2019 sales are projected ahead 4–6 percent not including Rockwell. Restructuring charges, an unfavorable contract dispute at Pratt & Whitney, a recall in the Climate unit and other drags kept net income slightly behind 2016, 3.5 percent behind, in fact. Projections call for earnings to rise approximately 8–10 percent annually through 2019, erasing the 2017 hiccup. Healthy buybacks in the 3–4 percent range will help per-share earnings more, while the dividend continues to rise in the mid-single-digit range.

Reasons to Buy

UTX had been a question mark for the past couple of years with the relatively tumultuous management and soft earnings performance. That was so 2015; we have observed a solid stretch since then, albeit with some continued shakeups on the horizon. UTX has become a much more efficient and focused company than it was just a few years ago—and it looks to be ready to continue along that path.

The current UTX is becoming more focused on good commercial (and nonmilitary) businesses. The recent surge in the airline industry will help the business going forward. The company's brands, particularly Otis, are well-known and well supported worldwide, and a return of strength in global construction should help its two largest businesses.

Reasons for Caution

Instability is good because it fosters necessary change, and it is bad because it distracts management from what it really should be doing. There had been a little of both going on here, and there's still some "newness" in today's business structure. The company is still sensitive to the health of the construction industry, and there is plenty of competition in most of its construction businesses.

If the recent airline boom falters, that too could bring UTX back to earth. Like all conglomerates, UTX is a complex business to manage, and the kinds of changes that are rumored—if they happen—may unlock a lot of value but may also bring some pretty big challenges to the management team. The company can also be vulnerable to headline risk, such as aviation accidents resulting from failure of its jet engines.

SECTOR: **Industrials** ❑ BETA COEFFICIENT: **1.08** ❑ 10-YEAR COMPOUND EARNINGS PER-SHARE GROWTH: **6.0%** ❑ 10-YEAR COMPOUND DIVIDENDS PER-SHARE GROWTH: **10.0%**

	2010	2011	2012	2013	2014	2015	2016	2017
Revenues (mil)	54,326	58,190	57,708	62,626	65,100	56,098	57,244	59,837
Net income (mil)	4,373	4,979	4,840	5,685	6,220	5,563	5,462	5,271
Earnings per share	4.74	5.49	5.34	6.21	6.82	6.29	6.61	6.60
Dividends per share	1.70	1.87	2.03	2.20	2.36	2.56	2.62	2.72
Cash flow per share	6.22	6.97	6.93	8.19	8.94	8.86	9.18	9.27
Price: high	79.7	91.8	87.5	113.9	120.7	124.4	111.7	128.5
low	62.9	66.9	70.7	92.1	97.2	85.5	83.4	106.9

Website: www.utc.com

AGGRESSIVE GROWTH

Valero Energy Corporation

Ticker symbol: VLO (NYSE) ❑ Large Cap ❑ Value Line financial strength rating: A+ ❑ Current yield: 3.5% ❑ Dividend raises, past 10 years: 9

Company Profile

Valero Energy is the world's largest independent oil refiner. The company owns 15 refineries and distributes primarily through a network of 7,400 retail combined gasoline stations and convenience stores throughout the United States (5,700 outlets), the UK and Ireland (900), and Canada (800). Most of these sales are under Valero's formerly owned retail brand names, which include the Valero brand itself but also Ultramar, Shamrock, Diamond Shamrock, and Beacon brands. The company owns the names and supplies the product, but in 2013 the company spun off the retail operations themselves into an independent public company called CST Brands. These outlets are located in all but four US states and the eastern half of Canada. Aside from unlocking capital and increasing focus on refining, the separation of these businesses allowed more refining sales to other channels and allows the retailers to source from their lowest-cost supplier—improving the performance of both.

Most of the 15 Valero refineries are located in the United States, centered in the South and on the Texas Gulf Coast (70 percent of total capacity) with others in Memphis, Oklahoma, and on the West Coast. Others are located in Quebec and Wales in the UK. The refining operations produce the full gamut of hydrocarbon products: gasoline, jet fuel, diesel, asphalt, propane, base oils, solvents, aromatics, natural gas liquids, sulfur, hydrogen, middle distillates, and special fuel blends to meet California Air Resources Board requirements. The company markets these products where the refineries are located, plus in the Caribbean and in Ireland.

Valero is strictly focused on downstream operations—now just the refining portion, no longer retail—and owns no oil wells or production facilities. Instead, they purchase a variety of feedstocks on the open market and can adjust those purchases to market conditions while using contracts and hedging tools to manage input prices to a degree—and rail transport along with existing pipelines to get it to the refinery. About half of feedstocks are purchased under contracts, with the other half on the spot market. Most of these refineries are legacy operations and have been in place for many years, as far back as 1908. The company has invested heavily in upgrading these refineries to improve capacity, efficiency, and environmental compliance and in recent years has grown its refinery mechanical availability rate to 96.9 percent and total availability excluding scheduled shutdowns to 99 percent—an excellent figure—but hurricane-related shutdowns cut actual utilization rates to 94 percent in 2017 from 95–96 percent in 2014–2016. The company has also added capacity in two plants to produce high-quality distillates from low-quality feedstocks and natural gas.

The company continues to develop its US logistics capabilities with the strategic goal of sourcing as much crude as it can flexibly from the least expensive sources. The emphasis has shifted from building out its railcar fleet a few years ago to developing and hooking into various pipeline projects to bring US crude into its refineries. Far more crude originates today in the US; the company now imports about half the amount of crude that it did back in 2006.

Bulk sales to other retail outlets, commercial distributors, and large-end customers like airlines and railroads are also important. The company also owns and operates 11 ethanol plants in the US Midwest, producing and shipping 1.4 billion gallons per year and a 50 percent interest in a 10,500 barrels-per-day renewable diesel plant.

Financial Highlights, Fiscal Year 2017

Higher retail fuel prices created a substantial 24 percent revenue gain in FY2017; however, higher crude prices and hurricane-related refinery shutdowns caused net earnings to remain largely flat (some reports may show a doubling of earnings, but this was because of a one-time Tax Cuts and Jobs Act effect). Oil and gasoline prices have risen gradually, and inventories remain high in 2018; for the years 2018 and 2019 the company expects modest 2–4 percent sales gains. Fine-tuned sourcing should improve the refining margins slightly; that and tax benefits for this capital-intensive industry are forecast to bring net profit increases in the 43 percent range in 2018 (against a soft comparison year) and another 2–4 percent in 2019.

In this sort of business, refining margins and throughput and the cash generated from that are most important; the company manages that margin and cash flow very carefully. Cash flows approaching $12 per share are expected to lead to continued strong dividend increases and active share buybacks (the company has bought back almost 25 percent of its float since 2010). While the dividend raise pace may slow some, Valero continues to be one of our strongest dividend aggressors.

Reasons to Buy

The profitability of this business, like other refining businesses, depends on the supply and cost of feedstocks and the wholesale and retail prices of finished products. In addition, the availability of refining capacity is also a factor; when markets get tight, it is extremely difficult to put another refinery on the ground to handle demand. These two factors can work together very favorably for Valero—lower input costs, no new competition—it's an oligopolistic dream and should bode well for profits for years to come, especially in today's new world of crude oil (over)abundance.

Flexibility is a key part of Valero's strategy. Rail transport has been providing excellent flexibility; now a more relaxed regulatory view of pipelines has energized their extension and operation. Valero will make the best of both worlds to bring in crude at the lowest overall cost and is ahead of its competitors in its ability to do so. Finally, one cannot overlook the commitment to cash returns to shareholders in the form of dividends.

Reasons for Caution

The refining business in particular is inherently volatile and complex, and what may appear today as an advantageous input and output pricing profile might disappear in a minute. Indeed, refined products are in a glut too, making future prices uncertain, and the recent allowance of crude exports makes less oil available in Valero's own backyard.

Gross, operating, and net margins can become very thin, typically in the 1–2 percent range—although much of Valero's recent success is due to breaking out of that range into the 3–4 percent range, helped along by the tax law. Refiners also endure the headline risk of refinery mishaps, a few of which have already come Valero's way in recent years. We now incur more risks in rail transport of crude and saw what can happen in recent mishaps (neither of which affected Valero directly). Also, the recent liberalization of environmental constraints on pipelines could come to an end if the Trump administration begins to lose its impetus in Washington.

SECTOR: Energy ❑ BETA COEFFICIENT: 0.99 ❑ 10-YEAR COMPOUND EARNINGS PER-SHARE GROWTH: 0.5% ❑ 10-YEAR COMPOUND DIVIDENDS PER-SHARE GROWTH: 23.5%

	2010	2011	2012	2013	2014	2015	2016	2017
Revenues (bil)	81.3	125.1	138.3	138.1	130.8	87.8	75.7	94.0
Net income (mil)	923	2,097	2,083	2,395	3,630	3,990	2,289	2,200
Earnings per share	1.62	3.69	3.75	4.37	6.85	7.99	4.94	4.96
Dividends per share	0.20	0.30	0.65	0.85	1.05	1.70	2.40	2.80
Cash flow per share	4.10	6.52	6.60	7.65	10.47	12.25	9.25	9.50
Price:　high	23.7	31.1	34.5	50.5	59.7	73.9	72.5	93.2
low	15.5	16.4	16.1	33.0	42.5	43.4	45.9	60.7

Website: www.valero.com

AGGRESSIVE GROWTH

Valmont Industries, Inc.

Ticker symbol: VMI (NYSE) ❑ Mid Cap ❑ Value Line financial strength rating: A ❑ Current yield: 1.1% ❑ Dividend raises, past 10 years: 8

Company Profile

Valmont Industries was founded in 1946 as a supplier of irrigation products and became one of the classic postwar industrial success stories, growing along with the need for increased farm output. It was an early pioneer of the center-pivot irrigation system, which enabled much of that growth and now dominates the high-yield agricultural business. These irrigation machines remain a mainstay of this most profitable product line, but the company has expanded on that core expertise in galvanized metal to make such familiar infrastructure items as light poles, cell phone towers and other utility structures, and those familiar high-tension electric towers that crisscross the landscape. As well, it provides such galvanizing services to other product manufacturers.

From the following product line summary, you'll get a good idea how Valmont plays in important areas of infrastructure and agriculture:

- Engineered Support Structure products (33 percent of FY2017 revenues, 20 percent of operating income)—Lighting poles, including decorative lighting poles, guard rails, towers, and other metal structures used in lighting, communications, roadway safety, wireless phone carriers, and other applications. Also includes products for the energy and mining industries including tubing and piping products, conveyance systems, grinding products, grates and screens for separation, windmill towers, and parts and products for human access like walkways and stair structures. Products are available as standard designs and engineered for custom applications as needed for industrial, commercial, and residential applications. If you've ever sat at a stoplight and wondered how a single cantilevered arm could support four 400-pound traffic signals, these are the folks to ask.
- Utility Support Structures (31 percent, 31 percent)—This segment produces the very large concrete and steel substations and electric transmission support towers used by electric utilities. This segment also includes offshore structures, once part of a separate Energy and Mining segment. We like this unit's prospects as utility infrastructure is replaced and modernized in the interest of grid efficiency, and now, aesthetic and environmental sensibility.
- Irrigation (23 percent, 44 percent)—Under the Valley brand name, Valmont produces a wide range of equipment, including gravity and drip products, as well as its center-pivot designs, which can service up to 500 acres from a single machine. Valmont also sells its irrigation controllers to other manufacturers.
- Coatings (10 percent, 16 percent)—Developed as an adjunct to its other metal products businesses, the coatings business now provides services such as galvanizing, electroplating, powder coating, and anodizing to industrial customers throughout the company's operating areas.

The company is a market leader in a number of segments including irrigation, power transmission poles, highway infrastructure, and certain coated products.

Financial Highlights, Fiscal Year 2017

Strength in most markets, especially energy and utility structures offset some weakness in the farm sector, offshore structures, and transportation infrastructure-driven Engineered Support Structures business; the net was a 9 percent revenue gain for FY2017. However, higher material costs (mainly steel) were chiefly responsible for a 2.7 percent drop in net earnings.

Continued economic recovery and increased infrastructure spending should lead to revenue gains in the 6–8 percent range for 2018 and 4–6 percent for 2019; increased volumes and operational improvements should lead to net income gains in the 13–15 percent range in 2018 and 11–13 percent in 2019. Modest buybacks will reduce the already-low share count (22.5 million shares) while the dividend may remain unchanged for the next couple of years as the company pays down long-term debt.

Reasons to Buy

We remain attracted to—and loyal to—the fundamental strengths of Valmont and its core businesses, and in particular their strategic importance to the interests of agriculture, water conservation, and infrastructure.

As much as anything we continue to view Valmont as a key infrastructure play. America's infrastructure needs to be replaced, as does infrastructure in much of the developed world. As for the less-developed world, that infrastructure needs to be built in the first place. We think, long term, that Valmont is in the right place to capture a decent share of this replacement business, including electric utility infrastructure—which in particular may be moving away from the traditional wooden telephone pole (as it has in most of the rest of the world) and as more aesthetic high-tension power poles come into favor. The original irrigation business should also do well in the long term as global food consumption increases and as agriculture, farmland, and farm commodity prices eventually strengthen—and as droughts in key "ag" markets persist. The company's continued emphasis on growth into new geographies should pay dividends as India and China begin to build infrastructure and adopt more modern agricultural methods. The company has announced its intentions to acquire a significant foreign supplier of utility structures, signaling an increased emphasis on overseas markets. We also like the relatively simple, straightforward nature of this business and the way the company presents itself online and in shareholder documents.

Reasons for Caution

Of course, the infrastructure "boom" may never really come, or it may not address markets that Valmont serves. The relatively small size and deep, large-scale manufacturing infrastructure of a company like Valmont makes it more vulnerable to cyclical weakness—although steadier public sector demand mitigates that somewhat. Raw materials costs and inflation in general are potential headwinds. Valmont presents plenty of long-term opportunity in our view, but that doesn't come without some risk.

SECTOR: **Industrials** ❏ BETA COEFFICIENT: **1.02** ❏ 10-YEAR COMPOUND EARNINGS PER-SHARE
GROWTH: **8.0%** ❏ 10-YEAR COMPOUND DIVIDENDS PER-SHARE GROWTH: **15.0%**

		2010	2011	2012	2013	2014	2015	2016	2017
Revenues (mil)		1,975	2,661	3,029	3,304	3,123	2,619	2,523	2,746
Net income (mil)		109.7	158.0	234.1	278.5	184.0	40.0	173.2	158.2
Earnings per share		4.15	5.97	8.75	10.35	7.09	1.71	7.63	6.95
Cash flow per share		6.46	8.80	11.40	13.27	11.39	5.74	11.35	10.71
Dividends per share		0.65	0.72	0.88	0.98	1.38	1.50	1.50	1.50
Price:	high	90.3	116.0	141.2	164.9	163.2	129.1	156.0	176.4
	low	65.3	73.0	90.2	129.0	116.7	92.3	96.5	136.0

Website: www.valmont.com

AGGRESSIVE GROWTH

Visa, Inc.

Ticker symbol: V (NYSE) ❏ **Large Cap** ❏ **Value Line financial strength rating: A++** ❏ **Current yield: 0.7%** ❏ **Dividend raises, past 10 years: 9**

Company Profile

If we wrote about a company with a 40 percent *net* profit margin and a global brand that was in the business of collecting small fees on every one of the billions of transactions worldwide (totaling about $10.2 *trillion* in 2017, up from $8.2 trillion in 2016); a company that required almost no capital expenditures, plant, equipment, or inventory; a company that brought almost $800,000 per employee in net profit (the company refers to this as "people light and technology heavy"); a company growing per-share earnings 20–30 percent a year; a company with a time-tested business model and absolutely zero long-term debt until recently (to fund the acquisition of its European counterpart)— would you believe that it existed? No. It must be a dream. Though the meteoric rise has slowed a bit, Visa continues to be many an investor's dream.

But it's all true, in fact. Founded in 1958 but not taken public until 2008, the Visa emblem has traditionally appeared on a majority of the world's credit cards—and now debit cards. In fact, there are about 3.2 *billion* such cards accepted at 46 million–plus merchant locations dispersed through 200 countries worldwide. According to BrandZ's 2017 Top 100 Most Valuable Global Brands Study, Visa is the number seven brand worldwide.

Visa operates the world's largest retail electronic payment network, providing processing services; payment platforms; and fraud-detection services for credit, debit, and commercial payments. The company also operates one of the largest global ATM networks with its PLUS and Interlink brands. In total, the company processes 111 billion transactions per year (which works out to about 3,500 transactions *per second*) in 160 currencies and estimates that it can process about 18 times that amount in a peak scenario—65,000 transactions per second—while being operational 99.999999 percent of the time!

For years, Visa has been synonymous with credit and credit cards, but in recent years it has become more of a digital currency company, stitching together consumers, retailers, banks, and other businesses in a giant global network. Really, Visa is a global payments technology business that not only develops and supplies the technology but also collects fees upon its use.

The shift from traditional cash and check forms of payment to debit cards and other digital forms has been growing at about a 12 percent annual rate, driven by the security and convenience of these transactions as well as a shift away from consumer debt to more "paid for today" debit transactions. Debit transactions now account for more than half the company's overall business volume, albeit at a small penalty, as average transaction sizes are smaller.

The company is an active innovator, with several initiatives in what it calls an "evolving payments ecosystem" and in network security. Mobile payment and mobile wallet innovations include "V.me" and "payWave" licensed products, and, not surprisingly in light of recent news events, the company is also working on new payment and card security initiatives. A new developer platform called Visa Checkout makes it easier for merchants to use APIs to integrate Visa payment into websites and mobile platforms, now for 15 million consumer accounts, and the company has partnered with Apple to create new connections with Apple Pay. A new mobile app allowing swipe-free payment at gas stations is but one example. The company is also very active in fraud prevention and into mining data to help merchants grow their businesses with a new techy-sounding "Visa Threat Intelligence" fusion platform to monitor and control security threats. Visa has now hired some 2,000 new IT professionals in the past two years—a 20 percent bump in the workforce—to work on these initiatives. This all shows how Visa thinks of itself as a data and IT company, not merely a financial services firm.

The business continues to grow rapidly overseas; with the 2016 consolidation of Visa Europe Limited some 60 percent of its revenue now comes from outside the US, far more than its rivals and providing the company's strongest growth driver at present.

Financial Highlights, Fiscal Year 2017

A robust global economy and improved transaction volumes led to a 22 percent revenue gain for FY2017. Reported net earnings gained almost 12 percent, and a 3 percent share buyback led to a 22 percent gain in per-share earnings. Current projections call for revenue growth in the 10–12 percent range through the end of the decade with improved margins and gains in net and per-share earnings north of 20 percent. The company continues to repurchase shares at about a 2–3 percent annual rate and has already retired a third of its float since going public in 2008.

Reasons to Buy

"The Power of Digital Currency" continues as Visa's apt corporate mantra. Simply, it's hard to come up with a better business model—a company that develops and sells the network and collects fees every time it's used. "Financial Inclusion" is another slogan, as they expand globally to provide payment technologies for everyone everywhere. It would be like Microsoft collecting fees every time a file is created and saved or an email platform charging fees for every message. Visa is in a great position to not only capitalize on overall world economic growth, as most companies should be, but also to capitalize on a shift in this growth toward electronic and mobile payments. Even as debt-conscious consumers pull back on using credit cards, debit card usage continues to advance. This reinforces one of Visa's big strengths—unlike most other financial services businesses, Visa is relatively immune to downturns, as it makes its money by processing payments, not by extending credit. On the growth side, the company is expanding its footprint in emerging markets, and there is plenty of innovation opportunity in this business. Overall, while Visa has traditional competitors (MasterCard, American Express, Discover) and new competitors like Square, it continues to have the strongest franchise, technology leadership, and pricing power at its back. Its volumes are double its nearest competitor—MasterCard.

Reasons for Caution

The company has pricing power, but as with many companies that do, that power has come under government, merchant, and public scrutiny; the company must tread lightly or face possible consequences. Litigation and regulatory actions have presented some occasional headline and profit risk and may be construed as a threat to the franchise—perhaps if it sounds too good to be true, it may be. But even after some legal and regulatory bumps, Visa has emerged rock solid. Competition from new technologies like Square—and who knows, Bitcoin and other cryptocurrencies?—lurks in the wings, but we don't think they pose a threat as of now.

Finally, with the steady success, good entry points have been hard to find.

SECTOR: **Financials** ❑ BETA COEFFICIENT:**1.01** ❑ 10-YEAR COMPOUND EARNINGS PER-SHARE GROWTH: **NM** ❑ 10-YEAR COMPOUND DIVIDENDS PER-SHARE GROWTH: **NM**

		2010	2011	2012	2013	2014	2015	2016	2017
Revenues (mil)		8,065	9,188	10,421	11,776	12,702	13,880	15,082	18,358
Net income (mil)		2,966	3,650	4,203	4,980	5,438	6,238	5,991	6,699
Earnings per share		0.98	1.25	1.55	1.90	2.27	2.62	2.84	3.48
Dividends per share		0.13	0.15	0.22	0.33	0.42	0.50	0.59	0.69
Cash flow per share		1.09	1.39	1.67	2.05	2.44	2.82	3.07	3.75
Price:	high	24.3	25.9	38.1	55.7	67.3	81.0	84.0	114.0
	low	16.2	16.9	24.6	38.5	48.7	60.0	65.1	78.5

Website: **www.corporate.visa.com**

GROWTH AND INCOME

Vodafone Group Plc ADR

Ticker symbol: **VOD** (NASDAQ) ❑ **Large Cap** ❑ Value Line financial strength rating: **B++** ❑ Current yield: **6.4%** ❑ Dividend raises, past 10 years: **5**

Company Profile

Vodafone Group is one of the leading providers of mobile telecommunications services in the international market (all current operations are outside of the US). The company's operations are organized in two groups: Europe and AMAP (Africa, Middle East, and Asia Pacific). Their top markets (rank ordered) are Germany, UK, Italy, Spain and Other European countries, which, taken together, account for some 60 percent of revenue. Asia, India, and Africa (where they operate as Vodacom), account for twenty other markets and 40 percent of revenue, including partner networks in fifty additional countries.

The Vodafone name is not well known in the US as a communications provider, but they are the second-largest mobile operator in the world, behind only China Mobile. They serve approximately 520 million customers with services such as cellular, paging, and other personal and business communications. The company was founded in 1982 and is headquartered in London, England.

Financial Highlights, Fiscal Year 2017

Following two consecutive years of minor revenue declines, Vodafone is on track for a 7 percent increase in revenues in FY2018. This, coupled with continued improvement in operating margins, should result in a doubling of net profit when compared to their most recent high-water revenue mark in FY2015. An emphasis on cost-controls over the past few years has won significant efficiency gains.

Vodafone is in talks to divest of its 42 percent interest in a joint venture in cell towers located in India. The value of the projected share-swap would be close to $5 billion. The company also received a favorable judgment in the tax court of India that reversed a large prior retroactive tax judgment.

Reasons to Buy

Activity in the telecoms industry as a whole over the past several years has been characterized by consolidation in existing markets and build-out at the margins. If anything, this model applies in the European markets even more so than in the more sparsely populated North American markets. The larger telecoms in Europe have been under pressure to grow revenue in saturated markets, and as a consequence, growth there has moderated somewhat. Developing markets are where the expansion will take place, and among world players, Vodafone is in the best position to take advantage.

The company is in a strong cash position and is aggressively pursuing opportunities in new markets and in markets where they have an existing presence. They are in talks to acquire certain European assets of Liberty Global (with whom they have an existing joint venture agreement), which would reduce competition in overlapping geographies. The company has seen significant increases in data traffic throughout 2017 (up 61 percent in Q3 alone) and large gains in 4G connectivity, which was up 57 percent to 20 percent of total connections.

Net customer adds through 2017 averaged over 300k per quarter. Vodafone's recent investments in network platform have put them in a good position to support continued growth in demand for both data and voice. Vodafone remains committed to strong organic growth, as opposed to buying up small players (and their problems). They continue to invest their capital wisely and are winning customer base via better service and competitive pricing.

These ADRs are fairly priced and well positioned for growth. We don't make a habit of "bargain hunting" here at *100 Best*, as we feel all of our recommendations provide value going forward, but when a stock we already like is trading at a "floor" price, we like it even more and see no harm in calling it out.

Lastly, Vodafone has remained committed to supporting a handsome dividend through business cycles of both "five bars" and "no connection." The current yield of 6.4 percent has remained largely unchanged as the business has slumped and recovered over the past few years.

Reasons for Caution

Although growth prospects in emerging markets look bright, India remains a difficult arena in terms of its highly competitive and closely regulated environment. A recent partnership agreement there should help to ameliorate worries somewhat. Also, the Liberty Global acquisition bears watching, as anti-competitive regulations in Germany will likely create some hurdles. We should note that the steep share price drop in 2014 was due to a significant shareholder distribution from the sale of VOD's large stake of Verizon Wireless.

SECTOR: **Telecommunications Services** ❑ BETA COEFFICIENT: **1.10** ❑ 10-YEAR COMPOUND EARNINGS PER-SHARE GROWTH: **NA** ❑ 10-YEAR COMPOUND DIVIDENDS PER-SHARE GROWTH: **1.0%**

	2010	2011	2012	2013	2014	2015	2016	2017
Revenues (mil)	73,414	74,267	67,112	63,654	62,496	59,001	50,965	49,230
Net income (mil)	14,042	12,080	11,621	7,706	2,261	1,935	2,406	3,865
Earnings per ADR	4.87	4.34	4.31	2.89	0.85	0.73	0.86	1.45
Dividends per ADR	2.39	3.81	2.80	3.02	1.82	1.71	1.53	1.77
Cash flow per ADR	9.37	9.10	8.58	7.66	6.19	5.88	5.36	6.05
Price:　high	52.3	59.9	55.1	72.3	72.5	39.5	34.7	32.0
low	33.4	44.6	45.7	44.8	28.6	30.6	24.2	24.3

Website: www.vodafone.com

GROWTH AND INCOME

Waste Management, Inc.

Ticker symbol: WM (NYSE) ❑ Large Cap ❑ Value Line financial strength rating: A ❑ Current yield: 2.2% ❑ Dividend raises, past 10 years: 10

Company Profile

You may refer to it as a "garbage company" if you want—we won't take offense. Waste Management continues to be the largest and steadiest hand in the North American solid waste disposal industry. In their own words,

"North America's leading provider of comprehensive waste management environmental services"; supporting this claim, they serve some 21 million municipal, commercial, and industrial customers in the US and Canada. Like most large waste firms, WM has grown over time by assembling smaller, more local companies into a nationally branded and highly scaled operation with a notable amount of innovation on several fronts in the core business and especially in material recovery—translation, recycling.

The business is divided into three segments:

- Collection, which accounts for 65 percent of the business, includes the standard dumpster and garbage truck operations. The company has about 600 collection operations, many of which have long-term contracts with municipalities and businesses. About 40 percent of the collection business is commercial, 30 percent residential, 26 percent industrial, and 4 percent other. For the industry, WM is considered an innovator even in its traditional collection operations; examples include the Bagster small-scale disposal units now sold through retail home-improvement outlets and 3,700 collection trucks converted to natural gas (some of which the company produces from waste). The company perceives itself as a world-class logistics company (and why not?) and has equipped its trucks with the latest in onboard computers, centralized dispatching, and routing processes, reducing collection costs as much as 1 percent per year.
- Landfill (15 percent of revenues). The company operates 248 landfills across North America, servicing its own collection operations and other collection service providers. Among these sites, there are 131 landfill-gas-to-energy conversion projects producing fuel for electricity generation. There are also five active hazardous waste landfills and one underground hazardous waste facility.
- Transfer, Recycling, and Other (20 percent). These operations perform specialized material recovery and processing into useful commodities. There are 310 transfer stations set up for the collection of various forms of waste, including medical, recyclables, compact fluorescent (CFL), and e-waste. The company has also pioneered single-stream recycling, where physical and optical sorting technologies sort out unseparated recyclable materials. Single-streaming has greatly increased recycling rates in municipalities where it is used and provides a steady revenue stream in recovered paper, glass, metals, etc., for the company. WM also further refines these materials into industrial inputs, e.g., glass or

plastic feedstocks in certain colors. In total there are 61 traditional and 43 "single-stream" operations, recycling some 14 million tons of commodities annually today, a figure expected to grow to 20 million by 2020. Despite the strategic importance of recycling and the new technologies applied, volumes and pricing have retreated as global demand has waned, in part due to new regulations imposed by China on the import of recyclable material. Recycling prices dropped about 8 percent in 2017. The company also sold its waste-to-energy gasification business, Wheelabrator Technologies, in 2014, so this business segment, now 20 percent of the business, was once 25 percent.

Financial Highlights, Fiscal Year 2017

Strong pricing (up 4.8 percent for the year), volume gains (up 2.9 percent), and minor acquisition effects drove FY2017 volumes some 6.4 percent higher, the largest annual revenue increase since 1998. Operational improvements in all facets of the business and a moderate share buyback led to a 10.4 percent increase in per-share earnings. The company expects revenue growth to moderate somewhat at 3–5 percent annually through 2019, but continued process improvements and strong positive tax effects will take per-share earnings 22–25 percent higher in 2018 and 5 percent higher beyond that. A rebound in recycled material prices could bring still better income results. High-single-digit dividend increases and modest buybacks should continue coming down the conveyor belt.

Reasons to Buy

WM is the strongest and most entrenched player in a business that isn't going away any time soon. "Strategic" waste collection, particularly with the high-value-add material recovery operations that have become a key part of WM's business, is not only here to stay but also will only become more important to residential, industrial, and municipal customers as time goes on. The current rebound in commodity prices foretells better recycling yields; we feel the "sweet spot" in this business is yet to come.

WM exhibits a lot of innovation in an industry not particularly known for it. WM's performance has indeed improved as operational improvements and lower fuel costs have taken effect and material prices have increased.

Regulation and regulatory compliance has always been a big deal for WM, but relaxed regulation likely in the Trump administration may reduce this burden, and now the tax cuts will help too. In all, WM is a slow, steady, safe, well-managed investment with decent cash returns to shareholders.

Reasons for Caution

WM does rely on acquisitions for a lot of its growth. In this business, that might not be so bad, for existing companies have captive markets and disposal facilities and can likely benefit from proven management processes and reduced overhead costs. As we've seen, the recycling operations, while cool and sexy, aren't always as profitable as one would think. A lot depends on China policy and the price of "new" materials. Additionally, any waste company runs the risk of going afoul of environmental regulations; WM has largely steered clear of trouble thus far (and has indeed been voted in as a "world's most ethical company" for the past ten years by the Ethisphere Institute—the only entry in the "environmental services" category), but there are no guarantees.

SECTOR: **Business Services** ▫ BETA COEFFICIENT: **0.70** ▫ 10-YEAR COMPOUND EARNINGS PER-SHARE GROWTH: **5.0%** ▫ 10-YEAR COMPOUND DIVIDENDS PER-SHARE GROWTH: **6.5%**

		2010	2011	2012	2013	2014	2015	2016	2017
Revenues (mil)		12,515	13,375	13,649	13,983	13,996	12,961	13,609	14,485
Net income (mil)		1,011	1,007	968	1,008	1,155	1,153	1,295	1,425
Earnings per share		2.10	2.14	2.08	2.15	2.48	2.53	2.91	3.22
Dividends per share		1.28	1.36	1.42	1.46	1.50	1.54	1.64	1.70
Cash flow per share		4.64	4.85	4.88	5.04	5.34	5.36	5.90	6.45
Price:	high	37.3	36.7	36.3	46.4	51.9	55.9	71.8	86.9
	low	31.1	27.8	30.8	33.7	40.3	45.9	50.4	69.0

Website: www.wm.com

GROWTH AND INCOME

Welltower, Inc.

Ticker symbol: WELL (NYSE) ▫ Large Cap ▫ Value Line financial strength rating: A++ ▫ Current yield: 6.4% ▫ Dividend raises, past 10 years: 10

Company Profile

Welltower, our first real estate investment trust choice added five years ago in 2014, invests primarily in senior living and medical care properties mainly in the US but also in Canada and the UK. The business—and we think it's a good business, not just a real estate portfolio—operates in three primary business segments. The first and largest is referred to as the Seniors

Housing "triple-net" segment and is involved primarily in owning senior housing properties, including independent, continuing care, and assisted living facilities, and leasing them to qualified operators like Sunrise Senior Living and Genesis Healthcare in return for a steady income stream. This segment currently owns 573 properties in the US in 40 states but is concentrated in high-cost urban areas mostly on the coasts and contributes about 20 percent of revenues and 43 percent of net operating income. There are now also 61 facilities in the UK and six facilities in Canada.

The second and fastest-growing segment is the Seniors Housing Operating segment, which operates some of the facilities owned by the REIT and others owned by third parties. It operates 443 properties in 35 states, 103 in Canada, and 53 in the UK and contributes about 68 percent of revenues and 40 percent of net operating income. The third major segment is Outpatient Medical, which owns and sometimes operates 270 outpatient medical centers including skilled nursing facilities in 35 states, contributing about 13 percent of revenues and 17 percent to net operating income. The company sold its last hospital and its life sciences facilities in 2015 and 2016 and has been repositioning its portfolio to focus more on seniors housing (now 72 percent of total revenue and 95 percent private pay versus 40 percent of revenue at 69 percent private pay in 2010). This has led to an ongoing campaign to sell certain properties and acquire others—which affected 2017 performance negatively. In total, Welltower owns and/or operates some 1,286 properties in three countries, housing some 210,000 residents and supporting 16 million annual outpatient visits.

Welltower employs a conscious and stated strategy of being in markets with high barriers to entry and with a more upscale, affluent retiree base—this is part of why we feel it is a good business, not just a real estate play. Markets such as Boston, New Jersey, Seattle, and major coastal California cities are territories for Welltower. The top five markets are New York, Philadelphia, Los Angeles, Boston, and greater London. A recent study concluded that 68–73 percent of seniors wanted to stay in their same city in the top ten markets in the US.

The average revenue per occupied room in the seniors operating segment is $6,891 per month, some 51 percent higher than the national senior housing industry average. In the markets in which WELL operates, the cost of the average single-family home runs 74 percent higher than the national average, and household incomes are 40 percent higher. Eighty-five percent of facilities are in the 31 most affluent US metropolitan areas. FY2017 occupancy rates are 85.8 percent in the seniors housing triple-net segment (86.5

percent last year), 86.5 percent in the seniors housing operating (88.7 percent last year), and 93.7 percent in the medical facilities segments (94.7 percent last year). The facilities are newer, more attractive, and desirable, as a trip through the company's website at www.welltower.com will show.

The strategy and focus are to "differentiate" and to provide an "infrastructure platform that emphasizes wellness and connectivity across the continuum of care"—or pleasant, well-appointed alternatives to the traditional facilities usually offered to both healthy and less healthy seniors.

REITs, obviously, play on the real estate market, and in the Welltower case, in the high-value-add REIT segment of healthcare. You're also investing in the aging population—which is expected to grow 40 percent by 2024 against a 9.1 percent growth in the population as a whole. In this case in particular, you're investing in the ability and willingness of the more affluent segments of the elderly population to spend for a pleasant retirement.

REITs are typically good income producers, as they are required by law to pay a substantial portion of their cash flow to investors. The accounting rules are different, and REIT investors should focus on Funds from Operations (FFO), which is analogous to operating income; net income figures have depreciation expenses deducted, which can vary in timing and not always be realistic. FFO support the dividends paid to investors.

Financial Highlights, Fiscal Year 2017

A step up in portfolio transitions and somewhat diminished occupancy rates combined to produce fairly weak FY2017 results for Welltower. Revenues were up less than 1 percent as several producing properties came offline; per share FFO dropped a full 7.5 percent. The company expects modest 4–5 percent revenue gains going forward into 2018 and 2019, but expenses related to asset transitions may keep the lid on net income and FFO until 2019; to that the company suspended its first dividend raise in years (not the entire dividend) in early 2018. Forecasts call for a soft 2018 with a recovery to normal profit growth patterns (and then some) starting 2019. Some of this is internal, with property transitions, some may be external, due to overcapacity in the market—unfortunately the company isn't telling us much.

Reasons to Buy

Welltower continues to be a solid, income-oriented way to play the steady growth and trends of the healthcare industry and the aging demographic. Rents—and rent growth—are better than average, and its income payout is stable and typically growing. Longer term, the company estimates that senior housing rent growth will exceed inflation by 1.7 percent, that the US population over 75 years of age will grow some 86 percent over the next 20 years, and the 85+ population will double—all factors supporting a healthy growth story in the seniors housing business. Strong growth in outpatient medical procedures and services will help that segment too.

Some 95 percent of revenues were estimated to be derived from private pay sources in 2018, up from 93 percent in 2017, 88 percent in 2016, 87 percent in 2015, and 83 percent in 2014. With the concentration on private-pay services, Welltower will avoid some of the exposure to Medicare utilization management initiatives and related cutbacks that many others in the sector are exposed to—and an improving economy will only help further. We like, and most in the industry agree, the expansion into the UK, which positions them well for other fertile pastures overseas. The company also avoids exposure to debt and interest costs better than most REITs, with a target debt of 40 percent of total capital (they have currently managed this down to 44 percent).

In sum, despite some recent hiccups, Welltower offers a good combination of high yield and safety with a modest long-term growth kicker mixed in for good measure.

Reasons for Caution

Because of their differences from ordinary corporations, it may be difficult to understand this investment, particularly the financial performance of REITs, especially a complex REIT such as this one, which has both traditional property investments and operating company investments. The 10-K Annual Report is overly complicated and not much help, but their investor presentations are pretty helpful.

There is mounting evidence of competitive pressure and oversupply in the seniors real estate market, but we feel confident that Welltower is playing in the stronger, more exclusive niches and wisely not taking on the "mass market" players head to head. One could also question, going forward, whether retirees will be as well-heeled as they are today, with deterioration in retirement savings and increased costs. Finally, there is increasing sensitivity to rising interest rates; the modest underlying growth and high yield makes the stock act more like a bond than a stock much of the time.

SECTOR: **Healthcare** ❑ BETA COEFFICIENT: **0.20** ❑ 10-YEAR COMPOUND FFO PER-SHARE
GROWTH: **2.0%** ❑ 10-YEAR COMPOUND DIVIDENDS PER-SHARE GROWTH: **3.0%**

	2010	2011	2012	2013	2014	2015	2016	2017
Revenues (mil)	680.5	1,421	1,822	2,880	3,344	3,858	4,281	4,316
Net income (mil)	84	156	295	93	505	884	1,078	513
Funds from operations per share	3.08	3.41	3.52	3.80	4.13	4.38	4.55	4.21
Real estate owned per share	58.4	72.5	66.9	74.9	69.5	75.8	73.3	70.4
Dividends per share	2.74	2.84	2.96	3.06	3.18	3.30	3.44	3.48
Price: high	52.1	55.2	62.8	80.1	78.2	84.9	80.2	78.2
low	38.4	41.0	52.4	52.4	52.9	58.2	52.8	63.1

Website: www.welltower.com

CONSERVATIVE GROWTH

Whirlpool Corporation

Ticker symbol: WHR (NYSE) ❑ Large Cap ❑ Value Line financial strength rating: A+ ❑ Current
yield: 3.0% ❑ Dividend raises, past 10 years: 7

Company Profile

Whirlpool is the world's leading home appliance manufacturer in a $120 billion global industry. The company manufactures appliances under familiar and recognized brand names in all major home appliance categories including fabric care (laundry), cooking, refrigeration, dishwashers, water filtration, and garage organization. Familiar brand names include Whirlpool, Maytag, Hotpoint, KitchenAid, Amana, Jenn-Air, Gladiator, and international names Bauknecht, Brastemp, Indesit, and Consul. A new and less "traditional" brand for this major "white goods" maker is Yummly, a digital recipe platform—acquired in 2017 that allows users to search for recipes based on a host of criteria including spices, cooking time, and nutrition— and will become an important ingredient in the evolving "connected kitchen." To that end, some recipes are set up to scan directly to some Whirlpool kitchen appliances, automatically setting cook times and temperatures and varying them through the cook cycle as appropriate.

The Whirlpool brand itself is the number one global appliance brand and is number one across all four major world geographic regions. The company is the leading manufacturer in seven of the world's ten largest countries.

Products are found in 97 million homes worldwide. Seven brands within the branded house generate over $1 billion in annual sales. Based on FY2017 sales, the product breakdown is about 29 percent refrigerators and freezers, 28 percent fabric care, 19 percent home cooking appliances, and 24 percent "other." About 46 percent of Whirlpool's sales come from outside North America: 23 percent in Europe/Middle East/Africa, 16 percent in Latin America, and 7 percent in Asia. Major investments in overseas brands include: Europe's Indesit (another billion-dollar brand) and China's Hefei Sanyo. The acquisition strategy keys on adjacent businesses, many to open or gain critical mass in international markets. Whirlpool estimates that through its acquisitions it now has access to 90 percent of the world's consumers.

In an industry not traditionally known for innovation, Whirlpool has striven to be an innovation leader in its industry ("Innovation at the Pace of Life" is one slogan). This has manifested itself both in new products, product platforms, and contemporary styling within those platforms; and in manufacturing and supply-chain efficiencies, such as a global platform design for local manufacture of washing machine products, recalling similar achievements in the auto industry. Such gains are key in this competitive, price-sensitive industry. The company also has initiatives to build lifetime brand loyalty and product quality, improve water and energy efficiency and quietness of operation, and add more interesting and decorative colors to some of its products. More recently it has marketed specialized "smart" appliances controlled by smartphones or even voice as part of a broader initiative to "connect" with the connected home; one example is the Whirlpool 6th Sense Live app, which allows owners to operate a washing machine remotely for convenience and to save energy ("Innovations That Connect" is another slogan proudly displayed on their website and annual report).

Overall, the strategy is to expand the business through innovation, brand strength, and geographic coverage; then to expand margins through supply-chain and cost-structure efficiency.

Financial Highlights, Fiscal Year 2017

For several years the company has ridden the coattails of an improving economy, an improved replacement cycle for old units, improved demand for today's more efficient appliances, and operational improvements. FY2017 was, however, a bit of an off year as material input costs rose by some $600 million and there were some challenges integrating new acquisitions in Europe and China. Revenues rose a modest 2.6 percent, but margins and net earnings dropped a bit over 5 percent. Price increases and some new fixed cost reductions and operational efficiencies are leading the way to a forecasted 9–10 percent earnings gain on a forecasted 3 percent revenue boost for 2018; this widens out to a 12 percent earnings gain on a 1–3 percent revenue gain for 2019. Dividends should continue to rise although not at the 10–20 percent annual rate seen in recent years, and share buybacks will continue leading to still stronger per-share earnings gains. Even with the 2017 softness, net profit margins have doubled in five years from the 3 percent range to around 5 percent now and going forward.

Reasons to Buy

Long a dull, boring business, Whirlpool has made shopping for an appliance more interesting and has profited handsomely from its efforts. If you shop for an appliance today—take washers and dryers, for example—they work better, they're more energy efficient, they use less water, and are more technology enabled. In short, they're better products, and guess what: they're more expensive and more profitable for the manufacturers too. Operational improvements, higher-product value add, and a gradual increase in premium brands have driven operating and net margins substantially higher. We continue to like the way the company wrings ever more profit out of a modestly growing or even flat sales base.

Now as the economy and employment strengthen globally, Whirlpool is in a particularly good position to capitalize on these tailwinds. More than most, Whirlpool used the Great Recession and ensuing recovery as a wake-up call and an opportunity to streamline its businesses and to put some real strategic thought into how to drive its brand assortment and international portfolio to achieve better results.

The company continues to innovate toward better and more connected products and internal processes. Long term, "smart" appliances, which can work together with smartphones and other residential management applications to deliver better, more energy-efficient results, will take center stage. Bottom line: Whirlpool has ever more to compete on than just price.

In addition, the company is building critical mass in overseas markets. Cash flows and investor returns are solid and rising as the company focuses on margin expansion and cash flow. More than most, the management team is a plus with a recognizable pragmatic and strategic approach to managing this business.

Reasons for Caution

By nature, the appliance business is highly competitive and cyclical. Many higher-income consumers have been opting for fancier, more expensive foreign brands, like Bosch and LG, a trend that could hurt if it continues. We believe that Whirlpool is countering this trend by adding elegance, advertising, and channel support for its top-tier brands and products—as well as a few "foreign" brands of its own. Trade wars look to bring a mixed blessing at this point; the company "won" some price protection on foreign "dumping" of laundry and other products—but tariffs on steel, aluminum, and other raw materials raise costs; it is difficult to predict the dynamics of just how the recent trade instability will affect WHR.

SECTOR: **Consumer Durables** ◻ BETA COEFFICIENT: **1.84** ◻ 10-YEAR COMPOUND EARNINGS PER-SHARE GROWTH: **7.5%** ◻ 10-YEAR COMPOUND DIVIDENDS PER-SHARE GROWTH: **7.0%**

		2010	2011	2012	2013	2014	2015	2016	2017
Revenues (mil)		18,366	18,666	18,143	18,768	19,872	20,891	20,718	21,253
Net income (mil)		707	699	559	810	907	987	1,085	1,025
Earnings per share		9.10	8.95	7.05	10.03	11.39	12.38	14.08	13.78
Dividends per share		1.72	1.93	2.00	2.38	2.88	3.45	3.90	4.30
Cash flow per share		16.91	16.54	14.05	17.53	18.80	21.43	23.51	23.65
Price:	high	118.4	92.3	104.2	159.2	196.7	217.1	194.1	203.0
	low	71.0	45.2	47.7	101.7	124.4	140.5	123.5	158.8

Website: www.whirlpoolcorp.com

AGGRESSIVE GROWTH

NEW FOR 2019

Zebra Technologies Corp.

Ticker symbol: ZBRA (NASDAQ) ◻ Large Cap ◻ Value Line financial strength rating: B++ ◻ Current yield: Nil ◻ Dividend raises, past 10 years: NA

Company Profile

Established in 1969 in Lincolnshire, IL (where they are still headquartered), as Data Specialties Incorporated, Zebra has grown organically and through more than a dozen acquisitions to become a leading provider of barcode reading, tracking, and labeling systems. Their most recent significant acquisition, the 2014 purchase of Motorola Mobility Solutions, also gave them a major presence in the RFID, mobile computing, and data capture services. The combined businesses bring to market what are known as AIDC products, an industry acronym for Automatic Identification and Data Capture.

The company reports business in two segments: AIT (Asset Intelligence and Tracking), which consists of the bulk of the existing product line prior to the Motorola acquisition, and EVM (Enterprise Visibility and Mobility), which represents the businesses that came in the acquisition, including RFID technologies, wireless handheld readers, mobile computing and software tools. As of FY2017 the company has largely completed its "One Zebra" program, the goal of which was to integrate what were fairly distinct but complementary businesses under one management structure and gain efficiencies where possible.

The bulk of their sales are in hardware platforms, including barcode scanners and imagers, mobile computers and tablets, RFID readers, and mobile and fixed specialty printers. They also sell supplies and accessories to support the hardware, as well as software platforms employed in device tracking and data analytics. End-users of Zebra's products include businesses engaged in retailing and e-commerce, transportation and logistics, manufacturing, and healthcare. Nearly 50 percent of the products are sold through distribution, with downstream VARs ("value added resellers"), independent software vendors and systems integrators reselling a customized package/product to the end user. On the Zebra website you can see applications for tracking everything from cardiac patients to shopping carts.

The company's mobile computing platforms are widely supported in a multitude of applications, including federal and state government and civilian agencies, military, law enforcement, education, and public health. Applications are in place for material inspection, code enforcement, identity management, and healthcare analytics, to name a few. The list is deep and broad. Lastly, Zebra also sells subscription services for software and hardware support, as well as in-house custom development services for applications or hardware not available in their standard line.

The company provides products and services in over 180 countries, with 114 facilities and approximately 7,000 employees.

Financial Highlights, Fiscal Year 2017

The company saw a 4.1 percent increase in sales for FY2017, with international sales accounting for roughly 60 percent of that increase. As for the two segments of the business, AIT sales grew 5.1 percent and EVM 3.3 percent, with gross margins slightly higher in AIT. Sales in North America and Rest-of-World were very nearly split 50/50, with noticeable growth in ROW for 2017.

Projections for FY2018 are for a 9–12 percent increase in net sales, assuming about a 2 percent favorable impact from foreign exchange and $85–90 million in interest expense. The company also expects to benefit from the new US tax code in FY2018 with a reduction on the order of five percentage points to a 16–17 percent tax rate, boosting earnings some 35 percent. Revenues for FY2019 are expected to increase 9 percent as well, with earnings increasing 7–8 percent.

Reasons to Buy

At first glance, this may be among the least sexy stocks in the 2019 issue (unless you're just crazy about industrial labeling and asset management). Bear with us, though, as we think there's an interesting story here.

If there's anything to be learned from the Amazonification (new word, copyright *100 Best Stocks*) of the North American retail business, it's the value of smart logistics. By providing reliable, predictable, and verifiable delivery of goods to consumers, Amazon was able to win over most of those customers who were not initially persuaded simply by a marginally lower price. Now, obviously, order fulfillment is only part of Amazon's automation and logistics story, but our takeaway for the purposes of understanding Zebra's possibilities is that the appropriate application of intelligence can be a significant differentiator in endeavors even as mundane as knowing where a box is, because that box represents value. This is where Zebra lives. They provide the tools (the picks and shovels, a model we love) to help many different types of businesses gain an understanding of how value flows (or doesn't flow) through their organization on its way to a customer.

Now, Zebra is not bringing us some earthshaking new technology. Yes, their products are high quality and are refined on a regular basis to provide enhanced performance and usability, but the core functionality of most of the things they make and sell, such as specialty high-speed printers and barcode and RFID scanners, have been with us for some time. The primary reason we find this company attractive now is not so much that they're discovering large new markets, it's that large markets are moving toward them.

Organizations around the world are coming to understand that smart logistics, smart asset tracking, smart inventory management, and many other benefits made possible by the fairly simple (and some not so simple) tools provided by Zebra and its resellers can have a significant and measurable impact on their bottom line. This is a message that's being beaten into them not just by Zebra, but in recent years by their own partner businesses and companies like IBM, UPS and others.

We think Zebra is in the right place at the right time. Their traditional barcode and printer products (AIT) are still the industry standard in many applications, and the EVM segment brings wireless data capture and automated tracking, mobile computing and services to support real-time applications. They have a strong partner ecosystem, global presence, and a solid brand. Sexy enough for us.

Reasons for Caution

The Motorola Mobility business did not come cheap. Although the acquisition closed in 2014, Zebra is still carrying some $2.1 billion in total debt attributable to the purchase on its books. The debt itself has run about 70 percent of capital recently, but the company has been successful in paying down $550 million over the past five quarters and has successfully restructured the bulk of the debt in 2017. There's still a fair amount of quarterly service to be paid, but the company is one year into an internal cost reduction effort that has shown results and should ease the burden somewhat.

SECTOR: **Information Technology** ❑ BETA COEFFICIENT: **1.30** ❑ 10-YEAR COMPOUND EARNINGS PER-SHARE GROWTH: **11%** ❑ 10-YEAR COMPOUND DIVIDENDS PER-SHARE GROWTH: **NA**

	2010	2011	2012	2013	2014	2015	2016	2017
Revenues (mil)	957	984	996	1,038	1,671	3,652	3,574	3,722
Net income (mil)	99.0	130	131	134	128	277	293	379
Earnings per share	1.73	2.40	2.53	2.63	2.49	5.31	5.60	7.05
Dividends per share	—	—	—	—	—	—	—	—
Cash flow per share	2.34	2.96	3.09	3.30	4.05	11.45	11.29	12.06
Price: high	39.3	44.5	41.9	55.2	86.0	119.5	88.0	117.4
low	24.1	28.2	31.8	40.0	52.6	63.9	46.1	81.0

Website: www.zebra.com

Appendix A

PERFORMANCE ANALYSIS: 100 BEST STOCKS TO BUY IN 2018

Company	Symbol	Price 4/1/2017	Price 4/1/2018	% change	Dollar gain/loss, $1,000 invested
3M	MMM	$191.33	$219.52	14.7%	$147.34
Abbott Labs (*)	ABT	$42.72	$59.92	40.3%	$402.62
AbbVie	ABBV	$65.16	$94.65	45.3%	$452.58
Aetna	AET	$133.32	$169.00	26.8%	$267.63
Allstate	ALL	$79.91	$94.80	18.6%	$186.33
Amazon	AMZN	$886.75	$1,447.34	63.2%	$632.18
Apple	AAPL	$143.71	$167.78	16.7%	$167.49
Applied Materials (*)	AMAT	$40.28	$55.61	38.1%	$380.59
Aqua America	WTR	$32.15	$34.05	5.9%	$59.10
Archer Daniels Midland	ADM	$46.04	$42.37	-8.0%	$(79.71)
AT&T	T	$41.55	$35.65	-14.2%	$(142.00)
Becton, Dickinson	BDX	$183.44	$216.70	18.1%	$181.31
Bemis	BMS	$48.86	$43.52	-10.9%	$(109.29)
Boeing (*)	BA	$180.47	$327.88	81.7%	$816.81
Campbell Soup	CPB	$57.34	$43.31	-24.5%	$(244.68)
CarMax	KMX	$59.22	$61.94	4.6%	$45.93
Carnival Corporation	CCL	$58.91	$65.58	11.3%	$113.22
CenterPoint Energy	CNP	$27.57	$27.40	-0.6%	$(6.17)
Chemed (*)	CHE	$200.37	$272.86	36.2%	$361.78
Chevron	CVX	$107.37	$114.04	6.2%	$62.12
Cincinnati Financial	CINF	$77.27	$74.26	-3.9%	$(38.95)
Coca-Cola	KO	$42.44	$43.43	2.3%	$23.33
Colgate-Palmolive	CL	$73.19	$71.68	-2.1%	$(20.63)
Columbia Sportswear	COLM	$58.75	$76.43	30.1%	$300.94
Comcast	CMSCA	$37.60	$34.17	-9.1%	$(91.22)
ConocoPhillips	COP	$49.87	$59.29	18.9%	$188.89
Corning	GLW	$27.00	$27.88	3.3%	$32.59
Costco Wholesale	COST	$167.29	$188.43	12.6%	$126.37
CVS Health	CVS	$78.50	$62.21	-20.8%	$(207.52)
Daktronics	DAKT	$9.45	$8.81	-6.8%	$(67.72)
Deere	DE	$108.86	$155.32	42.7%	$426.79

* = New for 2018

Company	Symbol	Price 4/1/2017	Price 4/1/2018	% change	Dollar gain/loss, $1,000 invested
Dentsply Sirona (*)	XRAY	$62.87	$50.31	-20.0%	$(199.78)
DuPont	DWDP	$61.26	$63.71	4.0%	$39.99
Eastman Chemical	EMN	$80.80	$105.58	30.7%	$306.68
Empire State Realty Trust	ESRT	$20.64	$16.79	-18.7%	$(186.53)
Fair Isaac	FICO	$128.95	$169.37	31.3%	$313.45
FedEx	FDX	$195.15	$240.11	23.0%	$230.39
First Solar (*)	FSLR	$29.55	$70.98	140.2%	$1,402.03
Fresh Del Monte	FDP	$59.23	$45.24	-23.6%	$(236.20)
General Electric	GE	$29.80	$13.48	-54.8%	$(547.65)
General Mills	GIS	$59.01	$45.06	-23.6%	$(236.40)
Grainger W.W.	GWW	$232.76	$282.27	21.3%	$212.71
Honeywell	HON	$124.87	$144.51	15.7%	$157.28
Illinois Tool Works	ITW	$132.47	$156.60	18.2%	$182.15
International Flavors & Fragrances	IFF	$132.53	$136.91	3.3%	$33.05
Itron	ITRI	$60.70	$71.56	17.9%	$178.91
J.M. Smucker	SJM	$131.08	$124.01	-5.4%	$(53.94)
Johnson & Johnson	JNJ	$124.55	$128.15	2.9%	$28.90
Kimberly-Clark	KMB	$131.63	$110.13	-16.3%	$(163.34)
Kroger	KR	$29.42	$23.94	-18.6%	$(186.27)
McCormick	MKC	$97.55	$106.39	9.1%	$90.62
McKesson	MCK	$148.26	$140.87	-5.0%	$(49.84)
Medtronic	MDT	$80.56	$80.22	-0.4%	$(4.22)
Microchip Technology	MCHP	$73.78	$91.36	23.8%	$238.28
Mosaic	MOS	$29.18	$24.28	-16.8%	$(167.92)
NextEra Energy	NEE	$128.37	$163.33	27.2%	$272.34
Nike	NKE	$55.73	$66.44	19.2%	$192.18
Norfolk Southern	NSC	$111.97	$135.78	21.3%	$212.65
Novo Nordisk	NVO	$34.28	$49.25	43.7%	$436.70
Oracle	ORCL	$44.61	$45.75	2.6%	$25.55
Ormat Technologies	ORA	$57.08	$56.38	-1.2%	$(12.26)
Otter Tail	OTTR	$38.15	$43.35	13.6%	$136.30

* = New for 2018

Company	Symbol	Price 4/1/2017	Price 4/1/2018	% change	Dollar gain/loss, $1,000 invested
Paychex	PAYX	$58.90	$61.59	4.6%	$45.67
Perrigo	PRGO	$66.39	$83.34	25.5%	$255.31
Praxair	PX	$118.60	$144.30	21.7%	$216.69
Procter & Gamble	PG	$90.03	$79.28	-11.9%	$(119.40)
Prologis	PLD	$51.88	$62.99	21.4%	$214.15
Prudential Financial (*)	PRU	$103.90	$103.55	-0.3%	$(3.37)
Public Storage	PSA	$218.91	$200.39	-8.5%	$(84.60)
Qualcomm	QCOM	$57.34	$55.41	-3.4%	$(33.66)
Quest Diagnostics	DGX	$98.19	$100.30	2.1%	$21.49
ResMed	RMD	$71.97	$98.47	36.8%	$368.21
C.H. Robinson	CHRW	$77.29	$93.71	21.2%	$212.45
Ross Stores	ROST	$65.87	$77.98	18.4%	$183.85
RPM International	RPM	$55.03	$47.67	-13.4%	$(133.75)
Schlumberger	SLB	$78.10	$64.78	-17.1%	$(170.55)
Schnitzer Steel	SCHN	$20.65	$32.35	56.7%	$566.59
Scotts Miracle-Gro	SMG	$93.39	$85.75	-8.2%	$(81.81)
Siemens (*)	SIEGY	$69.55	$63.92	-8.1%	$(80.95)
Southwest Airlines	LUV	$53.76	$57.28	6.5%	$65.48
Starbucks	SBUX	$58.39	$57.89	-0.9%	$(8.56)
State Street Corp.	STT	$79.61	$99.73	25.3%	$252.73
Steelcase	SCS	$16.75	$13.60	-18.8%	$(188.06)
Stryker	SYK	$131.60	$160.92	22.3%	$222.80
Sysco	SYY	$51.92	$59.66	14.9%	$149.08
Timken	TKR	$45.20	$45.60	0.9%	$8.85
Total S.A.	TOT	$50.42	$57.69	14.4%	$144.19
Tupperware (*)	TUP	$68.91	$48.38	-29.8%	$(297.92)
Union Pacific	UNP	$105.92	$134.43	26.9%	$269.17
UnitedHealth Corp.	UNH	$164.01	$219.87	34.1%	$340.59
United Parcel Service	UPS	$107.30	$104.66	-2.5%	$(24.60)
United Technologies	UTX	$112.21	$125.82	12.1%	$121.29
Valero	VLO	$66.29	$92.77	39.9%	$399.46

* = New for 2018

Company	Symbol	Price 4/1/2017	Price 4/1/2018	% change	Dollar gain/loss, $1,000 invested
Valmont	VMI	$155.50	$146.30	-5.9%	$(59.16)
Visa	V	$88.87	$119.62	34.6%	$346.01
Vodafone (*)	VOD	$24.75	$27.82	12.4%	$124.04
Waste Management	WM	$72.92	$84.12	15.4%	$153.59
WD-40, Inc.	WDFC	$109.00	$131.70	20.8%	$208.26
Welltower	WELL	$70.82	$54.43	-23.1%	$(231.43)
Whirlpool	WHR	$171.33	$153.11	-10.6%	$(106.34)

* = New for 2018

Currently available from Value Line for individual investors

THE VALUE LINE INVESTMENT SURVEY®
The signature publication from Value Line is one of the most highly regarded comprehensive investment research resources. Published weekly, it tracks approximately 1,700 stocks in more than 90 industries and ranks stocks for Safety™ as well as appreciation potential.

THE VALUE LINE INVESTMENT SURVEY® — SMALL & MID-CAP
The Small & Mid-Cap Survey applies Value Line's data and analysis protocols to an additional 1,700+ companies with market values from less than $1 billion up to $5 billion.

THE VALUE LINE INVESTMENT SURVEY® — SMART INVESTOR
This Internet version of The Value Line Investment Survey tracks approximately 1,700 stocks and offers sorting functions and custom alerts.

THE VALUE LINE INVESTMENT SURVEY® — SAVVY INVESTOR
The Internet counterpart of the preceding three Surveys, Savvy Investor includes every one of our nearly 3,500 stock reports plus updates during Stock Exchange hours.

THE VALUE LINE® 600
Provides stock reports from The Value Line Investment Survey on 600 large, actively traded and widely held US exchange-listed corporations, including many foreign firms, spanning more than 90 industries.

VALUE LINE SELECT®
Once a month, subscribers receive a detailed report by Value Line, recommending the one stock that has the best upside and risk/reward ratio. A less-seasoned promising issue is sometimes highlighted as well.

VALUE LINE SELECT®: DIVIDEND INCOME & GROWTH
A monthly, in-depth report recommending one dividend-paying stock, along with follow-up on numerous alternate selections.

THE VALUE LINE SPECIAL SITUATIONS SERVICE®
The Value Line Special Situations Service is designed for those seeking investment ideas in the small-cap arena. Both aggressive and conservative selections appear monthly.

VALUE LINE SELECT®: ETFs recommends one Exchange-Traded Fund each month.

A special 14-day trial of The Value Line Investment Survey—Smart Investor is available to individual investors with the code "100STOCKS" at www.valueline.com/100STOCKS.

551 Fifth Avenue, 3rd FL, New York, NY 10176
www.valueline.com
1-800-VALUELINE